On the
REVOLUTION *of*
READING

The Selected Writings of
KENNETH S. GOODMAN

Edited by

Alan Flurkey & Jingguo Xu

HEINEMANN
Portsmouth, NH

To the pursuit of "good knowledge" and to the teachers
and children who create it.

Heinemann
A division of Reed Elsevier Inc.
361 Hanover Street
Portsmouth, NH 03801–3912
www.heinemann.com

Offices and agents throughout the world

© 2003 by Kenneth S. Goodman, Alan D. Flurkey, and Jingguo Xu

The author and publisher wish to thank those who have generously given permission to
reprint borrowed material: credit lines for borrowed material appear in the text.

Library of Congress Cataloging-in-Publication Data
Goodman, Kenneth S.
  On the revolution of reading : the selected writings of Kenneth S.
Goodman / edited by Alan D. Flurkey and Jingguo Xu.
      p.   cm.
    Includes bibliographical references and index.
    ISBN 0-325-00542-7 (pbk. : alk. paper)
    1. Reading.   I. Flurkey, Alan D., 1955–   II. Xu, Jingguo.   III. Title.
LB1050 .G64   2003
418′.4—dc21   2002153975

Editor: Lois Bridges
Production service: TechBooks
Production coordinator: Sonja S. Chapman
Cover design: Jenny Jensen Greenleaf
Compositor: TechBooks
Manufacturing: Steve Bernier

Printed in the United States of America on acid-free paper
07   06   05   04   03   VP   1   2   3   4   5

Contents

Acknowledgments

Thanks goes to our families for the hours of "release time" spent at the computer. We would also like to thank Marie Ruiz of the Program in Language and Literacy at the University of Arizona for her assistance and her forbearance in responding to our endless requests. A note of gratitude goes to James R. Johnson, Dean of the School of Education and Allied Human Services, and Herman A. Berliner, Provost and Senior Vice-President for Academic Affairs of Hofstra University, for their support of this project. A special thanks goes to Lois Bridges, our editor at Heinemann, for her continued encouragement and faith in this project. Thanks also goes to Yetta Goodman, co-author with Ken on several articles in this book for her invaluable contributions to research and teaching. Finally, we would like to thank Ken Goodman for his vision, patience, and inspiration.

Introduction

The walk-up to Ken Goodman's home office behind the carport of his Tucson home is crowded with olive, pomegranate and bougainvillea. Crossing the threshold and looking over the adjoining desks of Ken and his wife Yetta Goodman, one can't help but be drawn to the panoramic view to the north of the looming Santa Catalina range—pink or ochre depending on the time of day. Just to the left of the window is a photograph of Albert Einstein. Beneath the photo is a quote:

> Great spirits have always encountered violent opposition from mediocre minds.

The sentiment applies to others besides Einstein, of course. Darwin and Copernicus come to mind—thinkers who were considered heretics in their day. And like the work of all visionaries, Goodman's model of the reading process has met with its share of opposition. In the opening of his book *Phonics Phacts* (Goodman, 1994), Goodman writes that few subjects have provided more heat and less light than that of phonics. Indeed, in the United States nearly 50 years of debate and discussion over the nature and pedagogy of early reading has ensued since Rudolph Flesch wrote *Why Johnny Can't Read*. Goodman's own work in explaining the role of grapho-phonics in the reading process has attracted considerable attention in the fields of education and applied linguistics and has generated its own share of heat. But this heat does not come from the friction of the so-called 'reading wars' debates—it comes from the novalike incandescence of something truly different, wholly new, and unforeseen.

It is worth noting that groundbreaking ideas were labeled "heresy" by those who were unable to appreciate the value of new insights. Goodman acknowledged this (with confessed immodesty) in the attribution of a statement by William James to his own work.

> The three classic stages of a theory's career. First a new theory is attacked as absurd; then it is admitted to be true, but obvious and insignificant; finally it is seen as so important that its adversaries claim that they themselves discovered it.
>
> —Gollasch, 1982, p. ix

And so that is what this book is about. It is about sharing Ken Goodman's scientific insights about the reading process—insights that will find a place next to the work of other great "heretics."

Why This Book? How This Book Is Organized

Since the mid-1960s Kenneth Goodman has published several books, book chapters, and journal articles for the reading research community and for teachers who might apply his insights to their classroom practices. This book brings together some of Goodman's most important writings that were originally published in journals or as chapters of books that would be difficult for readers to locate today. These pieces have been selected for their appeal to classroom teachers, reading specialists, administrators, researchers, and all who have an interest in understanding a comprehensive explanation of the reading process.

This book is organized into six parts that deal with key aspects of Goodman's model of the reading process: Part I: Theoretical Model and Process of Reading; Part II: Miscue Analysis: Research on the Reading Process; Part III: Text Analysis; Part IV: Reading as Language; Part V: Literacy Development; Part VI: Teaching and Curriculum. These sections explore a variety of topics including a detailed description of the model, discussions of its development and theoretical underpinnings, the research methodology that informs the model, and its subsequent influence on the fields of applied linguistics, reading research, and education. Each section begins with a groundbreaking article, followed by others arranged in a chronological order. As such, this book not only helps to explain what reading is and how the process works, it also provides the reader with an appreciation of the historical development of this influential and important work.

Underpinnings

It is important to understand the place that Goodman's work occupies in the history of reading research and reading education. In "Professional Connections: Pioneers and Contemporaries in Reading" (Herber, 1994), the first chapter of the International Reading Association's flagship publication *Theoretical Models and Processes of Reading* (Ruddell, R., Ruddell, M., & Singer, H., 1994), Goodman is named by his peers as one of the seven most influential writers and researchers in the 1945–present era of the field of reading.[1] Likewise, in her President's Address to the 1999

1. Herber's declaration is based on responses to a survey of acclaimed authors, researchers, and professionals in leadership roles in the International Reading Association and the National Reading Conference. Goodman's influential contemporaries included Richard C. Anderson, Jeanne Chall, Marie Clay, Dolores Durkin, P. David Pearson, and Frank Smith.

National Reading Conference, Linda Gambrell named Ken Goodman as one of eight researchers whose work was deemed most influential by members of the National Reading Conference[2] (Gambrell, 2000).

But merely knowing that his peers have come to value Goodman's work underplays key dimensions of the significance of his contribution to the field. The uniqueness of his contribution needs to be recognized. Along with fellow pioneers Frank Smith and Marie Clay, Goodman recognized that reading is most usefully described as a *psycholinguistic* process and that reading is best understood as it is studied in the context of its real-world use.

While other researchers have explored what is meant by reading-as-meaning construction, Goodman has applied his study to the reading and writing of written texts. But as a researcher and theorist, it is his explanation of how written texts are *constructed* by both writers and readers that definitively sets his work apart. Thirty-five years ago, Goodman set out with a key premise: If reading is language, then what's true of language must also be true of reading. According to this premise, the most useful, elegant and parsimonious descriptions of reading emanate when reading is viewed as a language process with both personal and social aspects. One of the consequences of this premise is spelled out by Goodman in "Reading: A Psycholinguistic Guessing Game" (Goodman, 1967). Specifically, he rejected the "common sense" notion that "reading is a precise process [involving] exact, detailed sequential perception and identification of letters, words, spelling patterns and large language units" (Chapter 2, p. 46).

Goodman's insights about the reading process are made available through a unique contribution—miscue analysis. As a research tool, miscue analysis is slow to be accepted by those branches of the research community that place a premium on experimentation and a mechanistic view of reading. Yet as a tool for assessing and evaluating the competence of individual readers (Goodman, Watson, & Burke, 1987), miscue analysis has proved indispensable to teachers.

The model that resulted from this linguistic perspective (psycholinguistic *and* sociolinguistic) is responsible for several major implications. Among them are that *all* language processes, expressive (speaking and writing) and receptive (listening and reading) are processes of construction. This crucial insight is embodied in the concept of the *dual text*—the text that the listener/reader constructs that parallels the oral or printed text.

Another implication is the rejection of the notion of "error" in oral reading. Goodman has shown that readers' unexpected responses occur

2. Gambrell based her findings on a survey of National Reading Conference members, primarily research professionals. Named along with Ken Goodman were Dolores Durkin, Marie Clay, Louise Rosenblatt, Frank Smith, Yetta Goodman, Donald Graves, and Marilyn Adams.

for a reason. They are not random, nor are they the result of laziness or inattention or deficiency; rather, they are artifacts of the natural process of meaning construction. These are miscues and through their analyses, the patterns they display provide a wealth of information about how the reading process works and how an individual reader makes use of strategies as he or she constructs meaning from a text. And because the workings of the reading process can be inferred from these patterns of miscues, Goodman has referred to them as "windows on the reading process" (Chapter 6).

It would be a mistake, however, to intimate that Goodman has worked in a vacuum. Goodman acknowledges other theorists who have provided insights that have assisted him in the development of his theory. Louise Rosenblatt's transactional theory and Michael Halliday's systemic functional grammar have provided essential input in the development of Goodman's socio-psycholinguistic transactional theory of reading. He has refined his theory over time moving even farther away from a word level of focus and analysis. But the gist of his theory has remained the same—the search for meaning is at the heart of all things that readers do.

Copernican Shift

The rise to prominence of Goodman's perspective on reading, and literacy-as-a-language process has resulted in what Thomas Kuhn, in *The Structure of Scientific Revolutions,* calls a paradigm shift—an entirely new way to look at a phenomenon (Kuhn, 1996). To get a sense of the magnitude of the shift away from focusing on words and their identification toward the focus on construction of meaning that Goodman's model provides, it is helpful to think in terms of another important scientific revolution. Goodman has likened this shift to the shift in thinking that Copernicus ushered in when he published *On the Revolution of Celestial Spheres,* which was published in 1543. Goodman writes:

> For thousands of years people saw the sun move across the sky from east to west, day after day. From this and other equally reliable data they built theories that placed the earth at the center of the universe. But finally, in the 16th century, Copernicus looked at the same evidence and saw something different. If the earth moved around the sun and rotated once each day as it did so, wouldn't it appear to those of us standing on the earth that the sun was moving? The revolution Copernicus launched changed the view of the universe and made it possible for humanity to understand many phenomena in new and productive ways. We could see things that we had looked at but had not seen before. Centuries later Piaget would answer researchers who

said "I only know what I see" by saying, "No, you only see what you know" (Chapter 1, p. 3).

This Copernican revolution in reading has moved us away from a view of the reader as passive and the text as controlling the reader. The reader is now seen as an active user of language (Chapter 1, p. 4).

Scientific revolution is a fitting way to describe the shift in thinking that Goodman's model provides. Goodman's work emerged in the 1960s when behaviorism dominated psychological explanations of reading.[3] Goodman's novel explanation for reading that made use of insights from linguistics met with some resistance from the mainstream. And because miscue analysis research represented a radical departure from experimental tradition, the validity of the data was questioned. New constructs, such as reading-as-meaning construction, the artifactual nature of miscue production in oral reading, and the construction of dual texts radically stood out against a backdrop of reading-as-precise-word identification. But such is the nature of a scientific revolution: Normal science proceeds until a theory is no longer able to satisfactorily explain observable phenomena. When a competing theory succeeds in supplying an explanation and subsequently wins support, the crisis is resolved and the revolution is complete.

In the years that have followed since its development in the 1960s, Goodman's model is revealed to be a watershed event in the history of modern education. In diverging from the mainstream, his insights about reading have had far-reaching educational implications for related theories of teaching, learning, language, and curriculum. Eventually these theories became the foundation for another revolutionary idea—whole language.

An Educator's Model of Reading

While it is true that Goodman's model has weathered criticism from those who would cling to cognitivist or behaviorist traditions, to rationalistic research or word recognition models of reading, for teachers the model's path has traced a different arc. Educators have found the application of linguistics that stem from Goodman's model to be particularly useful. And the model has had a lasting impact in the United States, Canada, Britain, Australia, New Zealand, and Latin America on how education is carried out.

Because Goodman's model was informed by research conducted in classroom settings using classroom materials, it has a special relevance

---

3. Along with Kuhn's book, read *Chaos: Making a New Science* by James Gleick (1987) to get a sense of dynamics of paradigm change.

for teachers. Teachers gravitate toward the clarity that the model's explanation provides. For many, after grasping the notion of reading-as-meaning construction and its implications, the response is "For the first time I understand what my readers are doing as they read. What I see my readers do makes sense to me." That's because Goodman's model shows *how* readers are making sense as they read, and readers' responses (their miscues) are evidence of the sense-making process. This profound revelation is powerful enough to make a difference in teachers' lives. It has the power to "make" careers for those who would become teachers, and revive the careers of veteran teachers who might otherwise have succumbed to the disillusionment that comes from not knowing how to make a difference.

As teachers learn to observe and appreciate readers' sense-making capabilities, they make an ideological shift away from a deficit-oriented view of "what a reader can't do" toward a view that appreciates the linguistic strengths that each reader brings to any literacy event as they construct meaning from a text. This is the essence of what Goodman calls *revaluing*.[4]

But it doesn't end there. For educators, understanding the reading process and revaluing readers is the beginning of a cascade of changes. Learning to appraise a reader's strengths leads teachers to think about how to support the development of reading, how to support the flexible and proficient use of reading strategies that readers employ as they read a variety of texts, and how to support language learning in general. This, in turn, points the way for teachers to rethink the received knowledge about teaching, learning, and curriculum that are a part of the cultural experience of how we "do school" and spurs the search for alternatives that are congruent with new understandings of how to support literacy and learning.

To suggest that Goodman's model has helped to fuel an educational movement is not an overstatement. While whole language has been correctly characterized as a grass roots, bottom-up phenomenon, the deep insights into the transactional nature of reading, language, and learning that follow from Goodman's model lay a theoretical groundwork that supports the invention and refinement of progressive classroom practices. Teaching for social justice, making expanded use of literature coupled with decreased dependency on programmed materials with unauthentic texts that make reading more difficult, curriculum-as-inquiry, and authentic classroom language studies that include retrospective miscue analysis and incorporate reading strategy lessons are educational innovations that have been influenced by the development of Goodman's model.

4. See *Revaluing Readers* (1982), Chapter 26.

The Future of Goodman's Model

Theory building that is original and on the leading edge is by nature "futuristic." And Goodman has said that his model was a bit ahead of its time. So was Copernicus' for a long while. Yet, it must be noted that Goodman's model has been used by scholars in many countries throughout the world to explore the reading process in Spanish, Portuguese, Hebrew, Arabic, Japanese, Chinese, and a variety of other languages written with both alphabetic and non-alphabetic scripts, thus confirming his assertion that the reading process he describes is universal ("What's Universal About the Reading Process," Chapter 4).

In the United States and some other English speaking countries, notably Britain and Australia, the prevailing political climate has precipitated a retrograde shift with respect to support for holistic teaching and the underlying theories of reading and language that support it. Goodman documents this shift in *In Defense of Good Teaching* (Goodman, 1998). But the looming presence of hostile politics doesn't alter the fact that the scientific work has been done. The key scientific discoveries about the psycholinguistic and sociolinguistic nature of the reading process have already been made and what remains is for the rest of the field to catch up.

In his 1992 Distinguished Educator Series article in *The Reading Teacher*, Goodman speculates about the future of whole language. While the subject of this book is Goodman's model of the reading process, the model and the pedagogical principles that it supports are inextricably linked. Exchange the terms *socio–psycholinguistic transactional model* for *whole language* in the following excerpt from the article in *The Reading Teacher*, and the quote still works.

> The future of whole language is the future of education, both in the United States and in the world. I am optimistic enough to believe that eventually whole language, in very much expanded and elaborated form, will be the basis for education everywhere. By that time it will have a new name, or perhaps no name: It will be what education must be.
>
> —Goodman, 1992, p. 198

We confidently assert that for the future of Goodman's model of reading, the best is still ahead. Advances in technology and the research conducted in a variety of languages have opened new lines of research on the reading process that promise to bring new discoveries and raise new questions extending the depth and breadth of Goodman's model. Current research that is predicated on assumptions and theories set forth by Goodman's model include investigations into the nature of aphasia, the role of eye movements and perception in oral reading and silent reading, the nature of efficient and effective reading, and the nature of reading in alphabetic and non-alphabetic orthographies.

The following quote of Edmund Huey is a favorite among researchers and dissertation writers. We present it here to celebrate what Goodman's model has done to extend our understanding of humankind's most remarkable feat.

> And so to completely analyze what we do when we read would almost be the acme of a psychologist's achievements, for it would be to describe very many of the most intricate workings of the human mind, as well as to unravel the tangled story of the most remarkable specific performance that civilization has learned in all its history.
>
> —Huey, 1908, p. 6

On a recent occasion when Goodman was asked to speculate on the ultimate fate of his theory, he offered the maxim that "good knowledge chases out bad." He fully expects that in future years there will be modifications and extensions to the model; however, we assert that for those who make use of the central tenets of the model to craft future research, the underlying principles provide a permanent foundation. This book is dedicated to the sharing of good knowledge.

References

Gambrell, L. 2000. "Reflections on Literacy Research: The Decades of the 1970s, 1980s and 1990s." *49th Yearbook of the National Reading Conference.* T. Shanahan and F. Rodriguez-Brown, eds. Chicago: National Reading Conference.

Gleick, J. 1987. *Chaos: Making a New Science.* New York: Penguin Books.

Gollasch, F. V. 1982. Foreword to *Language and Literacy: The Selected Writings of Kenneth S. Goodman.* Vol. 2, *Reading, Language and the Classroom Teacher.* F. V. Gollasch, ed. Boston: Routledge & Kegan Paul.

Gollasch, F. V. 1982. Introduction to *Language and Literacy: The Selected Writings of Kenneth S. Goodman.* Vol. 1, *Process, Theory, Research.* F. V. Gollasch, ed. Boston: Routledge & Kegan Paul.

Goodman, K. 1994. *Phonics Phacts.* Portsmouth, NH: Heinemann.

———. 1992. "I Didn't Found Whole Language." *The Reading Teacher* 46(3): 188–199.

———. 1982. "Revaluing Readers and Reading." *Topics in Learning and Learning Disabilities* 1(4): 87–93.

———. 1967. "Reading: A Psycholinguistic Guessing Game." *The Journal of the Reading Specialist* 6(4): 126–135.

————, ed. 1998. *In Defense of Good Teaching: What Teachers Need to Know About the Reading Wars.* York, ME: Stenhouse.

Goodman, Y., D. Watson, & C. Burke. 1987. *Reading Miscue Inventory: Alternative Procedures.* New York: Richard C. Owen.

Herber, H. 1994. "Professional Connections: Pioneers and Contemporaries in Reading." *Theoretical Models and Processes of Reading.* R. Ruddell, M. Ruddell, and H. Singer, eds., Newark, DE: International Reading Association.

Huey, E. B. 1968. *The Psychology and Pedagogy of Reading.* Cambridge: The M.I.T. Press.

Kuhn, T. 1996. *The Structure of Scientific Revolutions.* 3rd ed. Chicago: University of Chicago Press.

Ruddell, R., M. Ruddell, & H. Singer, eds. 1994. *Theoretical Models and Processes of Reading.* Newark, DE: International Reading Association.

Part One

Theoretical Model and Process of Reading

The theoretical model of reading by Goodman dates back to the 1960s and finds its root in the psycholinguistic approach to the study of reading. Influenced by Chomsky's view of reading as "tentative information processing," Goodman proposed his reading model in 1967, comparing reading to a "psycholinguistic guessing game." The idea was new and received great attention from researchers and teachers of reading at that time. The influence of the model spread beyond the borders of the United States. Even twenty years later the 1967 paper, "Reading: A Psycholinguistic Guessing Game," was still selected for a graduate reading course in Britain. Its inclusion with the other four papers in this section helps readers better understand the origin and development of Goodman's transactional model of reading.

In Goodman's transactional model, reading is regarded as a language process; therefore, it is observed from linguistic, psycholinguistic, and sociolinguistic perspectives. Since reading involves communication between the reader and the writer, writing and written texts are taken into account in Goodman's exploration of the reading process. Traditionally, reading has been taken for a passive receptive process with the writer's text guiding the reader. Good or poor readers are determined by how accurately they perceive the letters or words in a linear order. The role of meaning is diminished or even denied in controlled studies of aspects of reading. However, Goodman's Copernican revolution in reading has fundamentally changed the view of readers as passive receivers of graphic input. They are active in the construction of meaning.

Goodman's model of reading is reader-centered, system-based, and meaning-focused. According to Goodman, reading is in essence a unitary psycholinguistic process as writing in which the writer encodes meaning into the text. Writing, reading, and written texts are integrated constituents of the reading process. It is the reader that plays a leading role in manipulating the graphic input and cognitive strategies to construct the meaning. Meaning construction does not depend on the accurate identification of letters or words in sequence. It can be accomplished with cues from any of the three systems: graphophonic, lexico-grammatical, and semantic-pragmatic. Readers bring their own meaning to the text and construct a parallel text of their own while reading the writer's text. Reading is a dynamic process characteristic of transaction between the knower and the unknown. Making sense is essential to reading and typical of the reading process in all languages.

Goodman's model of reading is neither the result of armchair thinking nor the product of controlled studies of word recognition. Goodman's data come from studies of authentic reading and his theoretical model has been tested and validated by studies of reading in alphabetic and non-alphabetic languages. The model is built on reading reality and also intended to serve it in return by shedding light on the teaching of reading. Goodman's writings are always oriented toward teaching and rooted in life experiences. The connection of theory with the realities of reading and teaching strengthens Goodman's arguments and demonstrates the vitality of his theory.

Chapter One

Reading, Writing, and Written Texts
A Transactional Sociopsycholinguistic View

Kenneth S. Goodman
University of Arizona, 1994

A Copernican Revolution

For thousands of years people saw the sun move across the sky from east to west, day after day. From this and other equally reliable data they built theories that placed the earth at the center of the universe. But finally, in the 16th century, Copernicus looked at the same evidence and saw something different. If the earth moved around the sun and rotated once each day as it did so, wouldn't it appear to those of us standing on the earth that the sun was moving? The revolution Copernicus launched changed the view of the universe and made it possible for humanity to understand many phenomena in new and productive ways. We could see things that we had looked at but had not seen before. Centuries later Piaget would answer researchers who said, "I only know what I see" by saying, "No, you only see what you know."

This chapter first appeared in *Theoretical Models and Processes of Reading*, 1994, Ruddell, R., M. Ruddell, & H. Singer, (eds.), International Reading Association, Newark, DE, pp. 1093–1130. It is based on and updated from work published in "Unity in Reading" from A. Purves & O. Niles, (eds.), *Becoming Readers in a Complex Society* (83rd Yearbook of the National Society for the Study of Education, Part I), 1984. Chicago, IL: University of Chicago Press. Copyright (1994) by the International Reading Association. Reprinted with permission.

Such a Copernican revolution is taking place in our understanding of the written language processes. This small excerpt from a child's reading of a text illustrates this well:

> "Those white marks must mean
>
> $\textcircled{C}$ *sa-*
>
> 'John.' They mean me! |he said.
>
> *I* $\textcircled{AC}$ *understand*
>
> Now he |understood why the children
>
> *have*   *my*
>
> had been calling his name."

In a traditional view Ian has made five errors and regressed twice. That surely shows he is a careless and ineffective reader. But in an emerging transactional view of reading, Ian is seen as trying to make sense of the text. He is quite successful. In constructing his meaning he has constructed his own text parallel to the printed text. In his text he has moved the part after "he said" into the direct quotation. In English the dialogue carrier may introduce the quote, it may follow the quote, or it may interrupt it, usually at a sentence break. Ian chose the latter option in his construction. The author shifted after "he said" from John's first-person voice to the third-person voice of the unseen narrator; Ian kept it in first person without changing the referent, which is still John. So the pronouns must shift from third person (*he, his*) to first person (*I, my*). The tense must also shift from past (*understood, had been calling*) to present (*understand, have been calling*). We know Ian comprehended because his text has the same meaning as the original.

This Copernican revolution in reading has moved us away from a view of the reader as passive and the text as controlling the reader. The reader is now seen as an active user of language. The writer creates a text to represent meaning, but the text is never a complete representation of the writer's meaning. The writer leaves much for the reader to infer. Human communication is never perfect. That's because what readers or listeners understand depends as much on what they bring to the transaction as it does on what the author brought to the text. Meaning is in the reader and the writer, not in the text. The writer constructs a text with a meaning potential that will be used by readers to construct their own meaning. Effective reading is making sense of print, not accurate word identification.

The revolution has come to include writing too. Figure 1–1 shows a birthday card Aaron, a kindergarten child, made for his grandfather, whom he calls "Grampa Kenny." In it, Aaron has written the following:

HAPBE

BrSDA GrAPA

GHNE

Figure 1–1
Aaron's Birthday Card

Aaron knows that birthday cards are signed so he wrote this along the left margin, starting at the bottom and moving upward:

BY AarON.

Traditionally, if any attention were paid to this message it would have been dismissed as scribble or unsuccessful, rather than being Aaron's first comprehensible writing. Some in special education might have suggested, looking at his bottom-up signature and his reversed *s*, that Aaron is an incipient dyslexic. But in the revolutionary view, Aaron is trying out a written language genre: the birthday card. He has some sense of the conventions of birthday cards. Their function, he knows, is to express a conventional message, "Happy birthday," to someone (in this case, his grandfather). He invents spellings for the words he needs, which shows a developing control over the conventions of writing. We can see that he is already at the point in his writing development where he attempts to spell the full sound sequence he hears. That tells us a lot: he has the alphabetic principle; he knows that spelling patterns relate to sound patterns. In this writing, he is beyond some stages found in early writing: representing only initial sounds in words; letting single letters (usually consonants) represent syllables and leaving vowels out—that is, writing in strings of consonants. Though he has only produced a single conventional spelling (*by*), we can see Aaron is well on his way into writing.

In the new view we're able to see development where before we had seen only deviations from conventional spelling and language form. That makes it possible not only to understand the natural development of writing but to gain a new perspective on the writing process itself.

History of My Model and Theory of Reading

I joined this revolution in understanding literacy when I began to study the reading process in 1962. I found that when I asked readers like Ian to read whole stories that they hadn't seen before, they made miscues—they produced unexpected responses that didn't match the text. The miscues became, for me, windows on the reading process. I started my analysis with the assumption that miscues are caused in the same way as expected responses. The reader uses cues in the text to construct meaning. I came to consider reading as an active, receptive language process and readers as users of language. I compared the observed and expected responses, looking at the effect on graphophonic, syntactic, and semantic aspects of the text.

I realized that in order to describe what I saw readers doing I would need the methods and concepts of scientific linguistics. Starting with the structural, descriptive linguistics of Fries (1952), I began to build a model and theory of the reading process: how we make sense of print. Though I moved on to other linguistic theories, I continued to draw on structural linguistics when I needed to compare the grammatical functions of words in the expected and the observed responses.

I looked for help in the research literature, but I found an ironic contradiction that characterized the study of the reading process in this century. On the one hand, the reading process has been the subject of more attention in educational research than any of the other language processes. But that research has been largely atheoretical, treating reading as sequential word identification. On the other hand, until recent decades, it has been very much neglected as a focus of interest by scholars in other disciplines who study language and language development.

Each discipline has stayed in its narrow confines, tending not to learn from the other disciplines.

This dichotomy has resulted in a highly developed technology of reading instruction with a very shallow theoretical base. The technology isolates reading from the other language processes and from its functional use, treating it largely as an object of instruction in how to read words accurately. Research has focused on building the word-identification technology. That creates an illusion that the technology has a research base. That's the "reading research" Chall summarized in *Learning to Read: The Great Debate* (1967) and Adams summarized 25 years later in *Beginning to Read: Thinking and Learning about Print* (1990). Here in Adams's words is what research in reading is all about:

> Before you pick this book up, you should understand fully that the topic at issue is that of reading words. Before you put this book down, however, you should understand fully that the ability to read words, quickly, accurately, and effortlessly, is critical to skillful reading comprehension—in the obvious ways and in a number of more subtle ones (p. 3).

From this current but "pre-Copernican" perspective, Ian is not a good reader since he is not reading words accurately. Later in her book Adams states,

> We have seen again and again that skillful reading depends critically on the speed and completeness with which words can be identified from their visual forms. Yet, for the beginning reader, it is visual word recognition skills, it is the knowledge that makes the orthographic processor work and links it to the rest of the system, that are uniquely absent (p. 333).

Again, here is a pre-Copernican view that discounts what beginning readers and writers like Ian show they are learning about the orthography as they invent spelling in their early writing.

This word-identification technology led to massive instruction, often consuming half or more of the primary school day, focused on reading words or on phonic skills for word identification or a combination of both. The tendency was to treat children learning to read as beginners who were learning something new and unlike anything else they do. Paradoxically, the same shallow theoretical base led to an almost total neglect of the teaching of writing in primary grades. Beyond teaching handwriting, we couldn't figure out how to sequence or test writing development, so we didn't teach it much.

There have been some attempts to bring together scholarship from a number of foundational disciplines to create a theoretical base for reading instruction in understanding the reading process, reading development, and effective instruction. Notable is the work of Smith (1982). But these efforts have only recently begun to overcome the inertia built up in the instructional technology. And it is the teachers who have learned best the lessons of the Copernican revolution in understanding written language.

I came to realize from the miscues of the young readers I was studying that I needed to go beyond linguistics in studying reading to develop an adequate model of the reading process. If reading is making sense of written language, then it is a psycholinguistic process: a theory of reading must include the relationships of thought and language. By good fortune I had made the choice to study the reading of pupils from groups not served well by schools. I reasoned that if the readers were too successful they would mask the process I was studying. So the readers I studied included urban black and white pupils who spoke a variety of dialects. That made me aware that I needed to draw on sociolinguistics to understand the social variations in language and language use I was finding. From the beginning, then, my attempt to build a theory of reading required an interdisciplinary base.

The transactional sociopsycholinguistic theory and model of reading—and now of reading, writing, and written text—that I have built is grounded in the scientific analysis of the reading miscues of hundreds of readers of wide ranges of abilities and cultural and linguistic backgrounds. To date, in addition to my work and that of my colleagues, there have been several hundred research studies that have used miscue analysis. I built a taxonomy to fully analyze miscues and a theory and model to support the analysis; the miscues, in turn, served as the test of the theory and taxonomy (Goodman & Burke, 1973; Goodman & Goodman, 1978). If miscues could not be fully categorized and described, then the taxonomy and the theory had to be reconsidered. Such is always the relationship between theory and reality in science, whether one is talking about physics, biology, astronomy, or linguistics: theory must be continuously validated through testing against reality. In my case, reality was real readers reading real texts.

In 1964 I developed an elaborate research plan to build an inclusive model of the reading process and to develop applications for reading instruction. My employer, Wayne State University, gave me an award that made it possible for me to hold an invitational conference, the title of which was "The Psycholinguistic Nature of the Reading Process"; I later published the papers under the same title (Goodman, 1967). So few people were working in this direction that I could afford to invite everyone I knew about: Stanford linguist Ruth Weir didn't come but sent a young Richard Venezky, who had just defended his dissertation; Ruth Strickland at Indiana University sent a young Robert Ruddell.

The following year I presented my first miscue analysis research report at the American Education Research Association (AERA) meeting; I published the report in 1965 in Elementary English at the suggestion of Nila Banton Smith. As a side concern I looked at the reading of lists of words from the stories young readers read for miscue analysis. I found, to no one's surprise, that readers could read words in the story context that they couldn't identify on lists.

As I continued my research, the taxonomy I was developing for analysis of the miscues became more and more complex (Goodman, 1969). I was led more fully into how readers were using the grammar of the language. I had to go beyond descriptive analysis to the deep structures Chomsky (1957) and the transformational/generative linguists were talking about.

In this same period Jeanne Chall, who had heard me at AERA, recommended me to Harry Levin, a psychologist at Cornell who had one of the early federal research grants awarded for study of the reading process. During the month I spent at Cornell, Noam Chomsky came and spent a few days. He talked about reading as "tentative information processing." That concept brought together for me my insights into what I saw readers doing as they read. I translated his term into "the psycholinguistic guessing game" (Goodman, 1967). I saw readers tentatively and selectively using graphophonic, syntactic, and semantic cues as they predicted and inferred (guessed) where the text was going. I presented this first attempt at a complete, integrated model in 1967 at AERA.

Two major National Institute of Education-funded miscue analysis studies were completed between 1970 and 1980. The first involved readers of different levels of proficiency in 2nd to 10th grades. The second study looked at 2nd, 4th, and 6th grade readers in 8 populations: 4 bilingual and 4 representative of low-status dialects. This made it possible to refine the reading model and see it as generalizable over quite varied populations. I found influences of culture and language, but I also found quite diverse readers responding very similarly to common texts and producing some identical miscues at key points.

My model building reached the point where it was clear that the theory of reading must be expanded laterally to include writing and the nature of written texts. Abundant research in both writing and text analysis made this possible at that point. In philosophy and linguistics, speech act theory (Searle, 1969) emerged as a way of considering oral language in the context of its use and of the roles and intentions of the participants. The counterpart in written language is the literacy event, an event in which writer or reader transacts with and through a text in a specific context with specific intentions. The linguistic transactions in literacy events may be viewed from three vantage points:

1. We may look at the process by which writers produce the texts.
2. We may look at the characteristics of texts.
3. We may look at the process by which readers make sense of texts.

Because of the extensive miscue research database, I've been able to study in-depth such aspects of the reading process as word omission and insertion (Goodman & Gollasch, 1981), and pronoun and determiner miscues (Goodman, 1983; Goodman & Gespass, 1983). Many doctoral studies have used the same database to study a wide range of other aspects (Marek, 1985). I've also been able to study the nature of written text including text wording, cohesion, and text complexity through this database (Altwerger & Goodman, 1981). Y.M. Goodman and other colleagues have studied the writing process in a 2-year study of Native American pupils in Arizona (Goodman & Wilde, 1992). I've also been able to draw on the extensive studies she and others have done on reading and writing development (Goodman, 1991).

In 1984, I attempted to bring together the work done from the three perspectives within the context of the whole literacy event and a transactional view. Reading—particularly reading comprehension—and writing had become hot topics in the previous decade in a number of fields. Cognitive psychology, ethnography, linguistics, child language development, artificial intelligence (merged into cognitive science), semiotics, rhetoric, literature, philosophy, and brain study are some of these fields where intense activity took place. But the period could be characterized as multidisciplinary rather than interdisciplinary: there was little crossing over from discipline to discipline, there was little attempt made to relate the objectives of each discipline to the others, and there was too little awareness by scholars in each field of the current work in other fields or the historical work already done in reading and writing. Attempts to apply the insights gained in these fields to instruction have been piecemeal and unintegrated. I tried to distill from theory and research in a wide range of fields a unified theory of reading, writing, and texts. I sought the unity that existed in the current diversity. This unity comes together as a transactional sociopsycholinguistic view. If we are to understand written language we must integrate knowledge from many disciplines.

Most current writers in the several fields studying reading and writing have regarded them as interactive; I've come to consider them as transactive. Rosenblatt (1981) has drawn on Dewey's view that both the knower and the known are changed in the course of knowing. I've built on Rosenblatt's insight. The reader constructs a text through transactions with the published text and the reader's schemata are also transformed in the process of transacting with the text through the assimilation and accommodation Piaget has described. In a transactional view, reading is seen as receptive written language and writing as productive or generative. In the productive generative processes (which also include speaking), a text is generated (constructed) to represent the meaning. In the receptive processes of listening and reading, meaning is constructed through transactions with the text and indirectly through the text with the writer who is the producer of the text. Both generative and receptive processes are constructive, active, and transactional.

In "Unity in Reading" (Goodman, 1984), as I moved to include writing and text analysis in my model building, I was able to use information from literary criticism, critical theory, schema theory, artificial intelligence, semiotics, neurolinguistics, and Halliday's (1975) systemic-functional linguistics. The model has also had vertical expansion to include the importance of function, purpose, and situational context. It has expanded in detail to include explication of reference, cohesion, wording, and deliberate and nondeliberate choice of strategies. The theoretical base now includes schema theory, reader response, and critical theory. In understanding the nature of texts we can consider how text features influence reading. Miscue analysis has helped me to study text influences.

At present my theory and model of literacy are being reexamined in the light of classroom application. Knowledgeable whole language teachers are producing new insights about teaching and learning as they break new ground in their classrooms. This knowledge in turn helps refine our knowledge of literacy processes. As large numbers of children are freed of test and textbook technology, we see authentic literacy and literacy development at work.

The model of reading, writing, and texts must be grounded in more general theories of reality, language, cognition, society, and human development (see Figure 1–2). It need not fully include these more general theories but it must be consistent with them. Figure 1–2 shows this vertical grounding. In this grounding I draw heavily on the work of M.A.K. Halliday, whose systemic-functional linguistics is itself grounded in a sociocultural view of language.

Halliday's use of field, mode, and tenor is useful in examining literacy events in their sociocultural contexts. Very simply, *field* refers to the general content area of the literacy event; *tenor* refers to the social and pragmatic relationships between the writer and reader and others in the event; and mode is the language form or genre selected for the event. To Halliday, language development is both personal and social in functional contexts. I build on that view to add the context of language as personal invention and social convention. The theory is also grounded in a general psycholinguistic theory of cognition

Figure 1–2

Vertical Grounding of the Transactional Sociopsycholinguistic Theory
of Reading, Writing, and Written Texts

A sociocultural theory of human communication

- field
- mode
- tenor

A social-personal theory of language development

- invention
- convention

A psycholinguistic theory of cognition, comprehension

- schema theory
- learning how to mean

A theory of language

• functions	• levels
ideational	symbolic
interpersonal	lexico-grammar
textual	meaning

and comprehension. Schema theory is helpful as is Halliday's view of language development as "learning how to mean" through language.

The theory of language that the model draws on is Halliday's systemic-functional view with its major language levels—symbolic, lexico-grammar, and meaning—and the three functions language serves simultaneously—ideational, interpersonal, and textual. The ideational is what we might call the message. But every text also has an interpersonal function: what participants in the literacy event are trying to do to or for each other. The textual function makes the other functions possible. In turn, the form the text takes is at least partly determined by the ideational and interpersonal functions.

Halliday's language theory also has three main levels of analysis: the symbolic, which in written language I call graphophonic; the meaning, which for me includes the pragmatic and which in Halliday's terms is both ideational and interpersonal; and the grammar and lexicon (wording) together in what Halliday calls the lexico-grammar. Just as the textual function makes the other functions possible, the lexico-grammar is what makes a text fully functioning language. Halliday's study of language development shows that the symbolic level is directly linked to meaning until the lexico-grammar develops and fully formed language occurs.

Retreat from Consensus

In 1984, I had great hopes that what I saw as an emerging consensus in theory and research on the nature of written language in key fields would lead to more collaboration across disciplines and multidisciplinary agreement on the issues needing exploration. Instead, since that time research in some fields has tended to turn away from comprehensive theories and to focus on narrow perspectives within disciplines. I find the following trends discouraging:

- In psychology, behaviorism has been reborn as "connectionism" and new justifications of atheoretical or microtheoretical and reductionist research are being made.
- Artificial intelligence has merged into cognitive science and computers are being taught to deal with limited aspects of language with little insight into how real texts are generated and comprehended. Unable to teach computers to read and write, some researchers have settled for calling what they can teach computers "reading and writing."
- Some studies in reading development are being centered around a narrow and sterile concept of "phonemic awareness." All children who learn to understand oral language must be aware of the phonemes (significant perceptual sound units of language) or they could not comprehend or produce speech. Still, studies appear to show some children lack "phonemic awareness" in highly reduced language contexts.
- Some linguists still see oral language as innate and written language as learned in a more or less behavioral way. That causes them to reject natural language learning as possible or appropriate for written language.
- Other linguists have fixated on the differences between different language genres. They want to teach systemic-functional analysis of key genres—those they term *genres of power*—directly to children to give them powerful language.

It's not the purpose of this article to critique these narrow proposals and research trends. Rather, I urge that they be contrasted by readers with the comprehensive, integrated, and unified view of written language.

Unitary Psycholinguistic Processes

Though reading and writing appear to vary greatly as they are used in the wide range of functions and contexts they serve, they are actually unitary, psycholinguistic processes. In generating language, thought represents a view of reality and is in turn represented by language. The constraints of the brain, the reality being represented, the schemata of the speaker or writer, the syntax and lexicon of the language, and the situational and social contexts all shape the process. None of these constraints may be ignored or avoided without reduction of the text to nonsense, so there are no alternative ways of making sense in reading and writing. There is only one way to make a text representative of an author's meaning, and there is also only one way to make sense of a text. The unitary processes of reading and writing are flexible. They will vary with purpose, with audience, with content, with proficiency, with language, and with orthography, but they involve universals. There is thus diversity within unity in writing and reading.

The Locus of Meaning

Texts are constructed by authors to be comprehended by readers. The meaning is in the author and the reader. The text has a potential to evoke meaning but has no meaning in itself; meaning is not a characteristic of texts. This does not mean the characteristics of the text are unimportant or that either writer or reader are independent of them. How well the writer constructs the text and how well the reader reconstructs it and constructs meaning will influence comprehension. But meaning does not pass between writer and reader. It is represented by a writer in a text and constructed from a text by a reader. Characteristics of writer, text, and reader will all influence the resultant meaning.

The Writer and the Text

Language is universal in all human societies. The key human attributes that make language possible are the ability to think symbolically and the need for highly complex communication that derives from human interdependence. The fact that human societies develop oral language first is a matter of convenience. The earliest functions of language involve immediate interpersonal transactions. As long as both parties can hear, oral language works admirably for these functions. But language needs and functions eventually transcend face-to-face contexts as society becomes more mobile and complex. People eventually need to communicate over time and space. Furthermore, our ability to use and perceive symbolic systems is not confined to a single sense, that of hearing. Indeed, all our senses can and do serve as channels of communication. Written language is visual, but so is the manual sign language of the deaf. Many blind people learn to use tactile language. What is universal among people is the need and ability to create language. The form it takes depends on its functions and the characteristics of the people who use it.

In social history, written language is created when interdependence extends beyond the primary community as trade and political structures emerge. It results from the expansion of the culture beyond the ability of the oral tradition to preserve the culture and pass it on to ensuing generations. People growing up in a literate society need written language as their horizons expand beyond the home. Written language functions derive from these personal and social developments. Written language extends memory and communication. Narrative and expository forms emerge to serve the new functions.

Writers and Their Audiences

Texts are shaped as much by the writers' sense of the characteristics of their readers as they are by the writers' own characteristics. That's as true for a shopping list or a letter as it is for a newspaper report or a novel. A diary entry intended to be read only by the writer and addressed to an alter ego named "Dear Diary" may presuppose full knowledge on the part of the reader of any reference, however implicit. Detail will stem from a sense that the diary may be reread long in the future when the author/reader may have forgotten some of the events. Letters to close friends and family will assume a body of shared knowledge and experience. But as the distance between writer and reader grows, the writer will need to balance a sense of the audience with a sense of how much background and detail must be provided.

Other constraints on the writer. In every act of writing, writers are constrained by their own values, concepts, experiences, and the schemata they have built of them. The purpose of the particular text being created is always influenced by these personal characteristics of the writer, so that the text will reflect what the writer is as well as what the writer is trying to communicate. In literacy events there is a kind of unstated contract between the reader and the writer (Grice, 1975). From the writer's point of view, this contract means that the reader wants to understand and will try to do so. No text can be so successfully constructed by a writer that it can be comprehended without the reader actively trying to make sense of it. The writer can create only a potential for comprehending by making effective use of the forms and structures of written language to express articulate ideas appropriate for and comprehensible to the intended audience. An effective text is one that not only expresses the author's meaning, but is comprehensible to others. It must be a full enough representation of the meaning to suit the needs, background, schemata, and interests of the readers. That's the other side of the writer-reader contract: readers èxpect writers to be trying to say something sensible in a sensible manner.

Language—written language included—is part of a complex human culture. Its forms and uses are constrained by the values and customs of the culture. The culture develops textual forms and pragmatic constraints. Certain phrases, such as "very truly yours" or "once upon a time," become necessary parts of certain written language forms. But social constraints on the lexico-grammar of language are far more pervasive and subtle. Some apply to both oral and written language. For example, feminists have demonstrated how the English language incorporates the societal attitude of male supremacy. This attitude is much in evidence in written language and is a particular problem for writers who are attempting to use general third-person references but avoid masculine pronouns.

Still, any text is very much what the writer has made it. The writer is engaged in a living transaction with the text being created. To make a text comprehensible, the writer must create within the constraints of purpose, content, language, logic, structure, and form, and within situational and social contexts. But there is plenty of room within these constraints for the writer to develop a unique voice and style. The genius of language is that it becomes the supple servant of expression and not a straitjacket on it. Writing as a generative language process has much in common with speech. In both, a text is composed that suits the situation, intention, and audience. But speech usually involves oral feedback from the listener or some sort of visual response. Oral language is more recursive and cyclical as points are introduced and then reintroduced for further discussion and development. Its chief dimension is time—the sequence in which it is uttered.

The characteristics of written language stem from its functions and purposes and from its use of a two-dimensional medium and a visual input mode. Writers learn to use the strengths of the medium and to work within its limitations. They make use of the fact that texts can be constructed that are more or less durable depending on the purpose and the materials used. And they make use of the fact that they may be reviewed, reconstructed, and polished before they go to the intended audiences. Learning to express thought in writing involves developing control over suitable forms for the specific purposes of written language.

Characteristics of Texts

The text, as Halliday and Hasan (1975) have defined it, is the "basic unit of meaning in language." It is not simply a set of well-formed sentences composed of words or morphemes. A text must have a unity; it must represent comprehensibly a coherent and cohesive message.

Physical characteristics. The text must be sufficiently well formed that communication can take place without any direct contact between the reader and the writer. That constraint interacts with the physical constraints on written text, derived from its characteristics as a permanent, two-dimensional medium that must be visually perceptible.

Orthography. How a particular written language uses its two-dimensional space is arbitrary, just as which side of the road a society chooses to permit drivers to drive on is arbitrary. Although some forms of picture writing seem to have used the space in a nonlinear manner, most writing is linear—that is, it uses either horizontal or vertical lines (or both) that follow directional patterns. Historically, every possible pattern seems to have been used: left to right, right to left, or alternating directions of horizontal lines and top to bottom or bottom to top vertical lines.

Some languages have changed their conventions over time. Such a change was recently made in China, where horizontal left-to-right writing has replaced vertical top-to-bottom writing. Modern Japanese uses the traditional vertical writing and a horizontal alternative. Hebrew goes from right to left, but numerals are written left to right in the same texts. The characteristics of the orthography also vary within the limits that it must be both producible and visually perceptible; it must serve both the writer and the reader.

All orthographies ultimately represent meaning, but some are designed to relate to the oral language as well. Since oral and written language have different constraints that derive from the differences in the media, there can be no simple one-to-one correspondence between the two systems. However, some systems—such as alphabetic and syllabic orthographies—are designed to more closely provide correspondences, while others—such as ideographic systems, where characters represent ideas and concepts—make no attempt to provide correspondences to the sound system.

Systems that represent ideas will have many more symbols than alphabetic or syllabic orthographies and thus make writing more complex (but Chinese characters are composed of a repertoire of strokes so Chinese writing is not so complex as it seems). It's a common belief that alphabetic systems are much easier to learn and use than are other writing systems. But when one considers the level of literacy in Japan and China, it appears that nonalphabetic systems serve their users quite well. Japanese uses a very complex orthography that combines two forms of Chinese characters with a system of syllabic symbols; it uses the Roman alphabet freely to represent borrowings from European languages. Ideographic writing has an intrinsic advantage over other systems. Since it represents meaning directly, ideographic texts may be understood by those literate in the system regardless of what language they speak. Mathematics uses an ideographic system that has become almost universal across languages. Anyone who knows the system can understand $6 + 5 = 11$ or $2(a-b) = cd$.

Spelling. Languages that employ alphabetic writing can be read only by those who know the language. Furthermore, these languages stay as close as possible to a strict alphabetic principle with invariant relationships between units of oral and written language; if they didn't, each dialect community would spell words differently and even idiolect (personal language) differences would show up as spelling differences. That would mean that written texts might be less comprehensible if writer and reader had substantial phonological differences. So almost all alphabetic languages conventionalize spellings across dialects, because written language is intended for use beyond immediate dialect communities in wider language communities.

Because of standardization of spellings, the way the spelling relates to how a word is pronounced in any dialect becomes variable. For example, *almond* has at least four pronunciations in American dialects: /æmənd/, /ælmənd/, /omənd/, /olmənd/. For most dialects of English, words like *right, light,* and *night* have unnecessary *gh* elements; in Scottish dialects, however, the *gh* relates to an actual sound: /rikht/.

Furthermore, the phonology of living dialects is constantly evolving. Over time, the fit between sound and spelling will change unless spelling conventions are periodically changed, a matter not so easily accomplished even if it were desirable.

This situation of standardizing spelling across dialects is not unique to English. All languages are really groups of closely related dialects so no orthography can be a perfect alphabetic fit for any one dialect without being a very poor fit for the others. This is true even for the new orthographies created for preliterate peoples.

Besides compromising on dialect differences, conventional spellings involve trade-offs in how they will deal with characteristics of oral and written systems that correspond and those that don't. Oral languages involve morphophonemic shifts, changes in phonemes that take place when they are followed by others in succeeding morphemes. Consider these related words: *site, situate, situation.* The conventional English spellings preserve the derivational relationships even though the /t/ in *site* shifts to /č/ in *situate* and the second /t/ in *situate* shifts to /š/ in *situation*. The trade-off involves sacrificing phoneme-grapheme consistency in favor of maintaining semantic relationships. That's an advantage, particularly since the same morphophonemic rules also apply across word boundaries: *can't you* becomes /kæntčə/, for example. Compare also *education* and *would you,* where in both cases the /d/ shifts to /ǰ/. Strict consistency would require the same word to be spelled differently depending on which words followed it.

So standardized spelling is an important text feature. Readers expect a word to be spelled consistently, but they don't expect all similar-sounding words to be consistently spelled. English spelling conventions are complex but not as capricious as popularly believed. What adds to the complexity are the multiple linguistic roots—Germanic and Latin roots with substantial influences from other languages—of English. This leads to not one but several systems of correspondence rules in English orthography.

Many believe that it would be easier to learn to read and write English if its spelling were simplified. While it is possible that misspelling would diminish if spelling were simplified, there is no substantial evidence that English is harder to comprehend or to learn to read and write as a result of this complexity. Most spelling reformers have not faced the trade-offs required to achieve spelling simplicity. Moreover, there is no evidence that there must be close correspondence between orthography and phonology for a written language to be functional for its users. Arabic and Hebrew have served their users very well for many centuries with little or no representation of vowels in their orthographies. People tolerate and comprehend texts that are visually highly variable. All languages employ orthographies that include alternate writing forms: there are upper- and lowercase forms, cursive and print forms, and varied type fonts; some orthographies use different letter forms in initial, medial, or final positions; personal handwriting wanders far from a model of perfection. If people were intolerant of such variation, written language would be a less useful means of communication. In oral language, too, listeners are also able to tolerate considerable variation in dialect, idiolect, and voice quality. It is our ability to assign symbolic value to a wide range of distinctive features and shift the constraints and values in different contexts that makes both written and oral text work as well as it does.

Punctuation and other orthographic conventions. Oral language usually uses segmental phonemes as its symbolic building blocks. The phonemes are segments of a phonological string that follow each other in time. But oral language uses a suprasegmental system—intonation—to produce meaningful utterances of these phonemes. There are junctures, ways of telling where one unit ends and another begins, and variable patterns of pitch and stress that provide the prosodic contours that mark off and differentiate the syntactic patterns. Written language uses punctuation, including spacing between words, extra spacing between sentences, and special formatting of paragraphs to accomplish this purpose.

A speaker may turn any oral English statement into a question by using a different intonation pattern: "The book is lost" becomes "The book is lost?" Besides this compulsory intonation required for every utterance, optional patterns make it possible to change the meaning of an utterance in quite subtle ways. For example, shifting the stress from word to word in "Do you want me to rent a red car?" changes the question's meaning.

Subtle shifts in the intonation of oral language may clarify what would be ambiguous statements in writing. That's because punctuation is not nearly as full and flexible a system for creating the patterns of written language. A written English sentence starts with an uppercase letter and ends with a period, question mark, or exclamation point, but it has nothing corresponding to the oral English sentence's intonational contour that marks it as statement, question, or command from beginning to end. Written English employs a variety of means such as underlining, boldface, italics, and oversize letters to indicate where special stress appears in a text. None of these works quite as well as intonation.

Only the exclamation point in written language gives any sense of the emotional state of a writer. A listener gets all kinds of signals of the feelings, moods, and intent of the speaker from voice quality, facial expressions, and body movements, in addition to the intonation, volume and speed of the utterance. One 3rd grader became aware of this problem in writing when he wrote about his dog being run over, so he invented his own "sadlamation point" to be used after sad statements.

Because punctuation comes at the end of English utterances, it provides a means of confirming what the reader has already understood but it is not useful in making predictions since all types of sentences start with capitals. Spanish puts question marks and exclamation points at both ends of a sentence, which provides more help.

This difference between how oral and written texts mark patterns is the result of differences between the constraints of the oral and graphic media. The effect of the difference is that the written text must explicitly represent what intonation and the situational context provide in a speech act.

The syntax of written language is also affected by this difference. Intonation is so effective in avoiding ambiguity in coreference of nouns, subordination of clauses, and other complex discourse structures that oral sentences may be much longer, more complex, and more rambling than those in written texts. The syntactic rules aren't different in oral and written language, but the parameters of orthography require a different use of the rules to produce a comprehensible text.

When this effect of the greater ambiguity of written text is combined with the polishing and editing possible and usual in preparing written texts, the result is that written texts employ styles and use syntactic patterns that are notably different from those found in oral texts. Learning to write comprehensible texts involves learning to use the styles and syntactic sequences particular to written language; one common characteristic of texts produced by inexperienced writers is the use of styles and patterns which work more successfully in oral language.

Format conventions. Some of the format conventions that govern texts are intrinsic to the function and the content of the particular type of text; others are arbitrary social conventions. Text conventions may be very general, applying to all kinds of texts, or very specific, applying to single text types such as airline schedules, recipes, TV guides, or bibliographies. An example of a general format convention is putting margins at the top, sides, and bottom of the page. This may result from the need for binding space or from aesthetic preferences or both.

Paragraphing is another written-language convention. It is done at least partly to set apart viable discourse units, though there is considerable dispute in the professional literature about whether the paragraph is a definite and definable unit of English discourse. Magazine and newspaper editors follow the convention that a text must be periodically broken by white space; therefore they start new paragraphs sometimes even in the midst of clearly connected text such as a long series of names.

Some text formats very clearly result from the nature of the text's subject matter. Recipes, for example, often list ingredients in tabular form. List forms are used for shopping lists, telephone directories, and similar reference materials.

Consider the theater ticket as a text form. Its function and manner of use limit its size, structure, and content. Often it is torn into two parts at the time of entry into the theater, so some information must appear on both parts. Certain information is represented on the ticket for the ticket holder, but other information may be provided for the ticket taker. Some abbreviations may be used to economize on space. The highly conventionalized form of the ticket facilitates its usefulness for frequent theatergoers, but a first-time user may find it difficult to locate and comprehend information even if it is represented in large, clear type.

Airline tickets have some similarities to theater tickets, but again their function and manner of use, as well as the structure of the information they must represent, place strong constraints on them as texts. There must be a separate coupon for each flight segment, so multipart tickets are used uniformly across participating airlines. General information is imprinted on the ticket form and the rest is added by hand or by computer, or a form is stored in the computer, data is added, and then the entire ticket form is printed by a computer printer. Again, frequent flyers can comprehend a great deal of information from the tickets, and ticket agents can comprehend more. The novice flyer must often seek help to comprehend the ticket.

Today's airline tickets, business forms, and other documents are designed to be computer printed. Indeed, the computer has had as much impact on text formats as the typewriter had at an earlier time. Even newspaper formats have changed to fit the constraints of the computers that now generate them.

Economy of space is a constraint of most texts, even novels. The newspaper classified advertisement has found its way into folk humor because of its widespread use of inventive abbreviations to limit use of space and thereby reduce cost. The writer presupposes that the reader will be able to determine what is being represented within the limited context and assign meaning to the symbols. As in most texts, there is a trade-off possible in creation of the ad. The more pertinent knowledge the reader may be presupposed to have, the more concise and compact the text can be. However, the more we leave to the audience to infer, the more we limit the audience to those with the requisite schemata. Here's a recent example. Can you tell what is offered for sale?

Great buy! dblwide 3BR 2BA, lite & brite w/sep fam rm. Steal at $17,995 6245777agt.

In modern literate societies, many text forms have evolved among special populations for the sharing of large amounts of very specific information. Some common examples are stock reports, theater, restaurant and hotel guides, racing forms, weather reports, horoscopes, and menus.

While it is true that the form a text takes follows its function, it is also true that functions are both limited by and take advantage of forms. The two-dimensional space of written texts makes them admirably suited for tabular representation of large amounts of information. That means information doesn't have to be remembered: readers need only to know where to go for the information and how to use the directories, charts, or lists. The function of written language as an extension of memory is largely dependent on its ability to represent information in a consistent, convenient, and retrievable manner. That means that the role of memory in the preservation of social knowledge has been largely supplanted by written texts in literate societies.

Nonphysical text constraints. Written texts are often published. Professional editors and designers strive for consistency in format, style, and over all appearance in particular publications. That means establishing arbitrary standards in all aspects of text production. These standards interact with social conventions, shaped by them but also shaping them.

Cultures evolve text forms that become conventionalized and predictable by those who share the cultures. Such forms may be considered to have text grammars (recurrent and predictable structures). As indicated earlier, constraints of content and function interact with social need for the text to fall within a predictable form to facilitate its comprehension.

The macrostructure of any text derives at least partially from the relations among the amount of information to be presented, the information's intrinsic structures, and spatial constraints. The telephone book is an example: its physical list form is a function of the structure of the information it represents. Entries must include all the necessary information in a concise, space-saving format. But entries must also be sequenced in some consistent, logical manner to allow quick access to needed information. Tabular information is usually organized by numerical, alphabetic, or chronological sequencing systems. Phone books sequence names alphabetically on the premise that users know names and are looking for numbers. In recent years, phone books have been reorganized to separate individual from business entries, to divide cities into districts, and to provide more white space by listing each last name once followed by all entries for that name. The goal is (or at least ought to be) producing the text most easily comprehensible for its function and users. But, as with many texts, the interests of the writers and editors do not always coincide with those of the readers.

No matter what aspect of a text is used to sequence it, there is always the possibility that certain information will be hard to find, so indexes are often included in reference texts. The macrostructure of any type of written text is similarly shaped by the same kind of considerations as the types we've explored. A business letter has a rather specific purpose and an internal structure related to its purpose. There are conventions of greeting, closure, and amenities that must be observed. Addresses of the sender and addressee must be included, usually in conventional ways in conventional places. The letter must clearly and concisely represent its message in a comprehensible manner. But a letter that confines itself to a concise statement and does not follow conventional form and include expected amenities may carry some unintended connotations to the recipient. Consider these alternatives:

3497 Valley Rd.
Portland, AZ

Mr. George Bronson
5749 Sixth St.
Jonesville, PA

Dear Mr. Bronson,
      In reviewing our records we find an unpaid balance of $50 in your account. Since this amount appears to be overdue we would appreciate payment at your earliest convenience. If you have already remitted the payment, please excuse this reminder.
      We're grateful for your continued patronage.

Sincerely,
Henry Pope

Bronson, I want the $50 you owe me now! Henry Pope.

Newspapers include a variety of text types. Newspaper space is at a premium and is usually assigned on the basis of significance and priority rather than proportionate to amount of information being handled. Reporters often need to cut down on the length of an article because they have more to say than the available space permits. But sometimes a front-page story is assigned more space than is needed to present the available information because of the story's high interest value. That means reporters must find ways of filling the space. The sequence of events in a news story would seem to provide a natural scaffold or macrostructure for the narration, yet few stories follow such a straightforward structure. Reporters want to start with an angle, something that will catch the interest of the readers and provide a schema for following the story. They're also aware of the habits of newspaper readers, many of whom start many articles but seldom read them to the end. So the most important information must be put early in the story and ordered in terms of its significance. A given story may relate to a continuing event that has been in the news for several days or even weeks. Reporters must use ingenuity to find new angles and to provide a synopsis of past history without boring or insulting those who have been following the unfolding events.

News reports have structures and styles different from those of feature articles, columns, or editorials; each of these develops its own text features that serve its particular purpose and make it predictable for readers familiar with the genre. Editors and readers would be surprised or angered if a news story took a position on an issue or an editorial stuck to the facts and took no position. A feature article is used to develop "human interest" and uses stylistic text devices that would be unacceptable in a news story. A syndicated columnist strives to develop a highly personal style that will win a continuing readership. On the other hand, news editors strive for a consistent, impersonal style across all reporters.

Though different forms and conventions have evolved for each type of text, each time we focus on a particular kind of text we see the same factors at work. The form must efficiently serve the function and purpose of both writers and readers. There must be a predictable macrostructure or text grammar. The text must be organized so meaning is represented in a cohesive and coherent way. In narrative and expository texts topics must be established and elaborated on rhetoric and linguistic rules and conventions observed. Words, phrases, and syntactic structures must be chosen within linguistic and pragmatic constraints that will produce a comprehensible text.

The wording of texts. In every narrative and expository text there are two kinds of very frequent words. Some are frequent because they are the function words, pronouns, and copulas (BE forms) that the language constantly requires; the others are content words that may be quite uncommon in the language as a whole but are frequent in a particular text because of its subject matter. With Lois Bird, I studied the wording of several different types of texts (Goodman & Bird, 1982). We found that the 25 most-frequent words in each text account for between 35 and 40 percent of the running words (tokens). At the same time over half of the different words (types) in each text are used only once. In an adult essay, 75 percent of the words (types) occur just once. Most of the frequent content words are nouns. In narratives these are often the names of the main characters. It's the function words, pronouns, copulas, and a few repeated nouns that provide most of the text cohesion in both narrative and nonnarrative texts.

In nonnarrative texts the important ideas are represented by a variety of nouns, so particular nouns will not be used with the same frequency as the proper nouns in narratives. That's because authors avoid, when they can, using the same word repeatedly. This is also why verbs, adjectives, and adverbs are unlikely to be repeated frequently in any text. Authors use a variety of terms with related references to provide cohesive chains. In one story, a character moves toward another in the opening sequence. No term is used more than once in this chain: *drove, approached, opened, coming, parked, went up, take, got to, crossed, pushed through, went across.*

Producing a cohesive text requires repetitious references to the same key characters, concepts, attributes, or actions. English writers can avoid repeating the same content words, but they can't avoid repeating function words because language provides only a few words for common functions. Because common nouns usually require determiners, *the* is the most common word in virtually all texts, representing up to 10 percent of all the running words.

Readers expect texts to be worded so that the uncommon words can be defined by their references, their collocations, and their embedding in contexts composed of high-frequency, noncontent words. Language itself thus controls the word frequency of texts. Ironically, artificial controls on word frequency can make texts less predictable and therefore less comprehensible to readers.

What emerges in everything that has been said about texts is the same concept of diversity within unity that was emphasized in the discussion of written language transactions from the point of view of the writer. Texts are highly constrained, and yet they must be variable and flexible enough to serve any writer's purpose and make it possible for the writer to establish a personal style and voice.

Reading as Construction of Meaning

Though theories of reading as a process have existed at least since the time of Huey (1908), reading, as was said earlier, has tended to be regarded essentially as a task of identifying words as they occur in sequence, a task of translating written words to oral words before making sense of the text. I believe most research on reading as a process is converging on it as a process of meaning making. I call it a psycholinguistic guessing game, Smith (1982) emphasizes reduction of uncertainty in reading, and Spiro, Bruce, and Brewer (1980) focus on hypothesis testing. All of these views stress that reading is meaning seeking, tentative, selective, and constructive. They all place importance on inference and prediction in reading. Readers use the least amount of available text information necessary in relation to existing linguistic and conceptual schemata to get to meaning.

Dual Texts

In a transactional view, both the knower and the known are transformed in the process of knowing. The reader is transformed as new knowledge is assimilated and accommodated. The reader's conceptual schemata and values are altered through reading comprehension. Because the published text is a reality that does not change its physical properties as a result of being read, how can it change during reading? The answer is that the reader is constructing a text parallel and closely related to the published text. It stays the same yet is a different text for each reader. The reader's text involves inferences, references, and coreferences based on schemata that the reader brings to the transaction. And it is this reader's text that the reader comprehends and on which any later retelling is based.

From this perspective of dual texts, it is possible to treat characteristics of published text as real and thus the same for all readers. It is also possible to study the importance of real text characteristics in the reading process and still understand that what really matters is how the reader perceives and uses them in constructing a new, personal text with different but related characteristics. The reader is not attending to text construction as an end product, however. The reader's attention is very much on making sense. Construction of the text is a necessary concomitant of the construction of meaning. In this transactive view, the literary quality of the text remains highly significant. Great literary works have a depth that makes it possible to understand them, to construct them, at many levels. Once, when Robert Frost was being introduced to an audience of college students, his host went on in great detail about the marvelous allegorical references he saw in his favorite Frost poem: Triumphantly, he turned to the poet and said, "Isn't that so, Mr. Frost?" Quietly the poet replied, "Then again, it may just be about apple picking."

Why People Read

Within the broad functions of communication over time and space, people read written language for several different purposes. To understand how reading works, it is necessary to understand why people read. Here is one attempt to examine the major purposes of reading. The types of reading are not necessarily mutually exclusive.

Environmental reading. Functioning in a literate society requires coping with street signs, regulations (such as "Keep off the Grass"), directions, store logos, and other ways that written language occurs in the environment. In international situations, important notices are in several different languages or in a system of ideographs designed to be universally comprehensible. Environmental print is read not so much by choice as by necessity, and it is no wonder that preschool children acquire the ability to make sense of much of the print in their environment without formal instruction. Studies in a number of countries show widespread print awareness and response to environmental print among preschool children, even in poverty cultures (see, for example, Ferreiro & Teberosky, 1982; Goodman, 1980).

Occupational reading. An Educational Testing Service study shows that 87 percent of those gainfully employed in the United States read an average of 141.1 minutes per 8-hour workday. By time and by sheer volume, this occupational reading has to be the major purpose for reading for most people. It includes a wide range of text types and varies considerably from occupation to occupation. It is likely to be so highly integrated into job activities that it may not be considered reading per se. If one said to an office worker, "What have you been reading recently?" it's unlikely that the response would be "Sixteen interoffice memos, twenty-three letters, six reports, the drafts of several unfinished letters, three sets of directions for use of equipment and materials, eight labels on office supplies, and several assorted posters on job safety."

Because such reading is well integrated into the job it is relatively repetitious, readers bring a great deal of relevant background to the reading, and motivation to comprehend is high (under normal circumstances). Because of the specialized nature of occupations, however, texts may be all but incomprehensible to outsiders unfamiliar with subject matter, text conventions, abbreviations, and acronyms. In fact, some text may be expressly designed to be incomprehensible to outsiders. Some occupations, such as teaching, also require a great deal of reading outside of usual working hours.

Informational reading. Written language is an extension of human memory, so written texts become storehouses of information. Some have referred to the current historical epoch as the "age of information." Our culture produces too much information for even experts in particular fields to remember it all. Readers make frequent use of texts, such as phone numbers and TV schedules, to gain information for immediate use. They also seek information to satisfy longer range curiosity or personal needs.

In human memory, storing information and getting at it are two different things. This is also true of written language, though on a much larger scale. Informational reading involves knowing how to access the appropriate sources of information. This purpose of reading has become so important that computers have been harnessed to make information retrieval more efficient and speedy. We use computers for everything from storing, finding, and dialing phone numbers, to locating explicit information dealing with questions we are trying to answer. But this only shifts the mode of our reading from paper to computer screens or paper printouts of computer-generated information.

Recreational reading. A fourth major purpose for reading is to occupy leisure time pleasantly. This is a bit too simply put because many of the aesthetic reasons for reading come under this heading. What all recreational reading has in common is that it is done at the reader's discretion, for the reader's own enjoyment, and by personal choice. The text may be fiction or nonfiction, and it is possible that informational material, particularly that related to hobbies and leisure interests, may be read for recreational reasons.

In modern society there are many alternate ways of spending leisure time: watching television, movies, plays, or spectator sports; engaging in physical activities and games; socializing; and so forth. Few people confine all their leisure time to any one such pursuit. Schools need to understand that this competition for leisure time is a sociocultural reality. Children who learn to enjoy reading will choose to read when the choice is theirs. Those who learn to read but not to enjoy reading will rarely choose to read during leisure time.

Ritualistic reading. In virtually all cultures there are written texts that are read and reread for ritualistic purposes. That means that the act of reading itself is a ritual, akin to chanting in oral language, and that the purpose is not so much comprehension of the particular passage as fulfillment of a religious or cultural rite. The reading of religious sacred texts, sometimes in ancient languages and scripts, is a common example of ritualistic reading. The literacy event has an overall meaning to the participant to which the text does not relate in the usual manner. This is probably a major reason why there are cults within many religions and cultures that search for secret meanings in sacred texts.

This range of purposes for reading does not contradict the contention that reading is a unitary process. What it does demonstrate is that, within this single process, what a reader comprehends in a given literacy event is very much related to the reader's purpose.

Students are expected to read a lot in school. In a sense, this reading is occupational reading since it is part of their job as students; it is different in that it does not necessarily grow out of a functional act as most occupational reading does. Often instructional reading involves exercises that are not directly related to any personal language function of the students. The exercises seem, like ritualistic reading, to be ends in themselves.

A good deal of school reading seems to be informational. Too often, however, the information is not sought to satisfy the needs or curiosity of the student but to complete an assignment that does not give the student a clear idea about how to use the information once it is obtained. Even the reading of literature often involves works selected by the teacher or assigned within a fixed curriculum. If the student does not have some kind of personal purpose for the reading and does not exercise some choice in what is read, then the activity becomes an unnatural one and is not as likely to contribute to reading development. Of course, what can make the difference in any school reading activity is how sensitive the teacher is to the background and interests of the students, how the teacher involves the students in planning and selection of texts, and how highly motivated the students become.

Schools must be doing some things right: various indicators in recent times indicate that all types of reading, including recreational reading, are increasing. From 1950 to 1975 book circulation in American libraries increased from 2.47 to 4.36 books per person. Sales in that period rose from 6.8 to 8.6 books and pamphlets per person. During the 1980s, sales of children's books increased 500 percent, and in 1989 circulation in children's rooms of public libraries increased 50 percent. And one need only look at copy shops on every corner to realize the explosion of informational reading and writing. Modern societies are becoming increasingly literate in all respects (Bormuth, 1978).

Purpose and Intention

Readers have broad purposes for their reading. These may overlap: informational reading may be occupational or recreational, for example. Within broad purposes, however, each reader has explicit intentions for what will result from a specific literacy event. Just as the intentions of the writer are important in the creation of a text, the reader's intentions are important in its comprehension. Consider the effect on comprehension of the intention of each of these readers reading the same text:

- a professional proofreader reading the text for typographical errors
- a teacher reading it as a student's assignment
- an editor reading it for potential publication
- a critic reviewing it for his newspaper audience
- a student reading the text as a class assignment because on Friday there will be a quiz on it
- the same student reading it as a source of information for a term paper
- any of the above reading the text in a magazine found on a table in the barbershop or hairdresser
- any of the above reading the text on recommendation of a friend as something "You simply must read."

Obviously, a number of factors can influence the "contract" between the reader and the writer. Primary among these is whether the reader self-selects the text or it is assigned by someone else. Even within a similar purpose—gaining information, for example—different intentions may strongly influence comprehension. Reading to cram for an exam is different from reading for a term paper or to fulfill a burning desire to know more about something. The same reader may get different meanings from the same text read at different times because of different intentions.

Comprehending and Comprehension

Comprehension, at some level, is always the end product of any act of reading. During the reading, the reader is engaged in comprehending—that is, in trying to make sense of the text. The distinction between comprehending as a process and comprehension as a product is important and useful. Attempts to study and evaluate reading have generally focused on comprehension as a product measured by some type of postreading test of knowledge. This may take the form of explicit, factual, text-based questions, more general questioning, open-ended retelling by the reader following reading, or some combination of these. All of these are limited by what the reader is willing or able to report as well as by what has actually been comprehended. Since comprehending is a constructive process in which readers make sense of text, it goes on during reading and even long afterwards as the reader reconsiders and reconstructs what has been comprehended; thus, comprehension may be changed in the course of testing it. The reader may change what he or she understood on the basis of test questions that seem to require particular responses and views.

Miscue analysis and cloze procedures are means of examining comprehending as it takes place during the act of reading. In miscue analysis, oral reading miscues, points where observed and expected responses to the text do not match, are examined. The extent to which miscues result in still-meaningful text or are self-corrected if they disrupt meaning gives a strong indication of the reader's concern for and ability to make sense of text. Many studies of comprehending have been conducted through miscue analysis.

In cloze activities, words are deleted from the text and readers are asked to supply them. Examination of the relationship between actual and expected responses gives a similar insight into the reader's ability to maintain meaningful text. Such studies have been conducted by Chapman (1981), Anderson (1982), Cambourne and Rousch (1979), and Lindberg (1977). Cloze distorts text to some extent, but it provides a way of examining comprehending during silent reading, and it has revealed patterns remarkably similar to those found in miscue analysis in oral reading.

The relationships between comprehending and comprehension are not simple and isomorphic. What one knows after reading is the product of what one knew before the reading plus how well one read the text. Effective comprehending is essential to comprehension, but it is not sufficient. Correlations between measures of the two, as reported in the research studies mentioned, are moderate and significant but not high. Figure 1–3 presents a current view of the essential aspects of the model of reading I've been developing.

Language Cue Systems

In constructing their texts and comprehending, readers take information, in the form of cues, from the three levels of language Halliday (1975) describes. Learning to read is at least partly gaining control over these systems and their interactions in the context of literacy events. Readers select from these language cue systems interchangeably and their use is simultaneous and integrated. These cues are within the text and the reader. Readers must have schemata for orthography, syntax, and concepts presupposed by the writer in order to select, use, and supply the cues appropriate to a particular text.

The graphophonic system. Oral and written language may each be considered semiotic systems with symbols appropriate to the form: we have oral, phonological symbols for speech and orthographic symbols for writing. In alphabetically written language there is a set of relationships between the two systems, which we call phonics. This should not be confused with phonetics, the sounds of the language. Phonic relationships are never simple one to one (isomorphic). We may use spelling, sound patterns, or phonic relationships as cues in reading with patterns in one system invoking patterns in the other.

The lexico-grammatical (structural) system. The grammar of a language is the structure or system of the language. It makes it possible for the symbols to come together into a complete semiotic system to represent a full range of meaning relationships, including future meanings. Halliday (1975) puts the lexicon—the set of words of the language—as well as the morphology—the word structure—on the same level as the grammar of the language. The grammar is largely a matter of syntax or sentence structure. Language, according to early theories of Chomsky (1957), has a deep structure closely related to the meaning represented. A set of transformation rules relate the deep structure to the oral surface representation in speech or the written surface representation in writing. A major feature of that surface representation is sentence order. In English that's the main feature of syntax. The patterns assign grammatical functions to clauses, phrases, and words within the

Figure 1–3

Elements of the Transactional Sociopsycholinguistic Model of Reading

---

Language (Cue) Systems

graphophonic (symbolic)
  orthography   phonology
  phonics (relationships between semiotic systems)

lexico-grammatical (structural)
  syntax/grammar   morphology
      order of functions   wording
      inflections
      function words

semantic-pragmatic (meaning)
  semantic   pragmatic
      ideational
      interpersonal
      textual

Cognitive Strategies

initiate/recognize (act of reading)
sample/select
predict
infer
confirm/disconfirm
correct
terminate (act of reading)

Cycles

visual
    scan
    fix
perceptual
    image formation
    narrow window
    schema use
syntactic
    assign surface structure
    apply transformations
    assign deep structure
semantic
    assimilation
    accommodation

sentences: syntactic pattern makes clear which noun is subject, which is object. A series of bound morphemes, affixes, form an inflectional system that also indicates person, number, and tense in nouns and verbs. A third system in English grammar is the small set of function words, determiners, auxiliaries, prepositions, and so on that have no lexical meaning but make it possible to create sentence patterns to express virtually unlimited meanings. Together these syntactic features create the grammatical system of the language. Just as the writer must create a grammatical text to represent meaning, a reader must use grammatical features to create a grammatical text. A text cannot be comprehensible to a reader without being grammatical to that reader.

In a very real sense the last thing that happens as the sentences are uttered or written is the choice of the specific words that fit the requirements of the surface structure. For example, we assign the particular form of *to be* (*was, were, is, am, are, be, being, been*) after we decide the tense, person, and other grammatical forms. Language, then, is much more than a string of words. And to read the words, readers must first construct a grammar.

The semantic-pragmatic system. So, the semantic system of language is not simply a set of definable words; it is the whole system by which language may represent highly complex social and personal meaning. As stated earlier, how much knowledge is shared by reader and writer will strongly influence how the text is constructed and how successful the reader's comprehension will be. Ultimately the references and coreferences must be furnished by the reader in response to the text.

Pragmatic meaning is also part of this system. This is always partly textual and partly contextual. The subtle differences between the straightforward and the sarcastic, the profane and the profound, the humorous and the serious are found in cues in both the text and the context of the literacy event. Schemata in the reader must be evoked to achieve pragmatic comprehension.

Halliday (1975) sees three functions in language. The *ideational* carries the experiential meaning. When we talk of rocks and canyons we may bring somewhat different images to the text, but we share common experiences. The *interpersonal* function involves values, attitudes, and personal relationships between author and reader and among characters in a narrative. Pragmatics is involved in this meaning. Halliday's third function is *textual*. The syntax makes it possible to produce sensible sentences, and the transformational rules of the language generate these sentences. But a text is more than a set of well-formed sentences: it has unity; it is both coherent and cohesive. The cohesion of a text is part of the semantic system of the language. We signal in textual ways whether particular information is new or given; for instance, we use a pronoun instead of a noun phrase when information is already established. In an extended written conversation, authors don't repeat "he said" and "she said"; turn-taking keeps the reader informed of which character is speaking. In fact, there is a general rule of economy in oral and written texts that says already-given information need not be included in surface text. Listeners and readers know this rule and can supply the unstated information.

Cognitive Strategies

Readers use general cognitive strategies in reading. These strategies take on particular significance in the construction of meaning in literacy events.

Initiation or task recognition. Reading requires an overt decision to activate appropriate strategies and schemata. Usually this relates to a particular chain of events. A reader decides to read the morning newspaper with the general intention of finding out what's new or the specific intention of seeking a particular bit of information—the score of a football game, for example. Often, though, it is not until the reader recognizes something in the visual environment as a readable text that he or she uses an initiation strategy. An example is thinking that a dress has a decorative pattern and then realizing that the pattern is cursive writing.

Sampling and selection. The human brain is not the prisoner of the senses, nor does it process everything that the senses feed into it. In reading it seeks information, directing the eyes where to look and what to look for. It samples and selects from the environment and from the input the eyes provide just that information that will be most productive and useful. Efficiency in any cognitive process requires this selectivity; otherwise the thought processes would be overwhelmed by irrelevant data. This sampling and selection strategy is one of the most difficult aspects of human intelligence to simulate in a computer (Schank, 1982). It depends for its effective use on everything the reader knows relevant to language, to reading, and to the particular text in the particular situational context.

Inference. Inference is a general strategy of guessing—based on what is known—information that is needed but not known. Calling inference "guesswork" does not make it random or mystic. Our schemata and knowledge structures make it possible to make reliable decisions on the basis of partial information by inferring missing information. We would be incapable of decision-making if we had to be sure of all the necessary prerequisite information before making each decision.

There is some risk involved in inference since the inferences may prove to be wrong. But the risk in not making inferences is even greater. So readers are tentative in their inferences, depending on how confident they are of their ability to comprehend a given text. Level of confidence limits willingness to take risks, which in turn limits inferencing.

Inference applies to all aspects of reading and to all cue systems: readers infer graphophonic, syntactic, and semantic information; furthermore, they infer information that is explicit as well as implicit. The reader cannot know at any point whether needed information will eventually become explicit in the text. For inference to be confined only to nonexplicit information would mean that it could be used only after the text has been read. Clearly the strategy must be applied when it is needed during reading. If inferred information becomes explicit, then the reader confirms the inference and builds the level of confidence in the quality of the inferences made.

Prediction. Receptive language processing, both reading and listening, requires the ability to predict and anticipate what is coming; otherwise processing would in some sense always be retrospective, a gathering of information at some point after its values were assigned. But readers must have some sense when they start a syntactic pattern whether it is a question, statement, or command. They must know from the beginning of a word, phrase, or clause where it is likely to end. The prediction strategy makes the process flow smoothly as the reader constructs text and meaning. Predictions are based on both explicit and inferred information used in such a way that the reader is quite unlikely to be aware of what was explicit and what was inferred. Cognitive strategies interact in reading so that readers sample on the basis of their predictions and inferences and predict and infer on the basis of the sampling they are doing.

The prediction strategy is greatly facilitated if texts are predictable for the given reader; in fact, predictability is probably a more useful and theoretically sound concept than readability in considering the comprehensibility of a given text for a given reader.

Prediction and inference are related and overlapping, but they are nevertheless distinct strategies. A prediction is an assumption that some information not yet available will become available in the text. An inference is supplying information not yet produced in the text. Every text is an incomplete representation of meaning, so writers expect readers to make inferences. In both strategies readers remain tentative, however, aware that either prediction or inference may be contradicted by subsequent text cues.

Confirming and disconfirming. If inference and prediction involve risk taking and are limited by the level of the reader's confidence, then it is necessary for the reader to self-monitor during reading. The reader must expect consistency of new information with past inferences, predictions, and comprehending. The confirming/disconfirming strategy is what makes the self-monitoring possible. The reader is tentative to the extent of always being ready to accommodate disconfirming information. In general, confirmation must be on the basis of the meaningfulness of the text being constructed. Specifically, it is based on expectations being met and not contradicted.

Again, there is interaction of strategies and an economy of processing. The same information used to confirm past decisions is used to make new inferences and predictions. Carrithers and Bever (1982) report that eye-movement studies support the hypothesis-confirmation view of use of perceptual data in reading.

Correction. It doesn't do much good to know something is wrong if you can't do anything about it. Readers develop correction strategies for reconstructing the text and recovering meaning. Correction strategies are of two types: one is revaluing information already processed and making alternate inferences, predictions, and interpretations; the other is regressing in the text to gather more information. Correction can be almost simultaneous with an original decision, or it can come at a point quite remote in the reading from the original decision. An example of the latter would be the belated realization in reading a murder mystery that the prime suspect could not have committed the crime.

Termination. Just as a deliberate decision begins reading, a deliberate decision ends it. The termination strategy is used in a variety of ways. It doesn't happen only when the reader reaches the end of the text. Readers may terminate at any point anywhere along the way out of disinterest, inability to comprehend, boredom, lack of time, or a change in circumstance.

These strategies operate together in a dynamic search for meaning, a drive to make sense of the text. Though they are continuously available, some are more likely to occur at particular points in reading than others.

Cycles of the Reading Process

Reading involves a transaction between the published text and the reader. This transaction depends on visual input. Once the decision to read is made, light bouncing off print to the eye is processed optically and perceptually transformed so that the orthographic, syntactic, and semantic systems of language may be used.

As perceptual and linguistic processing occur, they affect the quality of the optical information since the eyes are being directed by the brain in an informed way; thus, reading is a cyclical psycholinguistic process. Perceptual processing depends on optical input, syntactic processing operates on perceptual input, and semantic processing depends on syntactic input. In this sense the cycles are sequential, each dependent on preceding cycles; but it is a sequence that resembles a merry-go-round in which an optical cycle follows and precedes a semantic cycle.

Furthermore, reading is goal oriented and the goal is always meaning. Each cycle is tentative and partial, melting into the next. Inference and prediction make it possible to leap toward meaning without fully completing the optical, perceptual, and syntactic cycles. Yet the reader, once comprehension is achieved, has the sense of having seen every graphic feature, identified every pattern and word, and assigned every syntactic pattern. Schema theory can explain this phenomenon to some extent. The reader is continuously assigning the highest level and most inclusive schema available to move toward meaning. The strategies and rules available to the reader serve as schemata for schema formation. Schema use is always tentative; that is, a schema is assigned and maintained as long as it's useful but is quickly modified or abandoned if disconfirmed. This is what Bartlett (1932) calls the schema "turning back on itself" in the process of its use. All this means that each cycle can be understood only in the context of the holistic process.

The visual (optical) cycle. The eye is an optical instrument with a lens like any other lens; it has an angle of vision and a focal length, and it cannot function in the dark. Because written text is two dimensional and linear, the eye must scan the text, but it can provide useful visual input only when fixations occur. Thus, any visual process could be considered as a series of snapshots or frames of film if the brain operated like a photo album, but it does not. We do not see our world as chopped into snapshots surrounded by fuzz, but rather, as Neisser (1977) says, as a three-dimensional and integrated whole.

It is easy to demonstrate that only a small circle of the page is in sharp focus at any one-eye fixation. Furthermore, since the reader of English knows the display is horizontally linear, it follows that more attention will be paid to the horizontal dimension of that circle than to the vertical, so the visual field becomes a flattened oval. But in reading, the schemata the brain is operating with make it possible to use information in the peripheral visual field if it is consistent with the reader's expectations.

Kolers (1969) has summarized well the role of visual information in reading: reading begins with seeing the text, but it is what one does with the visual input that is the difference between seeing and reading.

The perceptual cycle. In a famous study, Miller (1956) demonstrated that how much can be remembered from a brief visual exposure to a text depends on the brain's ability to organize the information into meaningful wholes. "Seven plus or minus two" units represents the range among different observers. But whether these units are graphic features, letters, words, or longer meaningful phrases depends on what schema the observer can use for the visual input function. Thus observers can "see" and remember whole sentences with the same ease and assurance as they can see a few randomly ordered letters.

Cattell (1947) demonstrated the same principle nearly a century ago. He showed that the same features used to recognize a letter could be used to recognize a word. Perception does indeed depend on selecting highly significant and distinctive features and inferring the wholes they relate to. But it is only in the context of the whole that the features are significant or distinctive. Noses, for example, vary considerably from person to person, and to recognize someone quickly we must certainly use these distinctive noses. Yet it would be very difficult to identify the noses outside the context of the faces.

One aspect of perception that must be understood is that learning what not to pay attention to is as important as learning what to attend to. Consider a driver approaching a busy intersection. Realizing that there is significant information in the visual field that requires that the car be stopped by applying the brakes depends on assigning great significance to one relatively small spot of red light and ignoring as insignificant all the other lights. In just such a manner readers must use their selection strategies to choose only the most useful information from all that is available. The reader cannot store all information as a computer might and then sort out which pieces are significant. If a reader attempted to do so, the system would overload and comprehension would be slowed or completely disrupted.

The syntactic cycle. To get to meaning, the reader must assign a syntactic structure to the text. From a transformational point of view, the clause is the most significant unit because meaning is represented in the deep structure as a set of clauses that are transformed into the sentences of the surface structure through transformational rules. The reader must construct both surface and deep structure to get to the clauses and their interrelationships and to get to the meaning. Halliday (1975) also considers the clause the most significant unit in relating grammar and meaning.

Consider this common primer sentence:

See Spot run.

To make sense of this, the reader must treat it as an imperative. That requires awareness that the sentence starts with a simple verb. Only by treating it as an imperative can the reader apply the rule that provides the deep structure subject (you) not present in the surface representation—that is, the reader sees,

[You] See Spot run.

This seemingly simple sentence has a complex verb-noun-verb form. That's because it's composed of two clauses. The second clause is the object of the verb *to see:*

[You] See <Spot run.>

Spot is the subject of the second clause, but the verb in the second clause is an infinitive with the usual *to* deleted. The underlying structure of the second clause is *Spot runs:*

[You] See <Spot runs.> = [You] See <Spot [to] run.> = See Spot run.

There is no way to get to the meaning of this text sequence without going through the syntax. But imperatives are a familiar part of language, even for young readers. They have developed the schema for this sentence type. This three-word sentence is syntactically complex but not nearly as complex as many sentences found in texts of all kinds, including material considered appropriate for use in reading instruction in the early grades.

Inference and prediction strategies play important roles in the syntactic cycle. The reader must have a syntactic pattern within which to give symbolic value to and organize the perceptual information. The reader uses the syntactic features and cues in the text to make the necessary inferences and predictions; so, perceptual information is used to assign a syntactic pattern and this pattern is then used to assign values to perceptual information.

Words cannot be recognized unless there is a grammatical context to put them in. Halliday (1975) refers to this language system as the lexico-grammar because words in context must have both syntactic and lexical references that are interdependent. Rather than the common-sense notion that the sentence can't be understood until the words are recognized, the words can't be known until the structure they are found in is assigned. The assignment of syntactic structures by readers is reflected in the intonation used in oral reading. Often readers will regress in oral reading to the beginning of a paragraph or sentence to change the intonation after changing their minds about the syntactic pattern.

The semantic cycle. The grammar of a language exists largely on the level of sentences, though there are some rules that are intersentential. But the grammatical system of a language, complex as it is, consists of a relatively small number of rules capable of generating an infinite number of sentences. Using syntactic rules, people have the ability to produce novel sentences that they have never uttered, heard, or read and be assured that they will be considered grammatical by others who know the language.

The semantic system of a language is much more complex than the syntactic. It must be capable of representing the full range of thoughts, feelings, and emotions of the users of the language as individuals and as social groups. Whereas all users of the language control its rules (though these vary somewhat from dialect to dialect), they cannot possibly control everything that the language can mean or the full range of vocabulary, phrasing, idiom, and style that authors of texts use in representing meaning. That's why no one could possibly comprehend the full range of texts that exist or can be created in any language. Writers and readers must share a base of knowledge and a set of semantic devices—including specialized styles, special terminology, special text formats, and special cohesive devices—to achieve a high level of communication through written language.

Piaget (1971) helps us to understand how meaning is constructed. It's easy to assimilate information as we read provided that it fits within our existing schemata. When there is a conflict between what we think we know and what we are learning, then accommodation must occur to rebuild those schemata. Readers must be capable of learning through reading in the sense of assimilating new knowledge to established schemata and also of accommodating existing schemata to new knowledge. But the ability of a reader to comprehend a given text is very much limited by the conceptual and experiential background of the reader, and there are strong limitations on how much new knowledge can be gained from a reading of a given text.

How well the writer knows the audience and has built the text to suit that audience makes a major difference in text predictability and comprehension. However, since comprehension results from reader-text transactions, what the reader knows, who the reader is, what values guide the reader, and what purposes or interests the reader has will play vital roles in the reading process. It follows that what is comprehended from a given text varies among readers. Meaning is ultimately created by each reader.

An extensive vocabulary is undoubtedly a characteristic of a reader capable of making sense of a wide range of texts. But it is a mistake to think that vocabulary-building exercises can produce improved comprehension. Language is learned in the context of its use. Word meanings are built in relationship to concepts; language facilitates learning, but it is the conceptual development that creates the need for the language. Without that, words are empty forms. So vocabulary is built in the course of language use, including reading. It is probably more accurate to say that people have big vocabularies because they read a lot than that they read well because they have big vocabularies.

Throughout this chapter the emphasis has been on reading as a meaning-seeking process. It is this search for meaning that preoccupies the reader and unifies the use of the strategies and cycles that the process requires. Meaning is both input and output in this process. That's why aspects of the process and how it works cannot be isolated from the ultimate goal of construction of meaning. Learning to read involves getting the process together. That's harder if instruction takes it apart.

Flexibility and Diversity Within Unity

It's not possible to read without using the strategies and cycles discussed earlier. It's not possible to read without engaging oneself in a transaction with a text and seeking to make sense of it. These are universal essentials to reading across text types, styles, languages, purposes, and orthographies. Readers develop special strategies and schemata for dealing with different text types, different purposes, and different languages with different orthographies. Novels have a macrostructure different from those of essays or informational texts, so readers need to develop a sense of text appropriate to each text type in order to use inference and predication effectively. German has a sentence structure different from English, and readers of each assign the syntactic structure appropriate to the language. Hebrew uses a different alphabet and directionality than English. Readers of Hebrew have optical and perceptual strategies for scanning from right to left and they infer vowels on the basis of orthographic, syntactic, and semantic information since vowels are not explicitly represented as they are in languages that use the Roman alphabet. All this requires flexibility and variability within the single process with universal characteristics that is required to make sense of print. And making sense of print is what reading is all about.

What's Known and Who Knows It

In the 25 years since I began building a model of the reading process a lot has been learned. Those concerned with literacy and the development of written language have an integrated and increasingly powerful knowledge base about reading, text and writing to draw upon. All of this is meaningless, however, if the knowledge is not shared and used by the professionals whose job it is to help people—particularly young people—become literate. Fortunately, teaching as a profession is coming of age. Not only are teachers aware of and making use of this knowledge base, but they are also taking responsibility for translating it into practical pedagogy and authentic literacy experiences for their pupils. Teachers are not satisfied being told by researchers or by basal textbook authors what to do and when to do it. They are making professional decisions on behalf of their pupils. They are designing curriculum and inventing methodology consistent with the sociopsycholinguistic transactional understanding of literacy processes. Knowledge is being produced at the chalk-face of education, where teachers and pupils confront the realities of teaching and learning.

The knowledge is now so widely shared and implemented that it has shaken the foundations of two of the educational institutions most resistant to change and new knowledge: the textbook-publishing and test-publishing industries. Both are aware that teachers are so knowledgeable that they will no longer accept the old basals and the old tests.

What an exciting time it is for researchers who are willing to toss aside the old paradigms, leave the laboratories, come into the classrooms, and join the Copernican revolution in literacy.

References

Adams, M.J. (1990). *Beginning to read: Thinking and learning about print.* Cambridge, MA: MIT Press.

Altwerger, B., & Goodman, K.S. (1981, June). *Studying text difficulty through miscue analysis* (Program in Language and Literacy, Occasional Paper No. 2). Tucson, AZ: University of Arizona.

Anderson, J. (1982). *The writer, the reader, and the text.* Paper presented at the 19th Annual United Kingdom Reading Association Reading Conference, Newcastle-upon-Tyne, UK.

Bartlett, F.C. (1932). *Remembering: A study in experimental and social psychology.* London: Cambridge University Press.

Bormuth, J. (1978). Value and volume of literacy. *Visible Language, 12,* 118–161.

Cambourne, B., & Rousch, P. (1979). *A psycholinguistic model of the reading process as it relates to proficient, average, and low-ability readers* (Tech. Rep.). Wagga Wagga, NSW, Australia: Riverina College of Advanced English, Sturt University.

Carrithers, C., & Bever, T.G. (1982). *Eye movement patterns confirm theories of language comprehension.* Unpublished manuscript, Columbia University, New York, NY.

Cattell, J.M. (1947). James McKeen Cattell, man of science. In A.T.A. Poffenberger (Ed.), *Psychological research* (Vol. 1, pp. 13–23). Lancaster, PA: Science.

Chall, J.S. (1967). *Learning to read: The great debate.* New York: McGraw-Hill.

Chapman, J. (1981). The reader and the text. In J. Chapman (Ed.), *The reader and the text.* London: Heinemann.

Chomsky, N. (1957). *Syntactic structures.* The Hague, Netherlands: Mouton.

Ferreiro, E., & Teberosky, A. (1982). *Literacy before schooling.* Portsmouth, NH: Heinemann.

Fries, C. (1952). *The structure of English.* New York: Harcourt Brace.

Goodman, K.S. (1965). A Linguistic Study of Cues and Miscues in Reading. *Elementary English, 42*(6), 639–643.

Goodman, K.S. (1967, May). Reading: A psycholinguistic guessing game. *Journal of the Reading Specialist, 6,* 126–135.

Goodman, K.S. (1969). Analysis of Oral Reading Miscues: Applied Psycholinguistics. *Reading Research Quarterly, 5*(1), 9–30.

Goodman, K.S. (1983). *Text features as they relate to miscues: Determiners* (Program in Language and Literacy, Occasional Paper No. 8). Tucson, AZ: University of Arizona.

Goodman, K.S. (1984). Unity in reading. In A.C. Purves & O. Niles (Eds.), *Becoming readers in a complex society* (83rd yearbook of the National Society for the Study of Education, Part I, pp. 79–114). Chicago, IL: University of Chicago Press.

Goodman, K.S., & Bird, L. (1982). *On the wording of texts: A study of intra-text word frequency* (Program in Language and Literacy, Occasional Paper No. 6). Tucson, AZ: University of Arizona.

Goodman, K.S., & Burke, C.L. (1973, April). *Theoretically based studies of patterns of miscues in oral reading performance* (Project No. 9-0375). Washington, DC: U.S. Office of Education.

Goodman, K.S., & Gespass, S. (1983). *Text features as they relate to miscues: Pronouns* (Program in Language and Literacy, Occasional Paper No. 7). Tucson, AZ: University of Arizona.

Goodman, K.S., & Gollasch, F.V. (June, 1981). *Word level omissions in reading: Deliberate and non-deliberate* (Program in Language and Literacy, Occasional Paper No. 2). Tucson, AZ: University of Arizona.

Goodman, K.S., & Goodman, Y.M. (1978). *Reading of American children whose language is a stable rural dialect of English or a language other than English* (Final Rep., Project NIE-C-00-3-0087). Washington, DC: National Institute of Education.

Goodman, Y.M. (1980). The roots of literacy. In M. Douglas (Ed.), *Forty-fourth year book of the Claremont Reading Conference.* Claremont, CA: Claremont Graduate School.

Goodman, Y.M. (Ed.). (1991). *How children construct literacy: Piagetian perspectives.* Newark, DE: International Reading Association.

Goodman, Y.M., & Wilde, S. (1992). *A community of writers.* New York: Teachers College Press.

Grice, H.P. (1975). Logic and conversation. In P.A.M.J.L. Cole (Ed.), *Speech acts: Volume 3, syntax and semantics.* New York: Academic.

Halliday, M.A.K. (1975). *Learning how to mean: Explorations in the development of language.* London: Edward Arnold.

Halliday, M.A.K., & Hasan, R. (1975). *Cohesion in English.* London: Longman.

Huey, E.B. (1908). *The psychology and pedagogy of reading.* New York: Macmillan.

Kolers, P. (1969). Reading is only incidentally visual. In K.S. Goodman & J. Fleming (Eds.), *Psycholinguistics and the teaching of reading.* Newark, DE: International Reading Association.

Lindberg, M. (1977). *A descriptive analysis of the relationship between selected prelinguistic, linguistic, and psycholinguistic measures of readability.* Unpublished doctoral dissertation, Wayne State University, Detroit, MI.

Marek, A. (Ed.). (1985, November). *Annotated bibliography of miscue analysis* (Program in Language and Literacy, Occasional Paper No. 16). Tucson, AZ: University of Arizona.

Miller, G. (1956, March). The magic number seven plus or minus two: Some limits on our capacity in information processing. *Psychological Review, 63,* 81–92.

Neisser, U. (1977). *Cognition and reality.* San Francisco, CA: W.H. Freeman.

Piaget, J. (1971). *Psychology and epistemology.* New York: Grossman.

Rosenblatt, L.M. (1981). *The reader, the text, the poem: The transactional theory of the literary work.* Carbondale, IL: Southern Illinois University Press.

Schank, R.C. (1982). *Reading and understanding: Teaching from the perspective of artificial intelligence.* Hillsdale, NJ: Erlbaum.

Searle, J.R. (1969). *Speech acts.* New York: Cambridge University Press.

Smith, F. (1982). *Understanding reading* (3rd ed.). New York: Holt, Rinehart.

Spiro, R.J., Bruce, B.C., & Brewer, W.F. (1980). *Theoretical issues in reading comprehension.* Hillsdale, NJ: Erlbaum.

Chapter Two

Reading: A Psycholinguistic Guessing Game

Kenneth S. Goodman
Wayne State University, 1967

As scientific understanding develops in any field of study, preexisting, naive, common sense notions must give way. Such outmoded beliefs clutter the literature dealing with the process of reading. They interfere with the application of modern scientific concepts of language and thought to research in reading. They confuse the attempts at application of such concepts to solution of problems involved in the teaching and learning of reading. The very fact that such naive beliefs are based on common sense explains their persistent and recurrent nature. To the casual and unsophisticated observer they appear to explain, even predict, a set of phenomena in reading. This paper will deal with one such key misconception and offer a more viable scientific alternative.

Simply stated, the common sense notion I seek here to refute is this:

"Reading is a precise process. It involves exact, detailed, sequential perception and identification of letters, words, spelling patterns and large language units."

In phonic centered approaches to reading, the preoccupation is with precise letter identification. In word centered approaches, the focus is on word identifications. Known words are sight words, precisely named in any setting.

This chapter is based on a paper read at the American Educational Research Association, New York, February 1967. It was first published in the *Journal of the Reading Specialist*, (6)4, May 1967, pp. 126–135, (now *Reading Research and Instruction*). Copyright (1967) by *Reading Research and Instruction*. Reprinted with permission.

This is not to say that those who have worked diligently in the field of reading are not aware that reading is more than precise, sequential identification. But, the common sense notion, though not adequate, continues to permeate thinking about reading.

Spache (*8*) presents a word version of this common sense view: "Thus, in its simplest form, reading may be considered a series of word perceptions."

The teacher's manual of the Lippincott *Basic Reading* (*6*) incorporates a letter by letter variant in the justification of its reading approach: "In short, following this program the child learns from the beginning to see words exactly as the most skillful readers see them . . . as whole images of complete words with all their letters."

In place of this misconception, I offer this: Reading is a selective process. It involves partial use of available minimal language cues selected from perceptual input on the basis of the reader's expectation. As this partial information is processed, tentative decisions are made to be confirmed, rejected, or refined as reading progresses.

More simply stated, reading is a psycholinguistic guessing game. It involves an interaction between thought and language. Efficient reading does not result from precise perception and identification of all elements, but from skill in selecting the fewest, most productive cues necessary to produce guesses which are right the first time. The ability to anticipate that which has not been seen, of course, is vital in reading, just as the ability to anticipate what has not yet been heard is vital in listening. Consider this actual sample of a relatively proficient child reading orally. The reader is a fourth grade child reading the opening paragraphs of a story from a sixth grade basal reader (*5*).

"If it bothers you to think of it as baby sitting," my father said, "then don't think of it as baby sitting. Think of it as homework. Part of your education. You just happen to do your studying in the room where the baby brother is sleeping, that's all." He helped my mother with her coat, and then they were gone.

hoped Ⓒ *a*
So education it was! I ~~opened~~ the dictionary and picked out a

↓   *PH*————   *He*
word that sound~~ed~~ good. "Phil/oso/phi/cal!" ~~I~~ yelled. Might

what it means   *1. Phizo*   *2. Phiso/soophical*
as well study ~~word meanings first~~. "~~Philosophical~~: showing calmness

his   *1. fort*   *2. future*   *3. futshion*
and courage in ~~the~~ face of ill fortune." I mean I really yelled it. I guess a fellow has to work off steam once in a while.

He has not seen the story before. It is, by intention, slightly difficult for him. The insights into his reading process come primarily from his errors, which I choose to call miscues in order to avoid value implications. His expected responses mask the process of their attainment, but his unexpected responses have been achieved through the same process, albeit less successfully applied. The ways that they deviate from the expected reveal this process.

In the common sense view that I am rejecting, all deviations must be treated as errors. Furthermore, it must be assumed in this view that an error either indicates that the reader does not know something or that he has been "careless" in the application of his knowledge.

For example, his substitution of *the* for *your* in the first paragraph of the sample must mean that he was careless, since he has already read *your* and *the* correctly in the very same sentence. The implication is that we must teach him to be more careful, that is to be more precise in identifying each word or letter.

But now let's take the view that I have suggested. What sort of information could have led to tentatively deciding on *the* in this situation and not rejecting or refining this decision? There obviously is no graphic relationship between *your* and *the*. It may be of course, that he picked up *the* in the periphery of his visual field. But, there is an important non-graphic relationship between *the* and *your*. They both have the same grammatical function: they are, in my terminology, noun markers. Either the reader anticipated a noun marker and supplied one paying no attention to graphic information or he used *your* as a grammatical signal ignoring its graphic shape. Since the tentative choice *the* disturbs neither the meaning nor the grammar of the passage, there is no reason to reject and correct it. This explanation appears to be confirmed by two similar miscues in the next paragraph. *A* and *his* are both substituted for *the*. Neither are corrected. Though the substitution of *his* changes the meaning, the peculiar idiom used in this dictionary definition, "in the face of ill fortune," apparently has little meaning to this reader anyway.

The conclusion this time is that he is using noun markers for grammatical, as well as graphic, information in reaching his tentative conclusions. All together in reading this ten page story, he made twenty noun marker substitutions, six omissions and two insertions.

He corrected four of his substitutions and one omission. Similar miscues involved other function words (auxiliary verbs and prepositions, for example). These miscues appear to have little effect on the meaning of what he is reading. In spite of their frequency, their elimination would not substantially improve the child's reading. Insistence on more precise identification of each word might cause this reader to stop seeking grammatical information and use only graphic information.

The substitution of *hoped* for *opened* could again be regarded as careless or imprecise identification of letters. But, if we dig beyond this common sense explanation, we find 1) both are verbs and 2) the words have key graphic similarities. Further, there may be evidence of the reader's bilingual French-Canadian background here, as there is in subsequent miscues (*harms* for *arms, shuckled* for *chuckled, shoose* for *choose, shair* for *chair*). The correction of this miscue may involve an immediate rejection of the tentative choice made on the basis of a review of the graphic stimulus, or it may result from recognizing that it cannot lead to the rest of the sentence, "I hoped a dictionary . . ." does not make sense. (It isn't decodable). In any case, the reader has demonstrated the process by which he constantly tests his guesses, or tentative choices, if you prefer.

Sound*s* is substituted for sound*ed*, but the two differ in ending only. Common sense might lead to the conclusion that the child does not pay attention to word endings, slurs the ends or is otherwise careless. But, there is no consistent similar occurrence in other word endings. Actually, the child has substituted one inflectional ending for another. In doing so he has revealed 1) his ability to separate base and inflectional suffix, and 2) his use of inflectional endings as grammatical signals or markers. Again he has not corrected a miscue that is both grammatically and semantically acceptable.

He for *I* is a pronoun for pronoun substitution that results in a meaning change, though the antecedent is a bit vague, and the inconsistency of meaning is not easily apparent.

When we examine what the reader did with the sentence "*Might as well study word meanings first,*" we see how poorly the model of precise sequential identification fits the reading process. Essentially this reader has decoded graphic input for meaning and then encoded meaning in oral output with transformed grammar and changed vocabulary, but with the basic meaning retained. Perhaps as he encoded his output, he was already working at the list word which followed, but the tentative choice was good enough and was not corrected.

There are two examples, in this sample, of the reader working at unknown words. He reveals a fair picture of his strategies and abilities in these miscues, though in neither is he successful. In his several attempts at *philosophical,* his first attempt comes closest. Incidentally, he reveals here that he can use a phonic letter-sound strategy when he wants to. In subsequent attempts he moves away from this sounding out, trying other possibilities, as if trying to find something which at least will sound familiar. Interestingly, here he has a definition of sorts, but no context to work with. *Philosophical* occurs as a list word a number of times in the story. In subsequent attempts, the child tried *physica, physicacol, physical, philosovigul, phizzlesovigul, phizzo sorigul, philazophgul.* He appears to move in concentric circles around the phonic information he has, trying deviations and variations. His three unsuccessful attempts at fortune illustrate this same process. Both words are apparently unknown to the reader. He can never really identify a word he has not heard. In such cases, unless the context or contexts sufficiently delimit the word's meaning, the reader is not able to get meaning from the word. In some instances, of course, the reader may form a fairly accurate definition of the word, even if he never recognizes it (that is matches it with a known oral equivalent) or pronounces it correctly. This reader achieved that with the word *typical* which occurred many times in the story. Throughout his reading he said *topical*. When he finished reading, a check of his comprehension indicated that he knew quite well the meaning of the word. This phenomenon is familiar to any adult reader. Each of us has many well-defined words in our reading vocabulary which we either mispronounce or do not use orally.

I've used the example of this youngster's oral reading not because what he's done is typical of all readers or even of readers his age, but because his miscues suggest how he carries out the psycholinguistic guessing game in reading. The miscues of other readers show similarities and differences, but all point to a selective, tentative, anticipatory process quite unlike the process of precise, sequential identification commonly assumed.

Let's take a closer look now at the components the reader manipulates in this psycholinguistic guessing game.

At any point in time, of course, the reader has available to him and brings to his reading the sum total of his experience and his language and thought development. This self-evident fact needs to be stated because what appears to be intuitive in any guessing is actually the result of knowledge so well learned that the process of its application requires little conscious effort. Most language use has reached this automatic, intuitive level. Most of us are quite unable to describe the use we make of grammar in encoding and decoding speech, yet all language users demonstrate a high degree of skill and mastery over the syntax of language even in our humblest and most informal uses of speech.

Chomsky (3) has suggested this model of sentence production by speakers of a language:

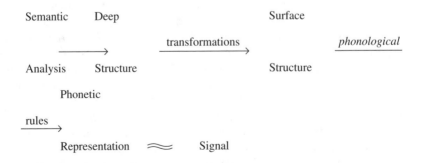

A model structure of the listener's sentence interpretation, according to Chomsky, is:

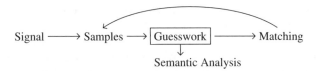

Thus, in Chomsky's view encoding of speech reaches a more or less precise level and the signal which results is fully formed. But in decoding, a sampling process aims at approximating the message and any matching or coded signal which results is a kind of by-product.

In oral reading, the reader must perform two tasks at the same time. He must produce an oral language equivalent of the graphic input which is the signal in reading, and he must also reconstruct the meaning of what he is reading. The matching in Chomsky's interpretation model is largely what I prefer to call a recoding operation. The reader recodes the coded graphic input as phonological or oral output. Meaning is not normally involved to any extent. This recoding can even be learned by someone who doesn't speak the language at all, for example, the bar-mitzvah boy may learn to recode Hebrew script as chanted oral Hebrew with no ability to understand what he is chanting; but when the reader engages in semantic analysis to reconstruct the meaning of the writer, only then is he decoding.

In oral reading there are three logical possible arrangements of these two operations. The reader may recode graphic input as oral language and then decode it. He may recode and decode simultaneously. Or, he may decode first and then encode the meaning as oral output.

On the basis of my research to date, it appears that readers who have achieved some degree of proficiency decode directly from the graphic stimulus in a process similar to Chomsky's sampling model and then encode from the deep structure, as illustrated in Chomsky's model of sentence production. Their oral output is not directly related to the graphic stimulus and may involve transformation in vocabulary and syntax, even if meaning is retained. If their comprehension is inaccurate, they will encode this changed or incomplete meaning as oral output.

The common misconception is that graphic input is precisely and sequentially recoded as phonological input and then decoded bit by bit. Meaning is cumulative, built up a piece at a time in this view. This view appears to be supported by studies of visual perception that indicate that only a very narrow span of print on either side of the point of fixation is in sharp focus at any time. We might dub this the "end of the nose" view, since it assumes that input in reading is that which lies in sharp focus in a straight line from the end of the nose. Speed and efficiency are assumed to come from widening the span taken in on either side of the nose, moving the nose more rapidly or avoiding backward movements of the eyes and nose, which of course must cut down on efficiency.

This view cannot possibly explain the speed with which the average adult reads, or a myriad of other constantly occurring phenomena in reading. How can it explain, for example, a highly proficient adult reader reading and rereading a paper he's written and always missing the same misprints. Or how can it explain our fourth grader seeing "Study word meanings first" and saying, "Study what it means"?

No, the "end of the nose" view of reading will not work. The reader is not confined to information he receives from a half inch of print in clear focus. Studies, in fact, indicate that children with severe visual handicaps are able to learn to read as well as normal children. Readers utilize not one, but three kinds of information simultaneously. Certainly without graphic input there would be no reading. But, the reader uses syntactic and semantic information as well. He predicts and anticipates on the basis of this information, sampling from the print just enough to confirm his guess of what's coming, to cue more semantic and syntactic information. Redundancy and sequential constraints in language, which the reader reacts to, make this prediction possible. Even the blurred and shadowy images he picks up in the peripheral area of his visual field may help to trigger or confirm guesses.

Skill in reading involves not greater precision, but more accurate first guesses based on better sampling techniques, greater control over language structure, broadened experiences and increased conceptual development. As the child develops reading skill and speed, he uses increasingly fewer graphic cues. Silent reading can then become a more rapid and efficient process than oral reading, for two reasons: 1) the reader's attention is not divided between decoding and recoding or encoding as oral output, and 2) his speed is not restricted to the speed of speech production. Reading becomes a more efficient and rapid process than listening, in fact, since listening is normally limited to the speed of the speaker.

Recent studies with speeded up electronic recordings where distortion of pitch is avoided have demonstrated that listening can be made more rapid without impairing comprehension too.

Though the beginning reader obviously needs more graphic information in decoding and, therefore, needs to be more precise than skilled readers, evidence from a study of first graders by Goodman (4) indicates that they begin to sample and draw on syntactic and semantic information almost from the beginning, if they are reading material which is fully formed language.

Here are excerpts from two primer stories (*1, 2*) as they were read by a first grade child at the same session. Ostensibly (and by intent of the authors) the first, from a second preprimer, should be much easier than the second, from a third preprimer. Yet she encountered problems to the point of total confusion with the first and was able to handle exactly the same elements in the second.

Note, for example, the confusion of *come* and *here* in "Ride In." This represents a habitual association in evidence in early reading of this child. Both *come* and *here* as graphic shapes are likely to be identified as *come* or *here*. In "Stop and Go," the difficulty does not occur when the words are sequential. She also substitutes *can* for *and* in the first story, but encounters no problem with either later. *Stop* stops her completely in "Ride In," a difficulty that she doesn't seem to know she has when she reads "Stop and Go" a few minutes later. Similarly, she calls (ride) *run* in the first story, but gets it right in the latter one.

Though there are miscues in the second story, there is a very important difference. In the first story she seems to be playing a game of name the word. She is recoding graphic shapes as phonological ones. Each word is apparently a separate problem. But in "Stop and Go" what she says, including her miscues, in almost all instances makes sense and is grammatically acceptable. Notice that as *Sue* becomes better known she becomes *Suzie* to our now confident reader.

A semantic association exists between *train* and *toy*. Though the child makes the same substitution many times, nothing causes her to reject her guess. It works well each time. Having called (train) *toy*, she calls (toy) *too* (actually it's an airplane in the pictures), not once, but consistently throughout the story. That doesn't seem to make sense. That's what the researcher thought too, until the child spoke of a "little red *too*" later in retelling the story. "What's a 'little red too,'" asked the researcher. "An airplane," she replied calmly. So a train is *toy* and a plane is a *too*. Why not? But, notice that when *toy* occurred preceding *train*, she could attempt nothing for *train*. There appears to be a problem for many first graders when nouns are used as adjectives.

Common sense says go back and drill her on *come, here, can, stop, ride, and;* don't let her go to the next book which she is obviously not ready to read.

But the more advanced story, with its stronger syntax, more fully formed language and increased load of meaning makes it possible for the child to use her graphic cues more effectively and supplement them with semantic and syntactic information. Teaching for more precise perception with lists and phonics charts may actually impede this child's reading development. Please notice, before we leave the passage, the effect of immediate experience on anticipation. Every one of the paragraphs in the sample starts with "Jimmy said" or "Sue said." When

RIDE IN

Run
~~Ride~~ in, Sue.
Run
~~Ride~~ in here.
Come   *here*
~~Here~~ I ~~come~~, Jimmy.
Can Come
~~And here~~ I (stop.)

STOP AND GO

Jimmy said, "Come here, Sue,
       too
Look at my ~~toy~~ (train.)

See it go.
             toy
Look at my lit/tle ~~train~~ go."
                         toy
Sue said, "Stop the ~~train~~.
             Come
Stop it ~~here,~~ Jimmy.
                             toy
Jimmy said, "I can stop the ~~train~~.
             toy
See the ~~train~~ stop."
                     too
Sue said, "Look at my ~~toy~~.
             toy
It is in the ~~train~~.
                 too
See my little red ~~toy,~~ Jimmy.
                 toy
It can ride in the ~~train~~."
                         toy
Jimmy said, "See the ~~train~~ go.

Look at it go."
       Suzie   *too*
~~Sue~~ said, "Look at my little red ~~toy~~.
                 toy
See it go for a ~~train~~ ride."
       Suzie   *too*
~~Sue~~ said, "My little red ~~toy~~!
       said   *too*
(C) Jimmy⌐my, ~~toy~~ is not here.
                 toy
It is not in the ~~train~~.
             toy
Stop the ~~train,~~ Jimmy.
                     too
Stop it and look for my ~~toy~~."

the reader comes to a line starting *Jimmy,* she assumes that it will be
followed by said and it is not until her expectation is contradicted by
subsequent input that she regresses and corrects her miscue.

Since they must learn to play the psycholinguistic guessing game
as they develop reading ability, effective methods and materials used

by teachers who understand the rules of the game, must help them to select the most productive cues, to use their knowledge of language structure, to draw on their experiences and concepts. They must be helped to discriminate between more and less useful available information. Fortunately, this parallels the processes they have used in developing the ability to comprehend spoken language. George Miller (7) has suggested ". . . psycholinguists should try to formulate performance models that will incorporate . . . hypothetical information storage and information processing components that can simulate the actual behavior of language users."

I'd like to present now my model of this psycholinguistic guessing game we call reading English. Please understand that the steps do not necessarily take place in the sequential or stretched out form they are shown here. [The model appears on pages 56–57.]

1. The reader scans along a line of print from left to right and down the page, line by line.

2. He fixes at a point to permit eye focus. Some print will be central and in focus, some will be peripheral; perhaps his perceptual field is a flattened circle.

3. Now begins the selection process. He picks up graphic cues, guided by constraints set up through prior choices, his language knowledge, his cognitive styles, and strategies he has learned.

4. He forms a perceptual image using these cues and his anticipated cues. This image then is partly what he sees and partly what he expected to see.

5. Now he searches his memory for related syntactic, semantic, and phonological cues. This may lead to selection of more graphic cues and to reforming the perceptual image.

6. At this point, he makes a guess or tentative choice consistent with graphic cues. Semantic analysis leads to partial decoding as far as possible. This meaning is stored in short-term memory as he proceeds.

7. If no guess is possible, he checks the recalled perceptual input and tries again. If a guess is still not possible, he takes another look at the text to gather more graphic cues.

8. If he can make a decodable choice, he tests it for semantic and grammatical acceptability in the context developed by prior choices and decoding.

9. If the tentative choice is not acceptable semantically or syntactically, then he regresses, scanning from right to left along the line and up the page to locate a point of semantic or syntactic inconsistency. When such a point is found, he starts over at that point. If no

Figure 2–1
A Flow Chart of Goodman's Model of Reading

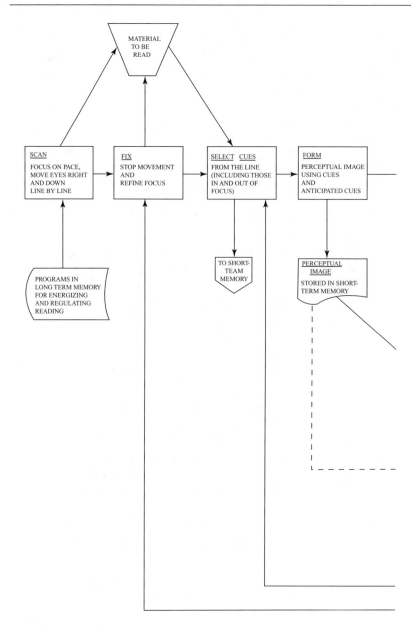

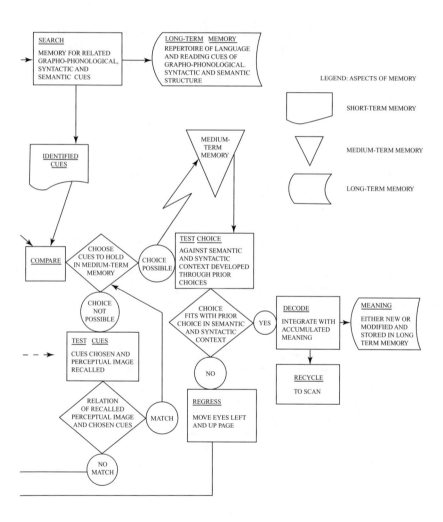

inconsistency can be identified, he reads on seeking some cue which will make it possible to reconcile the anomalous situation.

10. If the choice is acceptable, decoding is extended, meaning is assimilated with prior meaning, and prior meaning is accommodated, if necessary. Expectations are formed about input and meaning that lies ahead.

11. Then the cycle continues.

Throughout the process there is constant use of long- and short-term memory.

I offer no apologies for the complexity of this model. Its faults lie, not in its complexity, but in the fact that it is not yet complex enough to fully account for the complex phenomena in the actual behavior of readers. But such is man's destiny in his quest for knowledge. Simplistic folklore must give way to complexity as we come to know.

References

1. Betts, Emmett A. "Ride In," *Time to Play*, Second Preprimer, Betts Basic Readers (3rd ed.), Language Arts Series. New York: American Book, 1963.

2. Betts, Emmett A., and Carolyn M. Welch. "Stop and Go," *All In A Day*, Third Preprimer, Betts Basic Readers. New York: American Book, 1963.

3. Chomsky, Noam. Lecture at Project Literacy, Cornell University, June 18, 1965.

4. Goodman, Yalta M. College of Education, Wayne State University, doctoral study of development of reading in first grade children.

5. Hayes, William D. "My Brother is a Genius," *Adventures Now and Then*, Book 6, Betts Basic Readers (3rd ed.), Emmett A. Betts and Carolyn M. Welch. New York: American Book, 1963, 246.

6. McCracken, Glenn, and Charles C. Walcutt. *Basic Reading*, teacher's edition for the preprimer and primer. Philadelphia: B. Lippincott, 1963, vii.

7. Miller, George A. "Some Preliminaries to Psycholinguistics," *American Psychologist*, Vol. 20, No. 18, 1965.

8. Spache, George. *Reading In The Elementary School*. Boston: Allyn and Bacon, 1964, 12.

Chapter Three

Behind the Eye: What Happens in Reading

Kenneth S. Goodman
Wayne State University, 1970

A child, eyebrows knit, haltingly speaks as he stares intently at the small book he is holding, "See Tom. See Tom..." He stops, apparently unable to continue. "We haven't had that next word yet," he states in a troubled voice to his teacher.

"Mary is only seven, but she can read anything," says the doting mother to her friend. "Read us that article from the *Times*," she says to the little girl. The child reads an article on national politics, with great speed and animation, while the friend listens appreciatively. She stumbles occasionally, as the going gets rough now and then, but is apparently untroubled by the task. "Did you understand all that dear?" her awed listener asks. "She has a little difficulty putting it into words, but I'm sure she understands," interposes the mother.

"I give up," the weary graduate student mutters to himself as he sits at the small table in the library stacks. He's just finished his third reading of the article his professor has assigned. He forces himself to formulate, out of the conceptual jumble he finds himself lost in, a few questions to raise in class. "Maybe the class is too advanced for me," he wonders. "Why don't these guys write so people can understand?"

This chapter is reprinted from Kenneth S. Goodman and Olive S. Niles, (eds.), *Reading Process and Program*. Commission on the English Curriculum, Urbana, Illinois: National Council of Teachers of English, 1970, pp. 3–38. Copyright (1970) by the National Council of Teachers of English. Reprinted with permission.

"I can't make head or tail out of this damn thing." A best-selling writer is speaking long-distance to his attorney. "It's some kind of release I'm supposed to sign giving this producer the film rights to my latest book. But it's full of all kinds of parties of the first part and whereas's."

"Read it to me," says the lawyer. The author begins. "The undersigned, who shall be known as . . ." The attorney listens, interrupts a few times to ask for repetition, and is ready by the time his caller has finished to offer his legal advice. He clarifies the meaning of the document to the author, restates the legal terminology in phrases his client finds meaningful, dictates a clause to be added to protect the author's rights.

Reading is obviously involved in each of these episodes. But, at what point does it become reading and at what point does it cease to be reading and become something else, thinking perhaps, or concept formation, or the acquisition of knowledge?

Is the child who is limited to calling the names of word shapes he has been taught in any sense a reader? If he is not, at what point does he become one? Is it when he has a larger sight-word repertoire? How large? Is it when he has learned how to "attack" new words? If, like the hypothetical Mary above, he can "read" things he can't understand, is he reading?

To what extent must a reader arrive at the meaning the writer intended? If he must fully *comprehend,* then our graduate student is a non-reader. Even if a moderate level of comprehension is required he has fallen short of the mark. Are all readers then only semiliterate?

Who has read the legal document? The lawyer who is hundreds of miles away from it and who cannot even see it, or his client who holds it in his hand? Or did reading require both of their contributions? Shall we call what the author did reading, and his attorney's contribution interpretation? Or shall we say that the author was word-calling and the lawyer comprehending?

The issues which are raised in these episodes are neither simple nor easily answered. To a certain extent, of course, we can be arbitrary. We can define reading to be anything we choose. But if our definition is to be useful, it must be one we can use consistently; it must be inclusive of that which is relevant and exclusive of that which is not. It must also be productive. Definitions which are too narrow or too broad or too vague or too specific tend to cut off or dissipate inquiry rather than promote it. Further, a definition must be consistent with reality.

To move us toward a definition of reading, it may help to list certain evident aspects of the process:

- Reading begins with graphic language in some form: print, script, etc.
- The purpose of reading is the reconstruction of meaning. Meaning is not in print, but it is meaning that the author begins with when

he writes. Somehow the reader strives to *reconstruct* this meaning as he reads.

- In alphabetic writing systems there is a direct relationship between oral language and written language.
- Visual perception must be involved in reading.
- Nothing intrinsic in the writing system or its symbols has meaning. There is nothing in the shape or sequence of any letters or grouping of letters which in itself is meaning.
- Meaning is in the mind of the writer and the mind of the reader.
- Yet readers are capable through reading of reconstructing a message which agrees with the writer's intended message.

A Definition of Reading

At this point, we're ready to state a definition of reading: *Reading is a complex process by which a reader reconstructs, to some degree, a message encoded by a writer in graphic language.*

In this definition it is no more significant that the reader starts with graphic input[1] than that he ends with meaning. To understand this process, we must understand the nature of the graphic input. We must understand how language works and how language is used by the reader. We must understand how much meaning depends on the reader's prior learning and experience in the reconstruction of meaning. We must understand the perceptual system involved in reading. As we come to see the reader as a user of language, we will understand that reading is a psycholinguistic process, an interaction between thought and language.

Written Language: The Nature of the Graphic Input

Written English is, of course, an alphabetic system. It uses a set of letters almost directly adapted from the Latin. The Latin alphabet in turn was derived from the Greek. Most modern languages are written with alphabets derived from the same group of ancient, related alphabets. Alphabetic writing differs from other systems in that the system is a representation not of meaning directly, but of oral language. In

---

1. As we think of reading as an information seeking process, it will help to think of the graphic material as input and meaning as output. Oral reading produces speech as a second output.

original intent, the units of written language (letters) represented the sound units of speech rather than meanings as in pictographic and other systems.

Oral language is produced in a time sequence, but written language must be arranged spatially. Though various arrangements are possible, and used in other systems, in English print is arranged from left to right and top to bottom in successive lines. White space separates patterns of letters just as oral patterns are marked by intonation contours, pauses, pitch sequences, and relative stressing. Larger patterns require markings, punctuation, to set them off from other patterns. Again, intonational features are replaced to some degree in print by periods, commas, and other graphic signals. In this feature, as in a number of others, there is no one-to-one correspondence between oral and written language. The intonation pattern of a question like "Do you understand?" is distributed over the whole oral sentence, while graphically it is represented only by a capital letter at the beginning and a question mark at the end. It is marked as different from the statement form only at the end. (Contrast Spanish which puts a question mark at both ends.)

Relationships between Oral and Written English

While written language is a secondary form, both historically and in the personal history of any individual, it must be seen as a different but parallel form to oral language, since both for the literate user are fully capable of meeting the complex needs of communication. Written language has the advantage, only recently made possible for oral language, of being perfectable and preservable. Oral language on the other hand is more easily and more rapidly produced in a wider range of circumstances.

Having said that English uses an alphabetic writing system, we must now caution that the set of relationships between oral and written English is not a simple small set of letter-to-sound correspondences (or phoneme-to-grapheme ones, to use linguistic terms). For several reasons, to be accurate, we must say that the relationships are between patterns of sounds and patterns of letters. The most significant of these reasons is that spelling patterns are basically standard and stable while oral language changes over time and space.

Spellings are standard. Standard spellings were developed by printers in the early years of the development of printing and the spread of literacy. Though Americans may differ from the British in the spellings of a very few words like "labor" (labour), there is great agreement on word spellings among speakers of all English dialects. *Pumpkin* is the spelling whether one says *punkin, ponkin, pumpkin* or whatever. This is, of course, a considerable advantage, since written communication between speakers of diverse English dialects is made more effective. Any other arrangement would require establishment of a standard dialect upon which to base spelling. Subsequently either the dialect would need to be protected from change or periodical updating of the spelling system to catch up with the changes would be required. If this could be accomplished, the spelling system would be highly suited for the one dialect's speakers, but increasingly dysfunctional for all others. Change is always going on in language. It cannot in any case be closed off. No lesser man than Napoleon tried and failed to keep language from changing.

Oral language sequences. Another factor in making the relationships between oral and written English complex has to do with the nature of oral language sound sequences. For example, note these related words: *site, situate,* and *situation.* In *site,* we have a well known pattern with a vowel-consonant-e. (V-C-e) The *e* serves as a pattern marker. Notice that the relationship of the prior vowel to a sound is not clear without the rest of the spelling pattern. But when, through affixes, the word *situate* is formed, a sound sequence occurs after the /t/ which requires a shift in the oral form to a *ch* sound /č/. The same shift occurs in the word sequence *don't you.* We must either change the spelling to *ch* or retain the *t* and lose the close letter-sound correspondence. Similar shifting is required in moving to *situation* where the sound becomes *sh* /š/. The spelling system has alternatives. It may retain the close correspondence of sounds and letters and thus change spellings as the sounds shift. Or it may retain the letters even when the sound shifts and thus preserve the derivational character of the word relationships. The system tends to do the latter perhaps because speakers of the language seem to shift as required so automatically that they are not bothered by the spelling discrepancy. It simply sounds too strange to his ears for a speaker of English to say *situation* differently. This may be illustrated with this nonsense word offered in three alternate spellings: *boft, boffed, bofd.* The final consonant cluster is pronounced the same by native speakers of English. Because /f/ precedes the final consonant, the latter is produced as /t/; spelling cannot induce a speaker to abandon that pronunciation.

Much has been written about regular and irregular relationships between oral and written English. The distinction loses its meaning if we understand that the patterns of correspondence are complex, but systematic. Some examples above have already illustrated this complex regularity. Here is another: *s* may not frequently represent the sound *sh* /š/, but when it does, as in *sure* and *sugar,* the circumstances are consistent ones and it is thus every bit as regular in its representation as it is in *sister. Hymn, damn, bomb, sign,* appear irregularly spelled, but they are not so if we consider the "silent letters" relate to derived forms such as *hymnal, damnation, bombard, signal.*

A number of early applications to reading materials which stressed linguistics tended to apply a rather narrow view of regular letter-sound correspondence. The Bloomfield-Barnhart materials, the SRA Linguistic Readers, and the Harper-Row Linguistic Science Readers are examples. The Merrill Linguistic Readers, based on the work of C. C. Fries, had a somewhat broader view of regularity as represented in spelling patterns.

The Nature of Language

If we are to define and understand reading, we must understand the nature of language itself. Paradoxically, language is learned so early and so well that we tend to take its functioning for granted.

How Language Works

Language is always a means and only rarely an end in itself. We are so distracted, as we use it, by meaning (the end for which language is the means) that we are quite unaware of how language works to convey meaning. Consider, for example, a simple statement: *John hit Bill.* In either oral or written form, it is not the symbols, phonemes, or letters but the systematic structuring of these symbols that makes comprehension of meaning possible.

The listener or reader must recognize the patterns *John, hit,* and *Bill* and he must also recognize the pattern of patterns which makes a statement of relationships possible. The difference between *John hit Bill* and *Bill hit John* is in the sentence patterns or syntax. Nothing else tells the listener or reader whether Bill or John hit John or Bill. Grammar, the system of language, makes it possible for language to convey the most complex relationships humans conceive.

All language is patterned: the patterns are the sequences in which the elements may occur. In *John hit Bill,* it is pattern alone which tells the listener who was hitting and who was being hit.

In English, pattern is itself the single most important aspect of grammar. Other languages make more use of word changes (inflections) such as affixes to carry extensive portions of the grammatical system. In such languages the nominative and accusative endings might have differentiated the aggressor from the victim in the example above. English preserves such a system in its pronouns. *I hit him* and *He hit me* use different forms in grammatical cases. But notice that we still would not say *Him hit I.* Pattern is still preserved.

Certain English words and word parts serve as pattern markers. In a statement like *A man was feeding his dogs,* we have a pattern: A ____ was ____ing his ____s. The pattern markers, function words like *A, his,* and *was,* and inflectional endings like *ing,* and *s* set the pattern up. In themselves none of these elements carry meaning. But without the grammatical pattern they create, we cannot express even the simplest relationship between the words that do carry meaning.

How Language Is Used

When a child undertakes to learn to read at the age of five or six, he is already a skilled user of language. He has somehow learned to generate language to communicate his thoughts, emotions, and needs to his family and peers. Further, he is able to comprehend what other people say to him. To state that he has learned by imitation does not accurately represent the case. He has, in fact, devised language for himself which moves toward the norms of adult language because the more it does, the more effective he is in communication.

Moreover, he has not simply acquired a collection of words or sentences to use when the occasion is appropriate. He has learned the rules by which language is produced. Language is rule-governed. As long as a child can only produce language he has already heard, his language capability is severely limited. Infinite numbers of sentences are possible in a language. If a child had to hear them and learn them before he could use them, language learning would be a much slower process than it is. But a small number of rules govern language production. These are the rules that tell the child which noun to put before and which after a transitive verb when he runs up to a teacher on the playground and says, "John hit Bill." They are the rules that make it possible for him to say, "When I hit him, he hits me back," getting *hit* and *hits* in the right position and making one clause subordinate to another. They are the rules that make it possible for him to say things he has never heard anyone say before and be sure that other speakers of the language will understand.

Generating language. In speaking or in writing, meaning in the mind of the originator creates a deep language structure (a set of base forms) and activates a set of rules which transform that structure and generate a signal, either graphic or oral. This process must be a complete one. The signal must have a surface structure which is complete. All essential elements must be present, and extraneous ones must not be. We might

Figure 3–1
Spoken Language

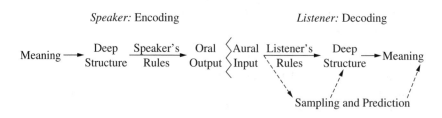

describe this whole process as *encoding*. A structured code signal has been produced. The user of a language has so well learned this encoding procedure that it is virtually automatic. Meaning, as a language user formulates it, literally creates an automatic chain of events which results in language code. A model of speech, quite simplified, is reprinted in Figure 3–1.

Note in this model that the speaker's output is not the same as the listener's input. What is said is not precisely what is heard, just as in reading what is written is not precisely what is read. This relationship might be compared to the relationship of fetus and mother. Her bloodstream nourishes the uterine wall from which the fetus draws its nourishment, through its own bloodstream. But, the two bloodstreams are not connected.

Note also that meaning is not in the oral output or the aural input. Meaning is only in the minds of the speaker and the listener. The listener (like the reader) must recreate meaning for himself from the input he has obtained.

Language has been learned by the listener in the context of experience as it was used in those situations by people around him. His ability to recreate meaning depends on his ability to associate those experiences and the concepts he has formed through them with the language.

The speaker in generating language must produce a sound sequence which is decodable by the listener. In this oral language signal, the sounds must be sufficiently well articulated and the structure sufficiently complete that the listener has all the information he needs.

At first appearances, it would seem that listening would be a kind of mirror image of speech with the process simply reversed to get from surface structure of aural language to meaning.

In fact, however, the listener may, through a process that combines sampling and prediction, leap to the deep structure and meaning without using all the information available to him. He acquires strategies as a language user that enable him to select only the most productive cues. His user's knowledge of language structure and the redundancy[2] of that structure make it possible for him to predict and anticipate the grammatical pattern on the basis of identifying a few elements in it. The context in which the language occurs, created by the previous meanings he has gathered, allows him to predict the meaning of what will follow. All these combine to make listening related to but a very different process from speaking.

Perception in Listening and Reading

Before we compare listening and reading, let's explore how perception operates in listening. Every language uses a small number of sound units, which some linguists label phonemes. These are in reality bundles of sounds which are treated by listeners as the same. Just as we call many different colors and shades of colors red, we hear many different sounds as /t/. Two colors could be quite similar, but one would be called red and the other orange, while two other more dissimilar colors might be both called red. In the same way the *phoneme* is a perceptual category. As a language is learned these categories become functional. The child learns to treat certain differences as significant and others as insignificant. *In short, he not only learns what to pay attention to, but, equally important, what not to pay attention to.* So the native speaker of Japanese learning English does not distinguish *late* from *rate* because he has learned to ignore a difference which isn't significant in Japanese. Similarly, a speaker of English has difficulty differentiating the Spanish *pero* (but) from *perro* (dog).[3]

Perception in language is and must be both selective and anticipatory. To be aware of what is significant in language one must ignore what is not. Perception, to be functional in listening, must be augmented by anticipation. The sounds are so fleeting and follow each other so rapidly that time does not allow for each to be fully perceived and identified. Mastery of the phonological system, however, and of the grammatical system as well, enables the listener to use partial perceptions and sample the input. Under some circumstances, of course, the partial perceptions may be too fragmentary or distorted and the listener may have to ask for repetition. But, to be quite blunt, what we think we hear is as much what we expect to hear as it is what we do hear.

2. Redundancy means, here, that each bit of information may be conveyed by several cues in the language. For example, notice in this sentence how many cues indicate the plural nature of the subject: *Two boys are eating their sandwiches.*
3. If you don't hear the difference, then you don't know Spanish phonemes, which is the point here.

Contrast the task of repeating even a short sequence in a foreign language with a comparable or longer one in a known language. The foreign language simply doesn't correspond to available perceptual categories, nor can we fit what we do catch into any system that would aid prediction.

Perception in language use cannot be viewed then as a simple series of sound perceptions or word perceptions. It must be understood in relation to the grammatical structure of the language, and to the structure of the meaning which is being communicated.

All that has been said in comparing speaking and listening basically applies to the parallel language processes, writing and reading.

The writer generates his signal in exactly the same way that the speaker does. In the last stage, these generative processes differ. In speech, a series of phonological rules determines the exact sound sequences which will be uttered. In writing, instead of phonological rules a set of graphotactic rules (spelling if you prefer) produces the exact grapheme sequences.

As we have indicated earlier, though both speaking and writing must produce complete signals, writing is usually polished and perfected to a greater degree than speech through editing by the author. Furthermore, the reader works from a more or less permanent graphic input while the listener must contend with input that in most cases perishes as it is produced. Rereading is possible. Relistening requires that the speaker cooperate in repeating what he has said.

But reading, like listening, is a sampling, predicting, guessing process. Proficient readers, in fact, learn to use the reading process much more rapidly than they normally use the listening process. Listening is held pretty much to the rate at which speech is produced. That, of course, is much slower than the processing of average proficient readers.

In the guessing game which is reacting, three types of information are used. Each has several subtypes. They are used in reading simultaneously and not sequentially.

Information Used during the Reading Process

I. Grapho-phonic Information
    A. Graphic Information: The letters, spelling patterns and patterns of patterns created through white space and punctuation. A word or suffix represents a graphic pattern; a phrase or sentence is a pattern of patterns.
    B. Phonological Information: The sounds, sound patterns and patterns of patterns created through intonation (pitch, stress, pause). Read any line on this page and note how these work.

   C. Phonic Information: The complex set of relationships between the graphic and phonological representations of the language. Notice here we are speaking of the relationships and not an instructional program for teaching them.

II. Syntactic Information

   A. Sentence Patterns: The grammatical sequences and interrelationships of language. The ____s ____ed the ____s, is an example of a sentence pattern common in English.

   B. Pattern Markers: The markers which outline the patterns.

      1. Function Words: Those very frequent words which, though themselves relatively without definable meaning, signal the grammatical function of the other elements. Examples: *the, was, not, do, in, very, why, but.*

      2. Inflections: Those bound morphemes (affixes) which convey basically grammatical information. Examples: *ing, ed, s.*

      3. Punctuation–Intonation: The system of markings and space distribution and the related intonation patterns. Pitch and stress variations and variable pauses in speech are represented to some extent by punctuation in writing.

   C. Transformational Rules: These are not characteristic of the graphic input itself, but are supplied by the reader in response to what he perceives as its surface structure. They carry him to the deep structure and meaning. If he is to recognize and derive meaning from a graphic pattern, he must bring these grammatical rules into the process.

III. Semantic Information

   A. Experience: The reader brings *his* prior experiences into play in response to the graphic input.

   B. Concepts: The reader organizes the meaning he is reconstructing according to his existing concepts and reorganizes experience into concepts as he reads.

   C. Vocabulary is largely a term for the ability of the child to sort out his experiences and concepts in relation to words and phrases in the context of what he is reading.

All of these kinds of information are available to the reader at the same time in graphic language. In the sampling process, they support each other much as they do in listening. Particular cues take on strategic importance in relation to the full array of information in the input which they could not have in isolation. In a list a word like *the*, for example, is a word with little or no referential meaning. It summons forth, from the reader's stockpile of information, no experiences or concepts. But put *the* into a sentence and it becomes a grammatical cue of some importance. In these sequences: *He hurried to farm* (his land) and *he hurried to the farm, farm* is marked as a noun in the second sequence by *the,* whereas in the first, *farm* is a verb and the reader will expect an object to follow.

The relationship between oral and written language is of more significance in reading than in listening. Particularly in learning to read the language he speaks, a child may draw on his oral language competence as he develops control over written language. The alphabetic character of the writing system makes it possible to match sound sequences already known with less familiar graphic sequences.

A possible simplified model for reading in early stages might look like this:

Figure 3–2
Early Reading[4]

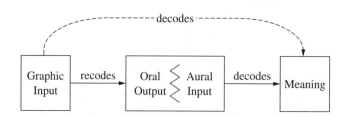

The child here recodes graphic input as speech (either outloud or internally) and then, utilizing his own speech as aural input, decodes as he does in listening. Notice the model assumes some direct decoding from print to meaning, even at early stages.

Some writers on the topic of reading have assumed that for instructional purposes these two aspects, recoding and decoding, are separable. And indeed, materials and methods have been built on that assumption. As a prereading program, instruction is provided to the child in matching letters and sounds (i.e., synthetic phonics, Sullivan's programmed reading) or in matching spelling patterns and sound patterns (e.g., Fries Linguistic Readers) or in matching oral names with graphic shapes (sight vocabulary). But in all of these types of recoding instruction, the reader is confined to words or word parts and may not sample the syntactic or semantic information that would be available

4. In this diagram, recode is used to mean going from code to code (aural to graphic); *decode* is reserved for processes that go from code (in either form) to meaning. In this sense, comprehension and decoding are virtual synonyms while word-calling and sounding-out are *recoding* processes. A third term, *encode,* is used to mean going from meaning to code (again either written or oral). In our early example of the writer and his attorney, the writer could only *recode* printed language as oral language. But the lawyer could *decode* from language to meaning. Then he could *encode* meaning in an oral language form his client could *decode* (comprehend).

in full language. What's more, the process is one in which meaning cannot result. Thus by our tentative definition given earlier, recoding in itself is not reading.

In any case, a second instructional phase would be needed to help the learner adapt his recoding strategies and techniques to the full language situation in which all information is available and decoding may result.

Reading does eventually become a parallel process to listening which then would have this appearance:

Figure 3–3
Proficient Reading

In this model, recoding has at best a supplementary role. The basic decoding is directly from print to meaning, though there is some echo of speech involved as the reader proceeds even in silent reading. At times, the reader may find it helpful to recode print as speech and then decode. (The reverse may also be true for literate speakers. They may occasionally "write it down," recoding speech as graphic input and then decoding.)

When silent reading becomes proficient, it becomes a very different process from oral reading. It is much more rapid and not tied to encoding what is being read as speech. In silent reading, the reader sweeps ahead, sampling from the graphic input, predicting structures, leaping to quick conclusions about the meaning and only slowing down or regressing when subsequent sampling fails to confirm what he expects to find.

Oral reading which is fluent and accurate may involve simultaneous recoding and decoding. But for most proficient silent readers, who don't have much occasion for oral reading, oral reading apparently follows this model:

Figure 3–4
Oral Reading

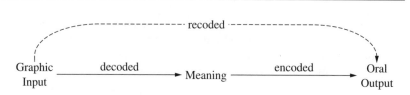

Primarily oral output is produced *after* meaning has been decoded and hence, though comprehension may be high, the oral output is often a poor match for the graphic input. The reader sounds clumsy and makes numerous errors.

The diagram on page 79 illustrates in some detail the psycholinguistic process which is silent reading. This model represents the *proficient* reader, but it also represents the competence which is the goal of reading instruction.

Reading is an active process in which the reader selects the fewest cues possible from those available to him and makes the best choices possible. If he is highly proficient, he will have good speed and high comprehension; reading will be a smooth process. If he is less proficient or if he is encountering unusually difficult material (as in the case of the graduate student in our early examples), reading will be less smooth and will involve considerable cycling back to gather more cues and make better choices.

Meaning is the constant goal of the proficient reader and he continually tests his choices against the developing meaning by asking himself if what he is reading makes sense. The process does not require that he perceive and identify every cue. In fact that would be both unnecessary and inefficient. But it does require that the reader monitor his choices so he can recognize his errors and gather more cues when needed.

Such traditional terms as *word recognition, sounding out,* and *word attack* stem from a view of reading as a succession of accurate perceptions or word identifications. Such a view is not consistent with the actual performance of proficient readers.

The Application of Reading

Reading, if it is successful, is, as we have shown, not a passive process. The reader is a language user who interacts with the graphic input. Successful reading yields meaning which becomes the means to further ends. The reader may follow directions, respond to questions, read further. The extent and direction of application depend on the nature and purpose of what is read. Literary materials, because of their aesthetic, stylistic qualities, yield a kind of pleasure and satisfaction which creates further appetite for literature. Plot and story line in literature propel the reader forward. "I just couldn't put it down," he may say.

Informational materials may have a similar effect; new knowledge leads to a desire for more knowledge. Or such material may meet a small but immediate need, as for example when the reader needs to clarify a particular fact in the encyclopedia.

Language and thought are interactive in reading, but at some point thought processes leap out and away from the message of the writer.

In this interaction a reader may be involved in cycles of reading, reflective thinking, flights of fancy and then more reading. In certain kinds of materials, recipes for example, the reader may follow a *read* and *do* cycle. He reads and then gathers his ingredients; then he reads again and performs step one and so forth.

Though reading and the application of the fruits of reading are separable, it must always be remembered that reading is never pursued for its own sake, even in literature. If the reader finds no "payoff," he will not continue to read. This is as true in the stages in which reading is being acquired as it is in the stages of proficient reading.

Materials used in the teaching of reading at all stages must necessarily be meaningful. Children with different purposes and interests will need a variety of materials to keep them reading. Ironically, development of reading competence is best achieved when the learner's focus is on the content of materials and not on reading itself. Social studies, science, mathematics, literature and other materials contribute well to the child's reading development while serving other curricular ends, if their conceptual load is not too heavy.

Adaptation in Reading

By the time he undertakes to become literate in his native language every child has acquired considerable competence[5] in its basic communicative use. The basic form of his language, that used in common discourse and conversation, is his means of communication, expression, thinking, and learning. It makes sense to start with this common discursive language in reading. Experience stories, directions, labels, signs are examples of early reading materials that use common language.

Children have not necessarily acquired the same kind of competence in dealing with other specialized forms of language. Literature utilizes one such special form. The language of literature has its own special set of rules and contingencies. Poetic license makes it possible for the poet to reverse some key language priorities for the sake of meter, rhyme, or mood. Similarly, literary prose employs structures and language devices differently from common language.

The strategies which the child has learned in listening transfer well to reading common language. To deal with literary language he will need to modify his strategies and perhaps acquire some new ones.

5. We use *competence* here, as some linguists do, to represent the basic, developed capacity for using language. *Performance* is a behavioral indicator of that *competence* but behavior should not be confused with the abilities that make performance possible.

A good deal of prereading experience with literature will help the child build a strong base for reading literature for himself. Some children grow up in a world of literature: they are surrounded by books; their parents read to them; they acquire favorites which they soon know by heart. By the time such children come to school, they have a feel for the peculiarities of literary language and a sense of what to expect from it. They can predict in literary language as they can in more common language. For the large number of children who lack such background, teachers can begin to build it through oral reading to the children and other devices while the more basic literacy ability is being built.

Subsequently, children can begin to read literary language. As they do so, they will necessarily modify the techniques and strategies they use in reading to accommodate the structure of literary language. Even then, it will probably make the most sense to start with literary forms and themes which are most like common language and move to literary forms which deviate more. Folk and fairy tales may be pleasurable to the child because of their familiarity. But the archaic language, the unusual structure, and the allegorical nature of their plots may combine to make them unsuitable for early literature reading. One possibility, of course, is to rewrite them for young children in order to eliminate these problems. A criticism of that approach is that in the process their qualities as literature may be lost and they may become dull and lacking in color and characterization. In a similar sense, adaptations of great works of literature for children too young to handle the original may make them more readable but destroy their essential merits. In both cases, such critics conclude it might be better to postpone reading such materials until the child's reading competence has reached a point where he is ready to learn to cope with the special demands they make on him.

Research into literary style is beginning to suggest that writers employ less common language structures frequently to achieve a sense of individuality and distinction. If this is true, then some specific assistance to children in recognizing and predicting these structures may greatly enhance their ability to read particular authors.

In the past several decades, a large and varied literature especially written for children of various ages has been produced. Such literature makes it possible to guide youngsters through material which they can select to suit their own interests and levels of ability. In the process, they will build their ability to deal with more sophisticated literature. A number of publishers have organized better selections in kits with multiple copies of each title and teacher guide material.

Schools present the learners with the need for dealing with a number of other special forms of language. Textbooks, in general, use language in special ways which vary from common language use. They tend, particularly in elementary and secondary schools, to present a very large number of topics, facts, and concepts rapidly and superficially. Reading to learn may well stimulate learning to read, but only if the concept load (roughly the number of new ideas presented) is not so heavy as to cause the reader to lose any sense of meaning. *Textbook reading, through the elementary years at least, probably requires considerable introductory, preparatory work on the part of the teacher.* Concepts and ideas can be introduced through demonstration, experimentation, concrete illustration. Vocabulary can be developed orally in relationship to these experiences. Then, and only then, is the child ready for the task of reading about the same concepts in the text. He reads them not so much to gain new concepts as to reinforce them. In the process, he learns to handle the unusual language uses of textbooks. If textbooks are well written and handled well in elementary schools, he may, by the time he is in high school, be able to initiate study at times through a textbook with the teacher following up and reteaching the concepts he meets in the books.

Another alternative is to change our thinking about how textbooks are used in elementary and junior high schools. Part of the problem with textbooks is that they move rapidly from topic to topic, a fact inherent in the nature of the task they undertake. Consequently, they present a large vocabulary of terms not well developed in context. Perhaps multimedia approaches would help; kits and coordinated packages containing film loops, audio and videotapes, transparencies, and other materials as well as reading materials could replace the single text. The texts could become elements in resource kits to provide more specific focus on single concepts or depth treatment of groups of related concepts.

Children will encounter problems in learning to deal with other kinds of reference books too. The need for reference skills, use of index, contents and glossary is obvious. Less obvious problems involve strategies for dealing with specialized vocabulary and language structures. Encyclopedias, for example, employ distinctive writing styles. There are also key problems for the reader in learning to modify his whole reading style to reference reading. Even graduate students do not always have effective techniques for selecting and reading from reference works only those portions germane to their needs. Skimming is one of several gross sampling strategies needed for specific use in some kinds of reference work.

Science, mathematics, social studies, music, art, industrial arts, home economics, in fact all school subjects, require learners to handle special kinds of language. It cannot be assumed that general reading competence leads automatically to these special abilities. Using a recipe, following a set of plans, interpreting a contour map, following a laboratory procedure—all present special reading problems. The abilities required must, of course, be developed in the context of the tasks. To pick an example, a reader can't learn how to read a recipe unless he is really making something. And the best test of the effectiveness of the reading will be the way the final product tastes. The implication is apparent. *Every teacher of whatever subject and level must be prepared to help children to meet new demands on their reading competence and to develop the special strategies which these demands require.*[6]

A special word needs to be said about vocabulary. Every time a learner pushes into a new field or into a new subject area within an old one, he encounters new vocabulary or new uses for old terms. That problem is a by-product of his quest for knowledge. The vocabulary is unfamiliar because the ideas and concepts it expresses are unfamiliar. Like new concepts, new vocabulary learned in relationship to the new knowledge must be built on the base of pre-existing vocabulary. If the new vocabulary is more effective in manipulating the new ideas it will be absorbed, and old language may be modified or set aside. *Vocabulary development outside of the context of new ideas and pre-existing language is not possible.*

What we commonly call a vocabulary problem is never simply a matter of putting a verbal label on an object. In reality, it may represent a variety of different problems.

1. The reader encounters a printed form he does not recognize for a word in his oral vocabulary. This is the simplest vocabulary problem since he has experiences and concepts to relate to his oral vocabulary.

2. The reader encounters a printed form which is not familiar and not in his oral vocabulary. But the concept is a known one. He has other language forms to express it. In this case the problem is to associate new language with old.

3. The reader encounters a printed form which is unfamiliar, has no oral counterpart for him, and represents a concept which is new to him. He may in fact lack relevant experience on which to base such a concept. This is the case in which vocabulary must follow conceptual development. Otherwise, we have a fourth possibility.

4. A written form is familiar and may even have an oral equivalent, but the reader has no meaning for it. Within narrow limits he may even use it to answer test questions correctly without understanding what he is reading.

5. The final possibility exists as readers become proficient. They may encounter printed forms and come to attach concepts to them without ever encountering them in oral speech. One does not have to be able to pronounce a word to understand it.

---

6. Of course it will also help to assure that materials children are asked to read are written well. Poor writing is not likely to be easily read.

Objectives of the Reading Curriculum

Once we have defined reading and discussed it as a process, a next step in considering reading curricula is to restate this process as a series of objectives. First, however, an important distinction must be made. That is the distinction between language competence and language performance.

Competence and Performance

Much has been said in curricular literature about behavioral objectives. In this view, the ultimate objective of instruction is always to change behavior (which we treat as a synonym for performance). But this view fails to take into account the concept that there is underlying all performance a basic competence. It is this underlying competence, and not the behavior itself, which we seek to build through education.

Above we delineated some variations involved in vocabulary. To use this as an example, in expanding vocabulary we must not mistake performance, the uttering of words, for competence, the understanding which must underlie the effective use of words. Too often school lessons change performance (behavior) but only superficially get at competence, and thus a change is a temporary or meaningless one.

While we must seek evidence in performance of the competence which learners have achieved, we must be very cautious of either equating performance and competence or of interpreting performance too directly and simplistically.

In language and reading this distinction is particularly important. Vocabulary, to continue the example, is going to develop in direct ratio to the experience and interest that a learner has. *Low vocabulary yield in the performance of children in certain task situations cannot be directly interpreted to mean that the child has a small vocabulary.* It may mean only that the topic or topics were not ones which interested him; it might also mean that for various reasons such as fear, unfamiliarity of the situation or the interviewers, or disdain for the task or teacher, the child simply did not perform in any way representative of his competence.

Here is another example: There are periods in the development of reading competence when oral reading becomes very awkward.[7] Readers who have recently become rapid, relatively effective, silent readers seem to be distracted and disrupted by the necessity of encoding oral output while they are decoding meaning. Ironically, then "poor" oral reading performance *may* reflect a high degree of reading competence rather than a lack of such competence.

7. Kenneth S. Goodman and Carolyn L. Burke, *Study of Children's Behavior While Reading Orally,* Final Report, Project S 425, USOE, March 1968.

Relevance

The language user, though he may be a beginner as far as literacy is concerned, brings to the task of learning to read the sum total of his life's experiences and the language competence he has already acquired. He has learned language well no matter what rung on the socioeconomic ladder his dialect occupies. To make it possible for each learner to fully capitalize on these resources the reading curriculum must be relevant to him. It must make it possible for him to build on his strengths, not put him at a disadvantage by focusing on his weaknesses.

All learners have had experiences. A learner is only disadvantaged if the school rejects his experiences as unsuitable to build learnings on while accepting those of other children. Similarly language difference is not a disadvantage unless the school rejects certain dialects and insists that a child must speak and read in a dialect in which he is not competent.

Remedial reading classes and clinics invariably have more boys than girls, more blacks than whites, more minority group youngsters than is proportional in the population these programs serve. This is not so much an indication of real weakness in these groups as it is of the failure of school reading programs to adequately reach them.

Too much time has been spent trying to find weaknesses and deficiencies in children that might explain their lack of success to learning to read. A flexible, relevant reading curriculum would capitalize on the strengths of children of both sexes and of all shapes, sizes, colors, ethnic and cultural backgrounds, dispositions, energy levels, and physical attributes. Every objective in reading must be relevant to the pupils we are teaching.

Comprehension: The Prime Objective in Reading

Essentially, the only objective in reading is comprehension. All else is either a skill to be used in achieving comprehension (for example, selecting key graphic cues), a subcategory of comprehension (for example, critical reading) or a use to be made of comprehension (e.g., appreciation of literature).

Comprehension depends on the successful processing of three kinds of information: grapho-phonic, syntactic, and semantic. A series of abilities is necessary to make this process successful. How these abilities operate within this process is illustrated in the tentative Model of Reading. (Figure 3–5).[8]

---

8. The author is indebted to William Gephart for the original flow chart for this model and to William Page for the current version.

Figure 3–5
The Goodman Model of Reading

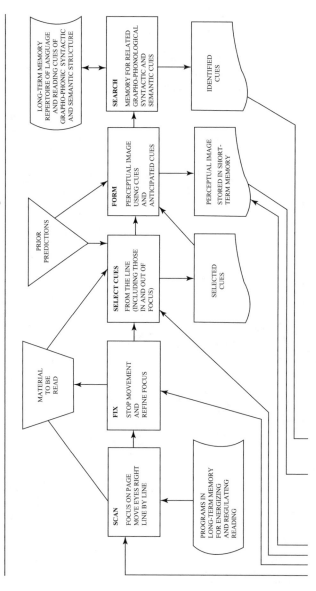

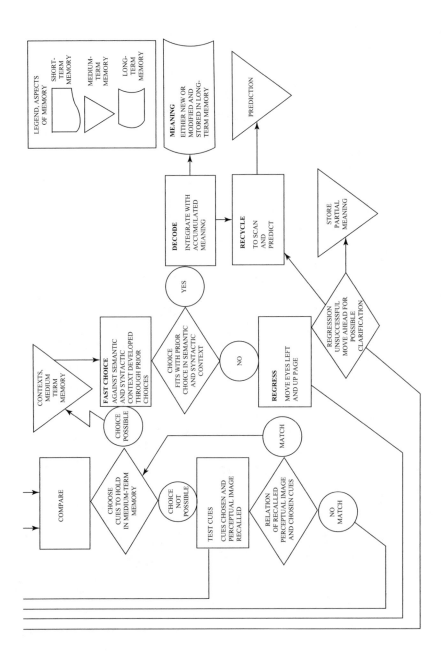

Reading instruction has as its subsidiary objectives development of these skills and strategies:

Scanning: The ability to move from left to right and down a page, line by line.

Fixing: The ability to focus the eye on the line of print.

Selecting: The ability to select from graphic input those key cues which will be most productive in the information processing. For example, initial consonants are the most useful letters in words.

Predicting: The ability to predict input on the basis of grammar and the growing sense of meaning from prior decoding. (Prediction and selection operate together since each is dependent of the other.)

Forming: The ability to form perceptual images on the basis of selection and prediction. The reader must combine what he sees with what he expects to see to form a perceptual image.

Searching: The ability to search memory for phonological cues and related syntactic and semantic information associated with perceptual images. The reader brings to bear his language knowledge and his experiential and conceptual background as he reads.

Tentative choosing: The ability to make tentative choices (guesses) on the basis of minimal cues and related syntactic and semantic input. It is crucial that the reader use the least amount of information possible to make the best guess possible. To do so, he will need well-developed strategies that become almost automatic.

Testing—semantic and syntactic: The ability to test choices against the screens of meaning and grammar. Literally the reader says to himself: "Does that make sense?" "Does that sound like language to me?" This involves the crucial ability to recognize his own errors when they are significant. Readers who do not use these two screens will tend to have low comprehension and will make little effective progress in reading, though they may become good word callers (recoders in the sense defined above).

Testing—grapho-phonic: The ability to test the tentative choice, if it has failed the prior test, against the recalled perceptual image and to gather more graphic information if needed. Note that it is only when the choice has been rejected on semantic or syntactic grounds that there is any need to resort to further grapho-phonic information. A miscalled word is most likely to be recognized as a mistake if it doesn't fit the meaning and grammar screens.

Regressing: The ability to scan right to left and up the page line by line if a choice is found unacceptable on prior tests. This involves the reader's recognizing that an anomaly or inconsistency exists in his processing to date and attempting to locate the source or point of error and then reprocessing. This is the device by which the reader corrects the errors he has recognized. A great deal of learning takes place through correction. The reader teaches himself new strategies and new insights as well as new words.

Decoding: When a successful, acceptable choice has been made, the reader integrates the information gained with the meaning which has been forming. This may involve assimilation of new meaning or accommodation of meaning previously decoded, or both.

Each of these abilities involves a set of strategies and techniques. Though phonic generalizations and sight words are learned and used in the reading process, it is the acquisition of key strategies which makes this knowledge develop and which makes it useful to the reader. In early reading instruction children will form associations between oral and written language (phonics generalizations). But only in the selection strategies, the perceptual image forming techniques, the grapho-phonic testing, and the semantic and syntactic contexts does this knowledge take on its true importance.

Some of the techniques we have tended to label word attack skills are useful. But, if we raise our sights from words to the whole reading process, these techniques will change their relative importance. Consider this short sequence:

> The boys stumbled into the house after their long hike. Mother said, "You must really be *fatigued*. Sit here and rest while I get lunch ready." When she returned with the food, Mother discovered they were so fatigued that they had fallen asleep.

Now, if we assume that *fatigued* is an unknown word to be "attacked," we will tend to employ phonics, structural analysis and other techniques that can work within the context of the word to achieve its recognition. This will be a problem, if, as is likely, the reader has not heard the word and therefore cannot match it with an equivalent.

If on the other hand, we are concerned about the same problem as it actually is encountered in the reading process, we will see that the meaning of the passage can come through rather clearly without the identification of this word. In fact, it is quite likely that in this short sequence the reader had become aware that the word must mean something like "tired." Should he assume another definition, *hungry* for example, subsequent reading might cause a correction. All of the syntactic and semantic information which the reader has going for him makes him relatively independent of the grapho-phonic information.

Developing Sophistication in Reading

Adequate functioning of the reading process depends on development in a number of areas, both mechanical and intellectual. A deficiency in any one of these can affect the quality of the child's reading and lessen its meaning for him.

Techniques and Strategies

If a reader does not develop independence in the use of the strategies and techniques required for adequate functioning of the reading process then special attention may be required. Cycles of skill instruction could be planned which would move the learner from language to a focus on the technique or knowledge which he needs and then back to language so that he can test the technique as he attempts to read.

To pick a simple example, suppose that a child is not aware that initial consonants are the most useful graphic cues. Instruction might help him by selecting from reading material words which start in various ways. Then the reader would return to the reading material to utilize the technique of selecting initial consonant cues.

If on the other hand children become overdependent on specific techniques, then again they can be guided within the full scope of reading materials to put the techniques in proper perspective in relationship to other techniques and available information. Suppose a child had become too reliant on initial consonants and was using neither meaning and syntax nor other graphic cues well. He could be helped to move away from his overdependence while the weak strategies were being developed at the same time.

Sequencing of skill instruction in reading has often been strongly advocated by publishers and curriculum workers. But the reading process requires that a multitude of skills be used simultaneously. As we have indicated, many of these skills are already employed by the learner in listening. *Any sequence will necessarily be arbitrary.*

Flexibility

In discussing adaptation, we indicated the need for developing general reading strategies and special reading strategies for literature, science, social studies and other language uses. The key to this development is experience of the learner with a wide variety of materials, and guidance from the teacher as it is needed to help develop specific strategies to handle the requirements of these special reading materials. This is only one kind of flexibility needed. A second kind of flexibility has to do with reading purpose. The reader needs to gain flexibility in the way his reading process functions in relation to the outcome he desires.

If he desires a high degree of comprehension with great detail then he will be more demanding of himself and more painstaking. If at the opposite extreme he is only concerned with getting a quick notion of the general drift of what he is reading, he will use test processes more freely, sample more widely, and not bother to worry about errors as he reads. If speed reading courses have any validity it must be in their ability to get readers to break out of a single inflexible reading style and into a more variable one.

A Sense of the Significance of Reading

A child who was a beginning reader was once asked why she thought it was important to know how to read. "You might park some place," she said, "and there might be a No Parking sign there. And a man might come out and say, 'Can't you read?' "

The story illustrates a small child's view of the great importance of being able to read in a literate society. An individual in a literate society has many, many encounters every day that require the comprehension of written language. Success with adult illiterates in building literacy has been achieved by building the instructional program around their most pressing needs: signs, applications, labels, directions, and other mundane things which readers take for granted.

A lesser, but still important motivation for the acquisition of reading comes from the pleasure and satisfaction it provides. This is not to say that simply by telling children how much fun reading is they can be motivated to learn. Rather, they can be led to discover this for themselves. The enjoyment of a good story will whet the appetite for more. The satisfaction of getting the information needed from a reference work will stimulate the reader to make greater use of reading as a source of information.

In aiding children to see the significance of reading, we should avoid the temptation of preselecting all the material for them. Children, like adults, have varied tastes and interests. What most children like or profit from may be totally uninteresting to one child. If a child is to find himself in reading, a wide range of topics, formats, and even quality must be represented in the material available to him.

In the multimedia world in which today's children become literate, reading need not be isolated from or exalted above other media. Television, movies, and radio can and do actually stimulate reading. Today's readers have seen and heard events that their parents and grandparents encountered only through their newspapers. They bring a much broader background and range of interests to reading than any earlier generations. Above all, motivation for reading requires that schools make themselves relevant to today's children.

Critical Sense

To read critically is to read skeptically. The reader asks himself not only, "Do I understand what this means?" but "Do I buy it?" Implicit in critical reading is a set of values and criteria which is constantly brought into play throughout the process.

Three things are requisite to developing critical reading competence. First, the reader must develop a set of appropriate criteria to judge what he is reading, or at least he must have general criteria which will help him deal with matters such as plausibility, credibility, ulterior motives of the writer or publisher, and so forth. Second, he must see critical reading as necessary and possible for himself. Third, he must be aware of the devices which writers use to appeal emotionally and subtly to him as a means of influencing him.

Much of the reading required of children in school deters rather than promotes critical reading. If there is always one right answer to a question, if the teacher settles an argument by pointing out that the book has given the information on page 38 (implying that books are never wrong), if children are led to believe that they are not competent to judge the merits of their social studies or science books, then the teacher cannot turn around and ask children to read an essay in their reading text critically. One either reads critically or one does not. *The strategies required to read critically must be developed for all reading tasks and not just for special ones designed for instruction.*

Some of the most effective users of language in our country are paid high salaries by Madison Avenue agencies to convince the public that they cannot possibly exist without their clients' products. The same *tactics* have been used with remarkable success to sell political candidates. Only a truly critical reader or listener can hope to ferret out fact from propaganda.

Conclusion

Everyone agrees that reading is a critical area in education. Everyone agrees that methods must be found and curricula developed to teach all children to read effectively. Energy and money are expended for materials, clinics, special teachers by school systems and by parents. That private clinics flourish and that schools are increasing their efforts are mute evidence that the problems of reading instruction have not been solved.

The state of reading instruction today is that of an art. Skilled teachers and specialists have the know-how to help *most*, but not all, of their pupils.

There is no simple breakthrough in reading just around the corner which will change instruction to a foolproof science. As more is understood about reading and learning to read, it becomes ever clearer how complex these processes are. No simple antitoxin can be injected into nonreaders to make them readers. But progress will come as misconceptions disappear in favor of sound understanding. Materials and curricula based on scientific insights will replace those built on tradition, trial-and-error and expediency. And a reading curriculum will evolve tied to an effective theory of reading instruction.

The basis for such progress now exists. If parents, teachers, and administrators can resist simplistic panaceas and keep up sustained efforts to achieve more effective reading instruction, then the next decade can be the one in which the major problems are solved.

Chapter Four

What's Universal About the Reading Process

Kenneth S. Goodman
University of Arizona, 1976

All human societies are linguistic. They have one or more languages which they use to communicate needs, wishes, concepts, emotions, experiences to each other. Humans use language, not only to communicate, but as a medium of thought and learning.

When human societies reach a point in their culture where communication is necessary over time and over space, then written language develops. Oral language is used in immediate face-to-face communication, but to preserve ideas for future generations, or to communicate over a wide distance, written language is needed.

Just as listening is a receptive oral language process, so reading is a receptive written language process. In productive language, speaking and writing, the language user begins with meaning and encodes it in language. In receptive language, the user starts with language and constructs meaning from it. The principal difference is that oral language use usually involves a speaker and listener interacting within each others hearing while in written language interaction, writer and reader may not even know each other. The writer may be far away, or even dead.

Reading is then the process of getting meaning from print.

This chapter is based on a paper presented at the First Japan International Reading Conference, 1976. Reprinted with permission of the author.

Miscue Research

In my research, I've sought to use the scientific insights of linguistics and psycho-linguistics to understand how the readers are able to process print, language in written form, to obtain meaning.

The basic research procedure has been to have a subject read aloud a complete story or other text he or she has not seen before. A text is chosen which will be somewhat difficult for the reader. The reader is informed that no help will be given during the reading and that he or she will be asked to retell what has been read upon completion.

The analysis focuses on the miscues of the reader. A miscue is an oral response to the text which does not match the expected response. All readers produce these unexpected responses, though some readers produce many more than others do.

In miscue analysis, miscues are examined by comparing the expected responses and the observed responses. I have been concerned for the similarities and differences in appearance, sound, grammar, and meaning, as well as for changes that result from miscues on the acceptability of the meaning and grammar of the resulting text. I have looked at spontaneous self-corrections of miscues by readers and am particularly concerned with which miscues lead to self-correction.

In the analysis I have assumed that nothing is accidental, that miscues represent the same process as expected responses except that the cues have somehow been used in an unexpected manner.

I have used the concepts of linguistics to describe the miscues and have also drawn on psycho-linguistics, the study of the relationships between thought and language.

Let's suppose that a reader reads the following sentence:

Japan is a country with a small land area, which has a large population.

A possible miscue could be the insertion of the word *large* before country. Insertions are often words which make sense and which appear elsewhere in the printed text. Another possible miscue is ending the sentence after *area* and at the same time substituting *it* for *which*. The result of the miscue is a transformed text which has acceptable syntax and meaning.

In the following example, the reader finds the miscue disrupts meaning and makes a self-correction, regressing to the point where meaning has been lost:

Japan is a country with a small land area, which has a large population.

In this case, the reader substitutes *was* for *has*. Both are verb forms of similar appearance. *Was* is very common, so it is something the reader might be expecting. When the reader realizes that meaning is lost, he knows something is wrong and self-corrects.

Miscues like these are like windows on the reading process since we can infer what the reader is thinking as the miscues occur.

What I've Learned About Reading English

In describing the process of reading English, I have learned to look beyond words. Language is a system for communication and the meaning of a sentence depends more on the sentence pattern and grammar than it does on the meaning of individual words.

There are 3 systems of cues that readers use to get from print to meaning:

Grapho-phonic: This is the system of letters, letter parts, and spelling patterns. Since English is written with an alphabetic writing system, it is also the system of relationships between the spellings and the sound patterns of oral English.

Syntactic: The syntactic system is the system that makes it possible to say the complex things one must with language. In English the order of the words in a sentence is the dominant feature of syntax. There are noun and verb endings, but these are not complex and only supplement word order. A noun is the subject of the sentence, because it is the subject position, not because of its ending. Some English words mark off the sentence patterns. They have grammatical functions with no real meaning: the determiners *a* and *the* are examples.

Semantic: The third cue system is semantic. The reader must bring meaning to the passage in order to take meaning from it.

Reading English is far more than recognizing letters and written words and matching sounds to them. It is a quest for meaning in which all three cue systems are used together.

Because reading uses our visual sense, it has an *optical cycle.* Light from the page reaches the lens of the eye. The eye, as an optical instrument, must stop or fix at a point in the print and focus. The eye's focus must be shifted along the direction of the graphic display. In English that is from left to right and down the paper.

Then a *perceptual* cycle follows in which the brain organizes the visual input, deciding what it is seeing. This is strongly influenced by expectation. Most of what we think we see is what we expected to see.

Following that is a *syntactic* cycle as the reader seeks to identify the sentence structure and the relationships of the words, phrases, and clauses to each other.

Finally, there is a *semantic* cycle. The reader constructs meaning.

The reader is most aware of the concern for meaning and each cycle melts into the next as the reader's focus stays on meaning.

Throughout these cycles the reader uses several different strategies:

Sampling: The strategy of sampling is one in which the reader selects out the most useful cues from all those available.

Predicting: Prediction, as we have already said, is an important strategy. The reader predicts shapes, letters, words, syntactic structures and meaning. These predictions create the framework in which sampling is possible.

Confirming is the strategy of deciding whether the predictions are acceptable, or not. If new information confirms the prediction the reading process moves forward. If it is inconsistent or contradictory, then the reader uses the *correcting* strategy. New information is sought, often by regressing, or information is reprocessed and a better prediction is made.

This brief statement of how I see the reading of English taking place leaves out much of the detail, but it serves to indicate that reading in English is very much a matter of using language to create meaning.

My research has convinced me that there is only one reading process for English. The differences that are found between proficient and poor readers is their relative ability to efficiently integrate the cycles and strategies so that they are able to effectively get meaning. Poor readers seem to get lost in the detail, they are less able to keep their focus throughout reading on meaning.

It has been traditional in teaching children to read English to build from part to whole, from letter-sound relationships to words, to meaningful wholes. I think this is quite wrong, that it violates both the evidence for how language is most naturally learned and that it turns written language from a meaningful whole to a set of abstract bits and pieces, which are hard for young children to learn and which lose their relationship to meaning.

If the language children are using to learn to read is natural, meaningful and relevant to them, then they will be strongly motivated to learn. They will be able to use their knowledge of oral language, and they will be able to judge their own success by asking themselves whether what they have read makes sense to them.

Reading Other Languages

So far I have been discussing reading and learning to read English. There is evidence from studies of children reading Spanish, Polish, German, and Yiddish that the same process is at work in these languages.

Lopez has found that children reading Spanish can read many words in a story that they were unable to recognize in a list. That result matches the result of my own research in English. Barrera found children reading in Spanish producing miscues which preserved meaningful syntactically acceptable language. She found that readers would sometimes change verb, noun, and adjective endings, so that they would be consistent, acceptable and meaningful.

The reader is dealing appropriately with the Spanish syntax and thus producing miscues which the same bi-lingual readers would not produce reading English, yet in both cases there is clear evidence of the reader predicting syntactic structures to get to meaning.

Romatowski found pupils bi-lingual in Polish and English, also effectively dealing with the difference in syntax, adapting the reading process to the linguistic and orthographic differences, but doing much the same things to get to meaning.

Hodes studied pupils bi-lingual in Yiddish and English. They were able to adapt to two different orthographies. Yiddish uses the Hebrew alphabet and is written from right to left, but the essential process of reading proved to be the same for both languages.

Hofer reports similar results in studying mono-lingual German children learning to read their native language.

I am unaware of any studies of children's miscues in reading non-alphabetic writing systems to date.

I would predict, however, that the basic process of reading would be the same as it is in alphabetic systems with necessary modifications for the differences in the writing systems. In alphabetic writing, there is a direct relationship of written and oral language. But they also are related through the meaning and syntax common to both. In non-alphabetic writing there is no direct relationship between print and speech, but both still are related through the meaning they represent and the syntax they use.

I would expect to find readers sampling from the graphic display, predicting syntactic structures and meaning, producing miscues, and correcting miscues when they produce unacceptable syntax and meaning.

In learning to read, I would expect pupils to be able to use syntactic and semantic context to assign meaning to new graphic symbols, so that there would not be any strong need for symbols to be formally taught as a prerequisite to successful reading. There seems to be no reason why any writing system should be learned any differently than any other for the purpose of reading with comprehension.

It is the search for meaning that motivates and unifies the reading process. Learning to read any system will be most successful when it is kept within the context of this search for meaning.

I believe the movement in reading through optical, perceptual, syntactic, and semantic cycles is universal in reading all languages regardless of the orthographies they employ. The use of sampling, predicting, confirming and correction strategies is also universal in all forms of reading.

Once learned, it is very unlikely that it is harder to read any language or any writing system than any other. Whether it is harder to learn to read any language or any writing system, alphabetic or non-alphabetic, is a harder question to answer. On the basis of the view of the reading process I have evolved, I believe that there are probably no important differences in the difficulty for people learning to read as long as the focus is kept on the relationships of written language to meaning during instruction. Learning to write in different orthographies is probably a different matter. The number and complexity of symbols and their forms in the writing systems may make it harder to write legibly and efficiently in some systems than in others. The invention and use of alphabetic writing systems with limited numbers of characters may be more useful to writers than readers. In fact, it may be that minimizing complexity may be a greater benefit to writers than the relationships between the symbols of speech and print alphabets establish. I ask the question in this regard, if alphabetic writing made learning to read much easier, wouldn't Japan have shifted totally to an alphabetic system, instead of the mixed system which prevails and seems to serve well, judging by the extent of literacy in Japan.

Needed Research

Clearly when I have gone beyond the discussion of how reading English works, I have argued on the basis of theory and implications of research and I have cited little direct research. The aspects, I believe to be universals of reading across languages and orthographies, must be verified, modified or rejected by direct research.

I believe that the methodology of miscue analysis is appropriate for research in reading any language. I think that analysis of the miscues of readers at varying levels of proficiency, reading, in each language, can help to explore the validity of my model of the reading process or any model for that language.

Such research can also illuminate how this process is varied or adapted by the readers to the particular characteristics of the language or writing system it uses.

Research is also needed on the relative ease of reading the same language written in different orthographies; again miscue analysis is a useful tool for such research.

The research I am suggesting is not simply for the sake of knowledge. Too many decisions about reading, writing and literacy are being made in the world today, without sufficient exploration of the realities of written language.

Good research should provide the sound basis for more effective literacy instruction in the world's schools.

Chapter Five

The Reading Process

Kenneth S. Goodman
Wayne State University, 1975

In a very real sense this paper is a progress report. Some years ago I decided that a major reason for the lack of forward motion in attempts to develop more effective reading instruction was a common failure to examine and articulate a clear view of the reading process itself. Knowledge, I felt, was non-cumulative in improving reading instruction largely because we either ignored the reading process and focused on the manipulation of teacher and/or pupil behaviors or because we treated reading as an unknowable mystery.

Ironically two opposite views were and still are widely found in the professional literature:

1. Reading is what reading is and everybody knows that; usually this translates to "reading is matching sounds to letters."
2. "Nobody knows how reading works." This view usually leads to a next premise: therefore, in instruction, whatever "works" is its own justification.

Both views are non-productive at best and at the worst seriously impede progress.

My effort has been to create a model of the reading process powerful enough to explain and predict reading behavior and sound enough to be a base on which to build and examine the effectiveness of reading instruction. This model has been developed using the concepts,

This chapter is based on a paper presented at the *Sixth Western Symposium on Learning, Language and Reading*, Bellingham, WA, 1975. Reprinted with permission of the author.

scientific methodology, and terminology of psycholinguistics, the inter-disciplinary science which is concerned with how thought and language are interrelated. The model has also continuously drawn on and been tested against linguistic reality. This reality has taken the form of close analysis of miscues, unexpected responses in oral reading, produced by readers of widely varied proficiency as they dealt with real printed text materials they were seeing for the first time.

The model isn't done yet. No one yet claims a "finished" model of any language process. But the model represents a productive usable view of what I believe, at this point in time, about the way the reading process works.

A Definition of Reading

Reading is a receptive language process. It is a psycholinguistic process in that it starts with a linguistic surface representation encoded by a writer and ends with meaning which the reader constructs. There is thus an essential interaction between language and thought in reading. The writer encodes thought as language and the reader decodes language to thought.

Further, proficient readers are both efficient and effective. They are effective in constructing a meaning which they can assimilate or accommodate and which bears some level of agreement with the original meaning of the author. And readers are efficient in using the least amount of effort to achieve effectiveness. To accomplish this efficiency readers maintain constant focus on constructing the meaning throughout the process, always seeking the most direct path to meaning, always using strategies for reducing uncertainty, always being selective about the use of the cues available and drawing deeply on prior conceptual and linguistic competence. Efficient readers minimize dependence on visual detail. Any reader's proficiency is variable depending on the semantic background brought by the reader to any given reading task.

Source for the Model

All scientific investigation must start with direct observation of available aspects of what is being studied. What distinguishes scientific from other forms of investigation is a constant striving to get beneath and beyond what is superficially observable. That involves finding new tools for making otherwise unavailable aspects observable. Such a tool is the microscope in all its variations designed to extend observation far beyond the limits of the human eye. Scientists also devise classification systems, taxonomies, paradigms as they constantly seek for essences, structures, interrelationships; they are aware of the distractions the obvious can cause and they are aware of how easy it is to overlook vital characteristics of phenomena they study.

The primary source of data for the view of the reading process presented here is observation of oral reading. But little can be learned from such observation if a naively empirical position is maintained. As the chemist must peer into the molecular structure, as the astronomer must ponder the effects of heavenly bodies on each other, as the ecologist must pursue the intricate web of interrelationships in a biological community, so the scientist in dealing with reading must look beyond behavior to process. Understanding reading requires depth analysis and a constant search for the insights which will let us infer the workings of the mind as print is processed and meaning created.

Oral miscue analysis is the tool I've found most useful in the depth analysis of reading behavior as I've sought to understand the reading process (Goodman, 1969).

Miscue analysis compares observed with expected responses as subjects read a story or other written text orally. It provides a continuous basis of comparison between what the readers overtly do and what they are expected to do. A key assumption is that whatever the readers do is not random but is the result of the reading process, whether successfully used or not. Just as the observed behavior of electrons must result from a complex but limited set of forces and conditions, so what the readers do results from limited but complex information sources and interactive but limited alternatives for their use.

When readers produce responses which match our expectations we can only infer successful use of the reading process. When miscues are produced, however, comparing the mismatches between expectation and observation can illuminate where the readers have deviated and what factors of input and process may have been involved. A simple illustration: there has long been concern over reversals in reading, changes in the sequences of letters, apparently involved in word substitution miscues. If *was* is substituted for *saw* there appears to be some kind of visual or perceptual aberration in the reader. Our miscue analysis data, however, tells us two things: (1) Such reversals are far less common in reading continuous texts than in word lists. (2) When such reversals do occur they are in only one direction: *saw* is replaced by *was* but virtually never is *was* replaced by *saw*. The reversal miscue must be influenced by factors other than the obvious visual or perceptual ones. Frequency, syntactic predictability and the range of semantic possibility clearly are involved.

In this depth miscue analysis several basic insights have emerged which have become foundational both to the research and to the model of the reading process:

- Language, reading included, must be seen in its social context. Readers will show the influence of the dialect(s) they control both productively and receptively as they read. Further, the common experience, concepts, interests, views, and life styles of readers with common social and cultural backgrounds will also be reflected in how and what people read and what they take from their reading.

- Competence, what readers are capable of doing, must be separated from performance, what we observe them to do. It is competence that results in the readers' control of and flexibility in using the reading process. Their performance is simply the observable result of the competence.

    Change in performance, whether through instruction or development, is important only to the extent that it reflects improved competence. Researchers may use performance or behavioral indicators of underlying competence but they err seriously in equating what readers do with what they are capable of doing.

- Language must be studied in process. Like a living organism it loses its essence if it is frozen or fragmented. Its parts and systems may be examined apart from their use but only in the living process may they be understood. Failure to recognize this has led many researchers to draw unwarranted and misconceived conclusions about both reading and reading instruction from controlled research on aspects of reading such as word naming, word identification, skill acquisition, and phonic rule development.

    Researchers, particularly, have tended to fall into the unexamined view that reading is recognizing the next words. An example is the study of reading acquisition by Singer, Samuels and Spiroff (1974).

    They concluded that words were more easily "learned" in isolation than in text or with illustration. They drew this conclusion from a study in which four (4) words were taught to a number of learners in three conditions:

    (a) in isolation.

    (b) in "context": each word was presented in a three-word sentence.

    (c) with an illustrative picture.

The key misconception in this study is that reading is a matter of identifying (or knowing) a series of words. It is then assumed that learning to read is learning to identify or know words. Further it is assumed that known words are known under all linguistic conditions. Implicit is the assumption that the task of "learning" four (4) words is representative of the general task of learning to read.

- Language must be studied in its human context. It is a uniquely but universally human achievement. That's not a humanistic assertion. It's a scientific fact. Human language learning and the general function of language in human learning are not usefully described with learning theories derived from study of rats, pigeons, and other non-language users.

A Revised Model

Three kinds of information are available and used in language, whether productive or receptive. These come from (1) *the symbol system* which uses sounds in oral languages and graphic shapes in written languages. For literate language users of alphabetic languages there is also a set of relationships between sounds and shapes; (2) *the language structure* which is the grammar, or set of syntactic relationships that make it possible to express highly complex messages using a very small set of symbols. The same syntax underlies both oral and written language; (3) *the semantic system* which is the set of meanings as organized in concepts and conceptual structures. Meaning is the end product of receptive language, both listening and reading; but meaning is also the context in which reading takes on reality. Listener/readers bring meaning to any communication and conduct themselves as seekers of meaning.

A model of the reading process must account for these information sources. It must also respond to the following realities:

Written language is displayed over space in contrast to oral language which is displayed in a time continuum.

Writing systems make arbitrary decisions about direction in using space. The reader must adjust to a left-to-right, right-to-left, top-to-bottom, or other arbitrary characteristic of written language.

Reading employs visual input. The eye is the input organ. It has certain characteristics and limitations as an optical instrument. It has a lens which must focus; it requires minimal light; it has a limited field; the area of view includes a small area of sharp detail.

Reading must employ memory: it must hold an image, briefly store information, retain knowledge and understanding.

Figure 5–1
Cycles

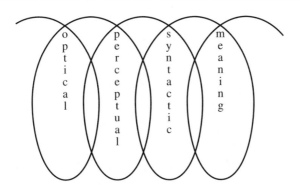

Cycles

Though reading is a process in which information is dealt with and meaning constructed continuously, it can be usefully represented as a series of cycles. Readers employ the cycles more or less sequentially as they move through a story or other text. But the readers' focus, if they are to be productive, is on meaning so each cycle melts into the next and the readers leap toward meaning. The cycles are telescoped by the readers if they can get to meaning.

Processes

As the readers move through the cycles of reading they employ five processes. The brain is the organ of information processing. It decides what tasks it must handle, what information is available, what strategies it must employ, which input channels to use, where to seek information. The brain seeks to maximize information it acquires and minimize effort and energy used to acquire it. The five processes it employs in reading are:

I. *Recognition-initiation.* The brain must recognize a graphic display in the visual field as written language and initiate reading. Normally this would occur once in each reading activity, though it's possible for reading to be interrupted by other activities, examining pictures, for example, and then to be reinitiated.

II. *Prediction.* The brain is always anticipating and predicting as it seeks order and significance in sensory inputs.

Figure 5–2
The Revised Model

Cycles	Inputs	Output
Start Recognize task as reading known language.	Graphic display. Memory: Recognition-Initiation Activate strategies in memory.	Optical scan cycle.
1. *OPTICAL* a. Scan in direction of print display.	Start: Memory: Strategies for scanning appropriate to graphic display. Adjust speed of scan to processing speed.	Optical fixation cycle. To memory: predict relation of information to direction of display.
b. Fix-focus eyes at point in the print.	Light reflects from graphic display. Visual field includes sharp and fuzzy input. Memory: Prior prediction of meaning, structure, graphic redundancy, expectation of locus of key graphic cues.	Perception cycle. To Memory: Cues for image formation.
2. *PERCEPTION* a. Sample-Select. Choose cues from available graphic display.	Fix: cues available in sharp and blurred input. Memory: Sampling strategies. Prior predictions and decodings to meaning.	To Memory: Selected cues. To Feature Analysis.
b. Feature Analysis: Choose features necessary to choose from alternate letters, words, structures.	Sampled features. From memory: Assign alloystem(s) (type style, cursive, etc.). Prior predictions.	Confirm prior prediction. Correct if necessary by return to scan, fix. If no system available, try best approximation or terminate; otherwise proceed to image formation.

c. *Image Formation* Form image of what is seen, and expected to be seen. Compare with expectations.	From: feature analysis, cues appropriate to allosystem(s) chosen. From memory: graphic, syntactic, semantic constructs. Prior predictions. Cues from parallel phonological system (optional).	If no image possible, return to feature analysis or prior cycle for more information. Confirm prior predictions. If correction needed return to prior cycle, scan back for source of inconsistency. If image formed, store in memory and go to syntactic cycle.
3. *SYNTACTIC CYCLE* a. Assign internal surface structure.	From image formation. From Memory: Rules for relating surface display to internal surface structure. Prior predictions and decodings.	If no structure possible, recycle to perception or optical cycles. If inconsistent with predictions, try alternate or correct by recycling and scanning back to point of mismatch. If structure is possible, go to deep structure.
b. Assign deep structure. Seek clauses and their inter-relationships.	From: Internal surface structure. From Memory: Transformational rules for relating surface and deep structures. Prior predictions and decodings.	If no structure possible try alternative. If still no structure, recycle. If inconsistent with prediction, correct by recycling. If deep structure possible, predict graphic, semantic, syntactic features. Go to Meaning. If oral reading, assign appropriate intonation contour. Terminate if no success.

(continued)

Figure 5-2
(Continued)

Cycles	Inputs	Output
4. *CONSTRUCT MEANING* a. Decode	From: Deep structure. From Memory: Stored experiences, conceptual constructs, lexicon. Prior predictions.	If meaning not acceptable, recycle to point of inconsistency. If no meaning possible, try alternate deep structure or recycle to seek more information. If still no meaning, hold all information in memory and return to scan. Terminate if no meaning results. If acceptable meaning, go to assimilate accommodate.
b. Assimilate/Accommodate If possible, assimilate. If not possible, accommodate prior meaning.	From: Decode. From memory: Prior predictions, prior meaning. Conceptual and attitudinal constructs.	If no assimilation possible and no accommodation possible, recycle to correct or obtain more information. If still not possible, hold and return to scan for possible clarification as reading progresses. Accommodations possible: modify meaning of story/text to this point modify predictions of meaning modify concepts modify word definitions restructure attitudes If task complete, terminate. If task incomplete, recycle and scan forward, predict meaning, structure, graphics.

III. *Confirmation.* If the brain predicts, it must also seek to verify its predictions. So it monitors to confirm or disconfirm with subsequent input what it expected.

IV. *Correction.* The brain reprocesses when it finds inconsistencies or its predictions are disconfirmed.

V. *Termination.* The brain terminates the reading when the reading task is completed, but termination may occur for other reasons: the task is non-productive; little meaning is being constructed, or the meaning is already known, or the story is uninteresting or the reader finds it inappropriate for the particular purpose. At any rate, termination in reading is usually an open option at any point.

These processes have an intrinsic sequence. Prediction precedes confirmation which precedes correction. Yet the same information may be used to confirm a prior prediction and to make a new one.

Short Circuits

Any reading which does not end with meaning is a short circuit. Readers may short circuit in a variety of ways and for a variety of reasons. In general, readers short circuit (1) when they can't get meaning or lose the structure; (2) when they've been taught or otherwise acquired non-productive reading strategies; (3) when they aren't permitted to terminate non-productive reading. Theoretically, a short circuit can occur at any point in the process. Here is a list of short circuits with successively more complex points:

Letter Naming: A very old method of reading instruction taught young readers to spell out to themselves any unfamiliar words. This short circuit still occurs but it is not too common.

Recoding: Since print is a graphic code and speech is also a code, it is possible for readers to concentrate on matching print to sound with no meaning resulting. Since the readers go from code to code such short circuits may be considered recoding. Recoding may take place on several levels. *Letter-sound recoding* is the most superficial. Sounds are matched on a one-to-one basis to the print. This sounding-out requires the readers to blend sounds to synthesize words. *Pattern-matching recoding* involves the readers fitting spelling patterns to sound patterns. Readers focus on features which contrast patterns such as rat–rate, hat–hate, mat–mate. Recoding is often by analogy: since *bean* looks like *mean* it must sound like it too. This recoding produces words or word-like utterances without requiring synthesizing. *Internal surface-structure recoding* involves using the rules needed to relate print to underlying surface structure. Instead of going beyond to deep structure, however, the reader generates an oral surface representation. This recoding can produce words and phrases with approximate intonation patterns.

Syntactic Nonsense. The readers may treat print as syntactic nonsense, generating an appropriate deep structure without going beyond to meaning. Even proficient readers resort to this short circuit when conceptual load is too great or when the lack relevant background. With this short circuit the oral reading may be relatively accurate and yet involve little comprehension. Because readers do employ this short circuit we have come to regard the separation of syntactic deep structure from meaning as a useful view.

Partial Structures. Readers may resort to one or more of these short circuits with alternating periods of productive reading. Furthermore, because the brain is always actively seeking meaning, some comprehension will often "leak" through even the most nonproductive short circuits. It will most likely result in fragments of meaning, a kind of kaleidoscopic view, rather than an integrated understanding.

I suspect that many of these short circuits result from instruction but the studies to demonstrate this remain to be done.

References

Goodman, K. Analysis of oral reading miscues: applied psycholinguistics. *Reading Research Quarterly*, 1969, *5*, 9–30.

Singer, H., Samuels, S. S., and Spiroff, J. The effect of pictures and contextual conditions on learning responses to printed words. *Reading Research Quarterly*, 1974, *9*, 555–567.

Part Two

Miscue Analysis: Research on the Reading Process

Kenneth Goodman began miscue analysis research in 1963. The trend in reading research up to that point had been to conduct word-focused studies that were detached from the reality of the natural act of reading. Isolated words or non-words were used as stimuli for responses in controlled experiments. However, the validity of these studies was questioned when applied to the teaching of reading. In view of the limits of word-focused research and its misleading implications for the teaching of reading, Goodman started to use miscue analysis as a tool to study the reading process. Miscue analysis studied real reading with real readers using real reading materials. Studies of miscue analysis included both "poor" readers and proficient readers, normal and perceptually handicapped readers, primary and high school students from urban and suburban areas, readers whose first language was English and those who spoke English as a second language, and readers who spoke a variety of dialects of English. The texts that were used included basal readers and trade books, authentic literature and controlled texts, science texts, social studies texts, fiction, and nonfiction. Both cross-sectional and longitudinal approaches were used in miscue analysis research.

Miscue analysis differs from traditional error analysis in several key respects. First, unlike error analysis, miscue analysis compares readers' observed responses that do not match expected responses during oral reading, and it studies these responses from linguistic and psycholinguistic perspectives. Given these perspectives, Goodman regards reading as a language process. Language is viewed as rule-governed and possessing discourse features. Second, miscue analysis does not hold reading to be an accurate rendering of text—an identification of words—as does error analysis. Readers are viewed as users of language who have developed control over language rules since childhood. Language's rules and discourse features (such as redundancy, for example) enable readers to use language cues selectively. This, in turn, makes inference and prediction possible. Third, miscue analysis does not view errors as undesirable events or weaknesses as does error analysis. Miscues are viewed as normal responses because all readers, beginning or proficient, make miscues in oral reading. Miscues reflect readers' effectiveness and efficiency as they construct meaning.

The chapters in this part show that, from the very beginning, miscue analysis was oriented toward theoretical model building and toward informing the teaching and evaluation of reading. Miscues were viewed as performance events in reading from which the nature of the reading process could be inferred. Had the analysis stopped at the performance level, then many important insights about the nature of reading might have gone undiscovered. But Goodman focused his attention on studying the *underlying competence* of the reader by using miscue analysis as a window for observing the process of reading. From one-to-one cause-effect relations to the analytical taxonomy of miscues, Goodman developed his theory of reading as a meaning-centered psycholinguistic process. The findings of miscue analysis help reform the teaching and testing of reading by shifting the focus from identifying words to constructing meaning.

Chapter Six

Miscues: Windows on the Reading Process

Kenneth S. Goodman
Wayne State University, 1973

Reading miscue research was undertaken for the express purpose of providing knowledge of the reading process and how it is used and acquired. In turn, this knowledge can form the basis for more effective reading instruction toward the achievement of the goal of universal literacy.

Some scholars see research as a quest for knowledge for the sake of knowledge. They see a sharp separation between research and the application of knowledge to the solution of real problems. This is a point of view which the authors of this work do not share.

We do not grudge the pure researcher his disinterest in the practical. In the course of our research we have frequently found uses for concepts that such pure research has produced. In interactions with linguists, psychologists, psycholinguists, and other academicians we have found it possible to raise issues and ask questions which stimulated them to conduct research and thereby provide further useful knowledge.

Now we are at a point in our research where we feel we know enough about how reading works that we can share with teachers and other practitioners some of our insight and their implications for reading instruction. Had our research not been reality oriented and rooted

This chapter originally appeared in *Miscue Analysis: Applications to Reading Instruction*, 1973, K. Goodman, (ed.)., ERIC Clearinghouse on Reading and Communication Skills, Urbana, IL: NCTE. pp. 3–14. Copyright (1973) by the National Council of Teachers of English. Reprinted with permission.

in our concern for the practical this task of translating research into application might have been more difficult. Because we worked with real kids reading real books in real schools, the practical applications of the lessons we have learned and even the research procedures we used are more evident. Everything we know we have learned from kids. Our purpose here is to show our fellow teachers how they also may learn from kids.

Miscue analysis, which will be explained below in some detail, must be viewed as part of a pervasive re-ordering and restructuring of our understanding of reading. It is a tool which in research has contributed to development of a comprehensive theory and model of reading; in the classroom or clinic it can be used to reveal the strengths and weaknesses of pupils and the extent to which they are efficient and effective readers. But it is only useful to the extent that the user comes to view reading as the psycholinguistic process it is. Miscue analysis involves its user in examining the observed behavior of oral readers as an interaction between language and thought, as a process of constructing meaning from a graphic display. The reader's use of graphic, phonological, syntactic, and semantic information is considered.

Fortunately, one of the most powerful uses of miscue analysis is in teacher education. In the process of analyzing the miscues of a reader, the teacher or potential teacher must ask questions and consider issues he may never have thought about. Was the meaning acceptable after the miscue? Did the reader correct the miscue if it was not? If a word was substituted for another word, was it the same part of speech? How close was it to the sound and shape of the text word? Was the reader's dialect involved? Through these questions, instead of the teacher's counting errors, the quality of the miscues and their effect on meaning are the central concerns. Miscue analysis then is rooted in a psycholinguistic view of reading (one that sees thought and language interacting), but it is also a way of redirecting the focus of teachers so that they may see reading in this new perspective.

When we try to understand how reading works, we must look beyond the superficial behavior of readers. We must try to see what is happening that is causing that behavior. When we teach reading we are trying to build the competence which underlies the superficial behavior, we are not trying simply to change the behavior.

A miscue, which we define as an actual observed response in oral reading which does not match the expected response, is like a window on the reading process. Nothing the reader does in reading is accidental. Both his expected responses and his miscues are produced as he attempts to process the print and get to meaning. If we can understand how his miscues relate to the expected responses we can also begin to understand how he is using the reading process.

Here is a sentence from one story used in our research, and the miscues one pupil produced in reading it:

$$\textcircled{C}$$

that

But I remember|the camera⑤moving close to the crib and

Barny　　　　　　　　　　　*some* $\textcircled{C}$ *words*

Mr. Barnaby bending over⟨and⟩saying soothing|things to

Andrew – but not too loud⟨ly⟩.

The reader omits a word and some word parts, inserts a word, substitutes other words, goes back at times to correct himself, and comes out with a meaningful sentence. We must be concerned with more than his superficial behavior. We must infer from it the process he has used and his competence with that process. He inserted 'that' but corrected when he realized the pattern he had created was not acceptable syntax. He omitted 'and' but did not correct because it was not a necessary element. We start in miscue analysis with observed behavior, but we do not stop there. We are able, through analysis of the miscues, to see the process at work.

Miscue Analysis

Miscue analysis as a research tool began in 1963. I started with the goal of describing the reading process. The most basic task in doing this seemed to be to have subjects read, orally, a story they had never seen before, one which was somewhat difficult for them.

Even in the very earliest research attempts, two things became clear. First, it was obvious that oral reading is not the accurate rendition of the text that it has been assumed to be. Readers, even good ones, make errors. Second, it was clear that linguistic insights, scientific views of language, were very much appropriate to describing reading behavior. The things the readers did were linguistic things—they were not random.

When a beginning reader substitutes 'a' for 'the' in a sentence like:

A

The little monkey had it.

the reader is substituting one noun marker for another. When a more advanced reader sees:

There were glaring spotlights.

and says:

There was a glaring spotlight.

that reader is processing language, he is not just saying the names of words.

In these early studies I naively looked for easily identified cause-effect relationships. For each miscue I looked for some 'one' cue. In this I was operating as others had done in research on error analysis. The difference was that I was using scientific linguistics to categorize the phenomena. So when I found myself saying a miscue had a graphic cause, I found myself aware that there also were grammatical relationships involved; 'lad' and 'lady' look quite a bit alike but they are also both nouns and they have related meanings. Both are kinds of people. So if a reader substitutes 'lady' for 'lad', which of these factors is the cause?

I was led then to development of an analytic taxonomy which considers the relationships between the expected response (ER) and the observed response (OR) from all possible angles. Each miscue is considered on all variables that are pertinent, and no attempt is made to establish a single cause-effect relationship. Reaching this point in understanding was dependent on coming to see that one had to look at the whole process and that the various kinds of information a reader used always interacted with each other.

This taxonomy was used then in studies of reader's miscues and modified continuously to deal with the phenomena we found in the actual reading of kids. The more we understood, the more we were able to modify the miscue analysis so that in turn it could deal more completely with the miscues. A recent version of the taxonomy appeared in the 'Reading Research Quarterly' (Goodman, 1969).

Miscue studies have now been completed on readers ranging from near beginners to proficient high school students. Miscue research studies have included black and white readers, urban and suburban, non-native speakers of English, pupils labeled perceptually handicapped and many others. Studies have been done of miscues in languages other than English. Studies have involved subjects reading basal texts, science, social studies, mathematics, fiction, and nonfiction. One series of studies followed a small group of readers over several years of reading development (Goodman, 1971).

In examining miscues, some variables have emerged as being more significant than others or more indicative of proficiency than others. It is possible then to get powerful insights into a child's reading or into the reading process in general using a less complete miscue analysis than the taxonomy.

In working with teachers, we have used a variety of less formal versions of miscue analysis. The 'Reading Miscue Inventory' is a published program for use of miscue analysis in classroom and clinical settings (Goodman and Burke, 1972). It concentrates on nine key variables and the patterns of miscues pupils produce. Many teachers are also applying miscue analysis to the use of traditional informal reading inventories for selecting stories from their current instructional materials to use in miscue analysis.

In all miscue analyses, procedures are relatively uniform:

1. **An appropriate selection for the pupil is made.**
   This is a story or other reading selection which is somewhat difficult for the pupil. He reads the entire story, so it must not be longer than he can handle at a single sitting. It must be long enough to generate 25 or more miscues (50 or more in the case of research studies). More than one selection may need to be tried to find one that is appropriate. The selection should have the continuity of meaning that unified stories or articles provide.

2. **The material is prepared for taping.**
   The pupil reads directly from the book. The teacher or researcher needs to have a worksheet on which the story is retyped, preserving the lines of the story exactly as they are in the book. Each line on the worksheet is numbered with page and line of the story, so that miscues may be identified as to where they occur.

3. **The reader is audiotaped and the code sheet is marked.**
   The reader is asked to read the story. Before he begins, light conversation puts him at ease. He is told that he will not be graded for his reading and that he will be asked to retell the story after he has read. He is also told that no help will be given while he is reading. He is encouraged to do the best he can to handle any problems. He can use any strategies he knows, he can guess or skip a word and go on. As he reads, the teacher or researcher follows, marking the miscues on the typescript. Too much happens for everything to be noted as it occurs, so the entire reading, including retelling, is tape-recorded. Later the tape is replayed to complete the marking of the miscues on the worksheet. The worksheet becomes a permanent record of the session. It becomes the basis for the miscue analysis.

4. **The subject retells the story.**
   After he has read, the subject is asked to retell the story without interruption. Following the unaided retelling, the reader is asked open-ended questions to probe areas he omitted in his retelling. These questions do not use any specific information which the reader has not himself reported. The teacher or researcher does not steer the reader to conclusions. The reader's mispronunciations are retained in the questioning. A comprehension rating is based on an analysis of the retelling.

5. **The miscues are coded according to the analytic procedure used** (Taxonomy, Reading Miscue Inventory, or other).

6. The patterns of miscues are studied.

Because miscue analysis gets at the process and goes beyond the superficial, it produces information that can become the basis of specific instruction. If the reader shows insufficient concern for meaning, the teacher can devote attention to building this concern. If a specific problem occurs, such as confusion of 'wh' and 'th' words (what, that; when, then; where, there), strategy lessons can be designed to help the reader cope with the problem.

In noting such a problem, the teacher can carefully find its limits. The reader does not interchange other words starting with 'w' or 't'. He does not mix words like 'whistle' and 'thistle'. Only these function words are confused. In this way, the teacher can design a lesson which will help the reader use meaning and grammatical structure to detect when he has made a miscue of this type. The instruction will help the reader correct when he makes the miscue, and in the process such miscues will begin to disappear as the reader makes better predictions.

The ability to use the information gained from miscue analysis in working with learners is, as was said earlier, dependent on the teacher's moving to a view of reading instruction consistent with views of reading as a meaning-getting language process.

What We Know About Reading

Reading instruction in the last four decades has been word oriented. Basal readers have been built on this word-centered view. Controlled vocabulary, a system of carefully introducing new words starting with those in very frequent use, has been the central organizing strand in reading instruction.

Phonics vs. whole word arguments are concerned with the best way to teach words. Miscue research has led us away from a word focus to a comprehension focus. As we have looked at reading from a psycholinguistic perspective, we have come to see that the word is not the most significant unit in reading. Word bound reading instruction must be reconsidered in light of what is now known about the reading process.

Three kinds of information are available to the reader. One kind, the graphic information, reaches the reader visually. The other two, syntactic and semantic information, are supplied by the reader as he begins to process the visual input. Since the reader's goal is meaning, he uses as much or as little of each of these kinds of information as is necessary to get to the meaning. He makes predictions of the grammatical structure; using the control over language structure he learned when he learned oral language. He supplies semantic concepts to get the meaning from the structure. In turn his sense of syntactic structure and meaning make it possible to predict the graphic input so he is highly selective, sampling the print to confirm his prediction. In reading, what the reader thinks he sees is partly what he sees, but largely what he expects to see. As readers become more efficient, they use less and less graphic input.

Readers test the predictions they make by asking themselves if what they are reading makes sense and sounds like language. They also check themselves when the graphic input they predict is not there. In all this, it is meaning which makes the system go. As long as readers are trying to get sense from what they read, they use their language competence to get to meaning. The extent to which a reader can get meaning from written language depends on how much related meaning he brings to it. That is why it is easier to read something for which the reader has a strong conceptual background.

Readers develop sampling strategies to pick only the most useful and necessary graphic cues. They develop prediction strategies to get to the underlying grammatical structure and to anticipate what they are likely to find in the print. They develop confirmation strategies to check on the validity of their predictions. And they have correction strategies to use when their predictions do not work out and they need to reprocess the graphic, syntactic and semantic cues to get to the meaning.

When a reader's miscues are analyzed, the most important single indication of the reader's proficiency is the semantic acceptability of his miscues before correction. The reader's preoccupation with meaning will show in his miscues, because they will tend to result in language which still makes sense.

Even when readers produce non-words, they tend to retain the grammatical endings and intonation of the real word which is replaced. If they cannot quite get the meaning, they preserve the grammatical structure.

Effective readers also tend to correct miscues which result in a loss of meaning. They do this selectively. They will often not even be aware they have made miscues if meaning is not changed. The reader, when he experiences difficulty, first asks himself what would make sense, what would fit the grammatical structure, and only after that, what would match the graphic cues that would fit into the twin contexts of meaning and syntax. This keeps the value of graphic information in proper perspective and does not cause the reader to use any more information than is necessary.

Readers who are inefficient may be too much concerned with word-for-word accuracy. This may show in their miscues in a variety of ways, such as:

1. High degree of graphic correspondence between expected and observed responses in word substitution even when meaning is lost;

2. Frequent correction of miscues that do not affect the meaning;

3. Multiple attempts at getting a word's pronunciation even when it makes little difference to the comprehension of the story (proper names or foreign words, for example).

When the conceptual load in a particular selection gets too heavy for the reader, he may begin to treat it as grammatical nonsense, manipulating the grammatical structure without getting to meaning. This may be reflected by a relatively high percentage of grammatical acceptability of miscues and relatively low percentage of meaning acceptability. If the reader is getting to the meaning, both should be relatively high.

In judging how proficiently a reader is using the reading process, a teacher might use a procedure something like this:

1. Count the reader's miscues.

2. Subtract all those which are shifts to the reader's own dialect; these are not really miscues since they are what we should expect the reader to say in response to the print.

3. Count all the miscues which result in acceptable meaning (even if changed) before correction.

4. Count all miscues which result in unacceptable meaning but which are successfully corrected.

5. Add the miscues in steps 3 and 4. The result is the total number of miscues semantically acceptable or corrected.

This last score, expressed as a percentage of all miscues, is what we have come to call the 'comprehending' score. It is a measure of the reader's ability to keep his focus successfully on meaning. It is a measure of the *quality* of the reader's miscues. What is important is not how many miscues a reader makes, but what their effect on meaning is.

Emergence of New Methodology for Reading Instruction

With the new, revolutionary way of viewing reading and learning to read, a new methodology is gradually emerging. This is not a psycholinguistic method of teaching reading. Psycholinguistics is the foundation on which sound methodology must be built, but psycholinguistic knowledge does not automatically translate into a method of teaching reading.

Nor is miscue analysis a method of teaching reading. It is a technique for examining and evaluating the development of control of the reading process in learners. It can, in the hands of a knowledgeable teacher, provide the basis for useful instruction. But it does not lead to a total method.

Rather, as we come to understand better the process we are trying to teach when we teach reading, we can examine current practices and methodology—keeping some, rejecting some, reshaping some, and adding some totally new elements.

What changes most is the perspective. But that is a pervasive change because it leads to a new set of criteria for judging what is of value in reading instruction.

This new perspective is process-centered, language-centered, meaning-centered. It requires a new respect for language, a new respect for the learner, and a new respect for the reading teacher.

Language is seen, in this developing methodology, as much more than the bag of words we used to think it was. It is a structured, systematic code which can be used to represent meaning.

The *learner* of reading has a highly developed language competence which is his greatest resource in learning to read. In fact, the key to successful reading instruction is as it has always been, in the learner. With a new respect for the learner, we can make learning to read and write an extension of the natural language learning the child has already accomplished without professional assistance.

The teachers in this new methodology have a new and very important role to play. The teachers must come to understand the reading process so well that they can guide the progress of the learners. The teachers must know the signs of progress and be able to provide appropriate materials and instruction to aid the child's growth in proficiency.

Miscue analysis can be of great use to the teachers in this role because of the specific and general insights it provides about the learner's strengths and weaknesses. His miscues reflect his control and use of the reading process.

In many diagnostic procedures the teacher is frequently advised to administer a dose of phonics regardless of the pattern the child has shown. Miscue analysis shows the process at work and will reveal changes in how this process is used.

One problem that plagues teachers is judging how much progress pupils are making toward reading proficiency. When we judge the progress of infants in learning oral language, we do it very simply. If they can make themselves understood, they are learning to talk; and if they can respond to what is said to them, they are making progress in listening. We judge, in other words, by the learners' success with the process as they use it. Reading also should be judged by the extent to which learners can understand an increasing range of written materials.

We let ourselves confuse published reading tests with the competence in reading they are trying to assess. The subskill tests, skill check lists and word lists do not test the ability to understand written language. They test, in large part, ability to perform with the abstract bits and pieces of language. Miscue analysis can bring us back to reality.

References

Goodman, K. 1969. "Analysis of Oral Reading Miscues: Applied Psycholinguistics," *Reading Research Quarterly,* Fall, pp. 9–30.

Goodman, K. *A Study of Children's Behavior While Reading Orally,* Final Report, Project No. S-425, Contract No. OE-6-10-136, U.S. Department of Health, Education and Welfare, Office of Education, Bureau of Research, 1971.

Goodman, Y. and C. Burke (1972). *Reading miscue inventory manual; Procedure for diagnosis and evaluation.* New York: Macmillan Pub. Co.; London: Collier Macmillan Publishers.

Chapter Seven

A Linguistic Study of Cues and Miscues in Reading

Kenneth S. Goodman
Wayne State University, 1965

This is a report of the conclusions to date of a descriptive study of the oral reading of first-, second-, and third-grade children. It is a study in applied linguistics since linguistic knowledge and insights into language and language learning were used.

Assumptions

In this study, reading has been defined as the active reconstruction of a message from written language. Reading must involve some level of comprehension. Nothing short of this comprehension is reading. I have assumed that all reading behavior is caused. It is cued or miscued during the child's interaction with written language. Research on reading must begin at this point of interaction. Reading is a psycholinguistic process. Linguistic science has identified the cue systems within language. The child learning to read his native language has already internalized these cue systems to the point where he is responding to them without being consciously aware of the process. To understand how children learn to read, we must learn how the individual experiences and abilities of children affect their ability to use language cues. We must also become aware of the differences and similarities between understanding oral language which uses sounds as symbol-units and written language which depends on graphic symbols.

Cue Systems in Reading

Here is a partial list of the systems operating to cue and miscue the reader as he interacts with written material. Within words there are:

Letter-sound relationships

Shape (or word configuration)

Known "little words" in bigger words

Whole known words

Recurrent spelling patterns.

In the flow of language there are:

Patterns of words (or function order)

Inflection and inflectional agreement (examples: The boy runs. The boys run.)

Function words such as noun markers (the, a, that, one, etc.)

Intonation (which is poorly represented in writing by punctuation)

The referential meaning of prior and subsequent language elements and whole utterances.

Cues external to language and the reader include:

Pictures

Prompting by teacher or peers

Concrete objects

Skill charts.

Cues within the reader include:

His language facility with the dialect of his subculture

His dialect (his own personal version of the language)

His experiential background (the reader responds to cues in terms of his own real or vicarious experiences)

His conceptual background and ability (a reader can't read what he can't understand)

Those reading attack skills and learning strategies he has acquired or been taught.

Procedures

The subjects of this study were 100 children in Grades 1, 2, and 3 who attend the same school in an industrial suburb of Detroit. Every second child on an alphabetic list of all children in these grades was included. There were an equal number of boys and girls from each room.

From reading materials, a sequence of stories was selected from a reading series not used in the school. With the publisher's permission the stories were dittoed on work sheets. A word list from each story was also duplicated.

An assistant called each subject individually out of the classroom. The subject was given a word list for a story at about his grade level. If the child missed many words, he was given a list for an earlier story. If he missed few or none he was given a more advanced story. Each child eventually had a word list of comparable difficulty. The number of words which each child missed on the lists, then, was a controlled variable.

Next the child was asked to read orally from the book the story on which his word list was based. The assistant noted all the child's oral reading behavior on the work sheets as the child read. The assistant refrained from any behavior which might cue the reader. Finally, each subject was to close his book and retell the story as best he could. He was not given advance notice that he would be asked to do this. The reading and retelling of the story was taped. Comparison between the structure of the language in the book and in the retold stories is underway utilizing the system of the Loban and Strickland studies.[1] It is not complete and will not be reported here.

Words in Lists and in Stories

One concern of the research was the relative ability of children to recognize words in the lists and read the words in the stories. The expectation was that children would read many words in stories which they could not recognize in lists. I reasoned that, in lists, children had only cues *within* printed words while in stories they had the additional cues in the flow of language. I was not disappointed.

1. Loban, W. 1963. *The Language of Elementary School Children: A study of the use and control of language and the relations among speaking, reading, writing, and listening.* Champaign: National Council of Teachers of English.
Strickland, R. 1962. "The Language of Elementary School Children: Its Relationship to the Language of Reading Textbooks and the Quality of Reading of Selected Children." *Bulletin of the School of Education,* Indiana University, 38, No. 4.

Table 7–1
Average Words Missed in List and in Story

		Also Missed in Story		
	List Average	Average	Percent	Ratio
Grade 1	9.5	3.4	38%	2.8:1
Grade 2	20.1	5.1	25%	3.9:1
Grade 3	18.8	3.4	18%	5.5:1

As is shown in Table 7–1, the children in this study were able to read many words in context which they couldn't read from lists. Average first graders could read almost two out of three words in the story which they missed on the list. The average second grader missed only one-fourth of the words in the story which he failed to recognize on the list. Third graders were able to get, in the stories, all but 18 percent of the words which they did not know in the list.

As Table 7–2 shows, except for a small group of first graders and a very few second and third graders, all the children in this study could read correctly in the story at least half of the words that they could not recognize on the lists. Sixty-nine percent of first-grade children could "get" two-thirds or more of their list errors right in reading the story. Sixty-six percent of the second graders could read three-fourths or more of their errors in the story. The comparable group of third graders could get better than four out of five. The children in successive grades in this study were increasingly efficient in using cue systems outside of words.

At the same time, as Table 7–3 shows, children in successive grades were making greater attempts to use word attack skills, here defined as responses to *cue systems within words*. About half of the listed errors of first graders were omissions. The children did not attempt to figure the words out by using any available cues. Second-grade children showed an increased tendency to try to "get" the word. This is shown by the somewhat higher percent of substitutions among the list

Table 7–2
Ability to Read Words in Context Which Were Missed on List*

	Less Than 1/2	More Than 1/2	More Than 2/3	More Than 3/4	More Than 4/5	N
Grade 1	11%	89%	69%	49%	26%	35
Grade 2	3%	97%	81%	66%	50%	32
Grade 3	6%	94%	91%	76%	67%	33

*Cumulative percents of subjects

Table 7–3

Total Errors and Substitution Errors on Lists

	List Errors	Included Substitutions		
	Average	Average	Percent	Ratio
Grade 1	9.5	4.9	52%	1.9:1
Grade 2	20.1	11.5	57%	1.7:1
Grade 3	18.1	14.3	79%	1.3:1

errors of second-grade children. Third graders showed a pronounced increase in the percent of substitutions among their list errors. Children in successive grades used word attack skills with increased frequency though not necessarily with increased efficiency.

There was no instance of a child getting a word right on the list but missing it consistently in the story. But often children made an incorrect substitution in the reading of the story in individual occurrences of known words. As Table 7–4 indicates, second and third graders made more than twice as many one-time substitutions per line read as first graders. Third graders made more substitutions per line than second graders. Three possible causes of these one-time substitutions may be:

1. overuse of cues within words to the exclusion of other cues

2. miscuing by book language which differs from the language as the child knows it

3. ineffective use of language cues.

Regressions in Reading

This study also was concerned with regressions in reading, that is repeating one or more words. No statistics are needed to support one observation: virtually every regression which the children in this study made was for the purpose of correcting previous reading.

Table 7–4

One-Time Substitutions for Known Words in Stories

	Average Substitutions	Average Lines Read	Substitutions per Line Read
Grade 1	3.7	50.2	.074
Grade 2	14.9	126.2	.118
Grade 3	16.9	118.7	.142

Table 7–5

Regressions in Reading

	First Grade		Second Grade		Third Grade	
	Per Child	Per Line Read	Per Child	Per Line Read	Per Child	Per Line Read
Word Only						
To correct word	2.40	.048	10.11	.090	10.30	.087
To correct intonation on word	.09	.002	.49	.004	1.42	.012
Total	2.49	.050	10.60	.094	11.72	.099
Phrase*						
To correct word by repeating phrase	1.54	.031	5.77	.052	7.54	.061
To rephrase	.29	.006	1.97	.018	1.03	.009
To change intonation	.52	.011	2.83	.026	2.76	.023
Total	2.35	.048	10.57	.096	11.33	.093

*For these purposes a phrase is considered *any* two or more consecutive words.

When a child missed a word on a list, unless he corrected it immediately he seldom ever went back. In reading the story, however, children frequently repeated words or groups of words, almost always to make a correction. Regressions themselves, then, were not errors but attempts (usually but not always successful) to correct prior errors.

If regressions are divided into two groups, word regressions—those which involve one word immediately repeated—and phrase regressions—those which include repeating two or more words—the two types each represent almost exactly half the regressions at each of the grade levels (see Table 7–5).

Regressions seem to function in children's reading about like this: if the child makes an error in reading which he realizes is inconsistent with prior cues, he reevaluates the cues and corrects his error before continuing. Otherwise, he reads on encountering more cues which are inconsistent with his errors. Eventually he becomes aware that the cues cannot be reconciled and retraces his footsteps to find the source of the inconsistency. Thus, regressions in reading are due to redundant cues in language. They are self-corrections which play a vital role in children's learning to read. In two cases errors go uncorrected:

1. if the error makes no difference to the meaning of the passage, and

2. if the reader is relying so heavily on analytical techniques using only cues within words that he has lost the meaning altogether.

A Preliminary Linguistic Taxonomy

In a third phase of the study I categorized all errors of the subjects according to linguistic terminology. This analysis produced the *Preliminary Linguistic Taxonomy of Cues and Miscues in Reading*. The Taxonomy will be published in a separate article.

It should be noted that the 100 subjects of this study, though all attend the same school and have learned to read with a fairly consistent methodology, exhibited virtually every kind of reading difficulty and deviation which I could predict linguistically.

Implications of This Study

There are several implications to be drawn from the description of the oral reading of these children. Some practices in the teaching of reading are made suspect.

1. Introducing new words out of context before new stories are introduced to children does not appear to be necessary or desirable.

2. Prompting children or correcting them when they read orally also appears to be unnecessary and undesirable in view of the self-correction which language cues in children.

3. Our fixation on eye fixations and our mania for devices which eliminate regressions in reading seem to be due to a lamentable failure to recognize what was obvious in this study: that regressions are the means by which the child corrects himself and learns.

4. Shotgun teaching of so-called phonic skills to whole classes or groups at the same time seems highly questionable in view of the extreme diversity of the difficulties children displayed in this study. No single difficulty seemed general enough to warrant this approach. In fact, it is most likely that at least as many children are suffering from difficulties caused by overusing particular learning strategies in reading as are suffering from a lack of such strategies.

5. The children in this study found it harder to recognize words than to read them in stories. Eventually I believe we must abandon our concentration on words in teaching reading and develop a theory of reading and a methodology which puts the focus where it belongs: on language.

Chapter Eight

Miscue Analysis: Theory and Reality in Reading

Kenneth S. Goodman
University of Arizona, 1976

More than ten years ago this researcher set himself a simple task: He wished to examine, from the perspective of modern linguistics, what happened when people read. It seemed logical to ask subjects to read material they had not seen before, so that what they did could be analyzed.

This examination of oral reading is not new. Analysis of reading errors in oral reading has been going on for several decades. What is new is the linguistic perspective which is applied. Error analysis had largely followed two assumptions. First, it was assumed that oral reading should be accurate and therefore that errors represented undesirable events in reading. Second it was assumed that errors grew from weaknesses or deficiencies in the reader. The number of errors was counted but little attention was given to qualitative differences among miscues or their effects.

In miscue analysis, from the very beginning, reading has been treated as a language process, the receptive aspect of written language and therefore the parallel process to listening. The reader is regarded as a user of language, one who constructs meaning from written language.

This chapter first appeared in *New Horizons in Reading, Proceedings of the Fifth IRA World Congress on Reading,* 1976, J. Merritt, (ed.), Newark, DE: International Reading Association. pp. 15–26. Copyright (1976) by the International Reading Association. Reprinted with permission.

Everything the reader does is assumed to be caused in this linguistic process. Unexpected events in oral reading thus reveal the way the reader is using the reading process itself. The term error is a misnomer then, since it implies an undesirable occurrence. The term miscue has emerged instead. A miscue is any observed oral response (OR) to print which does not match the expected response (ER). Miscue analysis reveals the reader's strengths and weaknesses and provides a continuous window on the reading process.

In this last sense miscue analysis is a uniquely powerful tool in linguistic and psycholinguistic research since it makes it possible to monitor a language process continuously as it proceeds.

Shifting the focus in this analysis from errors as undesirable phenomena to be eliminated to miscues as the by-product of the reading process has made possible a revolution in viewpoint in which both the reader and the reading process may be regarded positively. The reader, particularly of a native language, may be regarded as a competent user of language whose language competence is reflected in miscues produced as a proficient reader and at all stages of acquisition of reading proficiency.

By moving away from a simplistic view that reading must be accurate we are able to see, through miscues, how the efficient and effective reader operates. We can further define effectiveness in reading as the ability to construct a message (comprehend) and define efficiency as the ability to use the least amount of available cues necessary to get to the meaning. Miscues are produced in efficient reading but they are likely to either leave meaning unaffected or be corrected by the reader. As efficiency increases, frequency of miscues tends to decrease; but this is the result and not the cause of efficiency.

An Emerging Miscue Taxonomy

In early miscue research we sought simple cause-effect relationships. We began to recognize that there were graphic cues from the perception of the print itself, phonic cues which relate print to speech, syntactic cues which derive from the structure of the language, and semantic cues from the meaning. But we looked for a one-to-one cause-effect relationship. We tried to classify some miscues as grapho-phonic (combining the first two since the cues are the same), some as syntactic, some as semantic. We soon became aware that we could not fragment the process of reading, that every event involved the use of all three systems. Consider this example:

Text   Wait a *moment.*
Reader   Wait a *minute.*

The reader substitutes *minute* for *moment*. The observed response (OR) looks like and sounds like the expected response to some extent. But *minute* and *moment* also have the same grammatical function and mean the same thing. All of the three sorts of cues and their interactions contribute to the miscue. Furthermore the reader who is American is more likely to use *minute* than *moment* which the British writer has used. So the reader has shown that the influence of dialect is also at work.

A taxonomy for the analysis of oral reading miscues has emerged over a period of years in a series of studies. Each miscue is examined by asking a number of questions about the relationship of expected to observed response. All relevant questions are answered independently. What emerges then is the pattern of how the cuing systems are used in ongoing reading.

Here are the questions which are asked:

1. Is the miscue self-corrected by the reader?
2. Is the reader's dialect involved in the miscue?
3. How much graphic similarity is there between ER and OR?
4. How much phonemic similarity is there?
5. Is the OR an allolog of the ER? Typing and typewriting are allologs of the same word. Contractions are also allologs.
6. Does the miscue produce a syntactically acceptable text?
7. Does the miscue produce a semantically acceptable text?
8. Does a grammatical retransformation result from the miscue?
9. If the miscue is syntactically acceptable, how much is syntax changed?
10. If the miscue is semantically acceptable, how much is meaning changed?
11. Is intonation involved in the miscue? In English, changed intonation may reflect change in syntax, meaning, or both.
12. Does the miscue involve the submorphemic language level?
13. Does the miscue involve the bound morpheme level?
14. Does the miscue involve the phrase or free morpheme level?
15. Does the miscue involve the phrase level?
16. Does the miscue involve the clause level?
17. What is the grammatical category of the OR?
18. What is the grammatical category of the ER?
19. What is the relationship between function of ER and OR?

20. What influence has the surrounding text (peripheral visual field) had on miscues?

21. What is the semantic relationship between ER and OR word substitutions?

Miscue analysis using this taxonomy is suitable for depth research on small numbers of subjects. Typically, our research has involved 3–6 subjects selected because they have common characteristics. These subjects are asked to read one or more full selections. In our most recent research our subjects have been asked to read two stories. Comparing profiles on both stories adds to the depth of our insights into the process.

A simpler form of miscue analysis dealing with only the more significant questions has been developed by Yetta M. Goodman and Carolyn Burke. This form has been used in some research studies, but it is designed for use by teachers and clinicians as a diagnostic tool. It also has found wide use in teacher education as a means of helping preservice and inservice teachers to understand the reading process.

Psycholinguistics as a Base for Study of Reading

Reading and listening are receptive language processes. Speaking and writing are generative, productive, language processes. The reader or the listener is actively involved in the reconstruction of a message. He must comprehend meaning in order to be considered successful.

Meaning is not a property of the graphic display. The writer has moved from thought to language, encoding his meaning as a graphic display just as the speaker moves from thought to language encoding his meanings as a phonological sequence. The reader decodes the graphic display and reconstructs meaning.

Whether one wishes to understand reading as a process to teach initial literacy or to help readers become more effective, one must start from a base of psycholinguistics, the study of the interrelationships of thought and language. All the central questions involved in reading are psycholinguistic questions, because reading is a process in which language interacts with thought. Psycholinguistics is foundational to all understanding of the reading process.

In research and instruction, learning to read has been commonly equated with learning to match an alphabetic orthography with its oral language counterpart. Reading instruction has frequently either been minimal, considered to be complete once the orthography is mastered, or endlessly repetitious and barren for those learners who persist in not acquiring correspondences between oral and written language. Skills have been taught on the basis of tradition with no insight into their relationship to the basic function of reading, reconstructing the message. The result is the most common, persistent, and disabling reading problem in all cultures: people who have learned to respond orally to print but who cannot or do not comprehend what they are reading. Reading becomes a print-to-speech short circuit. Those who cannot get meaning from written language are just as functionally illiterate as those who never received instruction.

A Psycholinguistic Theory of Reading English

A theory and model of the reading process has grown out of research with young American readers of English. The theory has evolved as a means of interpreting the differences between OR and ER in order to understand the process of reading.

Behavior, whether linguistic or any other, is the end product of a process. The external behavior is observable and serves as an indicator of the underlying competence. Behavior can be observed but it cannot be understood without some theory of how it is produced. Seemingly identical behaviors may result from very different processing. Very different behaviors may prove closely related if they are seen within a theoretical framework.

Comparison of OR and ER in miscues is a powerful means of inferring the process readers are using in dealing with specific reading tasks. When reading is as expected, the process is not discernible, but when it has produced miscues, then the information used by readers and the ways in which they use it may be seen.

The following is the beginning of a short story as read by five relatively proficient readers aged 13–15. It will serve to illustrate the miscue phenomena and to introduce the theory of the reading process.

Miscues of Five Readers

Subject 1.   It must have been around

midnight when I drove home, and as I

approached the gates of the bungalow I

switched off the *C* | head lamps | *lights* of the car

on

so the beam wouldn't swing in through

the window of the side bedroom and

wake Harry Pope.

Subject 2.

It must have been around

midnight when I drove home, and *(as)* I ⓒ

approached the gates of the bungalow I

switched off the head lamps of the car ⓒ 2. *lights*

so the beam wouldn't swing in through

the window of the side bedroom and

wake Harry Pope.

Subject 3.

It must have been around

midnight when I drove home, *(and)* as I *As*

approached the gates of the bungalow I

switched off the head lamps of the car ⓒ *lights*

so the beam wouldn't swing *(in)* through

the window of the side bedroom *(and)* ⓒ

wake Harry Pope. *where* *was –*

Subject 4.

It must have been around

midnight when I drove home, and as I

approached the gates of the bungalow I ⓒ 2. *bung-* 1. *bung-*

switched off the head lamps of the car *(RS)*

so the beam wouldn't swing *(in)* through *Ⓘ* *Ⓘ*

the window of the side bedroom and

wake Harry Pope.

Subject 5.   It must have been around

midnight when I drove home, and (as) I

bagalog and

approached the gates of (the) bungalow I

lights

switched off the head lamps of the car

©

so the beam wouldn't swing (in) through

at   *of the*

the window of the side bedroom and

Henry

wake Harry Pope.

The first phenomenon which can be seen here is a common tendency among these readers to substitute *lights* for *lamps* in line four. The two words start with the same sound and letter but the relationship between the words is clearly semantic. Unless one assumes some kind of pervasive habitual association between these two words, one must conclude 1) that the readers are anticipating what they will in fact see, and 2) that they are more likely to expect *lights* than *lamps*. Notice, in fact, that subject 2 says *lamps*, rejects that in favor of *lights*, and then goes back to *lamps*. This is a good example of the reading process at work. This British writer has used the term *head lamps*. Our American subjects prefer the term *headlights* and have already predicted it. Subsequent graphic input, however, contradicts the prediction. Some of the readers reprocess, however they have already gotten the meaning from the initial processing and must have done so before they said *lights* if it is meaning which influenced their choices.

The words which are omitted by these five readers offer more insights into the process. *As* in line two is omitted by two readers, one of whom corrects. *In* in line five is omitted by three readers, one of whom corrects. Subject 1 substitutes *on* for *in*.

If we examine these for both cause and effect these insights emerge:

As may produce miscues (unexpected responses) because it follows *and* and introduces a dependent clause which precedes the independent clause it relates to. That requires that the *as* clause be processed, stored, and held until the following clause is processed before the meaning is fully clear. Omission of *as* changes the structure so that the hitherto dependent clause is independent conjoined by *and* to the preceding independent clause. A problem is then created since now there is no signal left as to the relationship between the new independent clause and the clause starting with *I* at the end of line three. The omission of *as* creates a sequence with an unacceptable grammatical structure. The reader who corrected seemed aware of this problem before he was aware of the precise omission because he repeated *and I* three times before a successful correction. The reader who did not correct inserts a conjunction *and* before *I* in line three producing parallel independent clauses.

Subject three omits *and* before *as* on line two. This conjunction turns out to be optional since the prior clause is independent.

The omission of *in* before *through* on line five results in little loss of semantic or syntactic information. The readers appeared to omit an element perhaps redundant in their American dialects. One substitutes *on* for *in* which may be more likely in her dialect in this context.

Subject five replaces *of the side bedroom* with *at the side of the bedroom*. In doing so he makes a minor change in the meaning but produces a new structure which is both meaningful and grammatical.

Subject three moves even farther away from the text at the end of the paragraph. He substitutes *where Harry Pope was* for *and wake Harry Pope*. Apparently he expected it to conclude with *sleeping*. He realizes his expectation is not borne out and regresses, reprocesses and corrects.

The miscues of these readers cannot be explained by viewing reading as a process of sequential letter or word identification. If it were so, then miscues would be more evenly distributed and be confined to words or word parts.

Even with the one word in this paragraph that did cause some recognition problems, *bungalow,* the problems cannot be seen simply as letter-sound (phonics) or word recognition based. It may be that the problem comes from a mismatch between the reader's definition (and concept) of a bungalow and the writer's. Americans commonly use bungalow to refer to a very modest house or vacation home. Furthermore we can't be sure that those readers who exhibited no difficulty with *bungalow* understood its use by this author in this context.

Several key concepts about the reading process are required to begin to explain the miscues of these readers.

1. Anticipation or prediction is an important part of the reading process.

2. Readers process syntactic or grammatical information as they read and this plays an important role in their ability to predict what they have not yet seen or processed.

3. Meaning is the end product of the reading process and effective readers are meaning-seekers.

4. Meaning is also input in the reading process. The success of the reader in comprehending is largely a function of the conceptual and experiential background he brings to the task and which his processing of the writer's language evokes in him.

5. Graphic information (letters, letter constituents, and patterns of letters) is by no means the sole input in the reading process. Nor is the matching of such information to phonological information a necessarily significant part of the reading process.

6. Accuracy in oral reading is not a prerequisite to effective reading. Comprehension is the basic goal and a focus on accuracy may be counterproductive.

The reader must begin with this graphic display and somehow decode it in such a way that he reconstructs the author's message.

Any passage may be analyzed for letters, words or meaning. The last focus is a much more efficient one in that the amount of information needed to get to the meaning is far less than if words or letters must be first analyzed. Thus, to be both *effective* and *efficient*, reading must be focused on meaning.

An effective, efficient reader uses the least amount of information necessary to reconstruct the writer's message. This is only possible if he is able to sample from available cues those which are most productive, that is, those that carry the most information. To do so he must use strategies which he develops that make it possible to predict and guess at the other available information without actually processing it. The reader's knowledge of the grammatical system of the language and the constraints within that system as well as the semantic constraints within the concepts dealt with constitute the parameters within which the reader's strategies are operating.

To get from print to meaning, the reader must treat the graphic display as a surface representation of an underlying structure. He must not only process the graphic display as a grammatically structured language sequence but he must assign an underlying or deep structure in order to process the interrelationships between clauses.

Consider, for example, the paragraph cited above as read by these subjects. This paragraph is a single sentence composed of clauses combined in complex ways so that the meaning of the whole is more than that of any one clause. Rewritten as a string of one clause sentences which express about the same meaning, it might read like this:

It must have been around midnight. I drove home at midnight. I approached the gates of the bungalow. (at the same time) I switched off the headlamps of the car. (in order that) The beam wouldn't swing in through the window of the bedroom. The bedroom was at the side. (in order that) The beam wouldn't wake Harry Pope.

The reader must deal with an underlying structure by interpreting signals in the surface structure because meaning relates not to the surface structure but to underlying structure.

The writer has produced the graphic display starting with meaning, assigning a deep grammatical structure, then transforming this deep structure by use of transforming rules and subsequently applying a set of orthographic rules to produce a surface representation in the form of a graphic display.

This process is much the same as speaking except that the final rules are orthographic rather than phonological. In use, the graphic display and oral language are alternate surface representations of the deep structure. Writing is not a secondary representation of speech. This is obvious in nonalphabetic writing systems. It is no less true in alphabetic systems even though there are direct relationships between the two surface representations.

The alphabetic systems are economical in that they are able to use a small number of symbols in patterned combinations to express an unlimited number of meanings, just as oral language does. And using the oral language symbols as a base for the written symbols is both convenient and logical. But if readers found it necessary to identify letters and match them with sounds or even identify word shapes and match them with oral names, then efficient reading would be slower than speech. But efficient readers use distinctive features of letters to move from print to deep structure and meaning. Their ability to identify letters or words they have read *follows* rather than *precedes* their assignment of deep structure and meaning. Once they know what they have read they also know the words they have read and their spellings. In this manner they *appear* to identify graphic elements much more rapidly than they could actually do so.

Essentially the same deep language structure underlies both speech and writing. There are, of course, different circumstances in which oral and written language are used. The former is much more likely to be in a situational context which may be indicated by gesture or which need no explanation. Written language, on the other hand, is most often abstracted from the situations it deals with. It must create its own setting and be a much more complete representation of the message to achieve effective communication. But these differences are more those of use than of process.

The reader samples the three systems of cues in order to be aware of and predict surface structure and induce deep structure and meaning.

The reader responds to what he sees or what he thinks he sees. His experience with and knowledge of the graphic symbols (letters), spelling patterns, sequencing rules and redundancies set up expectations. He is able to use distinctive features to form perceptual images which are partly the result of what he expects to see.

Subject five thought the name was *Henry* rather than *Harry*. The two names differ graphically in very minor ways. She had no reason to reject that having produced it since it fits both meaning and grammar constraints.

A minimum amount of syntactic information, that *as* is a marker of a clause for example, makes it possible to predict a surface structure and almost simultaneously begin to induce an underlying structure. Punctuation, part of the graphic cue system, comes mostly at the end of sequences in English and therefore is of little use except as a check on prediction. One must predict the pattern in order to process subsequent elements.

For a proficient reader to get directly to meaning he must draw on his knowledge of the patterns, rules, constraints, and redundancies of the grammatical system.

Even beginning readers in our research substitute *a* for *the*, an indication that they use grammatical as well as graphic cues. As the surface structure is predicted, the rules by which that structure is linked to the underlying deep structure are evoked and serve as additional cues.

Because of the limited number of patterns, the constraints within these patterns (only certain elements may follow certain others), and the redundancy of language (every cue does not carry a new bit of information) a reader is able to sample those cues which carry the most information and predict whole patterns on that basis.

Sampling, selecting, and predicting are basic aspects of reading. They require development by the reader of comprehension strategies which control the choice and use of cues and keep the reader oriented to the goal of reading which is meaning.

When miscues affect meaning the reader must be aware that they do and correct. He uses a set of confirmation strategies as he proceeds. He asks himself 1) whether he can predict a grammatical sequence on the basis of information processed, 2) whether he can assign a decodable deep structure, and 3) whether what he has decoded as meaning in fact makes sense.

As he continues to process information he is constantly alert to information which contradicts his prediction. As long as subsequent information confirms, he proceeds. If any contradictory information is encountered he must reprocess to reconcile the conflicting information. This may require a new hypothesis about what is coming. The problems with *as* that our subjects had and their subsequent responses illustrate this process at work.

Reading then becomes a sample, predict, test, confirm, and correct when necessary process.

The constant concern for meaning as output makes meaning input as well. The deep structure must be decodable; the reader must know whether what he had decoded makes sense. Furthermore, experience and concepts must be evoked to create a semantic context and a set of semantic constraints which correspond to the syntactic constraints.

Memory functions as a kind of highly cross-referenced lexicon feeding the most appropriate referential meaning into the processing to complete the set of semantic cues.

No person, however literate, is ever able to read all that is written in his native language. The ability to read any selection is a function of the semantic background one brings to it. Without substantial meaning input, effective reading is not possible. Literacy is by no means a constant for any individual for all reading tasks.

New Views of Old Questions

Miscue analysis and the psycholinguistic view of reading suggest the need for reconsidering old issues. Here, a few of these can only be listed. In each case the traditional view seems to be at odds with this new view.

1. Where should reading instruction begin? Not with letters or sounds but with whole real relevant natural language, we think.

2. What is the hierarchy of skills that should be taught in reading instruction? We think there is none. In fact, in learning to read as in learning to talk, one must use all skills at the same time.

3. Why do some people fail to learn to read? Not because of their weaknesses but because we've failed to build on their strengths as competent language users.

4. What should we do for deficient readers? Build their confidence in their ability to predict meaning and language.

5. Can anyone learn to read? Yes, we say. Anyone who can learn oral language can learn to read and write.

Some New Questions

There is still a lot to be learned about reading. Many new questions emerge as reading is seen from a new vantage point.

1. How does the difference in grammatical structure of different languages influence the reading process?

2. How does the reading process differ in nonalphabetic writing systems?

3. How do variations among readers in conceptual development influence their reading and their comprehension?

4. Can methods be devised for teaching people to read languages they don't speak? This question is of particular importance in countries where college texts are in languages other than the national language.

Perhaps the most basic question we need to ask is how can we put these new scientific insights to use in achieving the goal of universal literacy.

Part Three

Text Analysis

The traditional view of reading subordinates the reader to the writer's text and holds that meaning is accessed by accurately identifying words in sequence. Prior to Goodman's research, words in isolation had been the focus of controlled studies of reading. Word frequency had long been studied by analyzing a large corpus of words across a variety of texts, but little was known about word frequency in specific texts and the relationship between the two.

The first chapter in this part is a detailed study of word frequency in individual texts used for miscue analysis. Goodman and Bird found that more than half of the words in all six texts occurred only once, whereas only a small set of words occurred frequently. The extremely frequent words were few in number, including function words, *BE* forms, and pronouns. The results showed that word frequency is constrained by text, and word choice is the result of syntactic, semantic, pragmatic, and stylistic constraints. Goodman and Bird showed that the wording of a specific text is not random but predictable. Furthermore, any attempt to control vocabulary compromises the text's authenticity and makes the text less predictable.

In the second chapter, Goodman explores miscues made on determiners in three stories read by students from eight different American linguistic population groups. One of the findings of his study is that most of the miscues on determiners are function words, and they rarely switch with content words in noun, verb, adjective, and adverb categories. Another interesting finding is that miscues occur at a point of the clause where an article might be expected, but a pronoun, conjunction, or preposition could also be inserted. The point is a pivotal slot for word insertion that could lead to different syntactic structures.

The findings indicate that the readers did not process the written text in a linear order.

The two chapters in this part shed light on the study of reading from both the perspective of the written text and from the perspective of the reader. A key characteristic of text is that it is cohesive. Cohesiveness in syntax, semantics, pragmatics, and style allow readers to make better predictions when reading. With their intuitive understanding of the rules of language and knowledge of the world, readers are able to construct their own text that parallels that of the writer. The text that the reader constructs is the product of the transaction with the writer and construction of meaning. While we should have respect for the writer's text, we should have respect for the reader's text as well.

Chapter Nine

On the Wording of Texts: A Study of Intra-Text Word Frequency

Kenneth S. Goodman and Lois Bridges Bird
University of Arizona, 1984

Abstract.[1] This study examines word choice and frequency in six texts. Word frequency has been studied for almost a century but it has been studied across texts in large language corpuses in order to determine frequency in the language at large. Word frequency as a characteristic of specific texts has not been studied.

This study of infra-text word frequency shows that frequent words fall into two groups:

1. Words common across texts: function words, pronouns, and copulas (*BE* forms). These words are common because the syntax of the language requires them and because the sets of words that fit the text requirements are quite small.

2. Words common in the particular text because of the meaning the text represents. These may be quite uncommon in the language at large. These words are common because they provide the semantic

---

1. Some of the articles in this book were originally published with abstracts that precede the chapter. The abstracts have been retained to preserve continuity between the original article and the chapter as presented here.

This chapter first appeared in *Research in the Teaching of English,* Vol. 18, No. 2, May 1984, pp. 119–45. Copyright (1984) by the National Council of Teachers of English. Reprinted with permission.

cohesion necessary for the text to be a text. Their repetition maintains and extends text relationships.

Nouns, particularly proper nouns, are the only content words likely to appear very frequently in a given text. Other content words are rarely repeated more than a few times. This is largely for pragmatic and stylistic reasons. Authors deliberately avoid using the same word over and over. The language is rich in words with similar meaning, and English users value variation. So cohesion may be maintained without repeating the same content words.

This study raises questions about the use of word lists and controlled vocabulary in producing basal readers, judging and manipulating readability of texts, and building vocabulary.

Word Frequency in Texts and in General

The topic of this research report is really the wording of texts; Halliday (1978) considers "wording" the folk term for what he describes as the lexico-grammar of the language. As such the wording is both the final written representation of the meaning and the process by which the final selection is made. Which words constitute the visible text is certainly determined by the writer but only within strong lexico-grammatical constraints that the structure of language, meaning, and social communication provide.

But in the field of reading and in the history of reading research the focus on the wording of language has concentrated on *word frequency*, the frequency with which words occur in general in the language.

As with so many popular notions in education, study of the issue of word frequency is dominated by the original reasons it was considered important, and we have not looked objectively at the realities of wording as a text characteristic. Unless we examine how characteristics of coherent, functional, meaningful texts relate to choice and frequency of words in those texts, we cannot truly understand the significance of relative frequency of words in use. So, to put our study in an educational context and to examine current educational belief and practice, word frequency within texts is the focus of this article.

The Nature of Texts

Written language may be studied from three perspectives: the writer, the text, or the reader. The text, generated by the writer and comprehended by the reader, is the minimal unit of language fully capable of comprehensibly representing meaning (Halliday & Hasan, 1976, p. 1).

Texts have complex structures and sets of characteristics which derive from their social function: meaning cannot pass from writer to reader. It can only be constructed by readers from texts so constructed by writers that the texts have the potential to be comprehended.

The grammar creates the basic structure of the clauses and their interrelationships within and across the sentences of the text. It provides the set of rules by which clauses are structured, combined, and sequenced to produce a well-formed text.

Texts have semantic structures too. They have macrostructures or text grammars which derive partly from the meaning being represented: the plot and theme of a story, its sequence of events, and its characters, with their own experiences, thoughts, feelings, and goals. Partly these structures derive also from the culture: they are forms which become conventional within societies for certain genres and functions. A letter, formal or informal, must have a greeting such as "Dear Mary," for example. Semantic structures have pragmatic constraints: purposes, functions, and central realities determine the shape of texts.

Texts must be cohesive. They must hang together. Meaning and reference must be built on meaning and reference, and the parts of the texts must relate to each other and to the whole.

Further, authors establish personal styles or voices within these constraints. In fact, it is their control over the structures and constraints of texts that makes it possible for authors to achieve individuality. They know what can vary and what must be constant within texts.

One of the most visible characteristics of texts is their wording. In fact one common-sense misconception of written texts is that they are simply strings of words.

Clearly, wording is an important text characteristic. Clearly, also, wording is not random or at the whim of the writer. It is the result of the syntactic, semantic, pragmatic, and stylistic text constraints. Authors choose the words they use, but they make their choices within these constraints.

So wording is one of the most obvious text characteristics, but it is also one of the least studied by researchers of reading. That is because scholars, noting that word frequency varied from text to text, decided to collect large language corpuses and study word frequency in the language as a whole.

Now that the text as a unit is getting the attention it deserves, we need to look at intra-text word frequency. Only within a unified text can we clearly see the interplay of forces that determine the choice and frequency of words. Together with knowledge of other text characteristics, it becomes possible to understand how texts function in communication between writers and readers.

Purposes for studies of word frequency. Counts of word frequency were first compiled as a means of determining the readability of existing texts. The researchers were operating on the premise that words which occur most frequently in the language are more easily recognized, learned, and processed in reading than less-common words. So it seemed reasonable that the more high-frequency words a text contained, the easier it would be to read.

But early frequency studies showed that it is necessary to examine a very large corpus of language to obtain frequencies representative of the whole language. Later studies were based on awareness that the corpus analyzed must be broad and representative. Such grand-scale studies may or may not provide a list truly representative of "all" language. But such a large corpus of language containing many texts eliminates the very factors that constrain the choice and frequency of vocabulary in a single coherent text.

Word frequency as a feature of text. In this study we have put our focus on what grand-scale word frequency studies could not shed light on: what does word frequency mean in the context of a single coherent and cohesive text? We want to know what it is about language in use that produces variable word frequency. Such knowledge will help put the issue of vocabulary in its proper context (no pun intended). It will also help to define a text in terms of its wording, its use of vocabulary. This will provide knowledge of the relative importance of any particular word to the text and to text comprehension.

It will also suggest how vocabulary is developed through reading. John Carroll (1981) reasons that since good comprehension correlates with good vocabulary, then vocabulary development is essential to comprehension. An equally logical conclusion is that people who read a lot develop large vocabularies. So an important corollary question is, "What is there about word use and frequency in texts that could build vocabulary during reading?"

Our study is rooted in a psycholinguistic theory of reading and it draws on data from past miscue studies (Goodman & Burke, 1972; Goodman & Goodman, 1978).

In this study we have examined word frequency in six complete texts which have been used in miscue research. Our purpose is to determine not only the frequency with which words occur in each text but also to provide insights into why the text is worded as it is. We are seeking to understand how the vocabulary of the text relates to its other characteristics, and what constraints a complete text imposes on its vocabulary.

An Historical Summary of Word Frequency Research

Over a long period researchers have studied how word frequency affects readability. The word frequency variables selected to measure text difficulty were numerous: number of running words, percentage of different words, percentage of different, infrequent, uncommon, or "hard" words, percentage of polysyllabic words, vocabulary difficulty, vocabulary diversity, number of abstract words, number of affixed morphemes, and so on (Lorge, 1938, p. 22).

Klare characterizes the early period of readability research as follows:

1. primary attention paid to vocabulary (frequency) as a basis for predicting readability;
2. dependence upon Thorndike's Teacher's Word Book as the basis for determining vocabulary difficulty;
3. use of "relatively crude criteria of reading difficulty" (Klare, 1963, p. 44).

Everyone seemed to agree from the beginning that frequency of occurrence was important and to assume that common words are easier to recognize. So attention was focused on what should be the language sample from which the words were to be drawn. Everything from the Bible to popular adult magazines to the Buffalo Sunday newspaper were used. While some researchers used samples collected from written language, others (e.g., Horn, 1925) insisted that oral language was the best source. Still another variable was the age of the subjects from whom the language was collected. The subjects ranged in age from preschool to adult.

Although there was wide variation in the nature of the sample, the basic approach to the collection was the same. A large number of words were generated from a range of related texts from a particular source.

The utility of grand-scale word counts was essentially assumed and never seriously questioned. When people began to realize that word counts alone were not adequate for readability, attention gradually shifted to the development of readability formulas that incorporated other criteria, such as complex versus simple sentences, sentence length, and qualitative factors including obscurity and incoherence in expression. But basal texts continued to focus strongly on two factors: controlled vocabulary and repeated exposure, a contribution from behavioral psychology.

The essential weakness of all this word counting is that word frequency is treated as a phenomenon that exists independently of the text in which it occurs. Word frequency has been treated as a cause of text difficulty but not as a result of the characteristics of the text itself.

Early research established that very large amounts of text must be used to get some sense of the relative frequency of words in general. But using huge bodies of language, with millions of running words and thousands of different words, blots out the characteristics of a text which determine the choice of words and their frequency.

Though authors have some choice in the words they use in creating a text, there is always a considerable amount of constraint on that choice. Some syntactic features of the language are extremely constraining. Common nouns particularly in the singular in English almost always require determiners. So *the* and *a* are going to be very frequent in all English texts. *The* will be more frequent than *a* because *the* has an anaphoric quality: it is used with nouns already made definite in the text or context. Some semantic features of a text serve an essential and repeated purpose. If the text contains dialogue, *said* is likely to occur very often. This explains why it is often the most common verb in a text. But other semantic constraints derive from the message or meaning being represented. A story about a sheep dog defending her flock against predatory coyotes will make frequent use of some words not likely to be common in even several million words from school texts, several Sunday editions of the Buffalo Sunday paper, or many other sources. Such high- and low-frequency words do not necessarily make the text hard to read.

Description of the texts selected for this study. The six texts in this study include two middle-grade basal stories.

"Freddie Miller Scientist" (fifth grade) is a story that involves a boy whose amateur science adventures are always working out badly and getting him in trouble. One day, however, while Freddie is working on a bell for his mother, his sister gets stuck in the closet. He quickly improvises a flashlight which he lowers to his sister through a transom so she will be less scared while he goes for help. He becomes a family hero and the family agrees that his experimentation must be tolerated.

"My Brother is a Genius" (6th grade) is about a boy who combines his homework with pacifying his baby brother during babysitting. He reads soothing words out loud from the dictionary to him. The older boy decides also to use the baby as his school project. He sells a local television station on featuring eight-month-old Andrew on a television program as the "typical baby." It turns out however that Andrew has learned to say words such as "philosophical" and "intellectual" while listening to his older brother read the dictionary, and he begins to say them just before the program. The older boy saves the day by reading 'S' words from the dictionary to Andrew and getting him to sleep through the program. The story is told in the first person and the older brother is never named.

"Sheep Dog" is a selection from an eighth-grade literature book. It is the story of a heroic dog, Peggy, who single-handedly guards and saves a herd of sheep from coyotes after the shepherd dies and the coyotes kill her mate. She fights off the coyotes, almost losing her own life, and resists the temptation to kill a sheep for food even though she and her puppies are starving. Finally help arrives as she lies near death.

"Poison" is a story by Roald Dahl published in unabridged form in a twelfth-grade literature anthology. Its surprise ending is typical of Dahl's stories. Set in Bengal, the story centers around attempts to keep a man, lying in bed with a deadly snake on his abdomen, from being bitten. His housemate summons an Indian doctor who very meticulously soaks the sheet with ether to put the snake to sleep. When they feel the ether has had enough time to work they remove the covering sheet and blanket only to discover there is no snake there. Harry Pope, the potential victim, leaps from the bed uttering racial curses at the poor doctor.

"Ghost of the Lagoon," written by Armstrong Sperry, appears in its original form in a sixth-grade reader. In the story a boy, Mako, accompanied only by his dog, Afa, uses a harpoon to kill the great white shark, Tupa. The shark many years earlier killed the boy's father and has haunted the lagoon on the boy's island home and terrorized his people. Mako wins a reward and becomes a hero.

"Why We Need the Generation Gap" is an adult-magazine essay. It appeared first in *Look* magazine. It expresses the view that the difference in outlook and values of succeeding generations is not a simple matter of maturity vs. immaturity.

All six of these texts have been used in past miscue studies, and the word and grammatical function data were already available. In miscue analysis, readers are asked to read a complete story, somewhat difficult for them, that they have not seen before. The miscues, points in the oral reading where the observed response to the text does not match the expected response, are then analyzed according to a psycholinguistically-based taxonomy. That analysis has been reported elsewhere in several reports (Goodman & Goodman, 1978). Each of the texts used in these studies was coded grammatically, and both the text and the grammatical coding are stored in computer files. These files of texts used in past miscue studies range from pre-primer to adult material.

The particular texts for this study were chosen because they have intended audiences from fifth-grade readers to adults. All of them are natural texts in the sense that they were written for purposes other than reading instruction by authors in no way related to the research. They are complete, cohesive, and coherent. A non-fiction essay was included for contrast with the fictional texts. We have purposely avoided using beginning reading material as it tends to employ rigidly controlled vocabulary. Texts will be referred to by an abbreviated title, "Freddie," for example. Story numbers from the original database are listed in the references.

Table 9–1
Word Frequency: Types and Tokens

Text	Running Words	Different Words	Used Once	Type/Token Ratio	% Words Used Once
Freddie	1369	466	263	2.9	56.4
Genius	2030	645	336	3.4	55.6
Ghost	2775	809	457	3.4	56.5
Sheep Dog	3667	952	507	3.9	53.3
Poison	4208	883	499	4.8	56.5
Gap	1318	608	459	2.2	75.5

Word Frequencies within Texts

Operating from a theory that language controls its own vocabulary, we have examined word frequency in these texts. As the data will show, they have similar characteristics but are different too, depending on the author's purpose and style.

Table 9–1 provides some general data about word frequencies in the six texts. Text length in terms of total running words (tokens) is proportional to the grade level of the school selections. "Freddie," the fifth-grade story, has only 1,369 total running words. The sixth-grade stories, "Genius," and "Ghost," have 2,030 and 2,775 respectively. The story from an eighth-grade text, "Sheep Dog," has 3,667 words while "Poison," the adult short story from a 12th-grade anthology has 4,208 words. It is not surprising that the one text not intended for school use, the essay from a popular adult magazine, "Gap," is shorter with only 1,318 words.

The number of different words (types) also tends to increase in materials for more advanced readers but the increase is not proportionate. So types increase from 466 in "Freddie" to 604 in "Genius" to 809 in "Ghost" and 952 in "Sheep Dog." But in "Poison," the Roald Dahl short story, the number of types (different words) is actually lower than in "Sheep Dog," the eighth-grade selection. This relates to a steady increase in the type/token ratio for successively more advanced texts from a mean of less than 3 uses per type in "Freddie" to almost 5 in "Poison."

Common sense would suggest that the type/token ratio would decrease in more advanced texts, that proportionately more different words would be used causing the ratio of total words to different words (types) to go down. We might expect also to find the greatest effect of deliberate vocabulary control and repeated use of vocabulary in the two stories from the basal readers. In fact, the number of types does not increase as rapidly as length increases in the five narrative texts so there is a rising type/token ratio; that means that in less consciously-controlled narrative material, some words occur very frequently, in fact more frequently than in more controlled texts.

"Gap," the magazine essay, shows a very different pattern however with 608 types for 1,318 tokens and a ratio of only 2.2. This may represent a difference between non-narrative and narrative text. It suggests a concept worth looking at in future studies: different text genres have macrostructures which differ considerably in how they influence the wording, particularly the type/token ratio, of the texts. That could prove important in considering the readability of non-narrative materials, particularly school texts.

Words Used Only Once and Type/Token Ratio

In every word study, no matter how large the corpus, many words have been found to occur only once. In all of the texts in this study, more than half the types occurred only once. In fact all of the five narrative stories show similar percentages of word types used only once: 53.3 percent to 56.5 percent. The ratio, then, of words used once to total length is virtually constant over these texts. That makes even more interesting the rising type/token ratio discussed above. The number of unique words is proportionate to text length so the frequency of non-unique words increases to account for the increased length of the text.

One dimension of the wording of these narratives, then, is that more than half of the types occur only once. But an opposite dimension is that a small set of words occur extremely often. These few words account for about the same proportion of an increased number of words in the more advanced text so the type/token ratio goes up. What this shows is that the type/token ratio itself is not a predictor of text difficulty.

One could argue that the issue is not what proportion of words occur only once but how common or rare those words are. Indeed that is the rationale behind using the proportion of uncommon words in some readability formulas. A counter argument would be that a particular word cannot be of great importance to the comprehension of an entire text if it occurs only once in that text. The discussion below on which words are in fact common and uncommon will shed more light on this issue.

It is not surprising that better than 75 percent of the types in "Gap," the essay, occur only once considering the low type/token ratio. Again, this suggests a very different set of constraints on wording in this non-narrative text as compared to the narrative texts.

Frequent Words as Proportion of Total Words

To have a complete picture of relative frequency of these very frequent words in these six texts, we need to look at the number of different words (types) it takes to account for cumulative percents of the running words (tokens). This information is indicated in Table 9–2.

It takes only from 1 to 3 words in any of these six texts to account for 10 percent of the tokens. The most common word, *the*, accounts for between 3.9 percent ("Genius") and 9.9 percent ("Sheep Dog") of all tokens. (See Table 9–3.)

To account for 20 percent of the tokens takes only 5 to 8 different words. That is from 0.5 percent to 1.7 percent of the types. It takes 11 to 17 types to account for 30 percent of the tokens. This is only 1.2 to 3.4 percent of the types. To account for 40 percent of the running words takes only from 2.8 to 6.7 percent of the types. Both "Freddie" and "Gap" require a higher percent of the types to account for 30 or 40 percent of the tokens because of their lower type/token ratio. Between 6.6 and 8.1 percent of the types account for half of the running words in four of the narrative texts. But it takes 11.4 percent to account for 50 percent of "Freddie" and almost 14 percent of the types to account for half of the running words in the essay, "Gap."

Looked at another way, for 27 words in "Poison" to account for 40 percent of the total of 4,208 words, each of these 27 words occurs an average of 63 times. Each of the 58 words that account for the first 50 percent of "Poison" occurs an average of 36 times. Each of the 53 words that account for the first 50 percent of "Freddie" occurs an average of 12.9 times. And for "Gap," each occurs only 7.8 times. "Freddie," though a shorter, more controlled story, has a higher proportion of less-frequent words than the other narratives. In fact it seems as if in concentrating on controlling some words, the rest of the text may have become less cohesive. "Gap," the essay, has a higher proportion of infrequent words too, but that is because it is a different type of text.

Which Words are the Most Frequent in the Texts

So far we have looked only at numbers. A study of wording must look carefully at which specific words appear very frequently, which do not, and what text characteristics might account for their relative frequency. Table 9–3 shows the 25 most common words in each text (in four cases we include more due to ties).

The words on the list of the most frequent words in each text represent from 36 to 40 percent of the running words of each text.

Table 9–2
Number of Types Representing Cumulative % of Tokens

Text	Total Tokens	Total Types		Percent of Tokens Represented				
				10%	20%	30%	40%	50%
Freddie	1369	466	N of Types	3	8	16	31	53
			% of Types	0.6	1.7	3.4	6.7	11.4
Genius	2030	645	N of Types	3	7	14	26	52
			% of Types	0.5	1.1	2.2	1.0	8.1
Ghost	2775	809	N of Types	2	6	13	30	64
			% of Types	0.3	0.7	1.6	3.7	7.9
Sheep	3667	952	N of Types	1	5	11	27	64
			% of Types	0.1	0.5	1.2	2.8	6.7
Dog Poison	4208	883	N of Types	2	6	12	27	58
			% of Types	0.2	0.7	1.4	3.1	1.6
Gap	1318	608	N of Types	3	8	17	38	85
			% of Types	0.5	1.3	2.8	6.3	14.0

Table 9–3
Most Frequent Words in Order of Frequency

Rank	Freddie				Genius				Ghost			
	Word	n	%	Cum. %	Word	n	%	Cum. %	Word	n	%	Cum. %
1.	the	78	5.6	5.6	the	82	3.9	3.9	the	269	9.6	9.6
2.	he	40	2.8	8.4	I	80	3.9	7.8	of	86	3.0	12.6
3.	Freddie	37	2.6	11.0	a	65	3.1	10.9	his	67	2.4	15.0
4.	to	36	2.6	13.6	and	52	2.5	13.4	a	63	2.2	17.2
5.	a	29	2.0	15.6	he	51	2.4	15.8	and	59	2.1	19.3
6.	was	28	2.0	17.6	said	51	2.4	18.2	he	57	2.0	21.3
7.	it	26	1.8	19.4	to	48	2.3	21.5	to	55	1.9	23.2
8.	his	25	1.8	21.2	you	31	1.5	23.0	was	46	1.6	24.8
9.	in	19	1.3	22.5	Mr.	28	1.3	24.3	in	38	1.3	26.1
10.	that	18	1.3	23.8	my	28	1.3	25.6	Mako	35	1.2	27.3
11.	and	18	1.3	25.1	of	28	1.3	26.9	canoe	33	1.1	28.4
12.	I	17	1.2	26.3	baby	26	1.2	28.1	on	26	0.9	29.3
13.	you	16	1.1	27.4	Barnaby	25	1.2	29.3	it	25	0.8	30.1
14.	had	15	1.0	28.4	at	24	1.1	30.4	that	24	0.8	30.9
15.	of	14	1.0	29.4	was	24	1.1	31.5	boy	24	0.8	31.7

No.	Elizabeth				Andrew				Tupa			
16.	Elizabeth	14	1.0	30.4	Andrew	23	1.1	32.6	Tupa	24	0.8	32.5
17.	Miller	14	1.0	31.4	in	22	1.0	33.6	him	23	0.8	33.3
18.	with	13	0.9	32.3	his	20	0.9	34.5	Afa	22	0.7	34.0
19.	uncle	12	0.8	33.1	it	19	0.9	35.4	with	21	0.7	34.7
20.	mother	10	0.7	33.8	on	17	0.8	36.2	had	20	0.7	35.4
21.	at	10	0.7	34.5	as	14	0.6	36.8	into	18	0.6	36.0
22.	for	10	0.7	35.2	but	14	0.6	37.4	as	16	0.5	36.5
23.	father	9	0.6	35.8	for	14	0.6	38.0	water	16	0.5	37.0
24.	then	9	0.6	36.4	that	13	0.6	38.6	from	15	0.5	37.5
25.	this	9	0.6	37.0	typical	13	0.6	39.2	out	15	0.5	38.0
	Mrs.	9	0.6	37.6								
	like	9	0.6	38.2								
	said	9	0.6	38.8								
	she	9	0.6	29.4								

(continued)

Table 9–3 (*Continued*)

Rank	Sheep Dog Word	n	%	Cum. %	Poison Word	n	%	Cum. %	Gap Word	n	%	Cum. %
1.	the	370	9.9	9.9	the	259	6.0	6.0	the	73	5.2	5.2
2.	and	116	3.1	13.0	and	166	3.8	9.8	to	40	2.8	8.0
3.	to	110	2.9	15.9	he	137	3.1	12.9	and	35	2.5	10.5
4.	she	105	2.8	18.7	I	123	2.8	15.7	we	32	2.3	12.8
5.	her	105	2.8	21.5	to	117	2.7	18.4	will	32	2.3	15.1
6.	of	100	2.6	24.1	it	90	2.0	20.4	of	29	2.1	17.2
7.	a	76	2.0	26.1	his	85	1.9	22.3	in	24	1.7	18.9
8.	was	62	1.6	27.7	was	82	1.9	24.2	a	20	1.4	20.3
9.	Peggy	40	1.0	28.7	a	78	1.8	26.0	our	19	1.3	21.6
10.	it	36	0.9	29.6	of	73	1.6	27.6	that	17	1.2	22.8
11.	sheep	34	0.9	30.5	in	58	1.3	28.9	us	17	1.2	24.0
12.	in	33	0.9	31.3	Harry	45	1.0	29.9	have	16	1.1	25.1
13.	for	33	0.9	32.1	on	36	0.8	30.7	for	15	1.0	26.1
14.	had	31	0.8	32.9	you	36	0.8	31.5	is	15	1.0	27.1
15.	as	31	0.8	33.7	at	33	0.7	32.2	they	12	0.8	27.9

No.	Word	n	%	Cum %
16.	from	27	0.7	34.4
17.	on	27	0.7	35.1
18.	coyote*	24	0.6	35.7
19.	that	22	0.5	36.2
20.	at	21	0.5	36.7
21.	were	21	0.5	37.2
22.	he	20	0.5	37.7
23.	his	20	0.5	38.2
24.	down	19	0.5	38.7
25.	into	18	0.4	39.1
	coyotes*	18	0.4	39.5
	band	18	0.4	39.9

Word	n	%	Cum %
that	31	0.7	32.9
me	30	0.6	33.5
but	29	0.6	34.1
him	29	0.6	34.7
up	29	0.6	35.3
there	28	0.6	35.9
said	28	0.6	36.5
now	26	0.6	37.1
for	25	0.5	37.6
Ganderbai	25	0.5	38.1
my	25	0.5	38.6
not	25	0.5	39.1
out	25	0.5	39.6

Word	n	%	Cum %
when	12	0.8	28.7
be	10	0.7	29.4
I	10	0.7	30.1
on	10	0.7	30.8
with	10	0.7	31.5
children	9	0.6	32.1
it	9	0.6	32.7
all	8	0.5	33.2
their	8	0.5	33.7
are	7	0.5	34.2
from	7	0.5	34.7
can	7	0.5	35.2
who	7	0.5	35.7
one	7	0.5	36.2

*Two forms of the same word. It is traditional in word counts to treat such words as separate items. However, from a linguist's perspective, the two items are treated as forms of the same word.

Words Common Across Texts

The words on these lists account for better than a third of the running words in each text. Only eight words appear on all six lists. That is about one-third of the most frequent words in each list.

These are (with their mean rank):

the(1), *and*(4.5), *to*(4.5), *a*(6.3), *of*(8.3), *in*(10.8), *it*(12.8), *that*(15.5)

All of these eight words are function words. *It* and *that* can also function as pronouns.

Even *the*, the most common word in all 6 texts, ranges from 3.9 to 9.9 percent of the running words in each text. This illustrates a key feature of word frequency in connected texts: variability within constraint. The language requires the use of *the* but it permits sufficient variation to allow considerable range.

The most common words in these six texts may be divided for purpose of analysis into four groups:

1. Function words
2. Copulas
3. Pronouns
4. Content Words

Function Words

Function words in the lists of most common words include:

determiners (*the, a*),

verb markers (*was, had, were, will, are, is, can*),

conjoiners (*and, as, that, but, when*),

prepositions and particles (*to, in, of, with, at, for, into, from, on, up, out*),

others (*it, there, not*)

One simple reason for the frequency of many function words is that, while the grammar of the language requires their functions, there are only a few words in the language which can fulfill each function. Only a few words can be determiners. There are few conjunctions and other conjoining elements in the language; there are more prepositions, but they still represent a small finite set of words. Furthermore, while the language adds to its store of content words, it does not add to its store of function words. Yet they are a major element in the binding material which makes the language cohesive and coherent. To illustrate this, Table 9–4 shows the percentage of each type of function word in each of the six texts.

Table 9–4

Types of Function Words in the Six Texts

| | Percent of Running Words | | | | | |
	Freddie	Genius	Ghost	Sheep Dog	Poison	Gap
Noun Marker	8.7	7.7	12.8	12.3	8.2	7.3
Verb Marker	3.5	3.2	2.6	2.7	3.4	6.2
Verb Particle	3.1	2.8	2.0	2.3	3.8	2.8
Question Marker	0.3	0.2	0.1	0.1	0.3	0.0
Clause Marker	3.3	2.1	2.5	2.5	2.3	4.7
Phrase Marker	7.8	7.2	11.3	11.6	8.9	10.0
Intensifier	1.7	1.6	1.8	0.6	1.5	1.2
Conjunction	2.0	3.5	2.6	3.8	5.0	3.5
Negative	0.7	0.4	0.4	0.7	0.9	0.7
Quantifier	1.1	1.3	1.2	1.6	1.2	1.5
Other	0.4	1.2	0.3	0.5	0.7	0.7
Total	32.7	32.1	37.6	38.7	36.4	38.9

From 32 to 39 percent of each text's running words are function words. The terms we use in Table 9–4 to describe the various functions are those of C.C. Fries (1952). We prefer them for this purpose because of their descriptive reference to what they do.

Noun markers are few, mostly *the* and *a(an)*, but they represent 7 to 13 percent of the running words. The phrase markers (prepositions) are more common but still represent a small set of words, which also serve as verb particles. Contrast the use of *up* in "He ran *up* the street" with "He ran *up* the flag." In the former, *up* is a phrase marker, marking a prepositional phrase. In the latter, *up* is a verb particle, part of the verb, *ran up*. In these combined functions, this set of words represents from 10 to 14 percent of the running words in each text.

There is substantial variation from text to text in use of conjunctions; "Poison" uses two and a half times as many as "Freddie." But together with clause markers, which introduce subordinate clauses, conjunctions account for 5 to 8 percent of each text's running words. Again, a very small set of words in the language carries a big part of the running text, so such words are bound to be frequent in every text.

Copulas and BE Forms

The words which serve as copulas are the *be* forms. *Be, was, were, is, are* appear among the most common words in these six texts. These words also can serve as verb markers. Which *be* forms appear as copulas or verb markers and which other verb markers appear on the lists of most common words depends very much on the prevailing tenses in the text, which in turn are determined by whether the text is set in the past, present, or future. So "Freddie" and "Ghost" show only *was* and *had* among their most common words. "Genius" and "Poison" list just *was*. "Sheep Dog" has *was, had,* and *were*. But the essay "Gap" shows *will, have, is, be,* and *are* among its most common words.

Pronouns

Pronouns are clearly common among the most frequent words in each text. That is because the language requires the use of pronouns where the referents for noun phrases are established in the text or situational context. *It* is common in all the texts, but which other pronouns are used depends on characteristics of the text. This is well illustrated in "Sheep Dog." The central character is a female dog, Peggy. *She* and *her* occur 105 times each and tie for fourth and fifth most common word in the text. *He* and *his* occur only 20 times each.

"Genius" has predominately male characters and is told in the first person. So among its most common words are *I, he, you, my, his.* "Ghost" also has male characters but is told in third person so its common words include these pronouns: *his, he, him.* "Freddie" has both male and female main characters and quite a bit of dialogue. Its common words include *he, I, you, she, his.*

The essay, "Gap," uses a great many first person plurals to represent a generalized society: "When we . . . " So it is not surprising that these pronouns are among the most common words: *we, ours, us, they, I, their, who, one.*

Possessive pronouns are the only noun modifiers to appear among the most common words in any of the texts, with the exception of *Mrs.* and *uncle* which are not typical noun modifiers. Possessives can have a double anaphoric function since they replace the definite article at the same time that they link a noun to its possessor.

Pronouns are common text elements. They provide a lot of the cohesion by providing chains of reference. But which ones are common in any particular text depends upon text characteristics such as cast of characters, dialogue, and whether it is first-person or third-person narration.

It is not surprising that the words common across all the texts are mostly function words and pronouns, and that many of the words common in each text belong to these classes of words that have very few words to perform common syntactic and semantic functions.

Generally Uncommon Words Common in Particular Texts

All these text characteristics explain the frequency of function words, pronouns, and copulas. But they also explain the surprising infrequency of content words.

Frequent Nouns

Nouns are the only content words to appear in any number among the lists of most frequent words in Table 9–3. Here are the nouns that appear:

"Freddie": *Freddie, Elizabeth, Miller, uncle, mother, father.*

"Genius": *Barnaby, baby, Andrew.*

"Ghost": *Mako, canoe, boy, Tupa, Afa, water.*

"Sheep Dog": *Peggy, sheep, coyote, coyotes, band.*

"Poison": *Harry, Ganderbai.*

"Gap": *children.*

In each of the narrative texts, the most common noun is the name of one of the characters. In three of them it is the principal character, but in "Genius" and in "Poison" it is not the main character because these are first-person stories. In fact, in "Genius" the main character is never named. What is more surprising is that the most common nouns in these texts are not necessarily common in the language. Only *baby, boy,* and *children* could be considered truly common. And some really uncommon nouns appear among these most frequent words: *canoe, sheep, band* (the group of sheep) and *coyote and coyotes* (pair of antagonists).

"Gap" had only one noun, *children,* among its most common words. Only three nouns occurred more than four times in the entire text: *children* (9 times), *generation* (6) and *age* (5). It is apparently possible to write a coherent essay without using the same nouns very often, particularly when there are main ideas but no main characters.

Other Common Content Words

What about other content words? "Freddie" has a verb modifier, *then,* a kind of noun modifier, *Mrs.,* and the verb *said* in its most common word list. *Uncle* actually appears fairly often as a noun modifier. Mrs. Miller keeps telling Freddie he's "just like Uncle. . . ."

"Genius" has *said,* a verb, and *typical,* a noun modifier. The story centers around whether Andrew is a *typical* baby. *Had,* used as a verb, is the only non-noun content word among the most frequent list in "Ghost" and "Sheep Dog." *There* and *now* as verb modifiers are among the most common words in "Poison" and *said* is the only verb. *Have,* sometimes a verb, is the only non-noun content word on the "Gap" list.

Verb Frequency

Only five verbs in "Freddie" occur five times or more in the entire text. These are *said, thought, get, knew,* and *called.* In "Genius" the five most common verbs (six times or more) are *said, think, see, know,* and *go.* The five most common verbs in "Ghost" (occurring five times or more) are *saw, come, leaped, heard,* and *rose.* The contrast between this more active set of verbs and those in "Freddie" and "Genius" also shows in "Sheep Dog." The most common verbs in that text are *turned, saw, leaped, looked, made* (6 times or more). "Poison," with much tension about little action has these five more common verbs (13 times or more): *said, went, move, looked, stood.* Only these verbs occur three times or more in "Gap": *find, suspect, know, become, do, join, seen.*

While these verbs provide interesting insight into the content of each text, they show also that few verbs are frequent across texts and few verbs are frequent within texts. *Said,* of course, will be common where there is dialogue. Basal readers go out of their way to use alternatives to *said* in dialogue, but it will still occur relatively frequently where there is substantial dialogue. But it is possible for authors to tell coherent stories with considerable action or tension without repeating many verbs. That is because cohesion can be maintained through using synonyms, near synonyms and alternate phrasings.

Verb Modifier Frequency

Few verb modifiers occur with any great frequency in any of the texts. *Then* is relatively frequent in all texts except "Gap." *There,* sometimes a verb modifier, is also found with moderate frequency in most but not all of the texts. *Now* is found several times in three of the texts. Beyond that, the verb modifiers that occur more than two or three times are specific to the text. The five most common verb modifiers in "Ghost" (involving the killing of a shark) are *then, away, again, before, quickly.* "Sheep Dog" with the fighting of the *dog* and *coyotes* has a similar list: *then, again, slowly, forward, carefully.* And the very suspenseful "Poison" shows: *slowly, again, carefully, quickly, sharply.*

Noun Modifier Frequency

Noun modifiers other than possessive pronouns are even more varied. Few occur more than five times even in the longer texts. Not all of the

Table 9–5

Representations of Grammatical Categories

| | Percent of Running Words | | | | | |
	Freddie	Genius	Ghost	Sheep Dog	Poison	Gap
Pronouns*	9.3	11.6	4.9	6.7	11.8	6.9
Other Nouns	21.5	17.9	24.5	22.8	16.1	20.6
Total Noun Positions	30.8	29.5	29.4	29.5	27.9	27.5
Verbs	17.6	18.3	15.3	15.4	18.4	17.5
Noun Modifiers*	10.2	10.7	10.7	10.2	8.8	11.6
Verb Modifiers	4.6	4.0	4.8	4.1	5.8	3.1
Function Words	32.7	32.1	37.6	38.7	36.4	38.9
Indeterminate	0.0	7.0	0.2	0.1	0.3	0.0
Contractions	2.3	4.2	0.6	0.6	2.2	0.6

*Possessive pronouns are included as noun modifiers.

more common noun modifiers are adjectives. In "Sheep Dog," *coyote* and *sheep* are used five or more times as noun adjuncts. *Bedding,* verb derived, occurs five times ("the bedding sheep").

Again the lists of more common noun modifiers show their particularity to each text: "Freddie" shows Freddie's problem experiments: *dark, small, bad, proud, queer.* "Ghost's" list reflects the shark fight theme: *great, white, old, green, dead.* "Gap" has *human, political, Vietnam,* and *gold* (that's the Generation Gap).

Relative Frequency of Grammatical Functions

To put this information about the relative frequency of different grammatical categories of content words into perspective, Table 9–5 presents the distribution of each category in each text.

It is interesting to note that the percent of total noun positions in these six texts varies only from 28 to 31 percent. Yet the texts vary considerably in the proportion of pronouns in these noun positions; pronouns represent from 5 to 12 percent of the total running words. The two first-person stories, "Genius" and "Poison," have similar high pronoun percents, 11.6 and 11.8 respectively. These two stories have proportionately lower percents of other nouns, 17.9 and 16.1 percent respectively.

The rest of the variation in use of pronouns and nouns seems to reflect amount of dialogue and other stylistic factors. English sentences require nouns as subjects, direct and indirect objects, and objects of prepositions. The proportion, at least in these texts, seems to vary little.

But other factors, some of which the author may control, appear to decide how many nouns are replaced by pronouns.

Verbs show less variation, from 15.3 to 18.4 percent. "Ghost" and "Sheep Dog," the two texts with the lowest rate of verbs, have little dialogue because of identifiable text factors. In "Sheep Dog" there are no human characters in much of the story. In "Ghost" a considerable part of the story involves only the boy Mako, his dog Afa, and Tupa, a great white shark. So, whereas *said* occurs 51 times in "Genius" and ties for fifth most common word, it occurs only five times in "Sheep Dog" and twice in "Ghost." Representation of oral dialogue in written text requires a special grammar which includes an extra clause representing at least the speaker and some representation of the verb *said*.

The amount of dialogue present also seems to explain the variation in the relative amounts of contractions in each text since most of the contractions appear in dialogue. "Genius," with the most dialogue, has 4.2 percent contractions. "Ghost," "Sheep Dog," and the essay "Gap," with little or no dialogue, have only 0.6 percent contractions each.

There is a very specific textual reason for the percent of words with indeterminate grammatical function in "Genius." The central plot of the story is about an 8-month-old baby learning to say big words by listening to his older brother read words from the dictionary. So words like *philosophical* and *intellectual* occur as word names out of syntactic context and are classified as indeterminate. That adds up to 7 percent of the running words of the text, in contrast to negligible proportions for the other texts.

Noun modifiers and verb modifiers vary moderately in proportion from text to text, apparently for stylistic reasons. Possessive pronouns, included in noun modifiers, range from 2.2 to 3.5 percent of each text. The grammar of English requires neither noun modifiers nor verb modifiers to produce grammatical sentences. The meaning the author is representing may require a good deal of describing and qualifying, but the author's purpose and style determines just how much describing and qualifying will be in the text, since they are non-mandatory text features.

"Poison" contains a lot of terse dialogue. One central character, Harry Pope, thinks he has a poisonous snake resting on his abdomen so he is minimizing his speech and movements in order to avoid startling the snake. This leads to fewer noun modifiers. In the essay "Gap," there are more noun modifiers because the author uses a lot of embedding transformations to produce long, complex clauses and sentences. He also uses more adverbial clauses than adverbs. So he has a higher proportion of noun modifiers and a lower proportion of verb modifiers. His text is at the high end in use of function words, which also reflects its syntactic complexity. Table 9–4, discussed earlier, shows this text has the highest percentages of clause markers and verb markers among the function words.

To summarize this discussion of the distribution of grammatical categories in these texts, we can make the following statements:

The syntax requires some proportional distribution of these grammatical categories within the texts. But other text characteristics, including the semantic structure of the story and the author's purpose and style, produce variations among the texts in these proportions. Some very common grammatical functions can only be filled by a relatively small set of words, so these words are likely to be common in any text. Function words and pronouns (including possessive pronouns) are the principal examples.

On the other hand the categories of content words (nouns, verbs, noun modifiers, and verb modifiers) are much larger classes of words; they are often called "open" classes because the language is continually adding to them.

Still, the characteristics of particular texts exercise some constraint on the choice of words to fill these grammatical slots. In stories, proper nouns (the names of characters) are likely to be among the most frequent words. There is a similar but more moderate influence on verb frequency. Narratives with lots of action will select verbs of movement while suspenseful texts will choose another set.

Semantic and Pragmatic Text Features Influencing Wording

Rhetorical Value of Diversity

In the case of content words, there is a counter pressure to the factors causing some words to occur more frequently than others. That is the rhetorical value that authors in the English language place on using varied terms and alternate ways of representing the same referents. It is pragmatically unacceptable in English texts to keep using the same nouns, verbs, adjectives or adverbs over and over; writers even avoid using the same sentence patterns repeatedly. Authors deliberately vary their choice of words and structures to avoid repetition while still maintaining cohesion and reference.

Multiple Meanings

Lorge (1944) criticized word lists for their failure to account for multiple meanings of words. This criticism does appear to be a major shortcoming, especially when you consider that the many meanings of even a common word such as *run* fill a dictionary page. However, within the confines of the single texts we examined, multiple meanings for particular words seldom occur. In fact, in our six texts, we were able to find only one word, *allowance* in "Freddie," that has two clearly different meanings in the story itself. In one sentence, Mrs. Miller, chiding Freddie for ruining his sister's doll, says, "I want you to save half of your *allowance* for it each week." In the other, after Freddie has used his scientific ingenuity to free his sister from a dark closet, Mrs. Miller says proudly, "After this we must make some *allowance* for experiments that do not turn out so well."

While the multiple meanings of a given word may not occur in a single text, nevertheless the meaning of a word in a particular text may not be a common one. Any given reader may be unfamiliar with the unusual meaning. In "Sheep Dog," for instance, the author repeatedly refers to a *band* of sheep. Called upon to define *band* out of context, you might think of "band of gold," "rubber band," "brass band," and so forth, before naming *band* as a term for a group of animals. Likewise, you might be hard pressed to come up with the meanings out of context for *air* and *live* that appear in "Genius" in relation to television. Mr. Barnaby bemoans the fact that in five minutes they are going "on the *air,*" "with a *live* show." In "Poison," *draw* and its variations *drew* and *drawing* appear four times but never in the way one would probably think of first, to *draw* a picture. Rather, we find the following examples:

1. "He . . . *drew* his breath sharply through his teeth."
2. ". . . he stuck the needle through the rubber top of the bottle and began *drawing* a pale yellow liquid up into the syringe by pulling out the plunger."
3. "Shall we *draw* the sheet back quick . . . ?"
4. "Slowly he *drew* out the rubber tube from under the sheet."

Within a given text, an author may use words in unusual ways either frequently (*band* of sheep in "Sheep Dog") or infrequently (*body* of the island in "Ghost"). But the current meaning of any word is always relative to the context in which it is embedded.

Almost any word can be used metaphorically. The meanings of words used metaphorically may be quite different from more literal uses. The authors of our six texts employ metaphor to greater or lesser extents. The metaphorical uses of common words, *body* (of the island), *faces* (of the cliffs), *arms* (of the island) in the opening passage of "Ghost" are descriptively powerful but textually unpredictable. "Sheep Dog" begins with a string of vivid metaphors:

> The rays of the setting sun lingered over the high Arizona desert, touching the rocky tip of Badger Mountain and tinting the bold face of Antelope Rim.

What is clear is that the particular meaning of a word in a text, whether literal or metaphoric, may not be predicted from the meaning most common for the word in the language at large. Very frequent words may occur in particular texts with very infrequent meaning. Common words may be used in quite uncommon ways.

Text Cohesion

The wording of a text is strongly influenced by the need for the text to be semantically cohesive, that is, to have a unifying structure.

The information we have presented so far shows that syntactic cohesion requires some proportionate distribution of grammatical functions and that some words will be common simply because there are few words to fill very common syntactic functions. Determiners, prepositions, and pronouns are some examples.

We have also seen some evidence of the influence that maintaining semantic cohesion has on text wording and word frequency. But this is more complex as it relates to choice of content words, synonyms, and "pro" elements (words that can stand in place of content words or phrases such as pronouns, verb markers for verb phrases, prepositions for prepositional phrases).

We can illustrate semantic cohesion by looking at the opening lines of each text. Each author needs to accomplish a good deal in these opening lines to set up a cohesive text and create a semantic structure.

The authors use cohesive chains, words with the same or related meaning that extend through the text and bind the parts to a cohesive whole, in these openings. The opening lines show how the authors use wording to achieve the purpose of launching the readers into the texts.

"Freddie" starts with a lament: "Poor Freddie was in trouble again." The author, in the opening 22 lines, focuses on creating Freddie's character, his experimenting and the constant trouble this gets him into. Freddie's family is also introduced, and a sub-theme, his mother's comparing Freddie with his Swiss uncles, is also established.

In these opening lines we find six cohesive chains (frequency in parentheses):

Freddie (30):	*Elizabeth* (5):	*mother* (9):
Freddie (4)	Elizabeth (2)	mother (2)
He (5)	little	she (3)
his (5)	sister	I (2)
Freddie's	heartbroken	Mrs. Miller
you've		angry
I (4)		
you (4)		
your (2)		

him (2)
Tinker (2)

uncles (7):	*trouble* (7):	*chemistry* (4):
Uncle August	trouble	chemistry set
uncles (2)	turned green	experiment
Switzerland	poor	mixture
one	wrecked	chemicals
them	queer	
like Freddie	bad	
	sadly	

Four of the six cohesive chains in this opening section establish characters. The other two relate to the plot of the story: a boy's experimenting with chemicals gets him into continuous trouble. The 30 references to *Freddie* use 10 different words. This results from an abundance of dialogue: Freddie is referred to by name, by nickname, and by first, second, and third person pronouns. The semantic cohesion in "Freddie" results from some words being repeated while at the same time the author achieves variety by using alternatives, pronouns, and related terms.

In the opening 22 lines of "Genius" the author sets up the problem. A school-age boy does his homework while caring for his baby brother. The task, the situation, the older brother (the unnamed narrator), and the baby brother are established in six cohesive chains:

narrator (22):	*mood* (6):	*Andrew* (10):
you (2)	foolish	baby (4)
my (4)	ashamed	brother (2)
your (3)	yelled (2)	you (2)
I (11)	shouted	Andrew's
fellow	stay home	him
me		

baby's character (10):	*babysitting* (7):	*homework* (19):
silly	bothers	homework
sounds	it (2)	part
cry (3)	babysitting (2)	education (2)
disturb	disturb	studying
fault	stay home	dictionary
sleeping		word (3)
want		philosophical (3)
hold		study (2)
		meanings (3)
		definitions (2)

The main character here is referred to 22 times, almost all in first and second person, requiring only 6 words and no name. *Homework*, a key event throughout the story, has 19 references and 10 different words in these 22 opening lines.

"Ghost" begins by establishing the setting: "The island of Bora Bora, where Mako lives, is far away in the South Pacific." The author concentrates on the setting and on Mako, his young hero, in the opening 24 lines. There are seven cohesive chains:

setting (9):	*island features* (13):	*water* (6):
island (3)	far away	South Pacific
Bora Bora	rises	sea (2)
South Pacific	high	water
it (3)	(like) castle	surf
main body	waterfalls	lagoon
	faces	waterfalls
	cliffs	
	upward	
	crag (2)	
	edge	
	arms	
	reef	

Mako (13):	*Afa* (9):	*Mako's traits* (6):
Mako (4)	Afa (6)	clever
his (4)	they	made
he (2)	companions	spent
they	two	born
companions		hands
two		height

canoe (11):

canoe (2)
larger
outrigger
side
boat
tipping
large
hold
hollowing
tree

Thirteen references to Mako, individually or with his dog, Afa, require six words. Half the references are pronouns. The characteristics of Mako and the island use many references with only one word, *crag,* used twice.

The beginning of "Sheep Dog," quoted previously, also centers on establishing the setting. In the first 25 lines, the author creates both mood and setting while introducing sheep dogs at work. We find five cohesive chains:

evening (9):	*place* (9):	*sheep* (14):
rays	desert	band (3)
sun	rocky tip	sheep (3)
tinting	Badger Mountain	800
setting	bold face	lamb/s (2)
darkness	Antelope Rim	bleating
bedding down	basin	mass
night	Salt Creek	ewe
drowsiness	pool	her
dark	patch	far-side

dog/s (7):	*Peggy's traits* (6):
dog/s (3)	patrolling
two	urged
ears	alert
her	larger
mate	turned
	assured

These chains use many words once. Only *dog(s), band, sheep,* and *lamb(s)* occur more than once. The main character, a sheep dog, is not named until line 27 of the story. The author devotes the next 27 lines to establishing Peggy as the central character. In that sequence this chain occurs: *dog(s)* (3), *Peggy* (2), *she* (6), *her* (8), *breed, collies, coat, head, eyes* (2), *descendant, forepaw, toes, foot.* There are 29 references then to *Peggy,* more than one per line; yet even after her name is introduced, the author only uses it twice in this sequence using 14 pronouns instead.

"Poison" begins with creating the mood and establishing two main characters in the setting.

"It must have been around midnight when I drove home. . . ." There are six chains in the 26 lines:

narrator (16):	*Harry* (11):	*setting* (12):
I (12)	Harry Pope	home (2)
me (2)	his (2)	gates
Timber (2)	he (5)	bungalow
	he'd	window

Harry's	side bedroom
him	drive
	step/s (2)
	balcony (2)
	one

darkness (9):	*movement* (11):	*sleep* (8):
midnight	drove	wake
switched off	approached	awake (2)
beam	opened	dropped off
swing in	coming	quietly
light (2)	parked	lying
still on	went up	bed
dark	take	turn
switched on	got to	
	crossed	
	pushed through	
	went across	

Three words are enough to represent *Timber Woods*, the first person narrator, 16 times. But 11 different verbs are used to show his movement from car to house, with no one verb used twice. This shows again the text characteristics that make words both common and diverse in a connected text.

"Gap" starts with establishing two age groups: "Recently, I spoke with a man twice my age who expressed great faith in the future of American youth..."

Cohesive chains advance the two groups and set a tone for the essay.

youth (14):	*elders* (6):	*dispute* (8):
youth/s (2)	man	spoke
them	twice	expressed
years	he	envisions
troublemakers	maturity	wishful thinking
wrong	fathers	want
I	cynicism	accept
my		cynicism
American		pre-conception
they (2)		
age		
millions		
sons		

actions (5): *maturity* (6):

marching	shaving
risk	dropping hems
dropping	acculturating
fighting	family
shaving	mortgage payments
	yes

Each of these opening sequences illustrates how the need for semantic cohesion limits the writer's choices while allowing the writer to achieve such cohesion within a personal style and a richness of wording. The author builds a cohesive text by producing a controlled mix of function words, pronouns, and varied content words.

In each text, the author achieves the semantic and pragmatic purposes of the opening lines by staying within text constraints while still making use of rich language resources. In "Poison," few different words are needed to refer to the two characters, but 14 terms establish the house and 11 different verbs impel the reader into the story as Timber progresses to Harry's room.

The author can choose to use fewer terms, more common terms, or less varied terms. But authors seem to be aware that, as context builds, variety adds depth to the text meaning and builds stronger images and conceptualizations without making the text less comprehensible.

So in "Gap," when the author uses *baby food, weed killer,* and *convertible debentures* as examples of how youth may be acculturated, he knows that his readers can get his point without knowing exactly what a *debenture* is. The term may have been chosen deliberately to sound technical and boring.

Armstrong Sperry in "Ghost" prefers variety over repetition in representing the canoe and island and does not avoid uncommon terms such as *crag, reef, pandanus, surf, lagoon, outrigger,* when they seem appropriate. His purpose is to create a sense of setting, not to teach an island vocabulary. But, in fact, through his use of synonyms and related terms in cohesive chains, the author creates a context which makes it possible for readers to infer meaning and build vocabulary.

Conclusions

Our study of the wording of texts or, if you prefer, intra-text word frequency, as a text characteristic has demonstrated that there are some powerful text constraints on the wording of a given text and that general word frequency lists can, at best, tell only part of the story.

If words are frequent across texts it is because the language requires them to be. But words that are very frequent in all texts are very frequent indeed. They are few in total number and are likely to appear as function words, *BE* forms, or pronouns.

In word frequency lists, some content words will be considerably higher than others. That is because they are used in common ways to refer to common concepts and experiences. But in any particular coherent, cohesive text, which content words are common depends on the nature of the text. In narratives the common content words usually involve characters' names, some other important nouns, and a few other words needed to tell the story coherently.

But authors avoid using content words repetitiously for pragmatic and stylistic reasons. So cohesive chains are built of common pronouns, key content words, and a varied set of terms all semantically related in the context of the story. Many words—over half in each of the texts we studied—occur only once. Authors use them because they are needed to create the text, and the context will make clear their general if not their particular meaning.

Implications for Readability and Controlled Vocabulary

One of the most deeply rooted notions among teachers of reading is that controlled vocabulary, based on studies of relative word frequency, is necessary in instructional materials for developing readers. This study should help educators to understand why texts are worded as they are. Since the wording of any text is by no means random, readers can find it predictable without any external attempt to control vocabulary or limit the use of uncommon words. Such understanding should call into question the use of word frequency lists in judging readability and in structuring controlled-vocabulary basal readers.

When the word frequency list is used to judge readability of a text, it imposes the assumption that words are of equal difficulty regardless of where they occur, what their grammatical functions are, how they relate to text cohesion, and what kind of contextual support is provided.

When the frequency list is used to construct or rewrite texts it may make them strange and unpredictable. Words are not in texts because they are frequent. They are frequent because they are in texts and because the texts require them.

Artificially reducing vocabulary to create texts with low proportions of uncommon words tampers with the very factors that may contribute both to word frequency and text difficulty. There are good reasons why particular words occur in particular places in particular texts, and author's choice is only one of these reasons. Tampering with the wording of texts without understanding why words occur in texts the way they do may make texts less readable rather than more so.

Authors and editors would do better to focus on relating the content of texts to the audience rather than to focus on controlling vocabulary. A sense of audience and use of the natural constraints of the language will result in text wordings which are in keeping with the backgrounds of the intended readers and the strategies readers develop. New words are learned and definitions are broadened in the transactions between readers and appropriately worded texts. Then vocabulary results from reading; it is not the prerequisite for it.

Teachers concerned about vocabulary development would do better to focus on functional use of words and terms in the context of real texts than to resort to decontextualized lists or dictionary exercises.

A text, after all, is considerably more than the sum of its words.

References

Carroll, J. B., Davies, P., & Richmond, B. (1971). *The American heritage word frequency book.* Boston: Houghton, Mifflin.

Carroll, J. B. (1981, April). New analysis of reading skills. Paper Presented at the International Reading Association Conference. New Orleans.

Fries, C. C. (1952). *The structure of English: An introduction to the construction of English sentences.* New York: Harcourt, Brace and World.

Goodman, Y. M., & Burke, C. L. (1972). *Reading Miscue Inventory.* New York: Macmillan.

Goodman, K. S., & Goodman, Y. M. (1978, August). Reading of American children whose language is a stable rural dialect of English or a language other than English (Final Report, NIE-C-00-3-0087).

Halliday, M. A. K. (1978). *Language as social semiotic.* Baltimore: University Park Press.

Halliday, M. A. K., & Hasan, R. (1976). *Cohesion in English.* London: Longman.

Horn, E. A. (1925). The commonest words in the spoken vocabulary of children up to and including six years of age. In *Twenty-fourth yearbook of the national society for the study of education, Part I* (Chap. 7).

Klare, G. R. (1963). *The measurement of readability.* Iowa City: Iowa State University Press.

Lorge, I. (1938). Predicting Reading Difficulty of Selections for Children. *The Elementary English Review.*

Lorge, I. (1944). Word lists as background for communication. *Teachers College Record* (pp. 453–62).

Thorndike, E. L., & Lorge, I. (1944). *The teacher's word book of 30,000 words.* New York: Teachers College, Columbia University.

Texts Analyzed

S51* Moore, L. "Freddie Miller, Scientist," in *Adventures Here and There*, Eds. E. A. Betts & C. M. Welch. New York: American Book Company, 1965.

S53 Hayes, W. D. "My Brother is a Genius," in *Adventures Now and Then*, Eds. E. A. Betts & C. M. Welch. New York: American Book Company, 1965.

S59 Stovall, J. C. "Sheep Dog," in *Widening Views*, Eds. W. C. Sheldon & R. McCracken. Boston: Allyn and Bacon, 1966.

S60 Dahl, R. "Poison" in *Adventures in English Literature*. New York: Harcourt, Brace, and World, 1958.

S61 Rapoport, R. "Why We Need a Generation Gap," *Look*, January 13, 1970, p. 14.

S70 Sperry, A. "Ghost of the Lagoon," in *Open Highways*, Eds. H. Robinson et al. Glenview: Scott, Foresman, 1967.

*Numbers preceding titles are those used in the original database and in the related research reports.

Chapter Ten

Determiners In Reading: Miscues on a Few Little Words

Kenneth S. Goodman
University of Arizona, 1987

Abstract. The English system of determiners seems to be very simple, since there are so few articles, *the* and *a/an*. But it is more complex than it appears which serves pragmatic text functions: it is used to differentiate definite and indefinite noun phrases and to signal in a text whether particular information is given or new.

Using an existing data base from reading miscue research the miscues (unexpected responses) of readers in second, fourth, and sixth grades in 8 American populations were studied to understand the control of the determiner system by the subjects and how they used determiners in the reading of cohesive narrative texts.

Miscues were far less frequent than on general text words and they were limited to a small number of categories. There were almost no substitutions of nouns, verbs, adjectives and adverbs. A large proportion of the miscues were article for article substitutions. Omissions and insertions were much more common than for general miscues which reflects the use of null determiners in the English noun phrase.

The study strongly supported a model of reading that is transactional and constructive with readers generating their own text parallel

This chapter first appeared in *Language and Education*, Vol. 1, No. 1, 1987, pp. 33–57. Reprinted with permission of the author.

to the published text. It showed readers of all three age groups in strong control of the determiner system of English, which is not a surprise since it is necessary to the communicative use of the language.

A Few Little Words

The is the most common word in the English language. *A* (with its pre-vowel alternate *an*) is also very common. These words are common because of the way that the English noun phrase is constructed and because of the roles they play in making texts cohesive. They may seem to be trivial, yet the system of their use is highly complex and they are very useful to readers and writers as they construct texts and communicate through them.

In texts speakers/writers are trying to tell their listeners/readers what they want them to know on the basis of what they assume they already know. All languages must have structures and devices for reminding readers and listeners what they already know as they are presented with new information. Reference to people, places, events, ideas, and things must be established and maintained throughout the text. In English each noun phrase is structured so that it either presents information or presupposes it. The determiners are key elements in these structures indicating whether new or presupposed information is involved.

This study is concerned specifically with *the* and *a/an*, the articles or major determiners of English. Some less frequently occurring determiners are also examined. So the study deals with an aspect of texts that Halliday has labeled referential cohesion. It helps to provide a picture of how reference and relationship are established by readers in transactions with texts.

Stenning (1979) adopts a pragmatic view of the type of text relations involved in articles. He redefines the pragmatic relation as one between 'phrases, statements, and objects not a semantic property of sentence types'. That means that whatever relationships articles indicate are specific to particular contexts within texts.

As readers establish the text relations, their miscues reflect and reveal the use they make of the system. Because the noun structure system is so significant our theory would cause us to expect the miscues to reflect shifts in definiteness and reference and to vary in frequency depending on how the noun phrases are structured and how they are used.

Purposes of the Study

This study begins with an examination of the distribution of *the* and *a/an* in three texts. Then it examines the miscues produced on each text by second, fourth, and sixth grade pupils to answer these questions:

1. What relevant patterns of miscues do the readers of each text and of the three texts combined show?
2. How do these patterns relate to syntactic, semantic and pragmatic views of the referential functions of determiners?
3. What do these patterns show about how readers process the relational aspects of noun phrases?
4. Are these patterns consistent with a transactional, psycholinguistically based theory of reading?

The Miscue Data Base

Miscue analysis was developed as a system for analyzing the points in oral reading where observed and expected responses do not match. Readers' miscues (points where what readers do differs from what is expected) were used to understand the reading process and to develop a model and theory of that process. By reworking the database, the focus can be shifted from the readers to the text and the characteristics of the text may be considered from the point of view of the miscues they are involved in. This makes it possible to study the influence of specific text features on readers without the construction of artificial texts and the imposition of unnatural conditions on the readers.

From our miscue database we selected three stories used as common tasks across 8 linguistic population groups in a study reported in 1978 (Goodman & Goodman, 1978).

S44, *Kitten Jones,* was read by 24 second grade readers. S51, *Freddie Miller, Scientist,* was read by 32 fourth grade readers. S53, *My Brother is a Genius,* was read by 32 sixth graders. The eight populations were:

Dialect Groups:	*Bi-lingual Groups:*
Appalachian (Tennessee)	Navajo (Arizona)*
Downeast (Maine)	Arab (Michigan)
Rural Black (Mississippi)	Spanish (Texas)
Pidgin (Hawaii)	Samoan (Hawaii)*

*These groups did not read the second grade story, 544.

Our database provides us with quantity and quality of miscues as well as a complete listing of actual miscues at each text address. So we were able to examine all miscues on a given word wherever it occurred in the text.

Each subject in the original study read, orally, a complete text. The determiners are there because the authors, who had no part in the research, needed them or chose to use them in the writing. The texts have not been specially created or adapted for use in the research.

An Integrated Pragmatic-Grammatical View of English Determiners

To provide a base for understanding determiners in English texts this study draws on a 'pragmatic componential analysis' provided by Martin (1978) which expands on the view of Halliday & Hasan (1976). Martin's focus is on what a speaker (or writer) can do with the language and how the grammar of the language makes such use possible. Readers do things with texts. And in doing these things they use language structures. We'll explore the grammar of determiners in noun phrases before we return to pragmatic analysis.

The Grammar of Determiners

Quirk & Greenbaum (1973) provide a paradigm of English noun phrase structures. They begin by defining 3 classes of nouns. Examples are from the three texts in this study: S44, a second grade story; S51, a fourth grade story; S53, a sixth grade story.

1. Proper nouns: Usually these have no determiner.

   Example: Poor *Freddie* was in trouble again.

2. Count nouns: These are countable and so they have singular and plural forms. *The* and *a* may occur with singular count nouns. *The* or *null* articles may occur with plurals.

   Example: We get *a good education* in our school. And they encourage special *projects*.

3. Non-count nouns: *the* and *some* may occur with non-count nouns.

   Example: . . . playing on the *grass*

   Quirk & Greenbaum identify 6 classes of determiners as they relate to singular or possessive count nouns and to non-count nouns.

A. All three noun classes: *the*, Possessives, *whose, which, whichever, what, whatever, some* (Stressed), *any* (Stressed), *no*

B. Plural count and non-count: *null* article, *some* (unstressed), *any* (unstressed), *enough*.

C. Singular count and non-count: *this, that*

D. Plural count: *these, those*

E. Singular count: *a/an, every, each, either, neither*

F. Non-count: *much* (p. 62)

Article use is dependent on whether reference is specific or generic and definite or indefinite. Here are examples from the texts used in this study:

Generic reference for count nouns uses *a* or *the* for the singular and *null* for the plural:

> ...*a fellow* has to work off steam once in a while

> Might as well study word meanings first

Generic non-count nouns take only null form:

> ...nothing to do with *chemistry*

Nouns with both definite and specific reference take *the* with all three classes:

Singular count:	...in *the room* where your baby brother is sleeping...
Plural count:	It helps me to remember *the word definitions*...
Non-count:	He looked at *the butter*

Nouns with specific but indefinite reference choose *a* for singular count nouns and *some* or *null* for plural and non-count.

Singular count:	It will be a *a live show*
Plural count:	We could take *some moving pictures*
	We're setting up *lights and cameras*
Non-count:	There was a blast of *music*
	We must make some *allowance* for experiments...

Possessives do not take articles. Rather they absorb their function making the noun phrase definite. Nominative and objective pronouns do not take articles:

> I was only washing the doll to make *it* look like new.

A small number of common count nouns take *null* articles:

> at breakfast   to get *supper* ready

The Pragmatics of Determiners

With this grammatical framework we can now consider Martin's pragmatic framework. Martin describes noun phrases which presuppose information in discourse as *phoric* and phrases which do not presuppose as *non-phoric*.

Indefinite nouns are *non-phoric*. Definite nouns are made definite by some presupposed information and are therefore *phoric*. If noun phrases presuppose participant identity as in *the baby, that baby,* or *he* they have *reminding phoricity*. Other noun phrases have *relevance phoricity* because they presuppose the identity of participants related to the one referred to:

'where are you?' he shouted.

'In *the hall closet*' came Elizabeth's tearful reply.

'The *door* blew shut. *It's* stuck.'

In this sequence both *closet* and *door* are used for the first time in the text but *the* is used rather than *a* because houses have hall closets and closets have doors.

Reference may be to either the cultural or situational context in a speech act. If the reference is cultural what is presupposed is stored knowledge. Here's an example from S44, our second grade text:

'May we take pictures and send them to the contest?'

'Yes,' answered Mrs. Jones. 'I'll get *the camera* now.'

Though this is the first time *camera* occurs in the text the definite article *the* is used. That's because the author presupposes that readers will know that pictures are taken with cameras and that families generally have only one camera. This latter type of exophoric reference Martin calls *homophora*.

Situational context reference may be either *endophoric*, that is within the linguistic text or *exophoric*, relating to the context of the speech act or literacy event. *Exophora* in written texts often involves direct quotation:

I'm going to drop *this light* down to *you*.

In the example above *I* and *you* have their co-referents not in the text but in the participant roles in the speech act the author is representing. The reference for *this light* is also in the speech act since *this* is pointing to something both speakers could see and experience in the situational context. Otherwise *a* or *the* would be used.

Endophoric reference may either be preceding (anaphora) or following (cataphora). Most *endophoric* references are *anaphoric* because usually the co-referent precedes the phoric element in the text. But the co-referent can follow:

You just happen to do your studying in the room where your baby brother is sleeping.

The is cataphoric relating to the modifying element (*where your baby brother is sleeping*) in the same noun phrase.

Since *a/an* is used in indefinite noun phrases it is never phoric. That leads to a common oversimplification of the phoric role played by *the*. As Halliday & Hasan (1976:73) put it:

> There is a commonly held belief that the typical function of *the* is the anaphoric one: that it invariably specifies by reference back in the text...It should be stressed, therefore, that anaphoric reference is only one means whereby *the* achieves specificity and, even when it is anaphoric, more often than not there is no second mention of the same noun...

Here is an example from S51 where the anaphoric uses of *the* do not involve second mentions of nouns. Numbers indicating page and line in the original text precede each cited line (i.e. 215 is page 2 line 15):

215 'I want you to save half your allowance for it each week.'

219 After *the cut* in his allowance...

In our stories there are more exophoric uses of *the* than anaphoric or cataphoric. Furthermore, most of the anaphoric uses of *the* are multiple references to exophoric entities. For example the first reference to each of these entities uses *the* because they are homophoric, that is definite within the situational context:

> Mrs. Miller went to *the kitchen*...she opened *the refrigerator*...*the alarm clock didn't ring*

Subsequent references to these are anaphoric and exophoric as well.

When proper nouns occur in texts, since they are not phoric they do not signal whether they contain new information or old. Possessive nouns and pronouns relate nouns to other nouns but since they replace the articles they lose some of the phoric quality that the presence of the article provides. So the presupposed information provided by the use of *his, the, this,* or *a* in the same phrase will vary considerably.

Halliday & Hasan group the definite article *the* with other specific determiners including deictics and possessives:

> Essentially *the*, like the demonstratives, is a specifying agent, serving to identify a particular individual or subclass within the class designated by the noun, but it does this only through dependence on something else—it contains no specifying element of its own...It merely indicates that the item in question is specific and identifiable: that somewhere the information necessary for identifying it is recoverable. Where is this information to be sought? Again, either in the situation or in the text. (p. 70–71)

So readers must use their knowledge of the grammatical and pragmatic systems to infer cohesive relationships in order to construct their own sensible texts. The cues to these relationships vary considerably in how explicit they are. We can expect reader's miscues to reflect the inferences and predictions they are making as they transact with the text. We can expect readers to produce a small range of miscues where the text cues are ambiguous as they change the text to reflect inferences they have drawn. We can expect what they do with determiners to be far from random.

An Exemplary Passage

The section of text in Figure 10–1 provides a range of examples of phenomena relating to determiners. This passage will serve to illustrate the phenomena we're examining. There are a series of noun phrases in the passage which involve *the, his, another, a,* and *null* as determiners:

602	*the* cellar	603	*the* small battery
603–4	*his* mother's bell	604	*his* tool box
604	*another* battery	604	*a* ruler
604–5	*a* coil	605	of copper wire
605	*a* small bulb	605	tape

Figure 10–1
Determiners and Related Features
(An exemplary passage from S51 Freddie Miller, Scientist).

0601　　At once Freddie set to work seriously at something he
　　　　　　　　　　　　　　　to(c)
　　　　　　　　and　　　　　0　　he,0
0602 had started for fun. He ran to the cellar and picked up
　　some　　　　　　　,and(4/lc)　　　　　　　　this,0
　　a(10/lc)　　　and(c)　　　　　　　　the(2c)　the (2)　3(lc/luc)
0603 the small battery/he had intended to use for his mother's ⟨.⟩
　　　0(3)　this(c)　　　　　　　　　　　　　he,it,0 and (2/lc)
　　and　the(8)　　　and(c)　　　others　　and(2/lc) and (c)0
0604 bell. In his tool box he found another battery, a ruler,/　　a
　　and,0(2)　　　and(4),0　　　that(c)
　　,a(4) and　　　and(4/lc)　　of a a(3)
0605 coil of / copper wire,　/ a small bulb　/,　and / tape.

Note: 0 is used here to represent omissions. / indicates insertions.

In the second noun phrase (*the small battery*), ten of the 32 subjects who read the text substitute *a* for *the* with only the one correcting. They are treating the noun phrase as indefinite which is consistent with the fact that no battery has been previously mentioned. *The* here is cataphoric; the following clause makes the battery definite. It appears that *a* is substituted for *the* as a result of subjects deciding they are dealing with an indefinite noun phrase. Otherwise other instances of *the* would be as likely to show this shift.

In contrast to this strong miscue shift from definite to indefinite article, there is only one miscue on *the* before *cellar,* an omission. That was produced by a Maine subject and may represent a null form permissible in her dialect.

The two noun phrases with possessive *his* in the determiner position also show a contrast. There are two substitutions of *the* and one of *this* for *his* before *mother's.* But before *tool box* there is one corrected *this* substitution and 8 *the* substitutions. Shifts to *the* before tool box lose the relationship to *Freddie* represented by *this.* That information is not lost when *the* is substituted for *his* before *mother's* since there is only one mother in the text and the relationship is already well established. One subject substitutes *Mother's* for *his mother's* shifting to a possessive proper noun with a null determiner.

There is no ambiguity about whom *his* refers to in either case. Subjects shifting to *the* are rejecting the possession *his* attributes to Freddie. It appears that a fourth of our subjects can't accept the possibility that a boy can possess a tool box. What is presupposed by the writer does not match the cultural knowledge of at least some of the readers. At another text point 7 subjects replace *his* by *the* in this sequence:

Freddie hurried to *his* cellar worktable.

So it appears that the truth (to the reader) of a statement influences assignment and acceptance of text relationships.

Only one miscue involves *another battery.* One subject substitutes *others* for the two word phrase making the reference general but still indefinite.

The substitutions in the five noun phrases which follow on line 605 show a very different phenomenon. The readers are having some difficulty organizing the syntax of this string of noun phrases, a list of the things which were *found* in *his tool box.* All of these are nonphoric noun phrases. Three use *a* as the article before indefinite singular count nouns. Two use null forms before indefinite non-count nouns.

Some subjects use *and* to link the noun phrases, a common way of linking two or more parallel syntactic elements which these non-phoric noun phrases are. *And* is substituted for *a* twice before *ruler* (one correction). It is substituted twice before *coil* (one correction) and inserted once before *a coil*. *And* is substituted for *of* once before *copper wire* (thus making *coil* and *copper wire* separate findings). *And* is also inserted by 4 subjects before *a small bulb* with no corrections. It is substituted for *a* before *small bulb* 4 times with one correction. These interactions with *and* involve both insertions between noun phrases and apparent substitutions of *and* for *a*. The latter appears to be coincidental: *and* is inserted between phrases as *a* is omitted. Two related but separable phenomena are happening at the same point.

A large number of miscues in these indefinite noun phrases involve *a*. *A* is omitted once before *coil*. But *a* is substituted three times for *of* before *copper wire* with appropriate intonation again making *a copper wire* another separate noun phrase in the series. Two additional subjects delete *of* at this point in the text. *A* is omitted by one subject before *small* bulb. It is inserted 3 times before *tape*. That shifts *tape* from a non-count to an indefinite singular count noun, which it could be. Note that there are no substitutions of *the* for *a* in this series of indefinite noun phrases and only one shift from *a* to *that*. That one miscue, which moves to a definite noun phrase, is corrected. The readers seem to be aware that this is a string of indefinite noun phrases.

Miscue research requires each subject to retell the story after reading. Most subjects describe the making of the flashlight in considerable detail during their retellings. The miscues here reflect the complexity of this particular syntactic structure but they do not result in loss of cohesion or sense.

These miscues show the subjects' text construction at work. Though these substitutions, insertions, and omissions all relate to organizing this complex syntax, they involve shifts within the possible noun phrase structures and noun phrase sequences. They are not random even in the instances where a fully acceptable structure does not result. Subjects are concerned for cohesion and references even in the miscues.

What is going on in the reading of this passage is an attempt by the readers to deal with text cohesion and noun phrase reference. Sometimes only one or two subjects show a particular response involving articles. But sometimes a sizeable percent of our readers do so at the same point. What is perhaps even more impressive in the miscues of these 32 subjects is *what doesn't happen*. There are no similar looking or sounding words substituted with little or no relationship to the syntax or meaning of the passage.

There are no totally inexplicable miscues. The range of readers' observed responses is small. It's confined almost completely to elements which could fit the text the readers are constructing.

Several key points are demonstrated in this short passage:

1. Miscues show strong use of the article system by readers and conversely strong constraints of that system on the readers.

2. Article miscues mostly involve a very small range of alternatives. These alternatives derive from a small number of syntactically and/or pragmatically related structures.

3. Miscue patterns involving articles are text specific; they reflect the features of the text surrounding particular articles. So several readers may make identical miscues at any point in the text showing similar processing and inference in response to the text features.

4. Readers seem to be influenced by and concerned for both grammatical and pragmatic aspects of article use.

5. Patterns of correction reflect the readers' self monitoring and their concern for sensible text.

Frequency of Articles and Other Determiners

Table 10–1 shows frequency and percent of articles and deictics in the texts used in this study. There are similar proportions of articles in the three texts, 7.3% to 7.8%. The proportion of *the* to *a/an* uses in S44 and S51 are similar, about 6% of running words are *the* and about 2% *a* or *an*. But S53, the sixth grade story, has an unusually high frequency of *a/an* (3.3%) and low frequency of *the* (3.9%) compared to the other two stories and to other texts examined in other miscue research. In six texts examined in a study of intratext word frequency (Goodman & Bird, 1982) occurrence of *a* ranged from 1.4% to 2% of running words. In two of those stories *the* reached almost 10% of the running words.

The percent of running words that are common nouns for each story is 15.6% for S44, 14.2% for S51 and 14.4% for S53. Since *the* and

Table 10–1

Determiners: Frequency and Percent of Running Words in Three Texts

	S44		S51		S53	
	F	%	F	%	F	%
A	14	1.9	29	2.0	65	3.1
An	0	0	4	0.2	5	0.2
The	43	6.0	78	5.6	82	3.9
Some	0	0	1		3	0.1
Tot. Art	57	7.9	112	7.8	155	7.3

a will occur primarily with common nouns, those percentages suggest that there are comparable opportunities for articles to occur in the three texts. But S53 is a first person narrative. It has more pronouns and less than half as many proper nouns as the other two texts. And it has 2.9% possessive pronouns as compared to 2.2% for each of the other texts. More possessive pronouns means fewer articles since both cannot occur in the same noun phrases. The total percent of articles in the three texts would be very similar at around 8% if there were not a higher rate of possessives in S53.

It seems likely that the higher proportion of *a* and lower proportion of *the* in S53 compared to other texts is due at least partly also to the first person use. But it probably also reflects other stylistic features that result in use of more non-phoric noun phrases.

Miscue Patterns Involving *the* and *a*

In the next section of this report we'll consider quantitatively the miscues on the articles in the database produced by the readers. It is important to keep in mind the points summarized from the depth analysis discussed above. The quantitative data for the group can show broad outlines of phenomena involved but to fully understand those phenomena we need to look at particular text sequences and particular readers' miscues.

There are few points in the text where the majority of the subjects do not produce the expected response. But there is more to be learned by analyzing the unexpected responses than the correct ones. In comparing mismatches between observed and expected responses we can see what readers are doing.

Table 10–2 shows that the miscue rate on articles is about one-fourth of the general rate for these subjects on these texts. Miscues on articles are less than half as common as they are on pronouns (including

Table 10–2
Miscues per Hundred Words and per Hundred Articles

Story	Total Words	Total Articles	Total Miscues	Article Miscues	MPHW* Per Subj	MPHA** Per Subj
S44	698	57	2867	61	17.11	4.46
S51	1369	112	5830	143	13.31	3.99
S53	2030	155	8790	188	13.54	3.79

*MPHW = Miscues per hundred words
**MPHA = Miscues per hundred articles

Table 10–3

Distribution of Miscues Over Occurrences of *a, an* and *the*

	the	*a*	*an*
S44			
Instances without miscues	16	2	0
Instances with miscues	27	12	0
Total Instances	43	14	0
Mean Misc. per site w/Miscues	2.26	3.25	0
S51			
Instances without miscues	17	3	0
Instances with miscues	61	26	4
Total Instances	78	29	4
Mean Misc. per site w/Miscues	2.34	4.3	5
S53			
Instances without miscues	25	16	1
Instances with miscues	57	49	4
Total Instances	82	65	5
Mean Misc. per site w/Miscues	3.29	3.0	3

possessives) (Goodman & Gespass, 1983:22). This is not a surprising finding. The articles are small common words. But the structures in which they are found, as was pointed out above, are not all that simple. So the low rate of miscues reflect strong control of the determiner system by our linguistically diverse subjects.

The rate of article miscues for the second graders reading S44 is slightly higher, 4.46, than the rate of fourth graders on S51, 3.99, or 6th graders on S53, 3.79. But these rates are remarkably similar particularly considering that the second graders' overall MPHW was substantially higher than the fourth or sixth graders'. There is nothing in these figures to suggest any important differences between age groups in dealing with articles. The articles are present in similar proportions and subjects produce similar rates of miscues on them.

In the examples provided of multiple identical miscues the impression may be given that miscues occur at every instance in the text where *a, an,* or *the* occur. Table 10–3 demonstrates that there are many instances of these articles in all three texts where no subject makes a miscue. On the other hand, where miscues do occur they are likely to involve several subjects. Again this demonstrates the transactive nature of the process of reading. Every reader must transact with the characteristics of the published text within the constraints of the language. But what readers bring to the text is also part of the transaction. So the data shows variation within the constraints of the psycholinguistic process.

Tables 10–4 and 10–5 present summary data on miscues by all subjects on *the* and *a*. The tables show the two kinds of article miscues: 1. *For the article:* Miscues where *the* or *a* is the expected response (ER) to the text which is either replaced by another word or omitted. 2. *By the article:* Miscues where other expected responses (ER) are replaced by articles as observed responses (OR) or articles are inserted in the text.

In the tables miscues have also been categorized according to the grammatical function of the term substituted for the article or replaced by it. The proportion of all article miscues in each category is expressed as a percent of the total.

The data strongly demonstrates how highly constrained miscues on articles are. A very small set of words are substituted for or replaced by *the* and *a*. Considering the words in the language this is indeed remarkable. Virtually every one is a monosyllable. That shows graphic influence: subjects expect short words. But it also is due to the fact that the classes of words involved tend to consist mostly of monosyllables.

A number of words substituted for or replaced by *the* have graphic similarities to *the*: their, they, that, those, these, this, then, he, her, she. That might suggest graphic reasons for substitutions. And indeed our theoretical perspective says that there are interactions with all cue systems; grapho-phonic, syntactic and semantic. Treating graphic similarity as a sole-cause or even major cause could not explain several things: (a) Interactions with *a* as well as *the*. (b) Other dissimilar words (*his* for example) which appear in the miscues. (c) Relative proportion of miscues involving each word. (d) Variation of miscue frequency across instances.

Seven categories, excluding omissions and insertions, account for all but a very few of all miscues involving articles. All of the categories except pronouns are function words. *That means that nouns, verbs, adjectives and adverbs are almost never interchanged with articles in miscues.* Of the six function word categories four are also determiners: Other Articles, Quantifiers, Possessive Pronouns, and Deictics. Together these account for 51.3% of miscues on *a* as ER and 60.5% of those with *a* as OR in S44. For S51, determiners account for 51.9% and 56% of the miscues on *a*. For S53, these figures are 50.3% and 53.3%. Figures for *the* in S44 are 42.5% and 66.7%. In S51 determiner miscues on *the* are 51.2% and 61%. And for S53 they are 63% and 64.1%. Any syntactic change such miscues involve would be within the noun phrase but cohesive and pragmatic relationships could be changed by such miscues. The fact that so high a proportion of miscues on articles involve other determiners is itself strong evidence of the control readers have over these text features and the strong constraints English noun phrase constructions provide for the readers.

Table 10-4

Miscues with *the*: Frequency and Percent

	S44				S51				S53				Total			
	For % of		By % of		For % of		By % of		For % of		By % of		For % of		By % of	
Type	f	Tot.	f	Tot.	f	Tot.	f	Tot.	f	Tot.	f	Tot.	f	Tot.	f	Tot.
Article	16	26.2	20	19.6	45	31.5	50	26.0	79	42.0	52	21.4	140	35.7	122	22.7
Quantif.	0	0	1	1.0	1	0.7	5	2.6	0	0	4	1.7	1	0.3	10	1.9
Pronoun	10	16.4	4	3.9	16	11.2	24	12.5	14	7.5	12	4.9	40	10.2	40	7.5
Pos. Pron.	7	11.5	15	14.7	12	8.4	39	20.3	32	17.0	39	16.0	51	13.0	93	17.3
Deictic	3	4.9	33	32.4	16	11.2	27	14.1	8	4.3	65	26.7	27	6.9	125	23.3
Conjunct.	3	4.9	7	6.9	11	7.7	10	5.2	9	4.8	30	12.3	23	5.9	47	8.8
Prepos.	2	3.3	2	2.0	9	6.3	4	2.1	2	1.1	3	1.2	13	3.3	9	1.7
Other	7	11.5	11	10.8	2	1.4	6	3.1	3	1.6	0	0	12	3.1	17	3.2
Omission	13	21.3			31	21.7			41	21.8			85	21.7		
Insertion			9	8.8			27	14.1			38	15.6			74	13.8
Total	61		102		143		192		188		243		392		537	

Table 10–5

Miscues Involving *a*: Frequency and Percent

Type	S44				S51				S53				Total			
	For % of Tot.		By % of Tot.		For % of Tot.		By % of Tot.		For % of Tot.		By % of Tot.		For % of Tot.		By % of Tot.	
	f	Tot.	f	Tot.	f	Tot.	f	Tot.	f	Tot.	f	Tot.	f	Tot.	f	Tot.
Article	20	51.3	16	48.5	50	44.6	44	49.4	51	34.7	78	46.2	121	40.6	138	47.4
Quantif.	0	0	1	3.0	0	0	2	2.2	0	0	0	0	0	0	3	1.0
Pronoun	1	2.6	1	3.0	6	5.4	4	4.5	12	8.2	14	8.3	19	6.4	19	6.5
Pos. Pron.	0	0	3	9.1	7	6.3	2	2.2	23	15.6	10	5.9	30	10.1	15	5.2
Deictic	0	0	1	3.0	1	1.0	2	2.2	0	0	2	1.2	1	0.3	5	1.7
Conjunct.	3	7.7	1	3.0	7	6.3	6	6.7	9	6.1	20	11.8	19	6.4	27	9.3
Prepos.	8	20.5	2	6.1	7	6.3	8	9.0	11	7.5	9	5.3	26	8.7	19	6.5
Other	1	2.6	1	3.0	1	0.9	4	4.5	2	1.4	2	1.2	4	1.3	7	2.4
Omission	6	15.4			33	29.5			39	26.5			78	26.2		
Insertion			7	21.2			17	19.1			34	20.1			58	19.9
Total	39		33		112		89		147		169		298		291	

Quantifiers (principally cardinal numbers) have been shown as a separate category here because they comprise a category of miscues on articles that could be important but isn't. One view of determiners is that they are all forms of quantifiers (Stenning, 1979). *A/an* historically derived from *one,* and *one* still functions as an article in the Hawaiian Pidgin spoken by some of our subjects. Yet there are very few miscues involving articles replacing quantifiers and only one in the three texts of a quantifier replacing an article. Partly that may reflect the small number of quantifiers in the texts. But it also reflects little tendency for our subjects to treat articles and quantifiers as interchangeable.

Omissions and insertions comprise much higher proportions of article miscues than general miscues. In the larger study, these subjects' proportions of all miscues that are omissions are 12.2% on S44, and 10.4% on both S51 and S53. Insertions for the same groups are 3.7%, 3.9%, and 4.1% of all miscues for the respective texts. As Table 10.4 shows, about 21% of miscues on *the* are omissions in all three texts. Insertions of *the* are 8.8%, 14.1%, and 15.6% of miscues on *the* in the respective texts. Omissions are 15.2% of the miscues on *a* in S44, 29.5% of S51, and 25.5% of S53. Insertions of *a* are 21.2%, 19.1%, and 20.1% respectively.

The patterns of miscues on *a* and *the* are similar in that they involve the same categories but they differ in the proportions of miscues involving each category.

Almost half the miscues involving *a* in the three texts are other articles, chiefly *the.* That compares with 26–42% of miscues on *the* in which *a* is substituted for *the* and 20–26% of the miscues with *the* as the OR in which *a* is the text word replaced by *the.* This disproportion mainly represents more tendency for readers to interchange *the* with other determiners that keep the noun phrase definite than to interchange such determiners with *a* which would represent shifts from definite to indefinite noun phrases.

The figures on S53 stand out in one respect in Tables 10–4 and 10–5. Forty-two percent of the miscues on *the* in S53 involve substitution of *a,* much higher than for the other two texts. At the same time only 34.7% of the miscues on *a* in S53 involve *the.* The most likely explanation of this difference is the unusually high proportion of *a* to *the* in that text. Either the style or frequency or both seem to be causing subjects to shift more to *a* and less to *the* in S53 than in the other texts.

Possessive pronouns are more likely to involve miscues with *the* than *a.* This is consistent with what was said above about staying within definite noun phrases. There is even more striking evidence with deictics (*this, that, these, those*). Shifts, particularly from deictics to *the,* are very common but there are only scattered interactions between deictics and *a.* One could argue that graphic similarity plays a major role in these differences. *The* looks more like *that* and *this* than *a* does. But that would not explain the frequent interaction of *a* and *the* and the infrequency of *a* and *this* or *that*. Graphic similarities certainly play a role in miscues but it must be a minor one considering how constrained article miscues are.

These overall figures tell part of the story that readers' miscues reveal about how readers process articles and noun phrases and the passages in which they occur. But to see this process in true perspective we need to examine examples of the miscues summarized in each category. In the following section we'll look mostly at examples where a strong reader-text transaction is reflected through several readers making identical miscues at the same point in the text. And we'll also consider self-correction rates since they show a lot about reader's awareness of the effects of their miscues.

The Others

The category labeled *others* is as remarkable as any if only because of the very small number of scattered miscues that need to be treated as miscellaneous. Only in S44 is the percent of the whole above 10% for miscues involving *the*. (See Table 10–4.) Only a handful of miscues in the three texts on *a* are in this group.

It might seem that our second grade subjects' higher percent of *other* miscues on *the* could indicate less control over articles among younger pupils. But all 7 of the miscues on *the* are identical substitutions of *said* in this text sequence:

701 'Who took it?' Mr. Vine asked.

　　　　　　　　said (7,3 corr.)
702 'Our Kitten!' *The* Jones children said.

In this passage, *the* occurs before a proper noun. That's only because of the unusual use of the name as a noun adjunct to a head noun which is a common noun, *children*. Furthermore that noun phrase occurs in a dialogue carrier in an *object, subject, verb* sentence. Seven of the 24 readers of this text have rejected the definite article before the proper noun and transformed the sentence so the verb *said* follows the direct quotation. A strong prediction of a likely structure has dominated over an unexpected structure. However the readers are self-monitoring and three of the seven self-correct their miscue.

Self-correction by the readers of miscues of this type is higher than average for miscues involving articles and considerably higher than the correction rates for all miscues. That's as expected. These miscues involve substantial shifts in syntactic and semantic structures and are more likely to be disconfirmed by other text information and corrected.

The data here underscores 2 other important concepts:

1. What doesn't happen in reading is as significant as what does.
2. Minor phenomena may be infrequent but still be important in demonstrating the constraints on article use.

Articles for Articles

It's not surprising that a large proportion of miscues on articles involve substituting other articles. These are basically *a* for *the* and vice-versa but there are scattered examples as well involving *an* and *some*.

The shifts between *a* and *the* involve shifts from phoric definite noun phrases to non-phoric indefinite noun phrases and the reverse. That means that reference for the noun phrase could be changed. It was indicated above that about half of all miscues on *a* are interchanges with *the*, that is shifts to definite phoric phrases. In the exemplary passage cited earlier, 10 subjects said *a small battery* rather than *the small battery*. In this instance *the* is cataphoric, the noun phrase is only definite because it is made specific by a modifying clause which follows: *he had intended to use for his mother's bell.* Though the use of *the* cataphorically foreshadows the information that follows and which makes the noun phrase definite, its use is not obligatory in English.

In the same story this example of a shift by several subjects from *a* to *the* occurs:

$$\text{the (9)}$$

0524 'Listen, Elizabeth,' he called. 'I'll fix *a* light and drop it to you . . .'

The shift here is from an indefinite nonphoric *a light* (which subsequently turns out to be the homemade flashlight Freddie makes later) to what Martin calls homophoric *the*. Though no light has been mentioned in the text, parts of houses, including dark closets (where Elizabeth is) have lights. The readers' common inference (made by 9 of 32 readers) is that if somebody's stuck in a closet someone should turn on or fix the light.

Corrections on article for article miscues are not very high, below the mean correction rate for all miscues in each of the stories. Readers tend to correct when miscues produce conflicts and incomprehensible texts. Some article for article miscues do that and when they do corrections are higher. Most of the article for article miscues produce only subtle changes at the most and they are therefore not likely to be corrected.

Substitutions of articles for articles show clearly the readers' use of syntactic and pragmatic rules for generating definite or indefinite phoric or nonphoric noun phrases and thus they confirm the dual text view of the reading process (Goodman, 1983).

Article/Possessive Miscues

Miscues involving possessives and articles include a range of possessives and both *a* and *the*, though there are substantial numbers of miscues involving *a* and possessives only in S53, which, as was indicated earlier, has more instances of *a* in the text. In all three stories, the largest number of miscues involve *his*. Corrections of possessive/article miscues are variable depending on the text in which they're found. That will be illustrated below.

Several miscues result in less specific reference which may reflect the issue raised earlier of pragmatic reasons why readers might reject the implicit ownership:

the (8, 2 corr.)

S44 417–8 He printed them upstairs in *his* darkroom.

the (8, 2 corr.)

S53 317–8 As the lady led me toward *his* office.

Several subjects treat *darkroom* as two words showing their lack of the concept that a darkroom is not any dark room. That shift may or may not compound the shift from *his* to *the*. In the example from S53, lines 317–8, some readers may have rejected *his* because the sentence theme is feminine, though none shifted to *her*.

Shifts from the article to the possessive make the possession and reference more cohesive and make inferences more explicit:

his (6)

S51 210 He was always like one of *the* uncles.

our(3)

S53 604 . . . came to *the* house.

A series of sequences in S53 show readers responding with relatively consistent shifts:

his (7)

606–7 He leaned over the crib and wagged *a* finger . . .

his(3), your(1), a(5, 1 corr.)

608 . . . grabbing for *the* finger.

his(7)
824 He wagged *a* finger at Andrew.

his(4), your a(2)
826–7 ... still holding *the* finger over the crib.

The author uses the stylistic device of a finger appearing over the baby. Apparently some of our readers feel fingers must be attached to somebody. But notice that in some of these instances while some subjects are making the noun phrase more specific by replacing *the* by a possessive, others are making it indefinite by substituting *a*. Perhaps *the finger* sounds like it is the only one whereas *a finger* implies one of several, the usual case with fingers.

In most of the cases of possessive/article miscues shown above changes of meaning, cohesion, and syntax still leave the reader with syntactically acceptable, comprehensible text. Correction is thus not required. Where it occurs it is either triggered by specific aspects of the surrounding text or by the reader's discontent with some subtle inconsistency or both. That explains the variability of rates of correction, from almost none to quite high.

Article/Deictic Miscues

Use of *this, that, these,* and *those* are termed deictic here because they have the common characteristic of pointing either forward or backward in the text or exophorically at something in the situational context. The general effect of substituting deictic for an article would be to make the noun phrase and cohesion more explicit. The opposite shift would have the opposite effect. Most of the instances where several readers make the same shift involve substituting *the* for the deictic. Very few of these miscues involve *a* so they almost all stay within definite noun phrases.

Here are some examples of shifts to *the* from deictics:

the(8, 1 corr.)
S44 605 Kitten took *that* picture.

the (8, 2 corr.)
S51 302 ... something wrong with *this* dream.

Deictic miscues tend to involve dialogue and the deictic reference is to something in the speech act, not in the published text. An exception is the *dream* example above where the co-referent is not a previous occurrence of *dream* as a noun but a whole prior idea represented by several lines of text.

In S53, there is a particular stylistic use of the deictic to provide emphasis which is involved at several instances in multiple miscues.

the(14, 1 unsucc. corr.)
803 ... 'Bring *that* fine boy over ... '

the(12) my(1)
806 Get *that* baby over here.

The deictic use is subtle and large numbers of subjects shift to a simple definite noun phrase not losing cohesion as much as the stylistic emphasis.

Here's an example where the text is ambiguous and *that* could either be a deictic or clause marker. Six readers are treating *that studying* as a noun phrase:

the(6) Ø(1)
S53 702 I even found *that* studying made the time go faster.

Overall, correction rates are high for miscues involving articles and deictics but as the examples show rate of correction in any instance depends on the text and type of phenomenon that triggers the miscues.

Article/Pronoun Miscues

When a miscue involves an interchange of a pronoun with an article, it is because the reader is anticipating a common noun phrase where a pronoun occurs in the published text or vice-versa. Common noun phrases usually start with articles. Such miscues are likely to result in disrupted syntax and are therefore very likely to be corrected when the reader realizes a conflict exists. In fact, our data shows over half of all such miscues are corrected by all three grade groups. Totally, 52% of these miscues are corrected; that's a very high rate of correction; mean rate of correction for all miscues on all three texts is less than 20%.

Almost all the pronouns involved are in subject positions which suggests that these miscues involve the readers' assignment or maintenance of theme or topic through a text sequence.

Several different pronouns and all three pronoun persons are involved. *He/the* and *the/he* substitutions are numerous, suggesting a graphic similarity factor, but examples occur of other combinations with no such similarity. Past studies have made clear that graphic similarity may compound semantic, syntactic, and pragmatic factors but it is not explanatory by itself. If it were, all instances of *the* or *he* would have equal probability of exhibiting such substitutions and the data does not show such distribution.

Both *the* and *a* show pronoun interactions which means that both definite and indefinite noun phrases are involved. One factor that seems to trigger such miscues is prior text leading to prediction of a co-referential common noun phrase:

S44 109 Kitten Jones would not have changed her white fur

the(2, 2 corr.)
110 coat for anything. And *she* always...

Another triggering factor is the readers' anticipation of a syntactic structure other than the author's:

S53 305   Suddenly I jumped from
I(6,4 corr.) and(1), Ø
306 my chair, *a* wonderful idea implanted in my brain.

A few miscues, usually made by only one or two readers at any text occurrence, involve nominalized verbs in either the published or reader's text:

he(6, 1 corr., 1 unsucc. corr.)
S51 219 After *the cut in* his allowance,...

Pronoun-article miscues show prediction, inference, self-monitoring, and self-correction strategies at work.

Article/Conjunction Miscues

Miscues involving articles and conjunctions are most likely to involve *and* and either *the* or *a*. But there are examples in all three texts involving many other conjunctions: *or, but, so, than, then, when, what, as.*

Miscues on conjunctions seem to be coincidental, but only in the sense that conjunctions occur at the beginnings of clauses where readers may be anticipating noun phrases. Conversely, where conjunctions replace articles it appears readers are anticipating new conjoined clauses. Such patterns would suggest that readers will tend to correct such miscues as they disconfirm their predictions. And in fact correction rates are relatively high overall though they vary depending on specific text features. Here's an unusual instance, for example, where substitution of an article for a conjunction is not disruptive:

the(3)
S51 715 *but* Kitten loved her ball...

Most examples of such miscues do produce discontinuities however:

the(3, 2 corr.)
S51   725   Wait until you hear *what* happened . . .

These conjunction-article miscues show readers' prediction of syntactic structures and the self-monitoring that accompanies prediction.

Article/Preposition Miscues

Miscues involving articles with prepositions occur in all three texts but without great frequency. In the readings of S44 and S51 they are more likely to involve *a* than *the*. In S53 they involve *a* and *the* in similar numbers. Several prepositions are involved, more or less in proportion to their occurrence in the text. Like the miscues involving conjunctions, these miscues seem to involve the coincidence of prepositions occurring where noun phrases might be expected. Here are examples:

the(3)
S51   503   . . . was always tinkering *with* clocks in Switzerland

at(5, 2 corr.)
S53   528   He's home *a* lot.

Words which are prepositions are also used as verb particles. *To* often introduces infinitives. Here's an example from S53 which shows the readers' involvement with the *to* of the infinitive:

a(4, 2 corr.)
205   . . . has *to* work off steam somehow.

Another example occurs in S44:

402   She suddenly wanted

to (7, 1 corr.)
403 *a* drink and ran into the house.

As expected, considering how syntax and meaning are likely to be disrupted, there is a relatively high rate of correction for these miscues involving prepositions.

Articles and prepositions are both categories involving small words. That similarity may contribute to this type of miscue. If it were an important factor, such miscues would be far more numerous, however.

Table 10–6

Substitution, Omission and Insertion of Articles: Frequency and Percent of Correction

Word	*For*	*the*		*By*	*the*		*For*	*a*		*By*	*a*	
	f	c	%	f	c	%	f	c	%	f	c	%
S44												
Subst.	48	17	35	93	32	34	33	8	24	26	11	42
Omis.	13	1	8				6	2	33			
Insert.				9	1	11				7	1	14
Total	61	18	30	102	33	32	39	10	26	33	12	36
S51												
Subst.	112	25	22	165	37	22	79	13	16	72	16	22
Omis.	31	3	10				33	6	18			
Insert.				27	3	11				17	3	18
Total	143	28	20	192	40	21	112	19	17	99	19	19
S53												
Subst.	147	36	25	206	48	23	108	25	23	135	34	25
Omis.	41	5	12				39	9	23			
Insert.				38	0	0				34	3	9
Total	188	41	22	244	48	20	147	34	23	169	37	22

Table 10–6 shows data on omission and insertion of articles. As indicated earlier, English noun phrases may have null determiners: the absence of a determiner is itself part of the system indicating whether noun phrases are general or specific, definite or indefinite. So insertions and omissions could be regarded as substitutions involving interactions with the null forms.

Omissions and Insertions

One type of insertion involves a shift from generic mass nouns to specific singular count nouns:

S53   a(3)   a(3)

... of / copper wire   and / tape

Opposite shifts from specific count to generic mass involve some omissions:

S51   ⱷ   ⱷ(3,1 corr.)

not so bad with *the* light.   He tied *a* string ...

Here's an example of a shift from specific mass to generic mass:

Ǫ
S44 on *the* grass

Another type of insertion of the article occurs in idioms where common nouns have null determiners:

S51   the(4, 2 corr.)   the(4, 2 corr.)   the(3), a
. . . parts in /place . . . taped it in / place   in /place

S53   the (3)   the(6)
     in / front of him . . . the babies in / town

An opposite example occurs in S53:

Ǫ
311 It's just 3 blocks from *the* school

Plural indefinites can become definite with insertion of *the*:

S44
                the(2)   the
208 There will be / prizes for / children who take . . .

Conversely plural definites can be indefinite with omission of *the:*

S51   Ǫ (2)
509 Just as he got *the* parts . . .

A number of omissions of articles occur preceding adjectives in noun phrases following a copula. These appear to be anticipation that the adjective is a predicate adjective modifying the subject:

S51   Ǫ (6)   Ǫ (3, 2 corr.)
311 . . . who was *a* real chemist   324 must have been *a* terrible

Plurals often take null determiners. Transforming plural nouns to singulars usually requires insertion of an article and dropping the plural suffix. Here are some examples:

                the class(2)
S53   a class(3)
310   . . . soon as *classes* let out for lunch

One other type of article insertion transforms a proper noun to a common noun phrase. That would be unlikely except in the special uses of basal readers. The name of the kitten in S44 is *Kitten Jones*. The readers produce shifts like the one above where *the* replaced *but* before *Kitten* and this insertion:

> the (1 corr.)
> 405 / Kitten had been playing . . .

As Table 10–6 shows, there are low rates of corrections on article insertions, 0–18%, on the three stories, and average rates on the article omission miscues. That reflects the phenomena involved in these two miscue types. Correction rates for all substitution miscues involving articles are a bit above average, particularly for S44. This latter may reflect high correction rates for the higher proportion of miscellaneous, 'other' miscues in S44.

In early research on errors in reading, the researchers were perplexed by the omission and insertion of words as common as *a* and *the*. They tended to regard such errors as reflecting careless or overly rapid reading. The examples and data from this study indicate that these miscues represent all of the phenomena we would expect to find as readers transact with texts, given the role that articles play in English noun phrases and the active use of null determiners in the noun phrase system.

General Conclusions

This study shows the transactional nature of the reading process. The miscues are strongly constrained by both the general functions of the determiners and their specific functions in particular text sequences. At the same time the miscues show the readers' effective control of the syntactic, semantic and pragmatic rules for the use of determiners and how determiners relate to noun phrases.

Distribution of Articles and Other Determiners

About 15% of running words in all three texts are common nouns. About half of these are preceded by articles. Some minor differences appear in distribution in the three stories but these seem to have more to do with text characteristics than anything having to do with the grade level of the story. S53 has an unusually low proportion of *the* and high proportion of *a* as compared to these and other texts studied. That seems to relate to its first person narration and other stylistic features involved in using an unusual proportion of indefinite noun phrases which take *a* rather than the definite *the*. These three stories are all from the same controlled vocabulary basal reader series. Simply speaking, what this all adds up to is that to create a cohesive, coherent, and comprehensible text one must use a considerable number and variety of noun phrases in ways that will involve the full range of the English determiner system. To make sense of such a text a reader must control that system whether that reader is in the second, fourth, or sixth grade.

Miscues on Determiners

If readers at all three grade levels must control the determiner system to make sense of the texts, then there should be similar patterns of miscues across the three grade groups and texts. Basically that's what the study showed.

Earlier, four questions were raised to be considered in this study. The findings will be discussed here in relation to each of those questions.

1. *What relevant patterns of miscues do the readers of each text and of the three texts combined show?*

Relevant and constrained are the words that describe the miscue patterns shown by the readers at all three grade levels in this study. Miscues on the text in general are 3 or 4 times as likely as they are on articles.

The subjects in this study represented eight populations (six at the second grade level) of American children of extremely varying linguistic backgrounds. Each group either spoke English as a second language or spoke a low status rural dialect of English. Yet the miscue patterns were so constrained and so similar across groups that there was no reason to separate the groups to compare miscue patterns.

This does not mean that there are no differences between English dialects in their use of determiners and no first language influences among our bilingual groups in reading English. The important thing is that no strong deviant pattern of miscues unrelated to the structure of the English noun phrase or the determiner system showed for any of our linguistically diverse groups. They all reflected at least receptive control of the determiner system in their miscues. The miscue patterns they produced were narrowly limited to a small set of words substituted for or replaced by the articles and other determiners and very selective insertion and omission of determiners. Miscues on particular articles or other determiners in specific instances varied considerably from none to several different substitutions to identical miscues produced by several different readers. There is no way to explain these patterns except that they require strong control of the system.

Except for a very small number of miscellaneous miscues, all miscues on *a/an* or *the* fall into seven categories. Four of these are determiners. All are function words except pronouns. One thing this pattern demonstrates is that in miscue analysis as in all scientific inquiry what doesn't happen is as important as what does. Nouns, verbs, adjectives, and adverbs are rarely ever switched with determiners. Such an overwhelming finding can't be accidental. It must reflect important constraints on the reading process.

Half or more of all the substitutions for and by articles are other determiners (including other articles). *The* is more likely to replace *a* representing a shift from indefinite to definite noun phrase than vice-versa. Sixth grade readers of S53 showed an opposite pattern which probably reflects the unusual proportion of *a* to *the* in text. Possessives were more likely to be interchanged with *the* than *a* and deictics were rarely involved in miscues with *a*. Both of these show a tendency to maintain the definite nature of the noun phrase.

There was a high rate of self-correction among the miscellaneous miscues that did not fit into the more common categories. In fact correction patterns for categories of article miscues followed closely the pattern that miscues are most likely to be corrected when they disrupt the meaning and/or syntax of the passage.

Article to article miscues are not random. They involve a shift between phoric and non-phoric noun phrases. Shifts from *the* to *a* are often in cataphoric phrases where the noun phrase is not made definite until the modifier which follows. Shifts from *a* to *the* are often in situations where the reader could assume a homophoric referent, one implicit in the situational context.

Article/possessive pronoun and article/deictic miscues basically make co-references more or less explicit. Shifting from an article to a possessive pronoun increases cohesion and makes ownership, which may be implicit, more explicit. Conversely, shifts to the article from the possessive pronoun seem to show the readers' inability to accept explicit ownership on the basis of their schemas.

Deictics often have exophoric referents in the speech acts represented in direct quotation. Others are involved in special emphasis. Shifts to *the* keeps the noun phrase definite while losing the pointing to or pointing up quality of the deictic. Rates of correction on both possessive and deictic involved miscues are highly variable depending on their effect on the meaningfulness of the text.

Pronoun, conjunction, and preposition miscues involving articles have a coincidental aspect to them, not in the sense that they are random, but in the sense that they occur at points in the texts where a pronoun or a conjunction or a preposition could occur which happens to be the same place where a reader might expect an article to occur. These then are pivotal points in the text where the syntax could go in more than one direction. The miscues show the readers' use of alternative predictions.

Miscues involving prepositions are not common. They seem to be due to anticipation of an alternate syntactic pattern and they show high correction rates. Conjunction miscues also have this coincidental quality but their correction rate is more variable because substitution of a conjunction for a determiner at the beginning of a clause could produce an acceptable sequence with a null determiner.

Almost all miscues involving pronouns and articles occur in subject noun phrases. They often follow strong prior context or come before nominalised verbs. They involve both *a* and *the*. More than half of the pronoun/article miscues are corrected.

Omissions and insertions of articles are more likely than other text words. Since noun phrases may use null articles, omissions and insertions of *the* and *a/an* can be considered substitutions. They frequently change the definiteness, specificity or phoricity of the noun phrase. Corrections are lower than average for article insertions and average for omissions. That reflects the fact that the insertions are less likely to produce a sequence the reader finds unacceptable.

2. *How do these patterns relate to syntactic, semantic, and pragmatic views of the referential functions of determiners?*

The patterns of miscues summarized under question 1 are very much those we would have expected. They show the readers' use of syntactic, semantic, and pragmatic schemes as they transact with the published text. Some miscues show strong expectations of definite or indefinite noun phrases on the basis of the readers' own schemata; others show miscues reflective of strong syntactic patterns in the prior context. Others show the interplay of the text pragmatics and the readers' own values and beliefs. Whether a particular text instance produces no miscues at all or several identical miscues, close examination reveals the patterns are predictable in terms of how the text and the readers use the determiner system. Considering the linguistic diversity and age range of our subjects, there is remarkably little in the entire range of article and other determiner miscues that cannot be easily related to the syntactic, semantic, and pragmatic features of text transactions.

3. *What do these patterns show about how readers process the relational aspects of noun phrases?*

There should be no doubt from the patterns the subjects of this study have produced that they are dealing with the relational aspects of the noun phrases in the texts they're reading in pretty sophisticated ways. Noun phrases either present new information or provide readers with reminders that the information is presupposed to already be available to the reader. So the noun phrases are either phoric in the sense that they relate to information available elsewhere in the text or context or they are non-phoric. This difference will be indicated by the subtle difference between whether *the* or *a* precedes a particular noun or whether there is no determiner at all in the noun phrase.

The patterns of miscues the readers have produced demonstrate that readers are not simply processing the published text linearly. If they were doing so miscues would be more evenly distributed across instances of articles and other determiners, correction patterns would not show such differences and anticipation of noun phrase structures would not be so evident. The readers are transacting with the text. They are constructing their own texts as they seek to construct meaning. And they are building reference and co-reference into the readers' texts. Whether a phoric relationship is *endophoric* (to the text) or *exophoric* (to the context) the references and co-references must be established in the readers' texts.

The noun phrases the readers are producing and their relations are not simply those of the published text. They are generated by the readers in transaction with the published text. A miscue that re-places *the* with *a* is an indefinite noun phrase being used by the reader where the author has used a definite noun phrase. The phoric relation that the author has presupposed no longer exists in the readers' text. On the other hand, when a reader uses *his* in a noun phrase where the text has used *the,* the reader is building more explicit cohesive information into the text.

In the process of transacting with the text the readers are build-ing their own texts using resources from the published text and from themselves. The readers use their own linguistic, cultural and concep-tual base. So the process in which the readers are engaged is very much like that of the original writer and the noun phrases are generated in much the same way. The difference, and it is an important one, is that the readers have the published text and its characteristics as resources.

4. *Are these patterns consistent with a transactional, psycholinguistically based theory of reading?*

Readers, through their miscues, show anticipation of where the text is going, what the syntactic structures will be, where new informa-tion will be introduced and where old information will be presupposed or referenced. They construct texts consistent with their expectations but they continuously monitor themselves by checking the sensibility of the text they are constructing and by checking against the ensu-ing published text. When the text is unacceptable or disconfirmed by further transactions with the published text then the readers reprocess and reconstruct their text and the meaning they are building.

So the mismatches between the published and the readers' texts, which show as miscues, are windows on this constructive and reconstructive process. That's why the miscues on articles and other determiners show the narrow constraints they do. That's why several readers from diverse populations can produce identical miscues at one article occurrence and none at another. That's why so small a set of words in so few categories occur as substitutions for or by articles. That's why the miscues demonstrate the strong control our diverse second, fourth, and sixth graders have over the determiner and noun phrase systems of English.

Miscues on articles and other determiners have always been present within miscue data. But the reading process is exceedingly complex and general miscue patterns reflect this great complexity. Focusing on miscues on determiners shows more strikingly than general miscue analysis the transactional, psycholinguistic process at work. There is no way to account for the strength of the miscue patterns in a model that sees the reader processing each letter and word sequentially. This analysis shows that the process of reading must be a constructive one in which predicting, inferring, sampling, confirming, and correcting strategies must be at work.

References

Goodman, K. (1983) *Text Features as They Relate to Miscues: Determiners.* Occasional Paper No. 8, Program in Language and Literacy, University of Arizona, Tucson, July.

Goodman, K. and Bird, L. (1982) *On the Wording of Texts: A Study of Intratext Word Frequency.* Occasional Paper No. 6, Program in Language and Literacy, University of Arizona, March.

Goodman, K. and Gespass, S. (1983) *Text Features as They Relate To Miscues: Pronouns,* Occasional Paper No. 7, Program in Language and Literacy, University of Arizona, Tucson, March.

Goodman, K. and Goodman, Y. (1978) Reading of American children whose Language is a Stable Rural Dialect of English or Language other than English. Unpublished Research Report. National Institute of Education. U.S. Department of Health, Education and Welfare, August.

Halliday, M. and Hasan, R. (1976) *Cohesion in English.* London: Longman Ltd.

Martin, J. (1978) *Reference as Semantic Choice.* Unpublished paper, Sydney, Australia.

Quirk, R. and Greenbaum, S. (1973) *A Concise Grammar of Contemporary English.* New York: Harcourt, Brace, Jovanovich.

Stenning. K. (1979) Articles, Quantifiers, and their Encoding in Textual Comprehension. In R. Freedle (ed), *New Directions in Discourse Processing.* Norwood, N.J.: Ablex.

Texts Analyzed

S44: Plowhead, R. G. (1965) "Kitten Jones." In E.A. Betts & C.M. Welch (eds), *Beyond Treasure Valley.* New York: American Book Company.

S51: Moore, L. (1965) "Freddie Miller, Scientist." In E.A. Betts & C.M. Welch (eds), *Adventures Here and There.* New York: American Book Company.

S53: Hayes, W.D. (1965) "My Brother is a Genius." In C.A. Betts & C.M. Welch (eds), *Adventures Now and Then.* New York: American Book Company.

Part Four

Reading As Language

In Chapter 1, *Reading, Writing and Written Texts: A Transactional Socio-Psycholinguistic View*, Goodman comprehensively discussed his transactional model of reading from linguistic, psycholinguistic, and sociolinguistic perspectives. The chapters in this part explore each of these perspectives in detail and help the reader better understand the development of Goodman's model. As in the other chapters in this book, Goodman and co-author Yetta M. Goodman connect discussions of reading theory with a theory of teaching reading.

Working from a linguistic perspective, Goodman argues that reading is about language, not merely words. When words are organized into sentences or paragraphs, the meaning of the latter is different from the sum of the meanings of the former. Language in an orderly flow serves as a vehicle for communication. No consistent correspondence ever exists between the written and spoken representations of language. Words are easier to read in context than in isolation, and their meanings are determined by contexts.

In the chapters that describe reading from a psycholinguistic perspective, the reader is viewed as an "active language user" and "intuitive grammarian." Since language is rule-governed, the reader's intuitive knowledge of language rules enables him or her to use predicting and confirming strategies as shown in miscues that occur at pivotal slots of syntactic structures. Miscues are shown to be the byproducts of the reading process, and Yetta and Kenneth Goodman use schema theory to explain the generation of miscues. They find from miscue analysis that it is harder to comprehend short language sequences than long ones. Whether it is oral or silent reading, reading in alphabetic or non-alphabetic languages, Goodman believes that the reading process is essentially the same.

Reading is also studied from a sociolinguistic perspective. On the issue of dialect in learning and reading, Goodman argues against the ethnocentric view and stresses that "No language, and no dialect of any language, is intrinsically superior to any other in coping with any specific area of human knowledge or with learning in general." Dialects should not be seen as disadvantages, Goodman argues. They should be allowed for supporting children to learn to read. Children should be encouraged to control their learning by bringing their own cultures, values, knowledge, and experiences into learning. Yetta and Kenneth Goodman argue that in-school learning should be connected with out-of-school learning and that the forces personal invention and social convention are of equal importance in the roles they serve in language development.

Authentic reading cannot be studied from any one perspective. That is why some arguments of one chapter also occur in others in this part, albeit with a different focus. The chapters from the 1980s and 1990s show that Goodman's view on learning and reading continues to develop and be refined with the introduction of some new ideas and the updating of existing ideas.

Word Perception: Linguistic Bases

Kenneth S. Goodman
Wayne State University, 1967

For decades the teaching of reading in this country has focused on words. Word recognition became the target of instruction. Word recognition skills were isolated and taught through drill, exercise, and controlled material. Words were counted, sorted according to frequency of occurrence, and listed. The word list became the main criterion in developing sequence in the basal reading program. Recently the book industry has discovered a large, profitable market for trade books based on the word lists.

Beginning reading instruction has had as its prime goal the establishment of a basic sight vocabulary, an inventory of words which the child knows in any and all situations. Certain assumptions underlie this focus on words. Language has been considered to be composed of words. These words have been regarded as being real entities with relatively stable meanings. Words have been presumed to exist in speech, in writing, in lists, and in dictionaries. The dictionary has been regarded as the final authority on word meaning and pronunciation.

Recent language knowledge produced by linguistic scientists makes these assumptions highly untenable. The linguist tells us that words exist only in the flow of language. Language is a code, a stream of sounds or graphic signs which can be used in a symbolic system to

This chapter first appeared in *Education*, Vol. 87, May 1967, pp. 539–543. Copyright (1987) by Project Innovation. Reprinted with the permission.

convey ideas, thoughts or desires/messages to others. In speech we use a system of intonation, the elements of which are slight variations in pitch, stress and juncture to set off sounds or groups of sounds from each other and thereby create symbols and patterns of symbols. In similar manner the telegraph operator uses a much simpler system of juncture, long and short pauses between sounds his key produces, to demark one symbol from the next or one pattern from the next.

The Word Concept

Ancient scholars must have noted the perceptible pauses in language and become aware that the elements which they marked off were recurrent in the same or slightly varied form. Further, in recurrent patterns with other recurrent elements these elements had rather consistent functions and often had consistent relationships to meanings. In such a manner the word concept developed. It was a useful conceptual tool in language study.

Since this concept developed words in written language have been demarked by extra spaces. The ancients carried the word concept further, classifying words (or parts of speech) into categories according to functions. The grammar they produced was a conceptual scheme of how the language worked that was borrowed from Greek to Latin to English in relatively unchanged form.

Modern linguists, using better tools and more careful descriptive techniques, have found this conceptual scheme faulty. They have also found that the word concept is not as useful in language study as the morpheme, a marked-off language molecule or combining form, the smallest unit of language which can bear a relationship to meaning. (For example *meaning* is composed of a free morpheme *mean* and a bound one *ing*.) But morphemes as well as words have no existence apart from language. Neither words nor morphemes can be defined, pronounced or classified outside of the stream of language. This is not only true of homophones and homographs (words which are alike in speech or writing respectively). It is true of all words, for example, *white* (1).

Word Recognition

Outside of a language context can *white* be firmly defined? It is probably a color. But it could be part of a chicken egg. It could be a man's name. It could be a substitute for Caucasian. It could be the opposite number of black in chess or red in politics.

Can *white* be pronounced from a list? By and large speakers of a particular dialect would say *white* in a fairly uniform way when reading it from a list. But consider these sentences. *The President lives in the White House. I live in a white house. Is this the White house?* (The one the White family lives in?) The intonation used in saying *white* makes a critical difference in the meanings of these sentences.

Can *white* be classified? It is an adjective in this sentence: *They waved a white flag.* But in this sentence it's a noun: *White wins in two moves. White* can be inflected as a verb, *He will whiten my shoes,* or compared as an adverb, *Cheer washes whiter. White* can be classified only when it occurs in a language context.

If a word can't be defined, pronounced, or classified out of the flow of language it can't be recognized. Teaching children sight vocabulary is teaching them to name words, not to recognize them. When a child reads words from a list he is calling their names, and this task of calling the names of words from a list is a much more difficult task than reading.

In a study conducted by this writer, first-grade readers were able to read two out of three words in a story which they had been unable to name on a word list. Second-graders could read three out of four such words, while third-graders could get better than four out of five (2).

Two Contexts

With our preoccupation with words in early reading instruction we have tended to consider context as one among many aids to word recognition. But there are two basic misconceptions in this view.

First, it makes word recognition an end in itself. This it never is. The recognition of words merely contributes to the comprehension of meaning. A confusion of means and ends results in misplaced emphasis in research and instruction.

Second, the nature and complexity of what context is and how it operates has been largely ignored. In reality there are two distinct but interacting contexts; one is the semantic or *meaning* context, the other the syntactic or structural context. Most of the meager attention to context has been concerned with the influence of recognition of an unknown word on the meanings of other words in the sentence. The vital role of the language structure, the grammatical patterning of the language in making language comprehensible and in framing and delimiting and defining sentence elements has been overlooked. This is our concern here.

Comprehension, reconstructing the message of a language utterance, involves rapid automatic reaction not only to significant differences in sounds or letters, but also to a number of other signal systems which provide cues to meaning. The order of words (or morphemes), intonation, inflection, and key function words play vital roles in cueing meaning in English. If words are extracted from the flow of language, all or most of these cue systems are eliminated. The child is left with only letters, configuration, and memory to use in recalling the name of a word. In a sense asking a child to recognize a word out of the syntactic context is like asking him to identify a picture of the eye or ear or mouth of a familiar person. He uses these interrelated features in identifying the familiar person but he can't identify the features out of the context of the whole.

Children Know Grammar

Fortunately, when the English-speaking child begins the task of learning to read and write English he has already virtually mastered the structure of the language. He could not listen and comprehend or speak and be understood if he had not mastered that structure.

Consider this simple statement: *The dog bit the cat.* If a child hears this he has no trouble understanding the message it conveys. He knows which animal was the aggressor and which the victim. He hears and knows because he has learned the very common subject-verb-object sentence pattern in English. Nothing in modern English distinguishes cat or dog as subject from cat or dog as object, except the position of each in the pattern. It is pattern that makes it possible for these words to convey meaning; it is pattern that the child uses automatically to comprehend as he listens.

It is this same knowledge of English patterns which he uses in comprehending what he reads. In speech the very errors a child is likely to make indicate his growing control over the grammatical structure of language. Thus a young child might say, *"The dog bited the cat."* The verb is wrong but it represents his over-generalization of the most common way of indicating past tense in English.

Expectation and Perception

The child's deeply internalized knowledge of the system of sounds and grammar of the dialect of English he speaks sets up expectations which strongly influence his perceptions and, in fact, his ability to perceive. The reason we can follow a familiar language or dialect more easily than an unfamiliar one is that we are constantly able to anticipate the perceptual input. More than a little of what we think we perceived is what we guess we heard or saw. This is true of phonemes (the unit sounds of language). It is true of letters. It is true of words.

Language would be a hopeless jumble incapable of carrying meaning without structure and system. Thus the meaning of a sentence or paragraph is not the sum of the meanings of a sequence of individual words. It is a unity created by meaning-bearing morphemes (words if you prefer) organized and unified in a language structure.

This structure has deeply imbedded itself in the mind of children by the time they begin learning to read. They organize their aural perceptions through it as they listen to language. They must come to the point where they can organize their visual perceptions according to the expectations the language structure sets up as they read. This is essentially what we mean when we say they must perceive and read phrases and large sequences rather than letters and/or words. Four systems are operating in this perceptual process:

(a) *Pattern*. In English syntax, pattern is the most important system. There are a small number of basic patterns with many variations and transformations. In the earlier example, *The dog bit the cat,* we find the familiar subject-verb-object pattern. Children who cannot begin to describe nouns will invariably supply one if one is left out in this pattern: The. ... bit the. ...

(b) *Inflection*. This can be considered as one system of pattern markers. Some morphemes of English are bound forms; that is they never occur separately. Inflectional suffixes are bound forms that occur with certain classes of free morphemes: nouns or verbs for example. In: *The dogs chased the cats,* the *s* represents the plural noun morpheme and thus confirms that *dogs* and *cats* are nouns. Similarly, *d* marks the verb as past and confirms that chased is a verb.

(c) *Function* words are usually small relatively meaningless words that also serve as pattern markers. Together with the inflectional suffixes they set up the pattern and structure of the sentence and thus link together and define the relationship between meaning-bearing morphemes. *The ...... s are not ..... ing ...... s,* is an example of an empty structure. It has no meaning but it is capable of carrying meaning if meaning-bearing words are included.

(d) *Intonation* is the fourth language system. Through variations of pitch, stress, and pause speakers mark off units and patterns and communicate fine differences in meaning. Punctuation partly represents this in written language.

These four systems do not need to be taught to children who speak English. They have already learned them. They are the linguistic bases of perception in reading. It is only necessary that materials and methods make it possible for children to use what they know.

Research Insights

Here are some insights this writer derived from linguistically based research: Words are likely to be first perceived by children as recurrent elements in familiar wholes, then as familiar elements in new wholes composed of familiar elements and, finally, as known entities recognizable even out of language context. Children do not start reading with "word sense." The white spaces around words are not enough to make them perceive *a man* as two words and *away* as one word. They develop this sense slowly.

Inflectional suffixes (*s, es, ing, ed,* etc.) become meaningful entities very early for children. Other bound morphemes, derivational suffixes (*er, ation,* for example), are not recognized as language units until much later. Prefixes are not seen as sub-units until the child's reading ability is very well developed.

Certain function words, among them prepositions and articles, are perceived in reading not as graphic entities but as grammatical signals. Even beginners will substitute *a* for *the* for example: since there is no graphic similarity, it's clear that the child identifies the function rather than the letters themselves.

Perhaps the most significant insight from this writer's research is that children can literally teach themselves to recognize unfamiliar words as they read. They do this by regressing, by going back and gathering more information when they have made an error so that they can correct it. If we understand language structure as it relates to reading we may be able to help children teach themselves to read.

Bibliography

1. Smith, F. Brooks, Robert Meredith, and Kenneth S. Goodman. *Language in the Educational Process.* In press. (New York: Dodd Mead).

2. Goodman, Kenneth S. "A Linguistic Study of Cues and Miscues in Reading." *Elementary English* (October, 1965), pp. 639–643.

Linguistic Aspects of Reading

Chapter Twelve

Words and Morphemes in Reading

Kenneth S. Goodman
Wayne State University, 1969

As written language developed and the alphabetic principle evolved, graphic displays shifted from direct representation of meaning to representation of oral language. Letter sequences were designed to represent sound sequences. Much later the device of using extra space at appropriate intervals in written language to create segmental units was introduced and the already existent term 'word' was applied to these units.[1] Like spelling patterns, word boundaries stabilized and conventions grew up that were in fact much more resistant to change than comparable phenomena in oral language. As language analysis developed, particularly in the form of dictionary making, written language and not oral language became its vehicle. The word was indeed a useful unit. Its range of meanings could be recorded, its grammatical functions listed, its relationships to other words induced. Just as spelling was intended to reflect phonology so written words were intended to correspond to actual segments of speech (even the term 'parts of speech' suggests this). But initial inadequacies in understanding and transcribing the segmental units of oral language created a gap. As the word concept in written language codified and oral language continued to change the lack of fit between oral and written language on this segmental level widened.

This chapter first appeared in *Psycholinguistics and the Teaching of Reading*, K. Goodman and J. Fleming, (eds.), Newark, DE: IRA, 1969, pp. 25–33. Copyright (1969) by the International Reading Association. Reprinted with permission.

When linguists began to study segmental units in speech they found the need for a new term, 'morpheme,' to describe these units. Words, those conventional units of written language separated by white space, do not really exist in speech. The word has become a unit of written language.

All this of course would be of only academic interest, if it were not that much of the research on language and the teaching of language has been based on the assumption that (1) words are natural units of language (2) words in print correspond to words in speech. In reading in particular the focus on words has grown in great part from the mistaken assumption that they were the gestalts of language. Thus when Gray and others recognized that reading instruction had to deal with something more than matching letters and sounds they moved to a word focus. They took for granted that words were perceptible units even to beginning readers. Reading came to be closely tied to the acquisition of an expanding sight vocabulary, a repertoire of learned wholes. Though this is of course an oversimplification of what its detractors called the 'look-say' approach to reading, the best proof of how word centered it was is in the evidence from research that in reading tests based on this approach simple word recognition tests correlate quite highly with total scores. Such correlations have been interpreted as proving the validity of word recognition focus in reading instruction. On the contrary, all that they prove is that children tend to learn what they are taught. Ironically, if we test the ability to recognize words as evidenced by our ability to match their printed form with an oral equivalent, children given phonics training tend to do somewhat better than their sight word peers in the stages when the repertoires of the latter group are limited. Chall and others have taken this as evidence that phonics, as such, is a necessary base for early reading instruction. If one could equate language with words and reading was only a matter of finding the oral equivalent for the written form then this perhaps would be true. The question would be simply whether to use a method in which words were taught and the phonic relationships induced or discovered by the learners (word centered) or a method in which phonic relationships were taught and words were acquired through phonic attacks (phonics centered). In her recent comparison of studies of reading methods Chall used seven basic criteria.[2] Four of them involve word recognition in some sense, one is letter-sound correspondences, one involves speed and only one involved comprehension. The obvious focus was on the word as an end in itself. Thus 'the great debate' is caught within the confines of the word. If we can clarify the relationships of words to written language and to comparable (but not corresponding) units of oral language we may not only shed light on the phonics-word controversy but perhaps demonstrate that the debate is quite obsolete: a relic of the history of reading instruction.

Modern insight into the relationships between oral and written English on the letter-sound level has already shown that these relationships are much more complex than letters having sounds, or letters representing sounds or phonemes corresponding to graphemes. This complexity is not simply a case of regularities and irregularities as has been commonly assumed even by many linguists who turned their attention to reading. What appears as irregularity to the casual observer results actually from the different ways that phonemes (oral symbols) relate to oral language and graphemes (written symbols) relate to written language. As Venezky has indicated, we find regularity if we treat the symbols as part of separate systems each with a set of rules governing their patterning.[3] The relationships are between these patterned systems rather than between the unitary symbols themselves. Thus the common sounds in 'church,' 'situation,' and 'watch' are irregularly represented if we match one unit of speech to one of writing but quite regularly represented if we match patterns with patterns. Phonics, then, must be more broadly redefined if it is to have any meaning at all. We must see it as the complex set of relationships between the phonological system of oral language and the graphic system of written language. Such a definition will also help us to see that variations in the phonological system among dialects of English are accompanied by variations in the phonics relationships since the graphic system tends to be stable across dialects.

We must view words and morphemes also as segmental units which relate through rules to the patterned systems of which they are part. Both words and morphemes tend to take on a reality in our minds they do not quite deserve because of their apparent stability in a variety of linguistic settings. Instead of regarding them as useful constructs for dividing longer units of language (sentences, utterances, sequences of discourse) into segmental units we begin to regard the longer units as accumulations of words or morphemes.

In actuality, of course, these molecular segments have no existence apart from language structures. What we call their meaning is in reality the portion of the meaning of a larger unit that may be assigned to one segment. What we write in dictionaries is the range of possible meanings assignable to a given word in the sentences in which it may occur. As many entries are made in the dictionary for a word as there are ranges of meaning for the word. The meaning of a sentence depends on the words or morphemes that compose it but it is always more than the sum of their meanings. Similarly one may speak of the grammatical functions of words or morphemes but these are only the portions of the syntax of a sentence assignable to the segmental unit.

In Chomsky's view the syntactic component of language begins with a base consisting of context-free rules, the function of which is "to define a certain system of grammatical relations that determine semantic interpretation and to specify an abstract underlying order of elements that makes possible the functioning of the transformational rules."[4]

The end of the generative process results in choice of specific forms of morphemes in specific sequences that fulfill grammar-meaning-phonology constraints that have been imposed by the rules.

Here is a simple discourse that illustrates how this works

Mother: Mary, will you ask Jimmy to hang up his jacket?

Mary: Hey Jim, hang your stuff up.

Jim: I did.

Here each speaker is conveying essentially the same information concerning the hanging up of the jacket. The situation in which the discourse is occurring and its sequence evoke a set of rules that result in varying actual utterances. Jim, in fact, need only use a pro-noun and a pro-verb to represent the entire sequence: James hung up his jacket. He is able to communicate his response effectively with no resort to meaningful terms. Literally he cites an underlying grammatical pattern. Alternate responses could have been similarly communicated: "Yes, I will"; "No, I won't"; "I don't have to" (pronounced hafta). This last could elicit the following repartee:

Mary: You got to (gotta).

Jim: I don't either.

Mary: You do too.

Jim: Why?

Mary: Mom said so.

Only in the last do we get any new meaningful element and even there "so" represents "that James should hang up his jacket."

It could serve no useful function to describe in detail the sequence of rules required to produce these utterances. The important point is that language in its ordered flow is the medium of communication and not words or morphemes.

In receptive phases of language, reading and listening, we work backward from the surface structure deriving the rules and subsequently the deep structure. But we cannot and do not treat words in print or morphemes in speech as independent entities. We must discover the grammatical relations in order to determine the semantic interpretation.

Educated, literate speakers of language have learned to think of words as self-evident entities, and to impose the characteristics of written words on oral language. Their perception of language is influenced but this should not be confused with reality.

The remainder of this chapter will explore morphemes and words as segmental units, the lack of one-to-one correspondence between them and the implications for reading instruction.

Morphemes, Oral Language Molecules

Like the molecule the morpheme is the smallest segment which has all the basic characteristics of the larger system. The morpheme's capability of carrying syntactic and/or semantic information distinguishes it from smaller segmental units, phonemes, that must be integrated into morphemes before they can really be considered linguistic units (actually a few morphemes are only one phoneme ions).

It is useful to treat morphemes as being divided into two classes, free and bound. Free morphemes occur in a variety of settings with relative freedom from accompaniment of other specific morphemes. Bound morphemes occur in more limited settings and always in precise relationship to another relatively limited set of morphemes, usually free morphemes.

In 'walked,' 'walk' is a free morpheme and 'ed' is a bound morpheme, one of a small number of bound morphemes in English that carry primarily grammatical information. This bound morpheme ('ed') always occurs as a suffix of certain verbs. It has three basic variants (allomorphs); they occur in complementary distribution with the choice made on phonological grounds; the final consonant in the base determines the particular allomorph. This type of inflectional suffix is a remnant of what was once a more general aspect of English grammar.

Other bound morphemes serve derivational functions and carry more semantic information. The 'er' in 'worker' makes a noun of the verb 'work' and adds the 'someone who' meaning. Other bound morphemes take the form of semantic prefixes. The problem with these is that they range from old dead Latin bound morphemes to current more active ones. These dead forms have lost their ability to combine freely with all appropriate morphemes. In a sense they have lost their separateness. In verb formations English speakers seem to prefer to use common verbs with particles to produce discontinuous verbs rather than use older forms with prefixes. We don't 'dissect' we 'cut up.' We would rather 'eat up' than 'consume.' It's easier for us to 'tear down' than 'demolish.' Or at least it seems easier because this verb-particle system is a live one that can be used flexibly to handle meanings. There is even a tendency in English to supply redundantly another carrier of the same meaning as the prefix. Thus we say 'combine with,' 'reflect back,' 'attach to,' 'enter into,' 'descend from,' 'eject from,' 'provide for,' 'submerge under.' The bases that prefixes attach to are frequently not free English morphemes but also old Latin ones which only occur in such combinations and hence must be regarded as bound morphemes themselves. In a sequence like 'combinations' one can find five bound morphemes but no free morphemes.

The degree that particular bound morphemes will be apparent segmental units to any given speaker of the language and that he will be able to separate a given bound morpheme from a base form is variable. Most speakers treat words like 'descend' as single units.

Intonation, particularly relative stress, is very much involved in relating morphemes, and influences some phonological options. Verb-noun pairs such as 'produce/produce,' 'contract/contract,' 'record/record' are examples of how the relationship between morphemes produced by intonation affects meaning. In the sentence "All blackboards aren't black boards" we can distinguish by the relative stress, boards that are black from those that are for use with chalk. The closer relationship between the two morphemes in 'blackboard' than in 'black board' results in what we have called compounds (two free morphemes united). And of course we do represent that relationship in print by an absence of white space or a hyphen in place of the white space. But neither device consistently represents this compounding. 'Blood test' is a compound but it is not joined when used as a noun ("He took a blood test") and hyphenated when used as a verb ("We blood-tested our chicks"). We have 'eye doctor,' 'eyebrow,' 'eyelid,' 'eye-catching.' All have the stress pattern of compounds. The conventions of print do not directly correspond to the intonational devices of oral language.

One phase of intonation used to relate morphemes more or less closely is juncture; the length of pause between morphemes can be varied. 'Nitrate' has a different kind of juncture than 'night rate.' However these junctures are only relatively different and in the flow of speech it is often quite difficult to discern any difference. A speaker can of course intentionally exaggerate the juncture to be sure ambiguity is avoided. But is a certain toothpaste 'proved effective' or 'proved defective'?

What further complicates things is that morphophonemic rules cut across morpheme boundaries in the flow of speech. The same rule that operates in 'situation' applies to 'can't you' (cancha). We find 'education' and 'don't you' (doncha). Certain sequences involving these morphophonemic rules are so common that their constituents are apparently not distinguished by young speakers. 'Have to' (hafta), 'going to' (gonna), 'with him' (with'm), 'must have' (must'v), 'should have' (should'v) are examples. Only the meager set of contractions recognized in print represent this phenomenon and even those are avoided in some situations. One unit in speech is represented by two in print. The resulting problems affect both reading and spelling. The problem does not confine itself to children. Adults often have difficulty distinguishing segmental units in idiomatic or archaic expressions. Recently an undergraduate used this spelling in a paper I received: 'anotherwords' (in other words). Teachers are quite familiar with what happens when children are asked to write the Pledge to the flag or the national anthem. I must confess for many years I was saying 'in the visible' (indivisible).

Jones has indicated that the difficulty in determining junctures is not confined to the uninitiated. Phoneticians employed in her research study frequently could not find expected differences in pause length. Prepositions and articles on the basis of their limited privilege of occurrence and the junctures that separated them from the next morpheme behaved very much like prefixes.[5]

Any one can confirm the difficulty of using purely intonational cues in segmenting the flow of speech into free and bound morphemes by listening to a brief statement in an unfamiliar language and trying to guess how many units are heard by a speaker of the language. Native speakers do of course bring their user's knowledge of the language to bear on the same task. Stable units are perceived by them as segments of wholes.

Recent research on child language development has demonstrated that children at early ages do produce language that can be segmented into morphemes.[6] Berko has also demonstrated that children have mastered rules relating to inflectional suffixes, as demonstrated by their ability to produce the expected allomorph for nonsense bases she supplied.[7] It's obvious that parallel to their mastery of grammatical and phonological rules children are also acquiring a sense of language units. Parents are well aware of a stage when children begin to ask such questions as "What does ___ mean?", selecting a unit from language they have heard. Some of the funny sounding language children produce consisting of unsuccessful efforts at interchanging units are assumed to be equivalent by the child. It must be reiterated, however, that children speak in language, not words, and that the sense of morphemes does not precede their use of sentences. The whole is not a combining of parts; the part is differentiated out of the whole.

Words, Written Language Molecules

Words, unlike morphemes, are very easy to identify as units. One can pick up a page written in an unfamiliar language that employs words as graphic units and easily count the number of words. In producing written language identifying word units creates a more difficult problem; ultimately the producer of written language must remember what is and what is not a word.

To the literate, words are familiar units in language sequences and in non-linguistic settings. Words occur in lists, dictionaries, and in fact anywhere that we choose to put them. Of course one can recite a list of morphemes too. But that's not very common. The trouble is, again, that words are not the real entities that they appear to be. They retain their physical appearance as entities but they lose much of their semantic and syntactic quality as language units. A list of five words is not at all comparable to a five-word sentence. This confusion of words as entities and as units of written language has been evident in a great deal of reading research and practice. It has also been evident in much of the research on so-called verbal learning. Sometimes such research has even dealt with lists of word-like nonsense assuming that the ability to deal with such nonsense could be directly interpreted as language ability.

One-to-One Relationships

In the previous sections, some aspects of the lack of correspondence between words and morphemes have been pointed out. Problems with compounds, affixes and intonation were discussed. The illusion of a one-to-one correspondence between oral language units and written language units appears to stem from the treatment of words as entities. The oral name for the written word (in isolation from language) is assumed to be a unit of oral language.

In a sentence such as the following this illusion of one-to-one correspondence is illustrated: "I'm going to have to find a way to get away tomorrow." One word 'away' and two words 'a way' sound very much the same. Morphophonemic rules cut across morpheme boundaries in 'going to,' 'have to,' and 'to get.' The literate reader is not bothered by this lack of close correspondence, in fact he will, in general, not be aware of it. He thinks that he reads every word, one at a time.

But for one learning to read this lack of correspondence will cause problems. If he matches oral names with graphic word shapes he becomes a word caller and may lose the meaning. He is dealing with print arranged in words but he must make his associations on higher language levels if he is to comprehend.

Words in Reading

It is no great revelation to first grade teachers that children frequently don't have any idea what words are. Perhaps what has been said here will begin to explain why they don't. The implications of this understanding should lead in two directions; (1) Less word-centeredness in reading materials and instruction. (2) More careful development of word sense in beginners where it is necessary and possible.

Several simple steps can help to move the teaching of reading away from word focus. Essentially they involve shifting focus to comprehension; the goal of reading instruction becomes more effective reading for more complete comprehension. Instead of word attack skills, sight vocabularies, and word perception the program must be designed to build comprehension strategies. The presentation of words in isolation should be avoided wherever possible. Words are harder to read in isolation than in context and the isolation of words makes them ends in themselves.[8] Children learning to read should see words always as units of larger, meaningful units. In that way they can use the correspondences between oral and written English within the semantic and syntactic contexts. As children induce these correspondences they will develop the strategies for using them in actual reading. They will be spared the need for transferring the correspondences from non-reading to reading.

As proficiency develops in reading, silent reading should predominate so that written language will become parallel to oral language; the child will then learn to go from print directly to meaning with no need to resort to oral language.

The development of word sense is something that must be nurtured as reading progresses. Children will differentiate words from graphic language wholes just as they have learned to differentiate morphemes in oral language. First a learner knows a graphic sentence; then he knows familiar words in new sentences; finally he knows words anywhere including lists. Teachers can assist children by helping them to see phrases as subdivisions of sentences and words as recurrent elements within them.

Word meanings are also differentiated out of varied contexts. As the reader meets a word in various sentences he begins to form an idea of the part of the meaning assignable to that word. He then tests his definition in subsequent encounters. A dictionary can confirm his definition or sharpen it but it cannot supply a definition.

Conclusion

There will always be some problems in learning to read that result from the lack of close correspondence between the units of oral and written language. Instruction based on an understanding of language and language units can help to minimize these problems.

Notes

1. Introduction of white space to separate words did not take place until about the eleventh century. E.B. Huey, "The Psychology and Pedagogy of Reading," Macmillan, 1908, reprinted Cambridge, Mass.: MIT Press, 1968.

2. Jeanne Chall, "Learning to Read: The Great Debate," New York: McGraw-Hill, 1967.

3. Richard Venezky, English Orthography: Its Graphical Structure and Its Relation to Sound, "Reading Research Quarterly," vol. II, no. 3.

4. Noam Chomsky, "Aspects of the Theory of Syntax," Cambridge, Mass.: MIT Press, 1965, p. 141.

5. Margaret Hubbard Jones, Some Thoughts on Perceptual Units in Language Processing, in "The Psycholinguistic Nature of the Reading Process," Goodman, ed., Wayne State University Press, in press.

6. David McNeil, Developmental Psycholinguistics, in "The Genesis of Language," Smith and Miller (eds), MIT Press, 1966.

7. Jean Berko, The Child's Learning of English Morphology, "Word," vol. XIV, 1958, pp. 150–77.

8. Kenneth S. Goodman, A Linguistic Study of Cues and Miscues in Reading, "Elementary English," October 1965, pp. 639–43.

Psycholinguistic Aspects of Reading

Chapter Thirteen

To Err Is Human: Learning About Language Processes by Analyzing Miscues

Yetta M. Goodman and Kenneth S. Goodman
University of Arizona, 1994

Everything people do, they do imperfectly. This is not a flaw but an asset. If we always performed perfectly, we could not maintain the tentativeness and flexibility that characterize human learning and the ways we interact with our environment and with one another. This model of imperfection causes us as researchers not to worry about why people fall short of perfection; rather, we are concerned with why people do what they do and with what we can learn about language processes from observing such phenomena.

The power of language users to fill knowledge gaps with missing elements, to infer unstated meanings and underlying structures, and to deal with novel experiences, novel thoughts, and novel emotions derives from the ability to predict, to guess, to make choices, to take risks, to go beyond observable data. We must have the capability of being wrong lest the limits on our functioning be too narrowly constrained.

This chapter first appeared in *Theoretical Models and Processing of Reading*, 1994, Ruddell, R., M. Ruddell, & H. Singer, (eds.), International Reading Association, Newark, DE, pp. 104–123. It is based on and updated from work published in "Learning abut Psycholinguistic Processes by Analyzing Oral Reading" (*Harvard Educational Review, 47*(3), 317–333), and "To Err is Human" (*New York University Education Quarterly, 12*(4), 14–19). Copyright (1994) by the International Reading Association. Reprinted with permission.

Unlike the computer, people do not exhibit specifically programmed, totally dependable responses time after time. We are tentative, we act impulsively, we make mistakes, and we tolerate our own deviations and the mistakes of others.

If you doubt that perfection in human behavior is the exception rather than the norm, consider how intensely a performer of any kind— athlete, actor, musician, writer, reader—must practice to achieve anything approaching error-free performance. If you doubt our view of how people deal with mistakes, think about the proofreader who skips over errors in a text or the native North Americans who deliberately insert flaws in handicrafts to remind themselves that the crafts are the work of human hands.

Miscues: Unexpected Responses

For more than 25 years we have studied the reading process by analyzing the miscues (or unexpected responses) of children and adults orally reading written texts. Ken Goodman coined this use of the word miscue because of the negative connotation and history of the term error. The term miscue reveals that miscues are unexpected responses cued by readers' linguistic or conceptual cognitive structures.

We started with the assumption that everything that happens during reading is caused, that a person's unexpected responses are produced in the same way and from the same knowledge, experience, and intellectual processes as expected responses. Reading aloud involves continuous oral response by the reader, which allows for comparisons between expected and observed responses. Such comparisons reveal the reader's knowledge, experience, and intellectual processes. Oral readers are engaged in comprehending written language while they produce oral responses. Because an oral response is generated while meaning is being constructed, it not only is a form of linguistic performance but also provides a powerful means of examining readers' process and underlying competence.

Miscue analysis requires several conditions. The written material must be new to the readers and complete with a beginning, middle, and end. The text needs to be long and challenging enough to produce sufficient numbers of miscues for patterns to appear. In addition, readers receive no help and are not interrupted. At most, if readers hesitate for more than 30 seconds, they are urged to guess, and only if hesitation continues are they told to keep reading even if it means skipping a word or phrase. Except that it takes place orally and not silently, the reading during miscue analysis requires as normal a situation as possible.

Depending on the purpose of miscue analysis research, readers often have been provided with more than one reading task. Various fiction and nonfiction reading materials have been used, including stories and articles from basal readers, textbooks, trade books, and magazines. Readers have been drawn from elementary, secondary, and adult populations and from a wide range of proficiency and racial, linguistic, and national backgrounds. Studies have been conducted in many languages other than English and in various writing systems (Goodman, Brown, & Marek, 1993).

Betsy's oral reading of the folktale "The Man Who Kept House" (from McInnes, Gerrard, & Ryckman, 1964, pp. 282–283) is used throughout for examples (Goodman, Watson, & Burke, 1987). The story has 68 sentences, 711 words. Betsy, a 9-year-old from Toronto, was selected by her teacher as representative of students with reading difficulties. Betsy read the story hesitantly, although in most places she read with appropriate expression. Below are the first 14 sentences (s1–s14) from the story, with the actual printed text on the left and the transcript of Betsy's oral reading on the right.

Text	*Transcript*
s1 Once upon a time there was a woodman who thought that no one worked as hard as he did.	Once upon a time there was a woodman. He threw . . . who thought that no one worked as hard as he did.
s2 One evening when he came home from work, he said to his wife, "What do you do all day while I am away cutting wood?"	One evening when he . . . when he came home from work, he said to his wife, "I want you do all day . . . what do you do all day when I am always cutting wood?"
s3 "I keep house," replied the wife, "and keeping house is hard work."	"I keep . . . I keep house," replied the wife, "and keeping . . . and keeping . . . and keeping house is and work."
s4 "Hard work!" said the husband.	"Hard work!" said the husband.
s5 "You don't know what hard work is!	"You don't know what hard work is!

s6	You should try cutting wood!"	You should try cutting wood!"
s7	"I'd be glad to," said the wife.	"I'll be glad to," said the wife.
s8	"Why don't you do my work some day?	"Why don't you ... Why don't You do my work so ... some day?
s9	I'll stay home and keep house," said the woodman.	I'll start house and keeping house," said the woodman.
s10	"If you stay home to do my work, you'll have to make butter, carry water from the well, wash the clothes, clean the house, and look after the baby," said the wife.	"If you start house ... If you start home to do my work, well you'll have to make bread, carry ... carry water from the well, wash the clothes, clean the house, and look after the baby," said the wife.
s11	"I can do all that," replied the husband.	"I can do that ... I can do all that," replied the husband.
s12	"We'll do it tomorrow!"	"Well you do it tomorrow!"
s13	So the next morning the wife went off to the forest.	So the next day the wife went off to the forest.
s14	The husband stayed home and began to do his wife's job.	The husband stayed home and began to do his work.

Betsy's performance reveals her language knowledge. These examples are not unusual; what Betsy does is done by other readers. She processes graphophonic information: most of her miscues show a graphic and phonic relationship between the expected and the observed response. She processes syntactic information: she substitutes noun for noun, verb for verb, noun phrase for noun phrase, verb phrase for verb phrase. She transforms phrases, clauses, and sentences: she omits an intensifier, changes a dependent clause to an independent clause, shifts a *wh* question sentence to a declarative sentence. She draws on her conceptual and linguistic background and struggles toward meaning by regressing, correcting, and reprocessing as necessary. She predicts appropriate structures and monitors her own success based on the degree to which she is making sense. She develops and uses psychosociolinguistic strategies as she reads. There is nothing random about her miscues.

Reading Miscues and Comprehension

Since we understand that the brain is the organ of human information processing, that it is not a prisoner of the senses but controls the sensory organs and selectively uses their input, we should not be surprised that what is said in oral reading is not what the eye has seen but what the brain has generated for the mouth to report. The text is what the brain responds to; the oral output reflects the underlying competence and the psychosociolinguistic processes that have generated it. When expected and observed responses match, we get little insight into this process. When they do not match and a miscue results, researchers have a window on the reading process.

We have come to believe that the strategies readers use when miscues occur are the same as when there are no miscues. Except for s3, s8, and s9, all of Betsy's miscues produced fully acceptable sentences or were self-corrected. By analyzing whether miscues are semantically acceptable with regard to the whole text or are acceptable only with regard to the prior portion of text, it is possible to infer the strategies readers actively engage in. s2 provides a powerful example. Betsy reads, *I want you do all day,* hesitates, reads slowly, and eventually—after a 23-second pause—reconsiders, probably rereads silently, and self-corrects the initial clause in this sentence. The verb *said* in the sentence portion prior to her miscue and her knowledge about what husbands might say when they come home from work allowed her to predict *I want you. . . .* After she self-corrects the first part of the dialogue, she reads, *when I am always cutting wood* for *while I am away cutting wood* with confidence and continues her reading. These two substitution miscues (*when* for *while* and *always* for *away*) produce a clause that fits with the meaning of the rest of the story. The more proficient the reader, the greater the proportion of semantically acceptable miscues or miscues acceptable with the prior portion of the text that are self-corrected (Goodman & Burke, 1973).

In s12 Betsy produces, *Well you do it tomorrow* instead of *We'll do it tomorrow.* Although it seems that Betsy simply substitutes *well* for *we'll* and inserts *you,* the miscues are shown to be more complex when we examine how the phrase and clauses are affected by the miscues. Betsy substitutes an interjection prior to the subject *you* to substitute for the noun and the beginning of the verb phrase represented by the contraction *we'll*. In addition, Betsy shifts intonation to indicate that the wife rather than the husband is talking. Apparently Betsy predicted that the wife was going to speak to maintain the pattern of husband-wife conversation that is established by the author in the previous sections (s2 and s11). Although the author's intended meaning is changed, the sentence is semantically acceptable within the story.

A reader's predicting and confirming strategies are evident in miscues that are acceptable with the text portion prior to the miscues. Such miscues often occur at pivotal points in sentences, such as junctures between clauses or phrases. At such points the author may select from a variety of linguistic structures to compose the text; the reader has similar options but may predict a structure that is different than the author's. Consider these examples from Betsy's reading:

	Text	*Transcript*
s38	"I'll light a fire in the fireplace and the porridge will be ready in a few minutes."	"I'll light a fire in the fireplace and I'll . . . and the porridge will be ready in a flash . . . a few minutes."
s48	Then he was afraid that she would fall off.	Then he was afraid that the . . . that she would fall off.

Betsy's prediction of *I'll* instead of *the* in the second clause of the first example is logical. Since *and* often connects two parallel items, it is not an unreasonable prediction that the second clause will begin with the subject of the first. However, when *I'll* does not fit with the second clause, Betsy confidently disconfirms her prediction and immediately self-corrects. The miscue substitution of *the* for *she* in the second example is also at a pivotal point in the sentence. Whenever an author uses a pronoun to refer to a previously stated noun phrase, a reader may revert to the original noun phrase. The reverse phenomenon also occurs. When the author chooses a noun for which the referent has been established earlier, the reader may use that pronoun. Choosing a noun for which the referent has been established earlier, the reader may use that pronoun. Betsy was probably predicting *the cow* which *she* refers to. These miscues clearly show that Betsy is an active language user as she reads. Ken Goodman has done studies on the control readers have over determiners and pronouns in relation to the cohesion of text (Goodman, 1983; Goodman & Gespass, 1983).

The idea that miscues often occur at specific pivotal points in any text is important enough to provide an example from another reader. An Appalachian reader, while reading the sentence "By the time I got out and over to where they were," inserted *of the water* between *out* and

and. In the previous paragraph the male character is in the water. The author and the reader have similar options at this point in the grammatical structure. The prepositional phrase *of the water* is understood by the reader though not stated by the author and therefore may be omitted or inserted without changing the meaning. In this case, the reader makes explicit what the author left implicit.

Miscues that result in semantically acceptable structures are confirmed as acceptable to readers and, therefore, are less likely to be corrected than those that are not acceptable or acceptable only with the immediately preceding text. Miscues at pivotal points in the text are often acceptable with regard to the preceding text. Of the ten semantically acceptable miscues that Betsy produced in the first excerpt, she corrected only one (*all* in s11). However, of the six miscues that were acceptable only with the prior portion of the text, she corrected four. Such correction strategies tend to occur when the reader believes they are most needed—when a prediction has been disconfirmed by subsequent language cues.

Insights are gained into the reader's construction of meaning and the process of comprehension when we ask questions such as "Why did the reader make this miscue? Does it make sense in the context of this story or article?" Through such examination, it is possible to see the pattern of comprehending strategies a reader engages in.

We contrast comprehending—what the reader does to understand during the reading of a text—with comprehension—what the reader understands at the end of the reading. Open-ended retellings that always follow the reading during miscue analysis are an index of comprehension. They add to the profile of comprehending, which shows the reader's concern for meaning as expressed through the reading miscues. Retellings also provide an opportunity for the researcher or teacher to gain insight into how concepts and language are actively used and developed throughout a reading event.

Although the concept of retelling is common to present-day research, in the early sixties when we first used this concept, many questioned the term and the appropriateness of its use in reading research. Rather than asking direct questions that would give cues to the reader about what is significant in the story, we asked for unaided retelling. Information on the readers' understanding of the text emerges from the organization they use in retelling the story, from whether they use the author's language or their own, and from the conceptions or misconceptions they reveal. Here is the first segment of Betsy's retelling:

> Um . . . it was about this woodman and um . . . when he . . . he thought that he um . . . he had harder work to do than his wife. So he went home and he told his wife, "What have you been doing all day." And then his wife told him. And then, um . . . and then, he thought that it

was easy work. And ... so ... so his wife, so his wife, so she um ... so the wife said, "Well so you have to keep," no ... the husband says that you have to go to the woods and cut ... and have to go out in the forest and cut wood and I'll stay home. And the next day they did that.

By comparing our interpretation of the story with Betsy's retelling and her miscues, we are able to analyze how much learning has occurred during Betsy and the author's transaction. For example, although the story frequently uses *woodman* and *to cut wood, forest,* the noun used to refer to setting, is used twice. Not only does Betsy provide evidence in her retelling that she knows that *woods* and *forest* are synonymous, she also indicates that she knows the author's choice is *forest.* The maze she works through suggests her search for the author's language. Her oral language mazes are evidence of her intentions and self-correction patterns. Betsy seems to believe that the teacher is looking for the author's language rather than her own. Additional evidence of Betsy's concern to reproduce the author's language is seen in her use of *woodman* and *husband.* In the story, the woodman is referred to as *woodman* and *husband* eight times each and as *man* four times; the wife is referred to only as *wife.* Otherwise pronouns are used to refer to the husband and wife. In the retelling, Betsy uses *husband* and *woodman* six times and *man* only once; she called the wife only *wife.* Betsy always uses appropriate pronouns in referring to the husband and wife. However, when cow was the referent, she substituted *he* for *she* twice. (What does Betsy know about the sex of cattle?)

The linguistic and conceptual schematic background a reader brings to reading not only shows in miscues but is implicit in the developing conceptions or misconceptions revealed through the reader's retelling. Betsy adds to her conceptual base and builds her control of language as she reads this story, but her ability to do both is limited by what she brings to the task. In the story, the husband has to make butter in a churn. Betsy makes miscues whenever buttermaking is mentioned. For example, in s10 she substituted *bread* for *butter.* (Breadmaking is much more common than butter-making as a home activity for North American children.) The next time *butter* appears, in s15, she reads it as expected. However, in s18, *Soon the cream will turn into butter,* Betsy reads *buttermilk* for *butter.* Other references to butter-making include the words *churn* or *cream.* Betsy reads *cream* as expected each time it appears in the text but produces miscues for *churn.* She pauses about 10 seconds at the first appearance of *churn* and finally says it with exaggerated articulation. However, the next two times *churn* appears, Betsy reads *cream.*

Text	Transcript
s25 ...he saw a big pig inside, with its nose in the churn.	...he saw a big pig inside, with its nose in the cream.
s28 It bumped into the churn, knocking it over.	It jumped...it bumped into the cream, knocking it over.
s29 The cream splashed all over the room.	The cream shado [nonword miscue] ...splashed all over the room.

In the retelling Betsy provides evidence that her miscues are conceptually based and not mere confusions:

> And the husband was sitting down and he poured some buttermilk and um ...in a jar. And, and he was making buttermilk, and then he um ...heard the baby crying. So he looked all around in the room and um ...And then he saw a big, a big, um ...pig. Um ...he saw a big pig inside the house. So, he told him to get out and he, the pig, started racing around and um ...he di ...he um ...bumped into the buttermilk and then the buttermilk fell down and then the pig, um ...went out.

Betsy, who is growing up in a metropolis, knows little about how butter is made in churns. She knows that there is a relationship between cream and butter, although she does not know the details of that relationship. According to her teacher, she has also taken part in a traditional primary school activity in which sweet cream is poured into a jar, closed up, and shaken until butter and buttermilk are produced. Although Betsy's miscues and retelling suggest that she has only some knowledge about butter-making, the concept is peripheral to comprehending the story. All that she needs to know is that butter-making is one of the wife's many chores that can cause the woodman trouble.

For a long time, teachers have been confused about how a reader can know something in one context but not know it in another. Such confusion comes from the belief that reading is word recognition; on the contrary, words in different syntactic and semantic contexts become different entities for readers, and Betsy's response to the structure *keep house* is good evidence for this. In s3, where the clauses *I keep house* and *and keeping house* occur the first time, Betsy reads the expected responses but repeats each several times before getting the words right, suggesting that she is grappling with their meanings. In s9 she reads *start house and keeping house* for *stay home and keep house,* and she reads the first phrase in s10 as *If you start home to do my work.* The structure *keep house* is a complex one. To a 9-year-old, *keep* is a verb that means being able to hold on to or take care of something small. *Keeping house* is no longer a common idiom in American or Canadian English. *Stay home* adds complexity to *keep house*. Used with different verbs and different function words, *home* and *house* are sometimes synonyms and sometimes not. The transitive and intransitive nature of *keep* and *stay* as well as the infinitive structure *to keep* and *to stay* add to the complexity of the verb phrases.

In her search for meaning and her transaction with the published text, Betsy continues to develop strategies to handle these complex problems. In s14 she produces *stayed home*; however, in s35 she encounters *keeping house* again and reads, *perhaps keeping house ... home and ... is ... hard work*. She is exploring the concept and grammaticality of *keeping house*. She first reads the expected response and then abandons it. In the story *home* appears seven times and *house* ten times. Betsy reads them correctly in every context except in the patterns *staying home* and *keeping house*. Yet as she continues to work on these phrases throughout her reading she finally is able to handle the structures and either self-corrects successfully or produces a semantically acceptable sentence. Thus Betsy's miscues and retelling reveal the dynamic transaction between a reader and written language.

Through careful observation and evaluation, miscue analysis provides evidence of the ways in which the published text teaches the reader (Meek, 1988). Through continuous transactions with the text, Betsy develops as a reader. Our analysis also provides evidence for the published text as a mediator. Betsy is in a continuing zone of proximal development as she works at making sense of this text (Vygotsky, 1978). Because the text is a complete one it mediates Betsy's development.

The Reader: An Intuitive Grammarian

Reading is not simply knowing sounds, words, sentences, and the abstract parts of language that can be studied by linguists. Reading, like listening, consists of processing language and constructing meaning. The reader brings a great deal of information to this complex and active process. A large body of research has been concerned with meaning construction and the understanding of reading processes and has provided supporting evidence to many of the principles we have revealed through miscue analysis. However, there is still too little attention paid to the ability of readers to make use of their knowledge of the syntax of their language as they read.

Readers sometimes cope with texts that they do not understand well by manipulating the language. Their miscues demonstrate this. The work of both Chomsky and Halliday has helped us understand the syntactic transformations that occur as readers transact with texts. Such manipulations are often seen when readers correctly answer questions about material they do not understand. For example, we ask readers to read an article entitled "Downhole Heave Compensator" (Kirk, 1974). Most readers claim little comprehension, but they can answer the question "What were the two things destroying the underreamers?" by finding the statement in the text that reads, "We were trying to keep drillships and semisubmersibles from wiping out our underreamers" (p. 88). It is because of such ability to manipulate the syntax of questions that we decided to use open-ended retellings for miscue analysis.

In miscue analysis research, we examine the syntactic nature of the miscues, the points in the text where miscues occur, and the syntactic acceptability of sentences that include miscues. Readers often produce sentences that are syntactically, but not semantically, acceptable. In s10 Betsy finally reads, *If you start home to do my work* for the text phrase *If you stay home to do my work.* Her reading of this phrase is syntactically acceptable in the story but unacceptable semantically since it is important to the story line that the woodman stay home.

We became aware that readers were able to maintain the grammaticality of sentences even if the meaning was not maintained when we examined the phenomenon of nonwords. Such nonsense words give us insight into English-speaking readers' grammatical awareness because sentences with nonwords often retain the grammatical features of English although they lose English meaning. Betsy produces only 2 nonword miscues among the 75 miscues she produces. In s58 Betsy reads, *As for the cow, she hang between the roof and the gorun* instead of the expected response *She hung between the roof and the ground.* She repeats *and the* prior to *ground* three times and pauses for about 10 seconds between each repetition. She seems to be aware that the word *ground* is not a familiar one in this context, but she maintains a noun intonation for the nonword. This allows her to maintain the grammatical sense of the sentence so that later in the story when the text reads *the cow fell to the ground,* she reads it as expected without hesitation.

Use of intonation also provides evidence for the grammatical similarity between the nonword and the text word. Miscues on the different forms of *to* (as the initial part of an infinitive or as a preposition), *two,* and *too* are easy to clarify by paying attention to intonation patterns. Nonwords most often retain similarities not only in number of syllables, word length, and spelling but also in bound morphemes—the smallest units that carry meaning or grammatical information within a word but cannot stand alone (for example, the *ed* in carried). In one of our research studies (Goodman & Burke, 1973), a group of 6th graders read a story that included the following sentences: "Clearly and distinctively Andrew said 'philosophical.'" and "A distinct quiver in his voice." The nonword substitutions for each were different depending on the grammatical function of the word. For *distinctly* readers read nonwords that sounded like *distikily, distintly,* and *definely,* while for *distinct* they read *dristic, distink, distet.*

There is abundant evidence in miscues of readers' strong awareness of bound morphemic rules. Our data on readers' word-for-word substitutions, whether nonwords or real words, show that, on average, 80 percent of the observed responses retain the morphemic markings of the text. For example, if the text word is a noninflected form of a verb, the reader will tend to substitute that form; if the word has a prefix, the reader's substitution will tend to include a prefix. Derivational suffixes will be replaced by derivational suffixes, contractional suffixes by contractional suffixes.

Maintaining the syntactic acceptability of the text allows readers to continue reading and at the same time to maintain the cohesion and coherence of the text. Only a small portion of Betsy's substitution miscues do not retain the same grammatical function as the text word. Analysis of the word-for-word substitutions of 4th and 6th graders showed that their miscues retained the identical grammatical function over 73 percent of the time for nouns and verbs (Goodman & Burke, 1973). Function words were the same 67 percent or more of the time, while noun modifiers were retained approximately 60 percent of the time. In addition, an examination of what kinds of grammatical function were used for substitution when they were not identical indicated that nouns, noun modifiers, and function words are substituted for one another to a much greater degree than they are for verbs. Again this suggests the power of grammaticality on reading. Of 501 substitution miscues produced by 4th graders, only 3 times was a noun substituted for a verb modifier, and 6th graders made such a substitution only once in 424 miscues.

Evidence from miscues occurring at the beginning of sentences also adds insight into readers' awareness of the grammatical constraints of language. Generally, in prose for children few sentences begin with prepositions, intensifiers, adjectives, or singular common nouns without a preceding determiner. When readers produce miscues on the beginning words of sentences that do not retain the grammatical function of the text, we could not find one miscue that represented any of these unexpected grammatical forms. (One day we will do an article called "Miscues Readers Don't Make." Some of the strongest evidence comes from all the things readers could do that they do not.) These patterns are so strong that we have been able to detect manufactured examples in some professional texts. The authors have offered examples of errors readers don't make.

Readers' miscues that cross sentence boundaries also provide insight into the readers' grammatical sophistication. It is not uncommon to hear teachers complain that readers read past periods. Closer examination of this phenomenon suggests that when readers do this they are usually making a logical prediction that is based on a linguistic alternative. Although Betsy does this a few times, we will use an example from a story we used with 4th graders: *He still thought it more fun to pretend to be a great scientist, mixing the strange and the unknown* (Goodman & Goodman, 1978). Many readers predict that *strange* and *unknown* are adjectives and intone the sentence accordingly. This means that their voices are left up in the air, so to speak, in anticipation of a noun. The more proficient readers in the study regress at this point and self-correct by shifting to an end-of-the-sentence intonation pattern: Less proficient readers either do not correct at all and continue reading sounding surprised or try to regress without producing the appropriate intonation pattern.

Interrelations of All the Cueing Systems

Reading involves the interrelationship of all the language systems. All readers use graphic information to various degrees. Our research (Goodman & Burke, 1973) demonstrates that the least proficient readers we studied in the 6th, 8th, and 10th grades use graphic information more than the most proficient readers. Readers also produce substitution miscues similar to the phonemic patterns of text words. An examination of Betsy's word substitution miscues reveals that she pays more attention to the look-alike quality of the words than to their sound-alike quality. Although attention to graphic features occurs more frequently than attention to the phonemic patterns, readers use both systems to show that they call on their knowledge of the graphophonic system. Yet the use of these systems cannot explain why Betsy would produce a substitution such as *day* for *morning* or *job* for *work* (s13 and s14). She is clearly showing her use of the syntactic system and her ability to retain the grammatical function and morphemic constraints of the expected response. But the graphophonic and syntactic systems together do not explain why Betsy could seemingly understand words such as *house, home, ground,* and *cream* in certain contexts but not in others. To understand these aspects of reading, one must examine the interrelationship of all the cueing systems.

The integration of all the language systems (grammatical, graphophonic, semantic, and pragmatic) are necessary in order for reading to take place. Miscue analysis provides evidence that readers integrate cueing systems from the earliest initial attempts at reading. Readers sample and make judgments about which cues from each system will provide the most useful information in making predictions that will get them to meaning. All of the miscue examples we have cited point to the notion that readers monitor their reading and ask themselves, "Does this sound like language?" (syntactically acceptable) and "Does this make sense in this story?" (semantically acceptable). Finally, if they have to return to the text to check things, they look more closely at the print using their graphophonic knowledge to confirm and self-correct as they read.

As readers make use of their knowledge of all the language cues, they predict, make inferences, select significant features, confirm, and constantly work toward constructing a meaningful text. Not only are they constructing meaning, they are constructing themselves as readers.

Schema-Forming and Schema-Driven Miscues

Our analysis of oral reading miscues began with the foundational assumption that reading is a language process parallel to listening. Everything we have observed among readers from beginners to those with great proficiency supports the validity of this assumption. The analysis of miscues, in turn, has been the basis for the development of a theory and model of the reading process (Goodman, 1994, see Chapter 1, this volume, page 3).

What we have learned about miscues in reading has been applied to aspects of language such as spelling, composition, response to literature, and oral language development. Such research, liberated from the "perfection misconception," has demonstrated the linguistic creativity of humans. Errors children make as they develop oral language have provided insight not only into how the young learn language but into the nature of language—how it develops, grows, and changes (Brown, 1973). Children also invent schemata about the nature of written language as they become writers (Ferreiro & Teberosky, 1982; Goodman & Wilde, 1992). Invented punctuation and spelling are especially good examples of the ways in which children learn to control the relationship between the sound system of their dialects and the conventions of the writing system (Read, 1986; Wilde, 1992). Adults develop the craft of writing through making miscues (Shaughnessy, 1977). Rosenblatt (1978) has long argued for a transactional view of reader response to literature in which all response is seen as a transaction between reader and text which of necessity results in variation among readers as they proceed toward interpretation, evaluation, and criticism. The readers' schemata are vital to the transactions.

What we have learned from the study of oral reading miscues and what we have seen in research on other language processes can help to explain the generation of miscues. The concept of schema is helpful to explore how miscues are necessary to language learning. A schema, as we define the term, is an organized cognitive structure of related knowledge, ideas, emotions, and actions that has been internalized and that guides and controls a person's use of subsequent information and response to experience.

Humans have schemata for everything they know and do. We have linguistic schemata (which we call rules) by which we produce and comprehend language. For example, we know when to expect or produce questions and when a question requires an answer. We have schemata for what language does and how it works. With such schemata, we use language to control the behavior of others. We have conceptual schemata for our ideas, concepts, and knowledge of the world. We may reject a Picasso portrait because it does not meet our expectation or schema of the human face.

Our work has led us to believe that humans also develop overarching schemata for creating new schemata and modifying old ones. These we might call schemata for new schema formation. Chomsky's (1965) concept that the generation of language is controlled by a finite set of transformational rules is a case of a schema for schema formation. The rules determine and limit what syntactic patterns may be accepted as grammatical in a language; these same rules also make it possible for speakers to create new sentences that have never been heard before but will be comprehensible to others.

Conceptual schemata work much the same way, and they are also controlled by overarching schemata. That explains why we often use analogy and metaphor in making connections to well-known words and ideas when we talk about new experiences. An example is the use of the term *docking* for space travel. Conceptual and linguistic schemata are at work simultaneously. The schemata must all be in harmony. If more than one complexity occurs, the result is compounding; the possibility of miscues increases disproportionately.

The earlier discussion about Betsy's miscues relating to the concepts of *to stay home* and *to keep house* is a good example. Her complete retelling after reading indicates good understanding of these concepts. In order to build this kind of understanding, Betsy has to work hard during her reading. She relates her own limited knowledge of staying home and keeping house to the meanings she is constructing in transaction with the author. She has to develop control over the syntactic and conceptional complexity of *stay home* and *keep house* and add to her understanding of the relationship of *home* and *house*. She keeps selectively using the available graphophonic cues to produce both expected and unexpected responses. It is important to understand the complexity of thinking that Betsy has to use and that her miscues reflect. Much of children's language learning can be explained in terms of developing control over language schemata. With growing linguistic and conceptual schemata, children use language to predict, process, and monitor expression and comprehension.

Now let's reconsider a concept from miscue analysis: miscues are produced by the same process and in response to the same cues as expected responses. Putting that together with what we have just said about schema formation and use, we can consider miscues from the perspective of two schema processes: *schema-forming* or *schema-driven* miscues. And since schemata can be forming while we use our existing schemata, both processes can go on at the same time.

Piaget's (1977) concepts of assimilation and accommodation are pertinent here. A schema-forming miscue may be seen as a struggle toward accommodation, while a schema-driven miscue shows assimilation at work. Further, the effect of the miscue on subsequent language processing or intent may result in a disequilibrium, which may lead to reprocessing—that is, self-correction. Schemata may need to be abandoned, modified, or reformed as miscues are corrected.

A *schema-forming* miscue reflects the developmental process of building the rule systems of language and concepts, learning to apply those language rule systems, and delimiting them. For example, Susie responds to the printed name Corn Flakes on a box of cereal by pointing to each line of print successively while drawing out the word *ceeerrreeeeuuuull* until she finishes moving her finger. Although she has not yet developed the concept that English print is alphabetic, she shows through her unexpected response that she is developing a schema concerning a relationship between the length of print and the length of oral utterance.

The young child's development of the rules of past tense, number, and gender are reflected in the miscues children make in oral language (Brown, 1973). Rebecca, age 3, provides a good example when she says to her aunt, who is waiting to read her a story, "I'll come and get you in a few whiles." She shows her control of the schema for pluralization (*few* takes a plural) but she has taken *while,* which functions as a noun in the idiom *wait a little while* and has made it a count noun (*a few whiles*).

In the view of some scholars, a subject's production of language is dependent on whether the subject is dealing with old or new information. A schema-forming miscue is likely to involve new information, either linguistic or conceptual, which may not be easily assimilated. A schema-driven miscue may involve either old (given) information or new information in a predictable context. Furthermore, the schema, as well as the information, may be old or new.

A *schema-driven* miscue is one that results from the use of existing schemata to produce or comprehend language. In our research the concept of prediction has become important. Texts are hard or easy in proportion to how predictable they are for readers. They may use their existing schema to predict and comprehend, but sometimes the organization of the knowledge—that is, the schema on which the predictions are made—is so strong that it overrides the text and miscues occur. In the initial paragraph of a story that many adolescents and adults have read for us, the phrase *the headlamps of the car* occurs. The majority read *headlights* rather than *headlamps*. Many of those who do read *headlamps* indicate that they expected *headlights* and had to reread to accept *headlamps*.

Language variations also show evidence of schema-driven miscues. We shift dialects and registers when we move from formal written language to more informal styles or from one regional dialect to another. Tommy was overheard saying to his mother, a Texan, "Mom, Dad wants to know where the bucket is" and then to his father, a midwesterner, "Here's the pail, Dad." Tommy had learned to switch codes depending on the situation, and his schema-driven responses were appropriate to each parent. Understanding that dialect miscues are driven by schema may help teachers and researchers see them in proper perspective. A rural African American 4th grader in Port Gibson, Mississippi, was reading a story that included the line *the ducks walked in single file*. At this point in the story, mother duck was leading her babies in a proud and haughty manner. The child reading that line produced *the ducks walk signifying*.

The malapropisms that we all exhibit are also evidence of schema-driven miscues at work. We try to use schemata for word formation beyond word-formation limits. These result in miscues in listening as well as speaking. TV's Archie Bunker was upset because of the *alteration* he had had with a boisterous customer. We can't help relating the concept of schema-driven miscues to Tannen's (1990) work on conversations between men and women and among different ethnic groups. "I make sense of seemingly senseless misunderstandings that haunt our relationships and show that a man and a woman can interpret the same conversation differently, even when there is no apparent misunderstanding," she writes (p. 13). By understanding the reasons that underlie our misunderstandings perhaps we can form schemata that will help us "prevent or relieve some of the frustration" (p. 13).

In many cases it is not easy to separate miscues into schema-forming or schema-driven processes since they often occur simultaneously. At any particular point in time, it is fairly easy to explain the schemata that drive the miscues that occur. Schema formation, on the other hand, is less likely to occur at a single point and be easily discernible in a single miscue. The study of children's writing development allows us one way to observe the process of schema formation. It also reveals how both schema-forming and schema-driven miscues can occur in concert. An example from a story that Jennifer wrote in the 1st grade illustrates invented spelling that is driven by her linguistic schemata. Jennifer produced past-tense verbs about 20 times. Each reflected her invented phonic rules (and her awareness of the phonological rules of her own speech) since each had the letter *d* or *t* at the end, representing the appropriate phoneme. These spelling miscues included *rapt* (wrapped) and *yeld* (yelled). Her phonic schemata at this point led her to invent consistent spellings of single letters for single sounds. But a year later her spelling represented an awareness of the interrelationship of both the morphophonemic rules (past tense taking one of three forms depending on the preceding consonants) and the orthographic rule that spelling is not determined by sound in a simple one-to-one manner. Of 28 regular past tense verbs in a story she wrote in the 2nd grade, 25 were spelled conventionally. Jennifer was in a classroom where a lot of writing was encouraged but there was no direct teaching of spelling. During this year, she continually reformed her schemata and moved toward socially conventional ones.

Readers' miscues often can be driven by conceptual schemata, but at the same time readers can be forming new schemata. This is often revealed through the retelling as well as the miscues. In our research, we have had children read a story that has a significant concept represented by an unfamiliar but high-frequency word. One such word was *typical*. Although the children who read this story often reproduced oral substitutions for *typical* in the text (such as *tropical, type-ical,* and *topical*), they usually were able to explain the meaning of the word as it developed in the reading of the text. One Texas youngster said, "Oh, yeah, *tropical* means ordinary, just like all kinds of other babies. But, you know, it could also be a big storm."

Sometimes a new word represents a concept well known to the reader. In this case the reader must assimilate the new term to the old concept. Bilingual students often face this when they begin to read in a second language. We studied Arabic immigrant students who produced miscues on the word *plow* in a story they were reading, substituting *palow, pull, pole, polo, plew,* and *blow,* among other words and nonwords (Goodman & Goodman, 1978). However, they all were able to provide evidence that they had a "plowing" schema. One reader's example is representative: "Well, it's a thing with two handles and something pointing down. You got to pull it. But they don't push it with a camel. They push it with a cow. When the cow moves, the one who's pushing it got to go push on it so it goes deeper in the underground." In such a context we see both schema-driving and schema-forming processes taking place in a dynamic way. These 4th grade Arabic readers are new to English. They use their developing knowledge of English to produce unexpected responses to the word *plow* and their knowledge about plowing to show understanding of the concept (schema-driven).

At the same time, they add new knowledge as they encounter the English word for the concept (schema-forming). The example also indicates that the reader rejected the story element that a camel was used to pull a plow as implausible because of his conceptual schema.

We hope that our discussion of the role miscues play in language learning communicates to teachers and researchers that miscues are the positive effects of linguistic and conceptual processes rather than the failure to communicate or comprehend. If a language user loses meaning, she or he is likely to produce a miscue. If the language user chooses a syntactic schema different from the author's, a miscue will likely result. If a reader or listener interprets in a way different from the meaning intended by the speaker or author, a miscue will result. Miscues reflect readers' abilities to liberate themselves from detailed attention to print as they leap toward meaning. Readers make use of their linguistic and conceptual schemata to reverse, substitute, insert, omit, rearrange, paraphrase, and transform. They do this not only with letters and single words, but with two-word sequences, phrases, clauses, and sentences. Their own experiences, values, conceptual structures, expectations, dialects, and lifestyles are integral to the process. The meanings they construct can never be a simple reconstruction of the author's conceptual structures because they are dependent on the reader's schemata.

Risk-taking has been recognized as a significant aspect of both language learning and proficient language use. In risk-taking there is a necessary balance between tentativeness and self-confidence. Miscues reflect the degree to which existing schemata fit the existing circumstance and the level of confidence of the language user. In speaking a second language, speakers often show great tentativeness, consciously groping for control of developing schemata. As their confidence grows so does their risk-taking, and their miscues show the influence either of schemata for the first language (schema-driven) or of their developing schemata for the second language (schema-forming). An example of the former cautious type is this sentence from a native Spanish-speaking adult who is asking his English teacher for advice: "Ms. Buck, please, I hope I do not molest you." This oral miscue is driven by the speaker's schema for the Spanish *molestar* (to bother). In her response to the student, the teacher will provide information that will help the student form a schema to provide semantic limits for the English *molest.*

Oral and Silent Reading

We need to say a word about the relationship between oral and silent reading since much of miscue analysis research uses oral reading. The basic mode of reading is silent. Oral reading is special since it requires production of an oral representation concurrently with comprehending. The functions of oral reading representation are limited. It is a performing art used by teachers, entertainers, politicians, and religious leaders. We have already explained why we use oral reading in miscue analysis. But a basic question remains: Are oral and silent reading similar enough to justify generalizing from studies of oral reading miscues to theories and models of silent reading?

In our view, a single process underlies all reading. The language cueing systems and the strategies of oral and silent reading are essentially the same. The miscues we find in oral reading occur in silent reading as well. We have some research evidence of that. Studies of nonidentical fillers of cloze blanks (responses that do not match the deleted words) show remarkable correspondence to oral reading miscues and indicate that the processes of oral and silent reading are much the same (Anderson, 1982; Cambourne & Rousch, 1979; Chapman, 1981). Still, there are dissimilarities between oral and silent reading. First, oral reading is limited to the speed at which speech can be produced; therefore, it need not be as efficient as rapid silent reading. Next, superficial misarticulations such as *hangaber* for *hamburger* occur in oral reading but are not part of silent reading. Also, oral readers, conscious of their audience, read passages differently from when they read silently. Examples are production of nonword substitutions, persistence with several attempts at problem spots, overt regression to correct miscues already mentally corrected, and deliberate adjustments in ensuing text to cover miscues so that listeners will not notice them. Furthermore, oral readers may take fewer risks than silent readers. This can be seen in the deliberate omission of unfamiliar words, reluctance to attempt correction even though meaning is disrupted, and avoidance of overtly making corrections that have taken place silently to avoid calling attention to miscues. Finally, relatively proficient readers, particularly adults, may become so concerned with superficial fluency that they short-circuit the basic concern for meaning. Professional oral readers (newscasters, for example) seem to suffer from this malady. With these reservations noted, we believe that making sense is the same in oral and silent reading; in construction of meaning, miscues must occur in both.

Parts and Wholes

Too much research on language and language learning is still concerned with isolated sounds, letters, word parts, words, and even sentences. Such fragmentation, although it simplifies research design and the complexity of the phenomena under study, seriously distorts processes, tasks, cue values, interactions, and realities. Many years ago, Kintsch (1974) wrote as follows:

> Psycholinguistics is changing in character. ... The 1950s were still dominated by the nonsense syllables ... the 1960s were characterized by the use of word lists, while the present decade is witnessing a shift to even more complex learning materials. At present, we have reached the point where lists of sentences are being substituted for word lists in studies of recall recognition. Hopefully, this will not be the end-point of this development, and we shall soon see psychologists handle effectively the problems posed by the analysis of connected text (p. 2).

Through miscue analysis we have learned that, other things being equal, short language sequences are harder to comprehend than are long ones. Sentences are easier than words, paragraphs easier than sentences, pages easier than paragraphs, and stories easier than pages. We see two reasons for this. First, it takes some familiarity with the style and general semantic thrust of a text's language for the reader to make successful predictions. Style is largely a matter of an author's syntactic preferences; the semantic context develops over the entire text. Short texts provide limited cues for readers to build a sense of either style or meaning. Second, the disruptive effect of particular miscues on meaning is much greater in short texts. Longer texts offer redundant opportunities to recover and self-correct. This suggests why findings from studies of words, sentences, and short passages produce different results from those that involve whole texts. It also raises a major question about using standardized tests, which employ words, phrases, sentences, and short texts to assess reading proficiency.

Sooner or later all attempts to understand language—its development and its function as the medium of human communication—must confront linguistic reality. Theories, models, grammars, and research paradigms must predict and explain what people do when they use language and what makes it possible for them to do so. Researchers have contrived ingenious ways to make a small bit of linguistic or psycholinguistic reality available for examination. But then what they see is often out of focus, distorted by the design. Miscue analysis research makes fully available the reality of the miscues language users produce as they participate in real speech and literacy events. Huey (1908) said, "And so to completely analyze what we do when we read would almost be the acme of a psychologist's achievements, for it would be to describe very many of the most intricate workings of the human mind, as well as to unravel the tangled story of the most remarkable specific performance the civilization has learned in all its history" (p.6). To this we add that miscues are the windows on language processes at work.

References

Anderson, J. (1982, July). *The writer, the reader, the text.* Paper presented at the 19th annual UKRA Reading Conference, Newcastle-upon-Tyne, UK.

Brown, R. (1973). *A first language: The early stages.* Cambridge, MA: Harvard University Press.

Cambourne, B., & Rousch, P. (1979). *A psycholinguistic model of the reading process as it relates to proficient, average, and low-ability readers* (Tech. Rep.). Wagga Wagga, NSW, Australia: Riverina College of Advanced English, Sturt University.

Chapman, J. (1981). The reader and the text. In J. Chapman (Ed.), *The reader and the text.* London: Heinemann.

Chomsky, N. (1965). *Aspects of the theory of syntax.* Cambridge, MA: MIT Press.

Ferreiro, E., & Teberosky, A. (1982). *Literacy before schooling.* Portsmouth, NH: Heinemann.

Goodman, K.S. (1994). Reading, writing and written texts: A transactional, sociopsycholinguistic view. *Theoretical models and processes of reading.* R. B. Ruddell, M. R. Ruddell and H. Singer. Newark, DE, International Reading Association: 1093–1130.

Goodman, K.S. (1983, July). *Text features as they relate to miscues: Determiners* (Occasional Paper No. 8). Tucson, AZ: Program m Language and Literacy, College of Education, University of Arizona.

Goodman, K.S., Brown, J., & Marek, A. (1993). *Annotated chronological bibliography of miscue analysis* (Occasional Paper No. 16). Tucson, AZ: Program in Language and Literacy, College of Education, University of Arizona.

Goodman, K.S., & Burke, C.L. (1973, April). *Theoretically based studies of patterns of miscues in oral reading performance* (Project No. 9-0375). Washington, DC: U.S. Office of Education.

Goodman, K.S., & Gespass, S. (1983, March). *Text features as they relate to miscues: Pronouns* (Occasional Paper No. 7). Tucson, AZ: Program in Language and Literacy, College of Education, University of Arizona.

Goodman, K.S., & Goodman, Y.M. (1978). *Reading of American children whose language is a stable rural dialect of English or a language other than English* (Final Report, Project NIE-C-00-3-0087). Washington, DC: U.S. Department of Health, Education and Welfare, National Institute of Education.

Goodman, Y.M., Watson, D., & Burke, C. (1987). *Reading miscue inventory: Alternative procedures.* New York: Richard C. Owen.

Goodman, Y.M., & Wilde, S. (1992). *Literacy events in a community of young writers.* New York: Teachers College Press.

Huey, E.B. (1908). *The psychology and pedagogy of reading.* New York: Macmillan.

Kintsch, W. (1974). *The representation of meaning in memory.* Hillsdale, NJ: Erlbaum.

Kirk, S. (1974, June). Downhole heave compensator: A tool designed by hindsight. *Drilling-DCW,* 88.

McInnes, J., Gerrard, M., & Ryckman, J. (Series Eds.). (1964). *Magic and make believe* (Basal Program). Don Mills, Ont.: Thomas Nelson.

Meek, M. (1988). *How texts teach what readers learn.* Exeter, UK: Thimble.

Piaget, J. (1977). *The development of thought: Equilibration of cognitive structures.* New York: Viking.

Read, C. (1986). *Children's creative spelling.* London: Routledge & Kegan Paul.

Rosenblatt, L. (1978). *The reader, the text, the poem.* Carbondale, IL: Southern Illinois University Press.

Shaughnessy, M. (1977). *Errors and expectations.* New York: Oxford University Press.

Tannen, D. (1990). *You just don't understand: Women and men in conversation.* New York: Morrow.

Vygotsky, L. (1978*). Mind in society.* Cambridge, MA: Harvard University Press.

Wilde, S. (1992). *You kan red this! Spelling and punctuation for whole language classrooms, K–6.* Portsmouth, NH: Heinemann.

Psycholinguistic Aspects of Reading

Chapter Fourteen

Psycholinguistic Universals in the Reading Process

Kenneth S. Goodman
Wayne State University, 1970

Abstract. Literate speakers in any language have two alternative surface language forms which are realizations of the same deep structure and which represent alternate encodings of the same meaning. For the proficient reader, written language becomes parallel to speech and not a secondary representation of it. Listening and reading are processes in which the language user may sample, select, and predict from the available signal. Readers are users of language who process graphic, syntactic, and semantic information simultaneously. Readers develop strategies for the efficient sampling of the graphic signal in relation to the syntax of their language and the concepts and experiences with which the passage is concerned. The essential characteristics of the reading process are universal.

Reading is a psycholinguistic process by which the reader (a language user) reconstructs, as best he can, a message which has been encoded by a writer as a graphic display.

This chapter first appeared in the *Journal of Typographic Research* (now *Visible Language*), Spring 1970, pp. 103–110. It is based on a speech by Dr. Kenneth S. Goodman at the Second Annual International Congress of Applied Linguistics, Cambridge, England, September 1969. Copyright (1970) by *Visible Language*. Reprinted with permission.

Through research on children reading English who are native speakers of some dialect of American English, I have evolved a basic theoretical view of the reading process. It should be understood that some of what follows is an extension of and projection of a theoretical view into dimensions that go beyond the research on which it is based. In this sense, what follows is hypothetical; other scholars are invited to test and challenge the hypotheses in terms of languages and orthographies other than English.

Generative and Receptive Aspects of Language

It is ironic that although most researchers agree that receptive control of aspects of language precedes generative control, more attention has been given to the process of language production than to the process by which language is understood.

Many linguists have assumed that listening and reading are simply the mirror images of speaking and writing. They have assumed that since generative processes begin with meaning and result in a fully-formed phonological or graphic display that receptive processes begin with the encoded display and reverse the process, step by step, to get back to meaning.

In this too simple view, not enough consideration has been given to the variant nature of the productive and receptive tasks that are involved in language use. *In producing language,* the language user has thoughts which he wishes to express. In a transformational view, he creates a deep language structure which represents his meaning, applies a set of compulsory and optional transformational rules, and generates a surface structure. If the language user is literate, this surface structure may utilize a phonological signal and require the application of a set of phonological rules, or it may utilize a graphic signal and require use of a set of orthographic rules. The choice will be dictated, of course, by the language user's purpose.

The *receptive* process does start with the phonological or graphic display as input, and it does end with meaning as output, but the efficient language user takes the most direct route and touches the fewest bases necessary to get to his goal. He accomplishes this by *sampling,* relying on the redundancy of language, and his knowledge of linguistic constraints. He *predicts* structures, *tests* them against the semantic context which he builds up from the situation and the on-going discourse, and then *confirms* or disconfirms as he processes further language.

Receptive language processes are cycles of *sampling, predicting, testing,* and *confirming.* The language user relies on strategies which yield the most reliable prediction with the minimum use of the information available.

Neither listening nor reading are precise processes and, in fact, even what the language user perceives is only partly what he sees or hears and partly what he expects to see or hear. This is necessarily so not only because of the prediction in which the language user engages but also because he has learned to organize his perceptions according to what is and is not significant in the language. The language user must not simply know what to pay attention to but what not to pay attention to.

The producer of language will be most successful if the signal he produces is complete and well-formed. With such a signal, the receiver of language is free to utilize his sampling strategies.

The necessary concern for oral language which had been neglected for so long caused many scholars to dismiss written language—without adequate consideration—as a secondary representation of oral language. But written language in a literate culture is not simply a way of preserving and recording oral language. It designates streets, places, and directions; it labels and classifies. It makes communication possible over time and space.

A key difference between oral and written language is that speech is most commonly encountered within the situations in which it is most relevant. Speakers may rely on the situational context to make referents explicit. Listeners may infer from the situational context and from the movements, actions, and gestures of speakers a great deal of semantic information to augment and constrain what they derive from the language.

Written language tends to be out of situational context. The writer must make referents and antecedents explicit, he must create contexts through the language to replace those which are not present. He must furthermore address himself to an unseen and frequently unknown audience. He gets no immediate linguistic or visual feedback to cue him as to whether his communicative efforts are successful.

Written language is perfectable in that the writer may edit it to be sure he has said exactly what he wished to say. It isn't perishable in the sense that oral language is.

These differences should not obscure the basic similarities between the alternate language forms for literate language users, but they should make clear that reading and listening will employ variant psycholinguistic strategies to cope with the variant characteristics of the two forms. Reading employs a strategy of regression to reread, for example, whereas listening cannot employ a comparable strategy. The listener must ask the speaker to repeat and that is not always feasible.

One misconception which has caused considerable confusion in dealing with the reading process is the notion that meaning may be derived only from oral language. It is assumed by some that readers engage in a process of recoding graphic input as aural input and then decoding. While this may, in fact, take place in beginning stages of the acquisition of literacy among some learners, it is not necessary or characteristic of proficient reading. An analogy can be found in the early stages of learning a second language. The learner may be going through a process of continuous translation into his first language before he decodes. But eventually he must be able to derive meaning directly from the second language with no recourse to the first. Just so, the proficient reader becomes as skillful at deriving meaning from written language as he is from the aural form with no need to translate one to the other.

It must be remembered that oral language is no less an arbitrary code than written language. Neither has any direct relationship to meaning and the real world other than that which its users assign it.

Alphabetic writing systems have a number of virtues among which is that there is a built-in correspondence to the units and sequences of the oral language form. But this is not an unmitigated blessing. A writing system which is directly related to ideas and concepts has the virtue that it can be used for communication by speakers of different languages. The system of mathematical notation has that advantage. $6 + 9 = 15$ is a mathematical statement that will be immediately understood by speakers of a wide range of languages, whereas *six and nine equal fifteen* can only be understood if the reader knows English.

The Chinese writing system may indeed have its faults but it has the virtue of being understood by speakers of oral languages which are not mutually comprehensible. And, of course, the Chinese writing system— once it is mastered—does function quite well for its users. Alphabetic writing systems are not in fact necessary for literacy.

The Reading Process

The readers of English I have studied utilize three cue systems simultaneously. The starting point is graphic in reading and we may call one cue system *graphophonic*. The reader responds to graphic sequences and may utilize the correspondences between the graphic and phonological systems of his English dialect. I should point out that these are not phoneme-grapheme correspondences but in fact operate on morphophonemic levels (that is spelling patterns relate to sound sequences).

In English as in other languages the spelling system is fixed and standardized. This means that correspondences will vary from dialect to dialect and that over time changing phonology will loosen the fit of even the tightest alphabetic system.

The second cue system the reader uses is *syntactic*. The reader using pattern markers such as function words and inflectional suffixes as cues recognizes and predicts structures. Since the underlying or deep structure of written and oral language are the same, the reader seeks to infer the deep structure as he reads so that he may arrive at meaning.

The third cue system is *semantic*. In order to derive meaning from language, the language user must be able to provide semantic input. This is not simply a question of meaning for words but the much larger question of the reader having sufficient experience and conceptual background to feed into the reading process so that he can make sense out of what he's reading. All readers are illiterate in some senses, since no one can read everything written in his native language.

These cue systems are used simultaneously and interdependently. What constitutes useful graphic information depends on how much syntactic and semantic information is available. Within high contextual constraints an initial consonant may be all that is needed to identify an element and make possible the prediction of an ensuing sequence or the confirmation of prior predictions.

Proficient readers make generally successful predictions, but they are also able to recover when they produce miscues which change the meaning *in unacceptable ways*.

No readers read material they have not read before without errors. It must be understood that in the reading process accurate use of all cues available would not only be slow and inefficient but would actually lead the reader away from his primary goal which is comprehension. In fact in my research I have encountered many youngsters who are so busy matching letters to sounds and naming word shapes that they have no sense of the meaning of what they are reading. Reading requires not so much skills as strategies that make it possible to select the most productive cues.

These strategies will vary with the nature of the reading tasks. For example, literature has different characteristics than discursive language. The writer will use unusual terms and phrases rather than the more trite but also more predictable ones which would be used to express the same meaning in everyday conversation. The reader needs strategies that adjust to the very different constraints in literary materials.

Because reading involves visual input, characteristics of the visual system do affect the reading process. The material must be scanned from left to right, as English is printed, and the eye must focus at specific points since it cannot provide input while it is in motion. At each fixation a very small circle of print is in clear, sharp focus. Some have argued that only print in sharp focus can be used in reading. But there is a large area of print in the peripheral field at each point of fixation which is not seen clearly but is sufficiently seen to be usable in the sampling, predicting, confirming aspects of reading. The reader can, in fact, work with partial, blurred, even mutilated, graphic input to a considerable degree.

That, too briefly, is what my research has told me about the process of reading English among Native American speakers. I have no reason to believe that this process would vary except in minor degrees in the reading of any language. Whether the graphic sequence is from left to right, right to left, or top to bottom would be of little consequence to the basic reading process. The reader needs to scan appropriately but he will still sample and predict in much the same way.

With alphabetical orthographies the regularity of correspondence rules for letter-sound relationships is not nearly as important as many people have believed. Readers are able to use syntactic and semantic cues to such a considerable extent that they need only minimal graphic cues in many cases. They can tolerate a great deal of irregularity, ambiguity, and variability in orthographies without the reading process suffering. There is, in fact, a wide range in which an alphabetic orthography may exist and still be viable. Only minor adjustments in the reading process are required to deal with any unusual correspondence features.

An example in reading English is the variability of vowel representation. This is particularly confused since the unstressed vowel schwa may be spelled by any vowel letter. Readers learn to rely more heavily on consonants, particularly initial ones for their minimum cues and to use vowel letters only when other information is inadequate.

I confess to know nothing about problems of reading non-alphabetic writing systems, but I strongly believe that readers of languages which employ them will still be sampling using minimal graphic cues to predict grammatical structures.

Grammatical patterns and rules operate differently in each language, but readers will need to use their grammatical competence in much the same way. Some special reading strategies may result from particular characteristics of the grammatical system. Inflections are relatively unimportant in English grammar but positions in patterns are quite important. In a highly inflected language the reader would find it profitable to make strong use of inflectional cues. In English such cues are not terribly useful.

Semantic aspects of the reading process cannot vary to any extent from one language to another, since the key question is how much background the reader brings to the specific reading.

To sum up, it would seem that the reading process will be much the same for all languages with minor variations to accommodate the specific characteristics of the orthography used and the grammatical structure of the language.

Learning to Read One's Native Language

In the personal history of each individual in a literate society he learns first to control the spoken language and several years later to control the written language. He masters speech with no organized instruction. Normally he learns to read and write in school. It's puzzling that far less success is achieved in learning to read than in learning to speak.

Obviously there is not time to explore this vexing problem. But several key points need to be made:

1. Children who learn oral language should be able to learn to read.

2. Children who know oral language should be able to use this knowledge in learning to comprehend written language.

3. Reading instruction should center on comprehension strategies.

4. The reading process cannot be fractionated into sub-skills to be taught or sub-divided into code-breaking and comprehension without qualitatively changing it.

5. Reading instruction should use natural meaningful language within the conceptual grasp of the learners. (This implies of course that the content should always be relevant as well.)

6. Where it is at all feasible the child should achieve initial literacy within his own language (in fact within his own home dialect)!

Reading a Second Language

From my study of the reading process here are some implications I see for learning to read a second language:

(a) Learning to read a second language should be easier for someone already literate in another language, regardless of how similar or dissimilar it is.

(b) Reading will be difficult as long as the student does not have some degree of control over the grammatical system.

(c) Strong semantic input will help the acquisition of the reading competence where syntactic control is weak. This suggests that the subject of reading materials should be of high interest and relate to the background of the learners.

(d) Reading materials in early language instruction should probably avoid special language uses such as literature and focus on mundane, situationally related language such as signs, directions, descriptions, transcribed conversations, etc. This would depend, of course, on the background of the learner. Scientists should do very well with materials dealing with their own interests.

(e) It will always be easier for a student to learn to read a language he already speaks. For young learners this clearly suggests a sequence of early focus on oral language and later introduction of reading, even in situations where the second language will be the medium of later education. But the motivation and needs of older highly literate students may suggest that oral and written language receive equal attention even at early stages.

(f) As in learning to read a first language, reading instruction should always involve natural, meaningful language and instruction should avoid the trivial and keep the focus on comprehension strategies.

Sociolinguistic Aspects of Reading

Chapter Fifteen

Vygotsky in a Whole-Language Perspective

Yetta M. Goodman and Kenneth S. Goodman
University of Arizona, 1990

> *The best method [for teaching reading and writing] is one in which children do not learn to read and write but in which both these skills are found in play situations. . . . In the same way as children learn to speak, they should be able to learn to read and write. (Vygotsky, 1978, p. 118)*

In this passage, Vygotsky expresses his belief that written language develops, as speech does, in the context of its use. It indicates his holistic inclinations and his awareness of the need for learners to be immersed in language for literacy learning to be easy.

Such a view is the essence of whole language. Whole language is more than anything else a philosophy of education. It draws heavily on Vygotsky, among others. As we relate the developing conceptualizations of whole language to the work of Vygotsky, we will explore (1) what whole language is; (2) what it takes from Vygotsky; (3) how whole language can contribute to the application and development of

This chapter first appeared in *Vygotsky and Education*, Luis Moll, (ed.), Cambridge University Press, 1990, pp. 223–250. Copyright (1990) by Cambridge University Press. Reprinted with permission.

Vygotskian psychology; and (4) how it departs from or goes beyond Vygotsky.

What Is Whole Language?

Whole language is a holistic, dynamic, grass-roots movement among teachers. It is spreading rapidly in the English-speaking countries of the world and moving beyond to other countries. Though some of the key concepts of whole language have origins in the United States, particularly in the work of John Dewey (1938) and other progressive educationists such as Kilpatrick (1926), Counts (1932), and Childs (1956), and more recently in the work on reading and writing processes, other English-speaking countries came to whole language earlier and more pervasively than the United States. In Canada several provinces have whole-language policies, and implementation is widespread. Whole language in Great Britain is building on a number of holistic movements in education. The report of the Bullock committee, *A Language for Life* (1975), played a major role in innovation in schools in Britain as well as in Canada, Australia, and New Zealand. Though the term *whole language* is not used widely in Great Britain, the integrated day, language across the curriculum, and other school movements have led to widespread holistic school practices.

In Australia, drawing on European and North American sources, whole-language policies, methods, and materials have become dominant. New Zealand, however, has the longest continuous tradition of progressive, holistic education. Since the 1930s New Zealand educators have developed learner-centered curricula and school practices (Penton, 1979). This small country, perhaps the world's most literate according to multinational studies, never abandoned Dewey's progressive education concepts, and it has provided models of application for the rest of the world (Clay & Cazden, 1990).

The development of whole language in the United States has been held back by the strong influence of behavioral psychology in American schools. This influence has been felt through textbooks, particularly those used in reading instruction, through mandated norm-referenced tests, and through curricula organized around testable, behavioral objectives. Though teachers in the United States have the most degrees and the most years of education of any country in the world, these behavioral curricula, policies, and materials control teachers and make it difficult for them to apply their professional knowledge to decision making in their classrooms. With these constraints, teachers find it particularly difficult to respond to the characteristics and needs of individual learners.

Ironically, whole-language teachers in the United States have been strengthened as a result of their struggle against the behavioristic mandates that govern their teaching. They have had to examine their professional beliefs and values and, at the same time, build a knowledge base to support and defend their innovations. That is why whole-language teachers are reading Vygotsky individually and in support groups, thinking about his concepts, applying them in their classrooms, and using his arguments to defend their teaching and to understand what their pupils are doing.

Whole language, as it is emerging, draws on the antecedent movements in education that have taken positive, humanistic views of teaching and learning (Y. Goodman, 1989). These can be traced at least as far back as Comenius, who advocated vernacular schools and brought pictures and the real world into instruction (see Comenius, 1887). But whole language also draws on knowledge from all of the foundational disciplines: psychology, linguistics, anthropology, and sociology. It draws on interdisciplinary work in psycholinguistics, sociolinguistics, language development, artificial intelligence, and communication theory; and it draws on all disciplines that are concerned with language: literary criticism, semiotics, semantics, and language philosophy. This is not to say that whole language is eclectic. Rather, it integrates what it draws from these sources into a practical philosophy that provides the criteria for making all the decisions teachers, as practitioners, must make. This is no small undertaking. But whole language is in fact developing in such a sophisticated way that practice is getting ahead of theory and consequently knowledgeable whole-language teachers have much to teach psychologists, linguists, anthropologists, and others.

Whole-language teachers, with their focus on authentic learning experiences (Edelsky, 1986) and integration of subject matter with the language arts, create nonreductionist school learning environments. These environments are quite different from those experimental psychologists create in their laboratories or contrive in traditional classrooms. In these nonreductionist classrooms we are just beginning to see the potential for human learning and for the kinds of teaching that most effectively support learning. Key ideas of whole language concerning social contexts and literacy development, learning in and out of school, teaching and learning, and the relationship between teaching and learning draw heavily on Vygotsky while differing from some of his concepts.

Learning Literacy in the Context of Its Use

Language, written language included, is learned most easily in the context of use. When language is whole, relevant, and functional, learners have real purposes for using language, and through their language use they develop control over the processes of language. In authentic literacy events (Edelsky, 1986), events that have personal and significant meaning for the language user, there are transactions between the reader and the text in which the reader is continuously solving new problems and building and extending psycholinguistic strategies. Through these transactions text serves to mediate the development of reading and writing. We use the concept of text, as defined by Halliday and Hasan (1976). To them text is the basic semantic unit of linguistic interaction. "It has . . . a unity of meaning in context, a texture that expresses the fact that it relates as a whole to the environment in which it is placed" (pp. 293–295).

The whole-language view of literacy development is thus an immersion view. Children growing up in literate societies are surrounded by print. They begin to be aware of the functions of written language and to play at its use long before they come to school. School continues and extends this immersion in literacy. The school can be an even richer literate environment than the world outside of school. The teacher can serve as mediator between the learners and this literate environment. Each school experience can be an authentic speech or literacy event, "a complex cultural activity" (Vygotsky, 1978, p. 118). The teacher invites the participation of the learners and supports their transactions with language and the world.

Learning and Teaching

In *Crow Boy* by Taro Yashima (1959), an insightful author and illustrator of children's books, we are introduced to Chibi, a tiny boy in a village school in Japan, who has been an isolate, a "forlorn little tag-along," for 6 years. Even the teachers are pictured as uninvolved and distant from Chibi. When the children are in the sixth grade, Mr. Isobe, a new teacher, "a friendly man with a kind smile," introduces innovative experiences for the children. He often "took his class to the hilltop behind the school." He responds to Chibi differently as well.

> He [Mr. Isobe] was pleased to learn that Chibi knew all the places where the wild grapes and wild potatoes grew. . . .
>
> He was amazed to find how much Chibi knew about all the flowers in our class garden. . . .
>
> He liked Chibi's own handwriting, which no one but Chibi could read, and he tacked that upon the wall. . . .
>
> And he often spent time talking with Chibi when no one was around. . . .
>
> But when Chibi appeared on the stage at the talent show of that year, no one could believe his eyes. . . . "What can that stupid do up there?" . . .

Until Mr. Isobe announced that Chibi was going to imitate the voices of crows. (pp. 19–25)

Chibi learned from staring at ceilings, gazing out of windows, wandering the hills, and listening with great attention and interest to birds. But it wasn't until Mr. Isobe appeared in his sixth year of school that he found out that he could also learn in school and that what he had learned outside of school was important, valuable, and of interest to others. Mr. Isobe, like many teachers who call themselves whole language teachers now, saw no clear distinction between teachers and learners. He saw himself as a learner and believed that even the least of his pupils knew a lot and had a lot to teach him. He was a kid watcher who evaluated his pupils by talking with them, observing them, and transacting with them. Like Chibi, all children are whole-language learners. Unfortunately, also like Chibi, they don't often encounter whole-language teachers.

A basic tenet of whole language is that kids learn when they are in control of their learning and know that they are in control. Here is another point where Vygotsky and whole language come together. When children are immersed in real reading and real writing, they can read and write for purposes of their own and they are empowered.

In whole language, each learner builds on his or her own culture, values, and interest. Each builds on his or her own strengths: There are no disadvantaged. Such a view about learners is essential to literacy development, but is also essential to truly democratic education. Whole language opens up what Frank Smith (1988) calls "the literacy club" for members of both sexes and all classes, races, and language groups.

Whole language views learners as strong not weak, independent not dependent, active not passive. We believe such views are consistent with Vygotsky's views. Learners are capable of learning relatively easily what is relevant and functional for them. So the purpose of schools is to help learners to expand on what they know, to build on what they can do, to support them in identifying needs and interests and in coping with old and new experiences.

John Dewey (1902) provided considerable insight into the relationship between learning in school and learning outside of school. We learn by doing, he showed us. It becomes important then that students are involved in functional authentic activities in school. School is not preparation for life; it is life. Children can learn much more easily, therefore, when the knowledge is immediately useful; learning is more difficult if it has a more distant purpose. In Dewey's pragmatic philosophy there is no useful separation between ends and means in learning; what we learn today is the means of further learning tomorrow. There are no end products, no mastery goals; rather, each goal is part of the means to a new goal, a new schema, a new concept, a new view of the world.

The transactional view of learners in whole-language classrooms owes much to Dewey's views of education. He recognized the importance of integrating language, thought, and content in the thematic solving of everyday problems. Such experiences are authentic for learners. Learning by doing means that we learn to read by reading and to write by writing as we are using literacy for purposes that are important to ourselves. Skills cannot be isolated from their use; in fact, they develop most easily in the context of their use.

We see inconsistencies in Vygotsky's discussion (1978) of the authenticity of learning experiences in schools in his exploration of the similarities and differences between in-school and out-of-school learning. We will explore these similarities and differences in relation to Vygotsky's position throughout this chapter. On the one hand, Vygotsky establishes his position when he states:

> School learning introduces something fundamentally new into the child's development. In order to elaborate the dimensions of school learning we will describe a new and exceptionally important concept without which the issue cannot be resolved: the zone of proximal development. (p. 84)

On the other hand, Vygotsky contradicts his own statement that school learning alone activates the zone of proximal development when he discusses the role of play as a context in which the zone of proximal development is also activated.

> Play creates a zone of proximal development of the child. In play a child always behaves beyond his average age, above his daily behavior; in play it is as though he were a head taller than himself. As in the focus of a magnifying glass, play contains all developmental tendencies in a condensed form and is itself a major source of development. (p. 102)

The Role of Play

Vygotsky, like Dewey and Piaget, writes extensively about the power of play in the learning of children. In play children exercise their imaginations, but they also explore the roles of adults in common daily experiences.

When their play involves fantasizing, children draw on their experiences with stories, books, television, and films and on the special folklore that is passed on from each generation of children to the next. When our daughter Debra drove from Detroit to Tucson with her then

3-year-old son Reuben, she planned to stop at parks along the way for him to run and play to relieve the long stretches of sitting on the trip. She carefully packed toys and supplies for him to occupy himself. At the time his favorite playthings were the plastic figures from Masters of the Universe, which he also watched on television. Within minutes of arriving at a park he and other preschoolers were actively involved in imaginative play, easily fitting into the roles of He-man and She-ra as they opposed the imaginary forces of evil. They quickly lost any shyness and found common images and language to share their play.

At other times play appears more realistic as children play house or school or store or office. They pretend to be parents and children, teachers and pupils, gas station attendants, doctors and nurses, bus drivers, pilots, police officers, store clerks. As they do they adopt the appropriate language and engage in relevant activities. In both fantasy and realistic play situations children are involved in out-of-school experiences through which they are learning a good deal about the knowledge and culture of their peers and the adults in the society.

As Vygotsky suggests, play, itself, mediates the learning of children. Because they are "only" playing, they are free to risk doing things they are not yet confident they can do well. In social play, children transact with each other, mediating each other's learning. They learn to understand the meanings of the world as they play with their representations of the world. They build concepts of mathematics and science as well as language, including literacy. We believe that the concepts begun in play not only are the basis for scientific concepts but eventually become part of these concepts.

Social Transaction

Vygotsky helps us understand that as children transact with their world they are capable of doing more than they appear to be and that they can get much more out of an activity or experience if there is an adult or more experienced playmate to mediate the experience for them. We believe that all social interactions, not only those involving expert peers and adults, provide the opportunity for children to learn more about the world. There is growing evidence that collaborative learning between peers, regardless of ability, activates the zone of proximal development (Tudge, 1990). Pontecorvo and Zuccchermaglio (1990) have shown that peers of similar knowledge or ability cause reorganization of concepts as students argue and negotiate their solutions to various problems. Teberosky (1990) has shown how bilingual children learn about language through interactions with peers as they explore literacy events together.

We believe that zones of proximal development are created within the learners in the context of activities. Caring adults are sensitive to the directions in which children's curiosity takes them, their attempts to express needs or understandings, and the meanings they are creating. These adults track the development of the learners, and they are eager to help them learn. In fact, they take delight in the learning and in the developing ideas and invented language of the children. Teachers, as professionals but still caring adults, can be insightful kid watchers who sense from what kids *are doing* what they are *capable of doing.* They are able to involve learners in relevant functional activities and experiences that will stretch their capabilities, and they mediate the learners' transactions with the world in minimally intrusive ways, supporting learning without controlling it. They find opportunities to encourage learners to work in collaboration on a variety of problems that are important and meaningful to them.

Dewey, Vygotsky, and the Soviet psychologists who built on Vygotsky's work all emphasize the importance of activity and learning in the process of doing. In whole language the importance of authentic activities in which language, both oral and written, serves in real and functional ways is always stressed. In fact, the popular term *whole language* derives at least partly from a concern for keeping language whole and in the context of functional use.

Piaget (1977) has demonstrated that children are active and intelligent learners. They expect the world to make sense, so they continually seek order in the world as they transact with it. In coping with the physical world they shape the world and are shaped by it, in processes of assimilation and accommodation. Learners adapt to the physical world by building schemas to which they assimilate new knowledge. If there is a disequilibrium, if they cannot assimilate because of contradictions between existing schemas and new experience, then they must accommodate by modifying existing schemas or developing new ones.

The process of adaptation is one that can be supported by caring and insightful teachers, but it cannot be forced or controlled by teachers. In fact, teachers must be careful that they support real learning rather than forcing superficial behavior which may satisfy school requirements without real learning. Vygotsky cautioned against such superficial behavior as well. He provided research evidence that raises questions about "pedagogical movements that emphasized formal discipline and urged the teaching of classical languages, ancient civilizations, and mathematics ... regardless of the irrelevance of these ... for daily living" (1978, pp. 81–82).

David Bloome (1987) in his ethnographic studies calls this superficial behavior "procedural display." School becomes a place where you display the expected behavior by acting in acceptable ways without any real adaptation, without any real learning.

Learning Language and Learning Through Language

If we accept the concept that learning is different in school and out of school and that scientific concepts are learned only in school and spontaneous concepts only out of school, then we are put in the position of accepting the notion that experiences should be substantively different for school-learned concepts.

We believe, rather, that learning in school and learning out of school are not different. The same factors that make concepts easy to learn out of school make them easy in school: Learners build on experience, expand on schemas and rely heavily on language for development. We cannot accept the notion that the two kinds of concepts develop differently. Whole language assumes a single learning process influenced and constrained by personal understandings and social impacts.

We believe that scientific concepts begin as personal concepts that develop in individuals. These personal concepts are influenced by the social community, including the school community, which may or may not be scientific in nature. We use the terms *public* or *folk concepts* (Goodman, Smith, Meredith, & Goodman, 1987) to contrast with scientific concepts. Scientific concepts are derived from activities of scholars in various fields of study as they carefully consider the results of research and theory and incorporate them into explanations of phenomena and expansions of their own knowledge and ideas. Folk concepts are those that are carried by public means of communication, which may vary from accurate accounts of events to hearsay passed along in public places of work and commerce. They are the "commonsense" notions of a society, probably much the same as those concepts Vygotsky considered to be spontaneous.

Folk concepts can also be held up to scrutiny by their developers. They may or may not be accepted and corroborated by the scientific community. Many folk remedies have been supported by scientists once ways to study certain features became more accessible. Uses of herbs and spider webs as home remedies are examples.

Teachers can mediate concept development by providing opportunities for pupils to test personal, spontaneous, and scientific concepts. The water and sand tables found in many kindergartens and some first grades provide opportunity for children to explore concepts of volume, density, states of matter, categorization, and math, among others. But the process of concept development is a unitary one. Whether concepts are spontaneous or scientific, they are all learned in much the same way. For learners, a teacher may label a concept as scientific, but that doesn't mean they can or will learn it differently.

Vygotsky (1986) argues that

> to learn a foreign language at school and to develop one's native language involve two entirely different processes.... While learning a foreign language, we use word meanings that are already well developed in the native language and only translate them; the advanced knowledge of one's own language also plays an important role in the study of the foreign one, as well as those inner and outer relations that are characteristic only in the study of a foreign language. (pp. 159–161)

This is a major point of departure between whole-language advocates and ideas expressed by Vygotsky. We see only one language-learning process whether in school or out. Second-language learning is indeed facilitated by the "advanced knowledge" of the first language, but the process of learning is no different. In the last few decades, second-language and foreign-language programs have moved away from dual views and are now trying to organize instruction in the new language so that it is as authentic, natural, and contextualized as possible. Organizing schools to be like the most supportive learning and spontaneous social environments outside of school makes schools much more effective for learning.

We believe that Vygotsky was expressing the complex relationship between different kinds of knowledge of language. In our own work we have been aware that there are complex differences between being able to read, being able to talk about reading, and understanding the reading process. But it is the knowledge learners bring to the making of meaning, the knowledge and the relationships between the people in the environment who interact with the learners, and the particular environment itself that influence how easily and how well reading develops.

In his study of language development, Michael Halliday (1975) uses the phrase "learning how to mean." He describes the development of a range of personal/social functions which then stimulate the development of the forms of language. As learners experience the wide variety of functions and forms of language, they internalize the way their society uses language to represent meaning. So they are learning language at the same time they are using language to learn. They also are learning about language. But all three kinds of language learning must be simultaneous (Halliday, 1980). Thinking that we can teach the forms of language as prerequisites to their use is a mistake schools often make.

Halliday, like Vygotsky, has a social theory of language. In his systemic-functional view, the very form that language takes derives from the fact that it is used socially and that, through its use, language users, including children, create and learn the language conventions or social rules of language to make communication easy and effective.

It is equally important to recognize the central role that language plays in human learning. Language makes it possible to share experience, to link our minds and produce a social intelligence far superior to that of any one individual. We can learn from shared vicarious experience through language. Language, oral and written, can never be simply a school subject.

Centrifugal Force and Centripetal Force: Personal Invention and Social Convention

A common interpretation of Vygotsky's view of language development is that social experience is internalized and social language shapes the language of the individual. Though there can be no doubt that eventually the language of each individual must fall within the norms of the social language and that the way society organizes meaning and represents it strongly shapes the way the individual makes sense of the world, we believe that language is as much personal invention as social convention. Human learners are not passively manipulated by their social experiences; they are actively seeking sense in the world. The individual and society both play strong roles in language development.

Vygotsky (1986) describes the process of internalization: "An operation that initially represents an external activity is reconstructed and begins to occur internally" (pp. 56–57). We don't disagree with this concept of internalization. But we believe that there are also internal efforts to represent experience symbolically and that the reconstruction of external activity is simultaneously a reconstruction of internal activity.

There are two seemingly opposing forces shaping the development of language in individuals and in communities. Although they are opposing in a sense, they operate in an integral fashion. The metaphor we use to describe these forces comes from the concept of centrifugal and centripetal forces of physics. If a ball is twirled on a string, there is a centrifugal force pulling it away from the center. If the twirler lets go, the ball flies off in a straight line. The string transmits an opposing, centripetal force pulling it back toward the middle. As long as these are in balance, the ball will orbit the center.

In language, the centrifugal force is the ability of people individually and collectively to create semiotic systems, to invent new language, to deal with new experience, feelings, and ideas. This creative force produces change and makes it possible for language continuously to meet the developing and changing needs of its users. But if this force were unchecked, language would expand so rapidly that it would lose its social utility. People would soon be unable to understand each other at all.

The centripetal force that provides the counterbalance and relative stability is the social nature of language. If language were static and unchanging it would quickly inhibit its users in learning and in communicating their responses to new experiences. Change in language, whether temporary or permanent, may be initiated by individuals, but it must be understood and accepted by others in order for language to be effective. To serve its functions it must be comprehensible by others, not just by the speaker or the writer. In social transactions with others, learners experience the conventions of the social language. When language changes there is always balance between the creative force and the need to communicate. So the inventor moves toward the social forms and uses the social resources in making new inventions. Thus there is a centripetal force that balances the outward thrust of personal language.

Language development, then, can be viewed as being shaped by these two forces. There is an almost explosive force from within the children that propels them to express themselves, and at the same time there is a strong need to communicate that pushes the direction of growth and development toward the language of the family and community. This shaping is accomplished through the myriad language transactions that involve children with others. The language is generated by the child, but it is changed in transactions with others by their comprehension or lack of comprehension and by their responses. Thus parents, teachers, caregivers, siblings, peers, and significant others play vital roles in the language development of children. They are essential communicative partners, less role models than respondents, less to be imitated than to be understood and understanding.

Another way to view these two opposing forces shaping language is as a balance between invention and convention. Both invention, personal creation of language, and convention, the socially established systems and norms, are necessary for learning. Language is not learned by imitating adults or learning rules out of the context of language use. It is invented by each individual, and in the context of its social use it is adapted to the social conventions. Every language must have within it devices for change, but innovators must use the devices for change the language provides or risk not being understood.

Learners are not resistant to the social force in language. In fact, language comes about at least partially as a means of social participation. Infants sense the social functions of language before they understand the communicative functions. As they begin to represent their own needs and experiences symbolically, they are eager to be understood and to understand others. So they are accepting of the social conventions of language. But these conventions are implicit, not explicit. The rules by which language is governed can be inferred by learners, but they are never directly observable, never imitatable. Any attempt by well-meaning adults to make the rules explicit can actually inhibit learning. Rather, the child keeps inventing rules and trying them out until they work—until they come into balance with social conventions.

We believe that maintaining the balance between invention and convention in developing reading and writing is a major factor in whether pupils come to consider themselves as insiders or outsiders, members of the literacy club or excluded from club benefits (Smith, 1988). If all students are subjected to rigid curricula and interventionist teaching, some will survive and make their way into the club anyway. As they do they will be permitted more latitude in their reading and writing and will be able to balance their inventive energy against the conventions they find in their authentic literacy events. Because they belong to the literacy club, their in-school activities begin to look more like what they do outside of school. Other pupils, defeated by the rejection of their inventions, will be confused by the rigid conventions of textbooks and by the inflexibility of prescriptive language rules. These pupils will be excluded from the literacy club. The less they succeed, the less authentic will be their experiences and the less control they will be permitted. School life becomes alien to their out-of-school experiences. Ironically, the interventionist program is given credit for those who make it into the literacy club whereas the pupils who do not make it are blamed for their own failure.

Society values the inventions of some but not others. Established artists, writers, and scientists are supported. Art shows, book, drama, and concert reviews often praise the creative aspects of artistic works or performances. New discoveries of scientists are extolled on the front pages of newspapers. But a scientist whose discovery breaks with the dominant paradigm will not be easily accepted by his or her peers. Which concepts are scientific is not self-evident. Consider how long it took for Darwin's ideas about the scientific nature of biology to become established. The French Impressionists were vilified and unappreciated because they broke with the conventions of their time. Eventually their inventive energy was so strong, and they themselves so persistent, that new conventions emerged. The fact that these artistic nonconformists were also nonconformist in their life styles did not help their acceptance.

To this day, we are likely to reject and minimize the creative invention of some groups more than others. Poor people, minorities, teenagers, those from cultures outside the mainstream, and nonconformists in general are not expected to contribute in valued ways. Their lack of conformity to some social conventions defined by reference to the dominant culture is interpreted as ignorance, incompetence, or antisocial behavior.

The inventive abilities of young people of all ages are often treated as disruptive and antisocial. So school practice in all respects has tended to treat difference as deficiency and inventive strength as random weakness. Instead of understanding the ability of all pupils to learn and the need for them to make their own way to an equilibrium between invention and convention, we treat some as lacking in the requirements for admission to the literacy club and use interventionist strategies that become self-fulfilling prophecies: Eventually many accept the view of themselves as incapable; those that don't rebel or drop out.

The process of balancing invention and convention works better for young people outside of school than in the traditional school setting. Schools have traditionally narrowly defined conventions of behavior, of learning, of language, of thinking, even of dress. We believe that the difference between learning in school and out of school is largely an imposed one and an undesirable one. It ought to be easier to learn in school than out of school because in school there are professional teachers to mediate the learning. But instead of adjusting school to the learners we require them to adjust to the school.

Scientific concepts can be considered a type of social convention; they are conventional views shared by the best informed and most enlightened within the society. The process by which concepts are validated as scientific is itself highly conventionalized. The status of scientists gives their concepts a special status in society. But that also makes them resistant to displacement by better, alternate concepts, which may have to break with or defy the conventions. We believe scientific concepts are learned in the same way as other concepts, through the push and pull of personal invention and social convention.

Vygotsky certainly recognized the tensions between the individual and society. Wertsch (1985) says Vygotsky discusses the child's cultural development on two planes. "First it appears between people as an interpsychological category and then within the child as an intrapsychological category." We see this as more a transaction than a one-way sequence, with the social first and the personal following. Rather, the child invents in the context of authentic social experiences in which conventions are implicit. Over time the inventions come to conform to the social conventions.

Aaron, at age 4, provided a powerful example of invention when he wrote his "GRAPA GHENE" a birthday card. The card contains much evidence to support our contentions about the relationship of invention to convention, including his awareness of card giving for birthdays and the general form of birthday cards. But his spelling of GRAPA GHENE is a very strong example of how invention works in language development. What he is inventing is a spelling for *Grandpa Kenny,* his most common term for his grandfather. English does not represent the aspiration of /k/ in the initial position in *Kenny* (contrast the breathiness of the /K/ in *Ken* with the /k/ in *skill*). Aaron perceives this aspiration and draws on his knowledge of how it is represented in his own last name, *Hood*. At the same time that he invents the spelling GHENE, he shows his knowledge of a number of phonological and orthographic conventions.

Traditional methods in schools may get willing students to echo verbalizations of language conventions and scientific concepts and even manipulate them in narrow and controlled contexts. But for these to become internalized and operationalized by learners—for the social to become the personal—there must be room to invent, to test out, to experiment, and to reach personal-social equilibrium.

Collaboration in Whole-Language Classrooms

In whole language there is a reciprocal, transactional view of teaching and learning. Using transaction as Dewey did implies that in classroom transactions teachers and learners are changed. Wertsch (1985) quotes Vygotsky on this change in learners: "Internalization transforms the process itself and changes its structure and functions" (p. 81). The traditional idea that teaching can control learning or that each act of teaching results in a reciprocal act of learning in each learner is too simplistic. Teachers learn and learners teach, and as they transact each is changed. Both can resist this change by not committing themselves to the transactions. Whole language teachers recognize the power of classroom transactions and plan for them.

One key to teachers' success is building an atmosphere of mutual respect in their classrooms. These become social communities where teachers value each learner, help the learners to value themselves and each other, and win the respect of their students.

Whole-language teachers don't abdicate their authority or responsibility. But they lead by virtue of their greater experience, their knowledge, and their respect for their pupils. They know their pupils, monitor their learning, and provide support and resources as they are needed. They recognize that there must be collaboration between themselves and their pupils if an optimal learning atmosphere is to be created. Whole-language teachers believe that experiences and literacy events must be as authentic in the classroom as they are outside of it. Pupils must feel a sense of purpose, of choice, of utility, of participation, and of shared ownership in their classrooms and in what happens there. Even as young beginners they need to participate in decision-making and see relevance in what they are doing. The tenor of relationships between teachers and learners becomes one of trust and collaboration rather than conflict and domination.

New Roles for Teachers

In whole-language classrooms teachers are empowered. They are not reduced to powerless technicians administering someone else's work sheets, skill drills, and basal readers to powerless pupils. In turn they empower learners by valuing who they are and what they know, do, and believe. They support the learners in solving their problems and pursuing knowledge. The learners are involved and committed to the ongoing teaming events in their classrooms because these events are authentic and relevant and because the learners are empowered participants.

The teacher is an initiator. Whole-language teachers are initiators. Their roles are in no sense passive. They create authentic contexts in their classrooms and participate with their students in order to stimulate learners to engage in solving problems and identifying and meeting their own needs. As they do so they insightfully observe the learners so that they can recognize and even anticipate the learners' potential. These teachers know how to create conditions that will cause learners to exhibit and make the most of their zones of proximal development.

The teacher is a kid watcher. The whole-language teacher is skilled at observing kids at play and at work, knowing where they are developmentally, and seeing the naturally occurring zones of proximal development. We believe it is a mistake to think that teachers can control or even create zones of proximal development in learners. But whole-language teachers know how to detect the evidence of what learners are ready to do with support. If the teacher is not a successful kid watcher the zones will be missed, and so will opportunities for growth and learning.

The teacher is a mediator. Redefining learning requires us to redefine teaching. Optimal learning requires teaching that supports and facilitates it without controlling, distorting, or thwarting the learning. Vygotsky's (1978) concept of mediation is a useful way to view a major component of optimal teaching. The learner is in a situational context in which problems need to be solved or experiences understood. The teacher is present as the learning transaction takes place but in the role of mediator—supporting the learning transactions but neither causing them to happen in any direct sense nor controlling the learning. In this way the forces of invention and convention are unfettered, and the teacher supports the learner in achieving equilibrium.

In defining themselves as mediators, whole-language teachers understand that less can be more. They realize that helping a learner solve a problem is better than giving him or her an algorithm or a solution. In reading and writing, teachers interfere as little as possible between the text and the reader. Teachers mediate by asking a question here, offering a useful hint there, directing attention at an anomaly, calling attention to overlooked information, and supporting learners as they synthesize what they are learning into new concepts and schemas. They provide just enough support to help the learner make the most of his or her own zone of proximal development. Whole-language teachers do assume, as Vygotsky (1978) said, that "even the profoundest thinkers never questioned that what children can do with the assistance of others might be in some sense even more indicative of their mental development than what they can do alone" (p. 85). But whole-language teachers also know that assisting pupils in doing something is different from doing it for them or controlling what they do. Consider two classroom episodes:

1. A group of black inner-city fourth-grade pupils have read Langston Hughes's poem "Mother to Son" (Hughes, 1963, p. 67). The pupils discuss the poem. The classroom procedure involves a pupil leading the discussion; the teacher is a codiscussant. The teacher wonders what they think about the mother's saying "Life for me ain't been no crystal stair." Some of the pupils point out other references to stairs in the poem. The teacher shares with them her knowledge of the author's life and political beliefs. She suggests that the stairs represent the author's view of this woman's attempt to raise herself up from her difficult conditions. One boy asks, "She talkin' 'bout climbin' up to heaven?" They decide that the mother is contrasting her hard life to the religious idea of life as a beautiful crystal stair leading to heaven. In doing so they draw on their own knowledge of the likely experiences and religious beliefs of the mother. They share stories of their own mothers. "I never thought of this poem in quite that way," says the teacher.

2. An eighth-grade group in a working-class suburb plans a unit on evolution. The discussion and webbing of their knowledge of the concept introduce the controversy over the biblical view of creation. Two weeks after the unit begins one student tells the teacher that his minister would like to come in and debate evolution with the teacher. The teacher declines, explaining that studying a theory is different than

advocating it. The class discusses the situation and reaffirms that they are studying evolution as a theory. They decide to explore the role of theory in science and the difference between established fact and theory. The student is encouraged by the teacher and his classmates to bring into the study literature from creationists on the subject. The ensuing study is enlivened. The pupils search avidly for resources not only on evolution but on the history of the theory and the controversy over it. One group of students reads Irving Stone's (1979) biography of Charles Darwin and shares their responses.

In both of these examples, the teacher plays a crucial but not controlling role. The teacher is an initiator, selecting a poem to be shared, planning a unit, providing time for pupils to pursue a spontaneous question. The teacher is a kid watcher who considers not only where the pupils are but where they are capable of going in their learning. So one teacher is supportive and receptive as pupils relate their own schemas to Hughes's poem. The other teacher welcomes the fundamentalist challenge to the scientific concept. These teachers are not intervening in the learning; they are mediating it. The role of the teacher as mediator is an active one and reflects the teacher's understanding that teaching supports learning; it can't force it to happen.

In areas of controversy the teacher is not afraid to express belief but shows respect for the developing beliefs of the learners, whether they are based in personal, public, or scientific concepts. The teacher shares knowledge but knows that when learners can relate the new knowledge to what they already know and what they need to know they will understand why the knowledge is important, and they will be able to integrate the new knowledge with their existing schemas and conceptual systems. In building comprehension the teacher knows that the pupils' development of their own strategies is more important than whether they agree with the teacher. So the teacher helps the pupils to examine the available facts, to evaluate their own beliefs, and to find more information as they need it.

The teacher is by no means the only mediator in the whole-language classroom. By providing opportunities for pupils to self-evaluate, the power of reflective thinking as a mediating force is revealed. Reflecting on one's own learning is necessary for both the teacher and the learner. Dewey (Archambault, 1964), in his concern for reflective thinking, says: "Thinking enables us to direct our own activities with foresight and to plan according to ends-in-view, or purposes of which we are aware" (p. 212).

The teacher is a liberator. There is a vital difference between mediation and intervention. This difference controls whether the teacher liberates or suppresses the learners. In intervention the teacher takes control of learning, knows with great certainty in advance what learning will be acceptable, and thus undermines the learners' confidence in themselves; the teacher becomes the determiner of social conventions and the suppressor of invention. When invention is inhibited, risk taking is limited and zones of proximal development are unlikely to be revealed or explored.

Paolo Freire (1970) contrasts "banking" views of pedagogy with liberating views. The banking view treats learners as empty vessels. Teachers deposit bits of learning into their heads. Learners have no control over the process, nor are their needs or interests considered. Liberating pedagogy sees learners in a power relationship to society. If education is to help them to liberate themselves it must be empowering. The learners must own the process of their learning. They must see learning, including literacy and language development, as part of a process of liberation. Freire was successful in helping Brazilian peasants to become literate by using the ideas and concepts of their political movement in the texts they used in learning to read.

In a broader sense Freire was recognizing that learners learn best when they are free to control their own learning. This liberation is neither romantic nor abstract. Teachers cannot liberate pupils from society or from the constraints of social transactions. But they can remove the artificial controls of traditional schooling. They can encourage pupils to enter freely into speech and literacy events, authentic social transactions, in which language is a tool for communication. They can make their classrooms communities of learners in which a full range of language genres occur naturally and in which their own language and the language of their home cultures are completely accepted. In such a community pupils are free to invent ways of dealing with their functional needs and free to discover the conventions in authentic social language transactions.

Freeing pupils to take risks is a major concern of whole-language classrooms. In traditional classrooms, not only are pupils required to stay within arbitrary conventions in their oral and written expression, but they are penalized for their errors. Whole-language classrooms liberate pupils to try new things, to invent spellings, to experiment with new genres, to guess at meanings in their reading, to read and write imperfectly, to challenge textbooks, to pursue inquiry.

Our research on reading and writing has strongly supported the importance of error in language development (K. Goodman & Gollasch, 1982; Y. Goodman & Wilde, 1985). Miscues represent the tension between invention and convention in reading. They show the reader's use of existing schemas in attempting to comprehend texts. They also show how the text itself mediates learning. In whole-language classrooms risk taking is not simply tolerated, it is celebrated. Learners have always been free to fail in school. However, in whole-language classrooms they are free to learn from their failures with the support of their teachers.

Dewey relates failure to the power of thought:

> While the power of thought, then, frees us from servile subjection to instinct, appetite, and routine, it also brings with it the occasion and possibility of error and mistake. In elevating us above the brute, it opens the possibility of failures to which the animal, limited to instinct, cannot sink. (Archambault, 1964, p. 217)

The Role of Text and the Zone of Proximal Development

Whole-language teachers recognize that if their pupils are involved in authentic experiences the speech acts and literacy events will largely be self-mediating.

In the act of composing, for example, the writing of text mediates writing development as the language user seeks actively to make sense through the text being created.

For this self-development to take place, the written text must be authentic. That is, it must be whole with all the characteristics of real written texts created for real purposes in real contexts (keeping in mind Halliday and Hasan's [1976] definition of text as "a unity of meaning in context"). Vygotsky (1978) recognized writing as "a complex cultural activity." In contrast to his view on foreign-language teaching cited earlier, he says there is a "requirement that writing be taught naturally":

> Writing must be "relevant to life." ... Writing should be meaningful for children, ... an intrinsic need should be aroused in them, and ... writing should be incorporated into a task that is necessary and relevant for life. Only then can we be certain that it will develop not as a matter of hand and finger habits but as a really new and complex form of speech. (p. 118)

In our studies of children's writing (Y. Goodman & Wilde, 1985), a research project that followed the writing of six Tohono O'odharn Indian third- and fourth-graders over a 2-year period, we collected considerable evidence of how the developing written text mediates learning. We saw a continuously moving zone of proximal development in every piece of writing the children produced.

Gabriel, a third-grade Native American, decided that *foot* and *ball* needed to be placed closer together in the word *football* than the normal spacing between words. Observations of Gabriel in the act of composing over 2 years showed how he dealt with spacing and hyphenation as he gained control over the features of how compound words are represented in written English. In the act of producing text, Gabriel is inventing a way of representing in the written semiotic system phenomena that he knows he can represent in the oral semiotic system. In the process he discovers that there are not isomorphic conventions in the orthography for everything that can be represented in speech. In this research we found examples of the young writers developing control over genre variations, syntactic rules, spelling, and punctuation.

Another third-grader, Bill, also shows how the text serves as mediator. He invented a "sadlamation point" in a story about his pet dog who was killed in an automobile accident. He had realized there were no existing punctuation marks that represent sadness. When his classmates found out about his invention, they began to focus much more on the uses of punctuation in their writing. Bill's written text provided the opportunity for him to learn about the need for punctuation. Then Bill and the teacher became mediators for the other students' exploration of punctuation. Through writing conferences and other classroom discussions, all the members of the class became more conscious of the conventional uses of punctuation in their reading of books, advertisements, and signs in their environment.

In miscue research, where we analyze reading miscues (unexpected responses to written texts in oral reading), we became aware that every time we analyzed a reader's miscues in reading a whole story we saw learning and development (Goodman & Goodman, 1977). In miscue research, readers read a complete story aloud without aid from the researcher. Then each of the readers' miscues is analyzed using linguistic, psycholinguistic, and sociolinguistic criteria (Y. Goodman, Watson, & Burke, 1987). We have concluded that readers are developing new strategies, new vocabulary, new confidence in their ability to read during the reading itself without any discussion or aid from anyone else. In the reading of authentic texts, at all levels of reading proficiency, there are transactions between the reader and the text in which the reader is continuously solving new problems and building and extending psycholinguistic strategies.

Miscue research shows that reading is also a "complex cultural activity." John, a second-grader, was reading a story in which the word *oxygen* occurred a number of times (Y. Goodman & Burke, 1972). Each time he came to the word in his oral reading he omitted it but commented, "There's that word again," or "I think I'll skip that word." Later, during his retelling of the story, he was relating that men in the space station were feeling sleepy because the air was bad. He said, "They didn't have enough . . . oxygen! That's that word I didn't know! Oxygen!" Given the opportunity to think through the text while retelling the story, the meaning came together for him and he was able to identify a word that he thought he didn't know while he was reading earlier.

At no time did the researcher give John specific information. The text mediated his learning.

Transactions with written texts provide the problem situations that readers need to deal with. During these transactions texts become mediators as the reader takes control of the learning. We've marveled watching readers, often labeled as problem readers, move toward control of complex conventions that linguists are still struggling to understand and explicate.

Another example of text as mediator during reading is revealed through our analysis of Peggy's oral reading of *The Man Who Kept House* (1964, pp. 282–283). Peggy was chosen by her teacher for this analysis because she was supposedly reading below grade level (Goodman & Goodman, 1977). Her reading of the story shows how she learns the metaphor *keeping house* as a result of reading the story. In the next segment, where the text is shown on the left and Peggy's reading on the right, we see how she learns to read complex syntactic structure as she transacts with the text.

"If you stay home to do my work, you'll have to make butter, carry water from the well, wash the clothes, clean the house, and look after the baby," said the wife.	"..., well you'll have to make bread, carry... carry water from the well, wash the clothes, clean the house, and look after the baby," said the wife.

We don't show in this example the problem Peggy has with the beginning of the clause since it is not relevant to this discussion. She inserts *well*, suggesting that she is aware that this is an argument between the husband and the wife. She substitutes *bread* for *butter*, an expected and common miscue in this context. Peggy, like most other children her age, is much more aware of the process of bread making in the home than butter making. The substitution not only reveals her background knowledge but suggests that she is monitoring the text for comprehension since making bread is an alternate choice in "keeping house." She then quickly reads *carry*, followed by a 7-second pause. She then very slowly says *carry* again and cautiously reads the phrase *carry water from the well*. At this point her reading speeds up once again, and she reads the rest of the sentence with confidence and without hesitation. For many who are not familiar with miscue analysis procedures, it is easy to conclude that Peggy's problem is that she is having some difficulty with the word *carry*. However, it is more likely that Peggy, who has heard stories read to her but had never read a seven-page story before in her life, is having problems with the syntactic complexity of the sentence. The series of five phrases that end the sentence are all connected to the verb stem of the sentence, *will have to*. Peggy has to know that each of the phrases must start with *will have to—will have to carry, will have to wash, will have to clean,* and *will have to look after—*in order to read and comprehend this sentence. When she comes to the first verb that does not have the *will have to* stem, she hesitates, pauses, wonders about what the language of the sentence might be. Her intonation as she reads first cautiously and then confidently suggests that she has worked out the problem by reading.

Miscue analysis reveals that texts not only mediate the meanings and syntactic structures but allow the reader to work out strategies for comprehension as well. In a study of word-level omissions in children's miscues (K. Goodman and Gollasch, 1980), a fourth-grade Navajo reader had a very high percentage of omission miscues during the reading of a 12-page text. A close examination of her reading showed that for the first 23 lines she had utilized a strategy of pausing frequently, apparently waiting for the researcher to tell her what the following word was. Finally, she seemed to accept that this was not going to happen, and for the next 22 lines the pauses got progressively shorter and she omitted the following words and went on. She had switched to a new strategy, which we came to call "deliberate omission." Her motto seemed to have become "When in doubt, leave it out." But that strategy gave way to a third strategy because for the remaining 10 pages there were no pauses longer than 5 seconds and virtually no omissions. She produced a number of miscues, but they all showed use of comprehending strategies.

This example, besides showing how authentic texts can mediate reading development, also illustrates the perils of intervention. Had we responded to her pauses by supplying the following words we would have been assuming that she was pausing because (1) she didn't know them (in some absolute sense) and (2) she was incapable of resolving her difficulty. And we would have supported her strategy that the safest thing to do in reading when you are unsure is to wait for the teacher to tell you what to do. By not intervening we helped her help herself. We liberated the reader to work through her own zone of proximal development.

The Teacher's Role in Balancing Invention and Convention

Teachers have traditionally been seen as agents of conformity in the language use of their pupils. This role must be reconsidered to give sufficient room for invention and to let learners become aware of convention as it exists in social language. Too often teachers have rewarded conformity, punished experimentation and risk taking, and confused learners about conventions just as they were building some sense of them.

In fact, the rules taught in school were based on authority, a set of arbitrary rules established by textbooks or teachers, and not on scientific concepts about language in use. Learners often found it hard to apply the rules or confirm them in their own language experiences. For example, teachers have sometimes taught pupils that *and* and *but* may *not* be used to start sentences. *But* pupils often found examples of sentences that did start with these words in their reading. Too much intervention and direction by others, particularly teachers, can minimize invention and focus excessively and prematurely on the need for conventionality.

Everything we learn involves imperfection and error as we gain competence. Support for mistake making and hypothesis testing is one way teachers can mediate the balancing of invention and convention. "To err is human" is an old folk saying that illustrates how long people have been aware that error is a normal part of human learning. If language learning were purely imitative or purely innate it would be hard to explain the pervasiveness of error. But if we understand the role of invention then we can understand that as people move into equilibrium between invention and convention their errors reflect their progress. The 2-year-old who says "I faked it" has moved to a rule for past tense that is partway between his early inventions and the convention of adult grammar.

The 6-year-old who invents the spelling WAT for *went* has invented the alphabetic system whereby letter sequences represent sound sequences. Her spelling represents what she hears and her own articulatory system. The /n/ in *went* is nasalized, a feature that does not fit the phoneme she represents with <n>. But spelling conventions in English are the same across dialects, and therefore standard spellings cannot be dependably generated. For the sake of standardizing spellings across dialects the system sacrifices conformity to rules. The invented spellings represent the child's control over the basic principles of the orthography but not the many exceptions.

If the teacher treats all nonstandard spellings as equally wrong the insight into the learner's control of English spelling is lost. If the teacher insists on conventional language at all stages of development and during every phase of the composing process, then the whole balance between invention and convention is destroyed and the strength and creativity of the pupils in language learning is neutralized.

No invention is wholly the creation of the inventor. Every invention, whether one by a famous scientist that has broad impact on society or the child's invention of something known to every adult in the community, is built on transactions with others. As we quoted earlier, Vygotsky (1978) emphasized the child's development from the outside in. Our view, supported by literacy development research in the last decade and a half, shows how children's inventions based on social transactions transform written language and are modified until they coincide with the social conventions of written language (Y. Goodman & Altwerger, 1981; Ferreiro & Teberosky, 1982; Goelman, Olberg, & Smith, 1984; Teale & Sulzby, 1986). Thus the social becomes the personal through the tension between invention and convention.

Eleanor Duckworth (1987) comes to similar conclusions regarding personal invention:

> I see no difference in kind between wonderful ideas that many other people have already had and wonderful ideas that nobody has yet happened upon. That is, the nature of creative intellectual acts remains the same, whether it is an infant seeing things and reaching for them ... or an astronomer who develops a new theory of the creation of the universe. (p. 14)

Curriculum in Whole-Language Classrooms

Traditionally, classrooms have been organized to pass on the conventional wisdom, usually the wisdom of an educated elite, that ignores the knowledge, the culture, and the wisdom of large groups of people representing the less powerful gender, races, languages, and ethnicities. Accepting this fund of knowledge and belief is rarely considered as legitimate for schooling. That was as true in Vygotsky's era as in ours. Even after social and political revolutions, it has often been deemed sufficient to provide access to schools for all people while continuing to accept the traditional closed curriculum.

With the focus in whole-language classrooms on authentic experiences, learners are engaged in purposeful and meaningful uses of language, both oral and written. There is no artificial breaking down of language learning into sequences of abstract skills and no synthetic language designed to control vocabulary or focus on the form of written language out of the context of its functional use. Teachers are knowledgeable empowered professionals who empower their pupils.

Because of the emphasis on using the whole of language in meaningful situational contexts there is no disruption of the two forces, personal and social, that shape language and facilitate learning. Teachers are free to learn collaboratively with their pupils and are there to support and mediate the learning. There are no artificial limits on what can be learned, nor are there any school-imposed barriers to the literacy club. The curriculum is broad and open. It brings learners into contact with a full range of social conventions as they naturally occur, but it does not reduce itself to arbitrarily imposed and narrowly interpreted conventions.

This chapter is not the vehicle in which to explore all the ramifications of a whole-language curriculum; however, we do want to touch on those aspects of curriculum which we believe inform whole language and which have been informed by Vygotskian theory.

The Social Nature of Schooling

Social context is itself a powerful mediator. Classrooms are social organizations. They are necessarily different than other social groups pupils encounter since they bring numerous similarly aged people together. Their funding, staffing, and social-political status also constrain them. But it is possible to organize classrooms so that social interactions will be supportive, and bridges will be provided to the cultures and social values pupils bring to school. Students are capable of learning the conventions of new social contexts and new linguistic genres if the contexts are dynamic ones in which students are invited to participate and are free to be themselves. If, however, their learning in classrooms is too highly constrained, then all they will learn is a narrow set of behaviors. Some pupils will find themselves permitted to fail but not to be nonconformists.

Other pupils, highly motivated to do well in school, can literally play the "school game." They get satisfaction out of doing the school tasks and winning the praise of the teachers and the rewards of the system. And they continue to learn what they can in school and integrate it with what they learn outside of school. The success that many pupils have in traditional situations obscures the relationship between in-school and out-of-school learning. To understand the problems of traditional education and its failure to provide authentic learning situations we must look to those who do not succeed in the system. What we find is that disproportionate numbers of minorities, of the poor, of boys, and of nonconformists are among the low achievers. In all of these the inability of the system to adapt to the learners is the key. Pupils succeed in traditional controlled programs to the extent that they are willing and/or able to conform and accept nonfacilitative curriculum and teaching.

All human beings are capable of learning language and learning through language. If learning in school is as authentic as learning outside of school, then there are no disadvantaged groups. But not all groups are so motivated and culturally equipped for school that they can survive dysfunctional teaching and curricula.

Language Empowerment by Demystifying Language Processes

If the zone of proximal development is viewed as a source of positive development, then only certain kinds of teaching support the zone and in fact other attempts can disrupt, confuse, or negate the potential development. The informal literacy club (Smith, 1988) that exists in classrooms and schools accepts some pupils but excludes others. Social, cultural, and linguistic dues are required for membership.

Those pupils who find admission to the club easy learn to read and write with little trauma. They bring the right language and experience to school, and they can accept school experience even if it is somewhat dysfunctional. Others feel unwelcome, and the language and responses to school experience are interpreted as inappropriate. So they participate in a self-fulfilling prophecy: They appear to be stupid and unprepared for literacy. The school technology then classifies them as deficient, and a cycle of intervention begins that eliminates all invention and most of the authentic convention of functional language. The learners fail at this too.

These negative influences on the zone take many forms in schools and limit entry into the learning or literacy club. Often the negative influences come from particular views about the role of the teacher. One of these roles sees the teacher as diagnostician. In this role the teacher is involved in finding out what the learner doesn't know, letting the learner and the family know what is missing, and then setting up interventions that cause conflict with the learning because they are counterproductive.

Another view of the teacher disruptive to the development of the zone characterizes the teacher as an expert imparting knowledge and discipline. Teachers who accept this view make choices and assignments for students. They control what and how much is learned within a specified period of time. Specified skills in a particular sequence are considered prerequisite to learning, and the curriculum is, therefore, arranged to pass on information in specified ways. The teacher becomes so dominant that opportunities for mediation are lost and an autocratic social environment is fostered. The learner becomes dependent on the teacher for sources of information and for ways of thinking and doing. When the student responds as expected, learning is rewarded and students become more concerned with behaving in a particular way than learning through their own activated zone. Procedural display as described by Bloome (1987) is rewarded, invention becomes too risky, and learning is curtailed and moved toward a stultifying conformity, not simply toward social convention.

Behavioral learning theories support imitative, memorizing, and cloning activities that reduce the zone, trivialize it, narrowing the opportunities for students to expand on and develop to their fullest potential. Inauthentic activities become ends in themselves and are valued more than students' learning and development.

Views of learning often relate to theories of language. Teachers holding the narrow views of learning often have narrow and outdated models of the reading and writing processes. They therefore use artificial and conformist materials and methods that force students out of their naturally developing zones into transacting with artificially written texts. The students are forced into activities they are often unable to complete appropriately. Even students who have the sociocultural potential to join the literacy club can be excluded because they are not paying the proper classroom dues that include filling out work sheets, working quietly and alone, spending hours on meaningless homework, and doing what they are told without question or argument.

Because of unexamined beliefs about gender, race, or ethnicity, teachers' attitudes toward particular students often result in their not recognizing students' potential. In such situations, students' attempts at invention or interpretation of conventions are easily rejected because they do not fit the school's or the teacher's values, expectations, and knowledge.

A view of curriculum that rejects this negative teaching encourages teachers to organize the classroom environment so that students will have many opportunities to realize the extent to which they know and control language, the ways in which language controls them, and the significance of language to their lives. Such a curriculum not only supports the students' right to speak and read and write in their own variation of language but also helps students understand why there are those in society who are strongly opposed to multilingualism, multiculturalism, and multidialectalism in schools and in society.

The intuitive knowledge students have developed about language becomes more explicit as students examine the real things that they do with language as they use it. They are helped to view their errors in reading and writing as an important part of their learning and as part of the multiple interpretations that all readers and writers develop as they compose and comprehend texts. Students and teachers learn with each other and from each other as they explore each other's responses to literature and each other's attempts at composition.

In many schools in Great Britain, there is a language curriculum in place that includes many of the ideas suggested above. Introducing a text for students called *The Languages Book,* the editor writes:

> This book is about language and how people use it.... But everyone
> who reads this knows much more about language than can be put in a
> book. Everyone has managed the amazing job of learning at least one
> language—and, when you think about it, you use even one language
> in so many different ways that even one is a lot. So you're the expert;
> make sure you tell the others what you know about language and the
> way it works. (Raleigh, 1981, front matter)

Knowing that they know about language allows students to understand
that language is not a mystery understood by only a few experts but a
powerful tool to control and use in learning.

Authentic Language Experiences

With the focus in whole-language classrooms on authentic experiences,
learners are engaged in purposeful and meaningful use of language,
both oral and written. There is no artificial breaking down of language
learning into sequences of abstract skills and no synthetic language
designed to control the form of written language out of the context of
its functional use. The form of language is examined as it is necessary to
communicate to others. Reasons for language convention are explored
so that students have opportunities to choose when they want to be
conventional and when they are willing to take the risk to invent.

In one whole-language classroom such ideas were translated into
students studying utopian societies and organizing the whole classroom
into a town they wanted to establish. Class activities and daily routines
were carried out by the students. Students searched the literature to
discover what others had written about utopias and then wrote about
their own. They had a town meeting on a regular basis to establish the
laws of their classroom society. A publishing company, post office, library, museum, town meeting area, and store all became part of the
community the students organized and reorganized, discussed and de-
bated. The problems of the society such as noise abatement, traffic,
and disease control were a few of the issues the students explored, and
through their studies the students developed concepts concerning language, science, math, social studies, art, music, and other aspects of
academic and real life. They also found many opportunities to talk, to
read, and write, and to discover many conventions about how and why
they used the various functions and forms of language in the ways they
did.

Long before teachers began to use the term *whole language* there
were whole-language teachers like the above and like Mr. Isobe, the
Japanese teacher we introduced earlier. These were teachers who

understood that schools existed for the pupils and who trusted in their ability to recognize their students' strengths and knowledge.

Largely, these teachers were successful because they cared about their pupils and knew them well. Their empathy provided them with an intuitive sense of what sort of support their pupils needed. What whole language adds is a scientific base of knowledge about language, learning, and teaching amassed over several decades. Teachers can respond to their intuitions as professionals who thoughtfully examine what they learn from their students.

Such teachers are aware they need to know a great deal about their students and the communities in which their students live in order to provide for and support authentic opportunities for learning. Such teachers are sensitive to the total social context in which the student lives so that they know what criteria to use to establish authentic situations so that students' language learning is meaningful and functional to the students' life. This does not mean that a laissez-faire situation is allowed to exist. Rather, starting where the learner is assures that the teacher provides many different kinds of opportunities for the zones of proximal development to occur.

Dewey (1902) provides an important rationale for the need for a variety of opportunities for learning to occur. He explores the value of what he calls "the real symbols," which he states "are tools by which the individual pushes out most surely and widely into unexplored area." But then Dewey cautions that only when the symbol "stands for and sums up in shorthand actual experiences which the individual has already gone through can it really symbolize. . . . A symbol which is induced from without, which has not been led up to in preliminary activities, is . . . a bare or mere symbol; it is dead and barren" (pp. 24–25).

There are too many subjects, facts, and statements presented in school as symbols "induced from without." We believe that these kinds of presentations never allow learners to reach for the real concepts of any subject, and they are thereby seduced to remain with what Vygotsky (1986) might call pseudoconcepts.

Whole language represents a major departure from the kind of education that even Vygotsky seemed to take for granted. Schools have traditionally been regarded as places for inculcating conservative societal values and knowledge. The whole-language movement has historic roots in a continuous attempt since the beginning of formal schooling to move away from simplistic views of teaching and learning. In choosing to make schools fit learners, whole language draws on the best scientific knowledge of how learning and teaching work and how language relates to learning and teaching.

In a very real sense, now that there are appreciable numbers of classrooms and schools where whole language is developing, it is possible to reevaluate the whole discussion of in-school and out-of-school learning and the relationship between scientific and spontaneous concepts. When schools implement a whole-language philosophy, teachers are initiators, kid watchers, liberators, and professional mediators who support the pupils through their zones of proximal development. And even the most optimistic of theorists may have to admit that they have underestimated what learners are capable of achieving.

References

Archambault, R. D. (Ed.) (1964). *John Dewey on education.* Chicago: University of Chicago Press.

Bloome, D. (1987). Reading as a social process in a middle school classroom. In D. Bloome (Ed.), *Literacy and schooling* (pp. 123–149). Norwood, NJ: Ablex.

Bullock, A. (Chair) (1975). *A language for life: Report of the committee of inquiry.* London: Her Majesty's Stationery Office.

Childs, J. L. (1956). *American pragmatism and education.* New York: Holt.

Clay, M., & Cazden, C. (1990). A Vygotskian interpretation of Reading Recovery. In L. Moll (ed.), *Vygotsky and Education.* Cambridge: Cambridge University Press.

Comenius, J. (1887). *The orbis pictus* (English ed.). Syracuse, NY: Bardeen.

Counts, G. (1932). *Dare the school build a new social order?* New York: Day.

Department of Education (1985). *Reading in junior classes.* Wellington, NZ.

Dewey, J. (1902). *The child and the curriculum.* Chicago: University of Chicago Press.

Dewey, J. (1938). *Experience and education.* New York: Macmillan.

Duckworth, E. (1987). *"The having of wonderful ideas" and other essays.* New York: Teachers College Press.

Edelsky, C. (1986). *Habia una vez: Writing in a bilingual classroom.* Norwood, NJ: Ablex.

Ferreiro, E., & Teberosky, A. (1982). *Literacy before schooling* (K. Goodman, Trans.). Portsmouth, NH: Heinemann.

Freire, P. (1970). *Pedagogy of the oppressed.* New York: Seabury.

Goelman, H., Olberg, A., & Smith, F. (Eds.) (1984). *Awakening to literacy.* Exeter, NH: Heinemann.

Goodman, K., & Gollasch, F. (1980). Word omissions: Deliberate and nondeliberate. *Reading Research Quarterly, 16:*(1), 6–31.

Goodman, K., & Gollasch, F. (1982). *Language and literacy: The selected writings of Kenneth S. Goodman: Vol 2. Reading, language, and the classroom teacher* (F. V. Gollasch, Ed.). London: Routledge and Kegan Paul.

Goodman, K., & Goodman, Y. (1977). Learning about psycholinguistic processes by analyzing oral reading. *Harvard Educational Review, 40* (3), 317–333.

Goodman, K., Smith, E. B., Meredith, R., & Goodman, Y. (1987). *Language and thinking in school.* New York: Owen.

Goodman, Y. (1989, November). Roots of the whole language movement. *Elementary School Journal.* Vol. 90 No. 2 pp. 113–127.

Goodman, Y., & Altwerger, B. (1981). *Print awareness in preschool children* (Occasional Paper No. 4). Program in Language and Literacy. Tucson: University of Arizona, College of Education.

Goodman, Y., & Burke, C. (1972). *Reading miscue inventory: A procedure for diagnosis and evaluation.* New York: Richard C. Owen.

Goodman, Y., with Watson, D., & Burke, C. (1987). *Reading miscue inventory: Alternative procedures.* New York: Owen.

Goodman, Y., & Wilde, S. (1985). *Writing development: Third and fourth grade O'Odham (Papago) students* (Occasional paper No. 14). Program in Language and Literacy. Tucson: University of Arizona, College of Education.

Halliday, M. A. K. (1975). *Learning how to mean: Explorations in the development of languag*e. London: Edward Arnold.

Halliday, M. A. K. (1980). Three aspects of children's language development: Learning language, learning through language, and learning about language. In Y. M. Goodman, M. Haussler, & D. S. Strickland (Eds.), *Oral and written language development research: Impact on the schools.* Urbana, IL: National Council of Teachers of English.

Halliday, M. A. K., & Hasan, R. (1976). *Cohesion in English.* London: Longman.

Hughes, L. (1963). Mother to son. In A. Bomtemps (Ed.), *American Negro poetry* (p. 67). New York: Hill & Wang.

Kilpatrick, W. (1926). *Foundation of method.* New York: Macmillan.

The man who kept house. (1964). In J. McInnes, M. Gerrard, & J. Ryckman (Eds.), *Magic and make believe.* Don Mills, Ont.: Nelson.

Penton, J. (1979). *Reading in NZ Schools: A survey of our theory and practice.* Auckland: Department of Education.

Piaget, J. (1977). *The development of thought: Equilibration of cognitive structures.* New York: Viking.

Pontecorvo, C., & Zucchermaglio, C. (1990). A passage to literacy: Learning in a social context. In Y. Goodman (Ed.), *How children construct literacy: Piagetian Perspectives.* Newark, DE: International Reading Association.

Raleigh, M. (Ed.) (1981). *The languages book.* London: ILEA English Centre.

Smith, F. (1988*). Joining the literacy club.* Portsmouth, NH: Heinemann.

Stone, I. (1979). *The origin.* New York: Doubleday.

Teale, W., & Sulzby, E. (Eds.) (1986). *Emergent literacy: Writing and reading.* Norwood, NJ: Ablex.

Teberosky, A. (1990). The language young children write: Reflections on a learning situation. In Y. Goodman (Ed.), *How children construct literacy: Piagetian perspective.* Newark, DE: International Reading Association.

Tudge, J. (1990). Vygotsky, the zone of proximal development, and peer collaboration: Implications for classroom practice. In L. Moll (ed.), *Vygotsky and Education.* Cambridge: Cambridge University Press.

Vygotsky, L. S. (1978). *Mind in society* (M. Cole, S. Scribner, V. John-Steiner, & E. Souberman, Eds.). Cambridge, MA: Harvard University Press.

Vygotsky, L. S. (1986). *Thought and language.* (A. Kozulin, Ed. & Trans.). Cambridge, MA: MIT Press.

Wertsch, J. W. (1985). *Vygotsky and the social formation of mind.* Cambridge, MA: Harvard University Press.

Yashima, T. (1959). *Crow boy.* New York: Viking.

Sociolinguistic Aspects of Reading

Chapter Sixteen

Urban Dialects and Reading Instruction

Kenneth S. Goodman
Wayne State University, 1971

Perhaps the most easily observed and least understood characteristic of language is its immense variation. As one travels and encounters speakers in other parts of the country, differences in sound, vocabulary, and grammar are evident. Within a community differences in the language of social, economic, ethnic and age groups are heard but frequently misclassified as careless, sloppy, degenerate speech or even non-language.

The key to this strange anomaly is the deep-seated misconception that language is either right or wrong and that all deviations from right language are errors and deficiencies to be stamped out.

In dealing with the implications of dialect variation for reading instruction no insights are possible unless language realities are understood. Over time or space speakers of the same language develop differences which become systematic. This is a universal characteristic of language. All languages, English for example, are really families of related systematic variants, called dialects. Any two dialects may have a common ancestral dialect or they may themselves be derived from separate ancestral dialects.

This chapter first appeared in Kender, J. P., (ed.), *Teaching Reading—Not By Decoding Alone,* Interstate: Danville, 1971, pp. 61–75. Reprinted with the permission of Interstate Printers and Publishers.

Thus the major regional American English dialects are derived from different regional dialects in England and not from a single British dialect.

Social, economic, or ethnic groups in a given community may speak variations of a single regional dialect or they may speak dialects with different antecedents. Working classes in northern Midwest cities have been recruited from the South and Midlands while rural and more privileged groups tended to move from east to west. Each group brought their own regional speech.

Dialects in contact, like languages in contact, will influence each other. The amount of influence will depend on the extent of contact and the cultural, social, economic, and political circumstances. So in London, for example, extremely different dialects have exercised little influence on each other though their speakers lived within a few blocks of each other.

The speech of blacks in the United States tends to vary from that of whites in comparable social and economic strata within the same region. This may be the result of a process of language differentiation, due to patterns of segregation and migration. But it also could be, as some have argued, that it results from the influence of an ancestral plantation Creole, spoken at one period by slaves throughout the South, on the speech of present-day black Americans. This Creole had some roots in the languages of West Africa.

The history is less important than the present reality. Systematic language differences exist today. Because of the dynamic nature of American cities and American society the nature of urban language differences is particularly complex and fluid. Evidence can be cited for convergence, further differentiation, and change. But nothing in historical or comparative linguistics could support the expectation that dialect differences will ever cease to exist. In short, language difference is an expected, legitimate, universal phenomenon.

Each dialect is functionally the most useful for the speakers who have developed it. Speakers of other dialects will be somewhat less effective in dealing with the common life experiences of the group and somewhat less well understood than speakers of the native dialect. No language, and no dialect of any language, is intrinsically superior to any other in coping with any specific area of human knowledge or with learning in general. Any advantage one language form might enjoy over another is at the most temporary since each form can and does adjust to the needs of its users.

The myth of language deprivation has a variant based on the assumption that speakers of certain dialects are unable to learn or deal with abstract concepts. This myth derives from treating the speakers as poor speakers of someone else's dialect.

How Dialects Differ

Dialects differ in all aspects to some degree. Some aspects, vowels for instance, are easily observed while others are more subtle or get lost in misconception. Systematic difference often is treated as isolated error.

Sound variation, systematic phonological difference, is often what some people think constitutes the whole difference between a Southern and a Northern "accent." The term *accent* is not a useful one as a synonym for dialect since linguists use it to mean stress. It also results in confusing dialects of English with English influenced by another language.

Vowel difference is notable in the way speakers of English dialects would pronounce this list: been, bean, bin, Ben, being. Any two or more of these will be homophones (sound alike). Dialects of English vary in the number of vowels they use. Furthermore, there is not a consistent correspondence from one dialect to another. The vowel in the following group may be the same or the group may split in two (though not consistently for all dialects): *log, dog, fog, hog, cog, bog, frog,* smog, flog, grog, jog. Those italicized rhyme for this writer (the vowel is /ɔ/) while the others rhyme (the vowel is /a/).

/r/ and to a lesser extent /l/, particularly in final position, vary considerably in English dialects; a speaker from Maine and one from Michigan might hear each other's pronunciation of *media* and *meteor* as exactly opposite.

Consonants vary less notably than vowels but some variation does exist. Alternation of /ð/ and /d/ as in dis/this or /θ/ and /f/ as in nuffin'/nothing are examples.

Some consonants vary in certain sequences (Etna/Edna) or in clusters (Eas'side/Eastside) or final positions (col'/cold).

What complicates dealing with and accepting phonological difference is that there is an artificial phonology, sometimes based on spelling, that confuses many teachers on what is acceptable in any dialect. *Just* is assumed to be always pronounced the same and /jist/ is rejected. Most people would say /jist/ when it is in a phrase such as *just now*, and /just/ only when it is an adjective, *a just man. Can* is another word where artificial pronunciation is frequently advocated. I would say, "I *can*/kin/ open the *can*/kən/."

Grammar varies less among English dialects but the differences that result are most confusing to observers since there is the common assumption that a single set of grammatical rules applies to all English dialects.

Some differences are quite minor. Some Canadians might say "he was taken to hospital" or "he went to school." Most Americans would say "to *the* hospital" though they would agree on "to school."

In some American dialects one would say "I asked him to go" or "told him to go" but "I had him go." Others, notably Southern dialect speakers, would say "I had him to go."

Among speakers of some black American English dialects there is normally a deletion of the present tense of *be* in many cases: *He home, I here, She a good teacher.*

These same speakers may also not have an *s* form for third person singular verbs: I see, you see, he see.

It is used in some dialects where *there* may be used in others: It's a chair in the other room for you.

Conditional statements can appear very different because of different dialect rules. *If he does it* is equivalent to *Do he do it.*

Such examples are offered here to indicate the range of ways dialects vary in grammar; even minor differences between pairs of dialects are too systematic and extensive to describe fully here.

Some grammatical differences, particularly when compounded with others and with phonological and vocabulary differences, can lead to major problems of communication.

Vocabulary is another major difference. Speakers may use different terms for the same concepts or referents. An *elevator* in some dialects is a *lift* in others.

Even more commonly, range of meaning may vary. In one dialect a *frying pan* is identical to a *skillet*. In another a *skillet* is a special kind of *frying pan*, one made of cast iron. To others the latter is a *spider*. *Carry* varies its range of meaning so that "Carry Me Back to Old Virginny" doesn't mean the same thing to many people that it means in its original dialect.

Figure 16–1
Overlap of Meanings for Words in Different Dialects

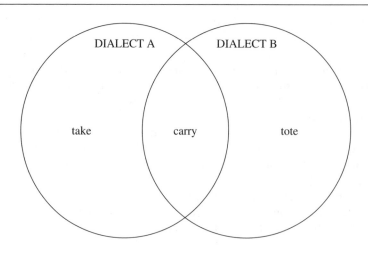

In this diagram notice that two dialects may have an overlap of meanings for *carry*, but dialect A uses *take* in some meanings where B uses *carry* and dialect B uses *tote* in some meanings where A uses *carry*.

Vocabulary differences are often overlooked where tenors mean almost but not quite the same thing.

Idioms in other people's dialects are easy to detect but those in one's own speech are frequently not thought of as idioms. Since idioms have unique meanings not suggested by the individual words they present rather special comprehension problems. *Mind your head* may not mean much to an American who sees it on a sign in England, but *watch out for your head* makes no more literal sense.

Dialects also differ in intonation. Pitch, stress, and pause patterns give a sense of poetry and music to other people's dialects. We are largely unaware on a conscious level of the same phenomena in our own speech. Yet without attending to intonational differences one could not understand the statement: All blackboards are not black boards. Unfamiliar intonation patterns make comprehension difficult since intonation keys phonological and syntactic patterns. Tuning in an unfamiliar dialect may in fact be mainly a question of picking up its melody.

The communication problems between speakers of different dialects are mutual; that is, a speaker of dialect A has about as much problem understanding a speaker of dialect B as the latter has in understanding him. Note that all speakers of different dialects have some communication problems; the problem is not confined to communication between blacks and whites.

An argument frequently used to support insisting on speakers of low-status dialects changing their speech is that they are hard to understand. To whom, though, are they hard to understand? Speakers of French are hard for English speakers to understand. But even little French children don't have much trouble understanding French.

Ethnocentrism permeates attitudes toward language. We think of our own speech as natural and that of others as funny-sounding. This gets entangled with feelings of superiority toward those in lesser social and economic hierarchies.

The speech of inferior people becomes inferior language. Good language is the possession of the superior social groups in society. In turn, strangers are classified socially according to the status of their speech.

Difference in language is not only, then, treated as linguistic deficiency, which it is not, but also as evidence of social inferiority, which it also is not. The twin doctrines of correctness and elitism are widespread in the general public. They are particularly found among educated people who believe themselves to be superior by virtue of their education and intelligence. Highly educated people frequently consider themselves the elite of society in all respects including language. Teachers are generally no exception. Elitist attitudes strongly influence their acceptance and rejection of their pupils' language. Many teachers are quite willing to accept simplistic characterization of low-status dialects as uncouth, sloppy, and incorrect. This is not to imply that they are undemocratic in their attitudes. They are frequently determined to help their unfortunate pupils become as good as they themselves are.

Attitudes toward the language of black people are quite similar to attitudes toward black people themselves. Racists have for a long time assumed observable language differences were the results of basic inferiorities among blacks and basic physical differences such as tongue, jaw, teeth, and mouth formations.

More enlightened people have explained what were assumed to be widespread language deficiencies among blacks as the result of cultural and environmental deprivation. Few liberally minded people are willing to accept the neo-racist conclusions recently advanced that blacks are genetically different in mental functioning from whites. They prefer to say that blacks are inferior because society has played nasty tricks on them. But the comparisons made are always to whites and it is the language of high-status whites that is treated as superior.

In such a view, the way to aid unfortunate blacks is to change them so that they are as much like whites as possible. A black pupil who speaks his own dialect of English effectively is to be treated like a deficient white.

All such attitudes are variations on a racist-elitist theme since all accept the language of a single status group and reject all others. The concept that poor people, black people, or people who are both could already possess language with any recognizable value is not even entertained.

Even many who have rejected as not possible the concept of cultural deprivation (human groups deprived of culture) have not rejected linguistic deprivation which is equally not possible.

Today's urban complex in America is a dynamic kaleidoscope of language. As population is recruited from south, midland, and rural areas, in general, it pours into center city or industrial suburb bringing transplanted regional, racial, class dialects. These interact with preexisting dialects as population moves physically toward more affluent outer circles of the urban complex and socially up the status ladder.

Until quite recently we have had no scientific studies of language patterns in urban areas. Even dialectologists were primarily concerned with the prestige forms in each geographic area.

Now, though studies have only begun to probe urban language patterns, we do have some basic insights.

Language differences do correspond to race and to social class within races. Pure distinct dialects are not actually found, however, in big cities. Forms dominant in the speech of one group are found in the speech of other groups but to a lesser degree. Swimming, sewing, running may tend to have /ŋ/ endings among one dialect group and /n/ among another but both forms will be found in all speakers. The extent of influence is apparently proportional to social distance. High status whites and blacks tend to be more alike in language than do speakers at other status levels.

Within the life span of urban individuals their language flexibility increases. They become capable of understanding a wide range of familiar dialects and are able to shift toward prestige forms in situations that seem to call for them. This reflects changing contacts more than it does direct teaching, though causes are not easily separable.

The urban classroom, whether in inner core or affluent suburb, will not be likely to present a homogeneous speech group. This will be extenuated where there is a range of backgrounds and socioeconomic levels. Areas of in-migration will present special patterns particularly where enclaves of speakers of transplanted dialects (Appalachian, for example) result. Even more complex patterns are presented when there are speakers whose native language is Spanish rather than English, as with Puerto Ricans and Chicanos. The Spanish dialect of these speakers is, as might be expected, as low in status as the English dialects they are most likely to learn.

Imposed Disadvantages

Many of the problems for speakers of divergent dialects in learning to read are avoidable and can be classified as imposed disadvantages.

If a child comes to school and finds his teacher either rejecting his speech outright or smiling and saying "We don't talk that way in school, dear," he becomes confused and ashamed about his language. The language base on which his literacy can be built is undermined or neutralized.

The confusion can be heightened if the teacher confuses teaching reading with attempts at changing the speech of the child. He reads. The teacher tells him he is wrong; but it sounds right to him. So there must be some secret set of rules to learning to read, some magic beyond his reach.

Teachers are not the only source of imposed disadvantage. Materials for reading instruction are peppered with misconceptions of language differences. Phonics programs almost invariably assume a single correct pronunciation for every word. Auditory discrimination exercises are designed to teach children to differentiate words which are the same to them—*pin* and *pen*, for example. To add to the learners' confusion, remedial and compensatory programs are designed to eliminate imaginary deficiencies. These hammer away at children's dialect differences and frequently have the result of inhibiting reading development.

Even when teachers do not overtly reject children's language they may create learning problems by not understanding the learners. If children can't make themselves understood or find they are continuously misunderstood with comic or tragic results they give up trying.

Imposed language disadvantages are accompanied by imposed cultural disadvantages. Materials and lessons often are built around experiences not common in the urban culture of the learners. Urban children, however poor, are not deprived of experience. If anything, their crowded, noisy environment bombards them with experience. But such experience, the learner finds, is not like the experience that characters in his book have. There is, in other words, a basic problem of reading programs being irrelevant to many urban learners. Teachers, like others, often make the assumption that children who speak low-status language do so because they are lacking in aptitude for learning. That is, they assume certain pupils are stupid simply because of their speech patterns. Furthermore, they confirm this belief by blaming the children for failure to make themselves understood. The result is a low expectation pigeon-holing of children before they even begin.

The vicious circle is reinforced by the use of tests of readiness and achievement which incorporate built-in bias against the low status language of the pigeon-holed children. Self-fulfilling prophecy gives the teacher an excuse for not expecting achievement among the urban poor and the tests conceal much of the actual progress the children do make.

Real Disadvantages of Speakers of Divergent Dialects

If the disadvantages that schools impose on speakers of dialects that diverge from high-status ones can be separated from actual problems in learning to read, then such problems will be much more amenable to study. In fact, it is likely that the problems will appear much less formidable obstacles to overcome.

Reading and Phonological Difference

Though sound systems vary from dialect to dialect, spelling, the written language patterning, is basically constant. *Pumpkin* is the spelling whether it's "punkin" or "pumpkin" in speech. *Picture* is the spelling whether the oral word sounds like *pitcher* or has a /k/ in it. In fact, the standardization of spelling across dialects is an advantage of English orthography. ITA or other spelling reforms would sacrifice some of that advantage since, in order to establish close correspondence between oral and written language in one dialect, they must move away in other dialects.

Words which sound alike, homophones, vary from dialect to dialect. The picture/pitcher example is an illustration of this variability. For/four also sound alike in some dialects and not in others. No one group of speakers derives any particular advantages or disadvantages from these similarities and dissimilarities.

There is in fact no reason why phonological dialect difference should be involved in reading problems. Phonics, defined as the set of relationships between oral and written language, will vary as much as the sound systems vary. The basic phonics problem in reading instruction is that children are often taught an irrelevant phonics, one based on someone else's sound system. If it is understood that phonics is variable then the problem will be largely eliminated.

Auditory discrimination tests are based on the two key misconceptions: (1) that there is a single right way to pronounce every word and (2) that children who can't discriminate between sounds or oral words are demonstrating an auditory problem. But there is no single correct pronunciation and children who don't perform well on auditory discrimination tests may simply be demonstrating their well-learned ability to ignore differences in sounds which are not significant in their own dialects.

Reading and Vocabulary Difference

There is not a single vocabulary shared by all literate users of English. Those who share a common interest or educational background in a particular field will share a particular vocabulary for that field but will differ in other fields. Doctors writing in medical journals will choose terms which are likely to be understood by other medical people. Hot-rod enthusiasts will be able to deal with the specialized vocabulary used in hot-rod magazines.

But each writer will draw on his own dialect in his writing and speakers of other dialects may in fact experience some comprehension problems that stem from vocabulary differences. Modern Americans have such difficulties reading Dickens and Shakespeare. Even Mark Twain used some terms differently than they are used in many current dialects of American English, particularly when he was trying to represent the dialect of the Mississippi River that Tom Sawyer and Huck Finn spoke. British and American people have some difficulty understanding the terms used in each others' newspapers.

Problems of divergent vocabularies are therefore not unique to speakers of low-status dialects. Personalized reading programs in which the language of the learners is used as a base and in which children are free to pursue their own interests in choosing reading materials can largely overcome this problem area. Two principles are important in expanding the vocabulary of learners: (1) Language cannot be learned in a vacuum apart from experience. Teaching isolated words in lists or having children do dictionary work on unfamiliar words is unlikely to have much pay-off. Vocabulary grows as it is needed to cope with new ideas and situations. (2) Bridges must be built between the existing vocabulary of the learners and terms used by others. If a child normally says bucket, the desirable goal is to help him know that some people call it a pail; the goal is not to insist on his abandoning his own term in favor of the other.

Sensitive teachers who listen carefully to children can anticipate vocabulary problems and build the necessary bridges. In a version of the *Three Billy Goats Gruff,* an old folk tale which retains, as do many such stories, the dialect form of an earlier era, the troll is tossed into the *bern.* Even teachers may need to find some term in their own vocabulary with which to match that. Reference is also made to curling stones. Canadian youngsters would be more likely to understand that term since curling is a popular sport in Canada.

What parent or teacher has not had to interpret the word porridge in *The Three Bears* for their children?

Reading and Syntactic Difference

Though syntactic differences between American English dialects are relatively minor, they are sufficient to cause some difficulties in communication. Phonological difference need not be a problem at all in reading; vocabulary difference is a problem to a greater extent but an easily recognized one; but syntactic difference is a more subtle and pervasive form of difficulty, particularly so since the role of grammar in comprehending language and particularly in reading is not well understood by teachers and text writers. Confusion over unfamiliar grammatical patterns is likely to be misunderstood as phonics problems or inability to deal with concepts.

Urban children, especially those who speak low-status dialects, have some advantage over rural children who live in more isolated linguistic communities. Such rural children may seldom encounter, face-to-face, speakers of dialects other than their own. The mass media may be their only awareness of speakers of other dialects. But the urban child comes into increasing contact with the varied forms of language spoken in his community as he grows older. Ironically, the inner-city child is more likely to acquire the ability to cope with the dialect differences within the urban complex than is a more privileged suburban child. He has both the need and the opportunity to do so since he frequently must comprehend speakers of higher-status dialects. He will not necessarily learn to speak in alternate ways. As he begins to develop pride in his own culture and heritage he may even disdain to do so, but he will come to comprehend these alternate language forms. Certainly by adolescence he will be able to handle the grammatical patterns of familiar dialects not his own whether he meets them in oral or written language.

The six-year-old reading beginner is not yet so facile, however. He may, in fact, be seriously hampered in learning to read materials which utilize grammatical patterns outside of his syntactic system. A key factor in learning to read is the child's ability to recognize written language as an alternate parallel form to oral language. The young reader must trust his linguistic judgment as he reads if he is to derive meaning. Beginners who encounter language forms that do not in fact sound like language to them are likely to have difficulty achieving this key understanding. Unnatural patterns in traditional pre-primers create something of the same problem for all readers. They are like no child's oral language.

Overcoming the Reading Problem for Speakers of Divergent Dialects

Several alternative solutions to the problem of language difference have been suggested. One is to teach all children so-called standard English before reading instruction. That approach has two key defects. It is a difficult time-consuming task which comes at an age before children have recognized any need to learn another language form. Many children would not succeed at all. Furthermore, the language skill which the child possesses in his own dialect would be ignored and his confidence undermined. He would be faced with the serious imposed disadvantage of having to acquire literacy in a dialect not his own.

An opposite approach is to literally teach the child in his own dialect by writing materials in that dialect. While that approach is quite sound and would probably work, there are problems in carrying it through which appear to be insurmountable. The most crucial of these is the variability of dialects within urban classrooms. To write materials in "black English" would require that a group of related American English dialects be standardized into a single dialect or treated as one dialect. While such a standard or composite would be closer to the actual dialect of many black children than the language of most current reading materials, they would still not be reading in their own dialect. Further, there are many black children whose speech is more like the eastern or midwestern dialects of their white neighbors. The thought of segregating children within the same school or classroom according to their dialects is not a pleasant one; it would most assuredly result in whites being segregated from blacks and both groups being sub-divided according to socio-economic status.

Teachers using materials written in dialects they don't themselves speak would be relatively ineffective. They would need to learn the dialects. If special dialect materials were used, a large-scale effort would be needed to overcome parental resistance. Parents would need to be educated to the facts of language difference and be convinced that the effort was in the best interests of their children.

If producing materials in the dialects of the learners was the only effective solution to the problems of teaching children with divergent dialects to read, then these problems would have to be overcome.

There is, however, another solution. It involves accepting the dialect of the learners and building on it while eliminating imposed disadvantages. Here are the elements of such an approach.

1. Early reading instruction would utilize language experience materials. They would be composed by the children, in their own language about their own experiences. Language differences within classrooms would be treated positively and alternate forms of experience stories would be developed if children desire them.

2. Relevant materials would be utilized at all stages of instruction.

3. As children move into reading published materials they would be encouraged to read in their own dialects. Teachers would be careful to avoid confusing the child by rejecting his shifts toward his own dialect as he reads.

4. The movement of urban children toward the comprehension of the range of dialects in their community would be encouraged and their ability to cope with a range of unfamiliar dialects in print would also be encouraged.

5. Throughout such a program teachers would try to anticipate possible sources of difficulty stemming from differences in vocabulary and grammar.

6. Most important, teachers would guard themselves against introducing elitist, racist views of language into their classrooms.

In such a program it should be possible to work with children, not at cross purposes to them; to build on language, not reject it; and to find strength in children where previously only weakness was seen.

Part Five

Literacy Development

While the core tenets of the theory remain unchanged, Goodman has developed and elaborated on his model of reading over time. In doing so, key insights into how human beings learn to construct and use written texts as members of literate societies have also been developed and nurtured. Drawing from the work of Piaget, Vygotsky, and most notably from Michael Halliday and his theory of systemic functional linguistics, the chapters in this part relate to the personal and social nature of written language learning.

Goodman's work has been instrumental in pointing the way to a theory of how reading and writing are learned. The chapters in this part show how, in the best scientific tradition, Goodman's theory directed him and his colleagues to the clinical and ethnographic research insights that lead to the development of an explanation of language learning. A key concept about learning in this explanation is that learning develops as a result of the tensions between the forces of personal invention (developing hypotheses, imposing order, making sense) and social convention (forms which are socially imposed).

In explaining how written language is learned, Kenneth and Yetta Goodman highlight the interrelationship of reading and writing, and show how each process supports the development of the other. They suggest that understanding the personal and social uses of reading and writing points the way to constructing school programs that support literacy development. Goodman & Goodman write that "[such programs need] to be built on the full range of personal uses of written language so that literacy may develop in the context of natural functional use" (page 330). Furthermore, "[t]hrough engaging in a large amount of varied reading and writing, children will develop a sense of control over them and will find a personal significance for becoming literate. Focusing on activities where reading and writing take place almost simultaneously helps children realize the one process supports the other and that they are capable of controlling them both"(page 336). And just as it is known how literacy develops and what is required to support that development, it is also known that control of the materials that separate the skills of literacy from the functional use required to control those skills impedes the development of literacy.

This part concludes with *Learning to Read Is Natural,* a classic chapter that draws the parallels between the functional uses of oral and written language and how the development of written and oral language processes parallel each other. The naturalness of written language learning is a recurring theme whose central premise is that control of function precedes control of form:

> We believe that children learn to read and write in the same way and for the same reason that they learn to speak and listen. That way is to encounter language in use as a vehicle of communicating meaning. The reason is need. Language learning, whether oral or written, is motivated by the need to communicate, to understand and be understood (page 353).

The assertion of the "naturalness" of literacy learning sets Goodman apart from other theorists of his generation when it comes to applying these insights in the service of teaching and curriculum (Part VI).

Chapter Seventeen

Language and Learning: Toward a Social-Personal View

Kenneth S. Goodman
University of Arizona, 1988

Preface

In American academic and pedagogical circles, views of learning have been strongly dominated by the behavioral learning theory rooted in the work of Thorndike and Skinner. Particularly in applications to schooling and learning within schools, behavioristic learning theories have dominated. Our basal readers are still strongly rooted in Thorndike's laws of learning; our methodology texts see teaching as "changing the behavior of pupils" by providing hierarchically arranged skill and sub-skill stimuli. Our ever-present tests, both norm-referenced and criterion-referenced, are built on a behavioral view of learning as the sequential acquisition of a hierarchy of skills and sub-skills.

Even some who call themselves cognitivists tend to see learning as divided into behaviorally acquired skills followed by the development of "higher order thinking skills." So in studying reading, for example, they can separate learning the skills of reading from learning to comprehend texts.

This chapter first appeared in the *Proceedings of the Brisbane Conference on Language and Learning*, July, 1988. Reprinted by permission of the author.

When it comes to language learning, the major controversy has been between behavioral psychologists, who view language learning as being simply another example of being conditioned by stimuli to develop a set of skills, and linguists and psycholinguists, who do not reject behavioral definitions of learning but counter that language is not learned at all but is in fact innate in human beings.

Thus, the controversy is between nature and nurture views. Those who believe that language is not learned at all, but innate, have no reason to offer a theory of language learning. Rather, they focus their attention on the search for language universals to prove their innatist's views. Some also see developing written language, learning to read and write, as quite different from oral language development. Oral language is innate, but for them written language is learned; it is an abstract, secondary representation of speech.

The exception, among innatists, is Steven Krashen (1983), who avoids using the term learning, which he leaves to the behaviorists; he prefers to talk about language acquisition, which he applies to development of both oral and written language. In both, it is exposure to natural "comprehensible input" which produces acquisition. That leads him to a natural approach to teaching in which teachers try to approximate real world conditions in their classrooms using meaningful written texts to provide comprehensible input.

Piaget has offered an alternative view of learning, which assigns an active role to learners as expecting the world to make sense, constructing schemas of the world, and testing these in the context of experience. But ironically even those attempting to apply Piaget in American schools have tended to see language and literacy development as acquisition of skills. Piaget cannot be blamed for misapplication of his psychogenetic theories, but he did not himself elaborate a theory of language development.

Emilia Ferreiro (1982), a student of Piaget's, studied beginning literacy development using Piagetian concepts and Piagetian research design. She finds children are aware of written language in their literate environment, and they are using the same hypothesis testing strategies they use in other kinds of learning.

There are two sources that have offered explanations of language learning based in more social views. The first is the work of Lev Vygotsky (1978), who as a Marxist saw human learning as strongly socially based and language learning as the internalization of the social forms. The second is the work of Michael Halliday (1978), who views language itself as a social semiotic—a means by which societies symbolically represent their shared meanings. In Halliday's studies of language development, he has drawn on a developing social theory of language learning.

Learning language is, to Halliday, learning how to mean. It is characterized by the development of personal-social language functions, and the form language takes is shaped by the functions of language. He calls his theories of language *functional-systemic.*

In Halliday's (1975) work, language development is a response to the development of language functions. Several separate functions are differentiated in young language learners, and these eventually lead to the three adult functions of language: ideational, interpersonal, and textual.

Halliday finds that there are three simultaneous kinds of language learning: we learn language, we learn through language, and we learn about language. Each is dependent on the others. A critical concept is that language is learned not as a sequence of skills but as a whole in the context of its use. It is thus important to study language learning as language is studied within the situational contexts in which language is used.

In this chapter I will draw on Piaget, Vygotsky, Halliday, and others in a statement of my own view of language learning and of the role of language in general learning. This is not a full statement of the social theory of language learning. It focuses on a particular concept that is foundational to this view of language development: the shaping of language by centripetal (personal invention) and centrifugal (social convention) forces.

It will be clear as this concept is developed that I see oral language and written language as parallel semiotic forms in literate societies. They share a common lexico-grammar, but they utilize different symbolic systems. With one using a system of audible sounds displayed in a time continuum and the other using a system of legible graphic characters displayed—usually linearly—in two dimensional space, there cannot be an isomorphic relationship between the units or sub-systems of oral language and written language even in alphabetic systems. Each of the two systems is used for a set of functions; each develops a set of registers and genre in a given society and culture. Some are unique to oral language, such as the telephone conversation; some are unique to written language, such as the time-table; and some overlap with either oral or written language or both used, depending on the context and purpose. In some cases, oral language is written down (as in transcribing an oral conversation), and written language is spoken (as in reading a paper at a conference).

But whatever is true of language in general is also true of written language, and that includes the role of personal invention and social convention in their development. Like oral language, written language is learned in the context of its use.

What Must a Social-Personal Theory of Language Learning Do?

From my perspective a useful language learning theory must satisfy the following requirements:

1. It must explain both how and why language develops.
2. It must account for the central role of language in human learning.
3. It must be consistent with a comprehensive theory of language.
4. It must account for the learning of both oral and written language.
5. It must deal with learning both outside and inside school.
6. It must deal with language development of all people and not just selected populations.
7. It must be consistent with good research and help differentiate good research from bad.
8. It must inform and inspire pedagogy.

Finally a social-personal theory must pass a critical test. It must be productive of insights and generate theories of curriculum and instruction which will be liberating and empowering. Neither theory nor research is ever value-free. All theory, however scientifically supported or carefully reasoned, serves different groups in society unequally. Behavioral language learning theory made it possible to dehumanize and operationally condition human beings, justifying mental and physical interventions in their lives in the name of improving them. Innatist theories made people the helpless victims of their heredity, limited in advance. It offered schools a very limited view of their ability to help language learners expand their competence, and it suggested to researchers that learning how to talk was no more interesting as a research topic than learning how to walk. Both theories minimized the creativity of the learner and the impact of society and culture on language development.

Why Language Is Learned

To understand human language and its development we must understand why human language develops. If anything is innate in human beings it is our ability to think symbolically, that is, to let signs and systems of signs represent aspects of reality as we experience them. This ability is totally recursive, so that signs may represent signs, and relationships between different aspects of reality may be used metaphorically to represent the relationships of other aspects of reality. What this means is that we may reflect on experience using symbolic language and thus continue to learn from and integrate experience long after it occurs.

But this ability to think symbolically would be insufficient to explain language development. Why don't each of us over our lifetime evolve our own personal language system different from everybody else's? The answer is that we are very much social beings, born dependent and mutually interdependent for our welfare and for our survival throughout our lifetimes. Human society is extremely complex, and we need a high level of interaction to make it operate. Language is the means of this interaction. That means that idiosyncratic semiotic systems are not enough. The system must be a shared social one in order to communicate and share our experiences, needs, feelings, emotions, and ideas. Through language, both the individual and the society grow. Through language, we can link our minds, greatly magnifying the intelligence and ability to learn of any one of us. Through language, we share meanings and life views. Through language, the culture is created and expressed.

In a real sense, each of us invents our own semiotic system but we do so within the social context; we use the linguistic resources available to us in that social context and language becomes both personal and social. It is the medium of social interactions and transactions. But it is also the medium of thought, learning, and personal expression.

Social-Personal Creation of Language: Centrifugal Forces (Personal Invention) and Centripetal Forces (Social Convention)

Since language serves both personal and social functions it must be understood as social-personal invention. Each human being creates language—a means of representing the world and his or her experiences with it. But each human being does that within a social context and makes use of the linguistic resources in that social environment. Eventually, the personal language of each individual comes safely within the social language: the symbols, the grammar, the ways of representing the world for the individual are those of the society in which that individual functions. But the creative force never diminishes, and it plays a key role in all subsequent language development. So, in a real sense, personal language is the product of society and social language is the product of the individuals who speak it. Neither ever loses its dynamic quality; both personal and social language change to meet the functional needs of their users.

In the beginning all human beings use a variety of physical motions and oral sounds to get attention and participate in social settings. Crying and making noise, as well as waving and moving body parts, result in getting adult attention. Caring adults are quick to draw inferences from these noises and motions, and thus the infant's needs are attended to. Language is in fact social, that is, interpersonal, before it is communicative in any linguistic sense. Think of the 6-month-old baby sitting in a high chair at the family dinner table. As the conversation develops, the baby's vocalizing gets louder and louder and more persistent. The tiny child sees vocal noisemaking as part of every social experience and joins in on the noise.

Hearing children begin to specialize in oral communication because adults respond in more complex ways to their sounds, and they move toward the phonology of the language community because those sounds are most productive of adult response. Profoundly deaf children, with no access to the speech sounds surrounding them, will specialize in gesture and body movement, often inventing an elaborate set of signs which caring family members become good at interpreting. If the deaf child should be growing up in a deaf home in which the home language is in fact a sign language, then his or her invention will move toward the symbol system of the adult language, again because of the more elaborate responses those evoke in adults.

Oral language has developed in all known human societies because it is a facile and convenient means of face-to-face communication for hearing people. Sign languages are somewhat less convenient because we can only see in one direction, while we can hear in all directions. In fact, we can hear sounds from sources we can't see. While all this may seem self-evident, I've included it to emphasize that language development depends on both personal and social resources and that the function of the language, both personal and social, largely constrains the forms it will take.

As individuals and societies grow and change they encounter new experiences, new needs, new understandings, and new values which require new language. The ability to create language is always available and at work; the invention of language is a never-ending process.

Languages do in fact change continuously. Partly this is in response to new societal experiences and needs. If languages couldn't change, they would quickly become inadequate for full communication. But change in language is also partly due to continuous reinvention by individuals and groups who may lack access to the existing resources—or who reject them—and who therefore invent new alternatives. New language, though it may follow conventions within the social language for how language may be created, is almost always the creation of individuals, and it moves from them into small sub-groups in society and then eventually into the social language. Though emperors, parliaments, and linguistic authorities have tried to create language by fiat or committee they have not been able to stem or shape the course of human invention in language change.

Some linguistic invention is short-lived and remains quite local. Other invention may move in widening circles and become quite stable and socially accepted. Total innovation is rare in linguistic invention. Only scientists and product manufacturers have the means of coining new words. It's more convenient for individuals to use the resources available in the linguistic community. If a baby should use sounds that are not within the phonology of the speech community they will be interpreted by family members and neighbors within their phonemic system, and the children will hear their sounds echoed in the phonemes of the language. It is not that infants imitate adult speech sounds— that would require a control over the full articulation features of the language. Rather they begin to specialize in the sounds that caring adults respond to best, putting their inventive energies into controlling the most useful articulatory mechanisms.

Language development starts with differentiation of functions, and the means of expressing those functions are then invented and differentiated. Halliday (1975) detected two functions very early in the speech of his son, who is called Nigel in the report of his study. These functions were expressed with different intonation patterns. Requests or questions had one intonation, and comments on the world had another. The former required some kind of adult response and the latter didn't.

All of the systems of language are invented by the learner. Early language has only two systems: symbolic (usually sounds) and meaning. Such language can convey a simple set of comments or needs. But for more complex relationships, a third system is required. In Halliday's view, the grammar grows out of the functions that the language performs in social contexts. What children do in inventing this system is experiment with a wide range of partial systems for organizing their expressions to deal with the functions. Grammar is never explicit in language. It is a set of rules, which even linguists must infer from close examination of the language in functional use. In their inventions, children make use of the linguistic resources around them. They use sequences from the ones they hear. But they invent the rules by continually modifying their expressions toward those which are best understood by adults around them. This can be seen again as an interplay between two forces, personal invention and adult convention, which eventually are in equilibrium at the point where the personal language is broadly within the social language.

As complex as the grammar is, it is relatively finite compared to the complex way that the language is used to represent the meanings the society assigns to the world. No user of the language controls the full lexicon of the language. That means that all language users encounter unfamiliar word uses and phrasings and that new terms are continuously being invented for meanings that have already been represented by other language users. Children invent their own meanings and then modify them to match the ones they hear around them. Again, they use available linguistic resources, so it is not surprising that they invent meanings for familiar words which do not coincide with conventional meanings. Similarly, it is not surprising that English words have different meanings in different dialects of English and that different dialects use different words to express similar meanings.

In a common sense view, children develop language by imitating first the sounds, then the words, and then the sentences of adult language. In reality, language development involves the invention of all three systems in the context of social use. Only in social use is it possible for the two forces, invention and convention, to shape language and achieve equilibrium. Vygotsky (1978) sensed this when he recognized that inner speech and personal language use is internalized from the social language use. The mechanism by which social language becomes inner speech is this balancing of invention and convention by language learners. Halliday (1975) recognized the two forces at play when he stated that learning language is learning how to mean.

So language develops from whole to part and not from part to whole. The systems of symbols and rules develop as invention and convention come together in experiences with authentic functional texts in situational contexts. Meanings develop in the context of social transactions in which learners are participants and observers.

One powerful means of expanding language and assigning meaning is metaphor. It is the most open means of inventing language for both the individual and the community. In a real sense, when babies let the sounds they make represent animals or objects in the environment (such as *choo-choo, owow, meow*), they are already using metaphor. Metaphor is also the most open system for invention of language. Through abductive reasoning, characteristics and interrelationships are transferred by analogy from one object, set of objects, or field of meaning to another. Contrasts such as *hot/cold, sharp/dull,* and *sweet/bitter* are transferred abductively to quite different fields. Whole ranges of terms from sports, games, and occupations are transferred to new fields. Consider how the parts of the bodies have been applied by analogy to everything from furniture (*head* and *foot* of the bed, *arms* of chairs, *legs* of tables) to geographic features (*headwaters, arm of a river, shoulders of roads, foothills, Grande Tetons*). Halliday (1986) has demonstrated that languages also use grammatical metaphor, using one grammatical form (such as nominal groups) to express another (such as verb processes).

Metaphoric invention can be spur of the moment and never repeated, or it can become so widely used that its users stop thinking of it as metaphor. Again it is the balance between personal invention and social convention that makes the difference.

The Nature and Need for Convention in Language

Language could not serve its social and communicative functions if there were not social agreement on the essentials of the three systems: shared meanings, lexico-grammar (including rules and word choices), and symbol systems (phonology for speech and orthography for writing). For the society and the individual, these systems must be complete enough to cope with communicating virtually any experiential meaning. From the learner's point of view, these complex systems constitute arbitrary social conventions: joining in on how people mean things to each other requires controlling the conventions. That's not the same as being controlled by them, which would then stifle invention and limit growth and change in language.

Though language functions create parameters for the range of possible ways a particular oral language can deal with a particular function, choices within those options vary in arbitrary ways from language to language. For example, French and Spanish put adjectives after nouns, and English puts them before nouns. Different cultures choose between available ways of representing functions within the parameters.

Social pragmatics also determine necessary functions that require linguistic conventions. If, in the culture, the tenor of relationships between people of different age or different social positions requires more and less formal manners of communication, then the language will provide conventions that reflect the cultural views. Formal and informal second person pronouns in Spanish or honorifics in Japanese are examples of such linguistic pragmatic conventions.

Achieving Equilibrium Between Personal Invention and Social Convention

Balance and tension between internal, personal, and external social forces are necessary for human development. The task of personally creating an entire language system would be far too difficult and time-consuming for any individual. And as we have indicated, it would seriously complicate social participation by the learner. The learning creative, centrifugal force (invention) and the social need for shared form and shared meaning (convention) are both necessary for learning. The conventions are never self-evident in the language the learners experience; grammatical rules control the word order for example, and provide for tense, clause structure, and complex clausal relationships. So the learner hypothesizes inventing personal rules and trying out these on the speech community. But the learner draws on the linguistic resources of the language community in these inventions and moves toward the conventions of the language to be better understood while engaging in continual social transactions in social-situational contexts.

The many sub-systems of conventions in language are experienced in these social contexts by the young learners. As their linguistic inventions interplay with these conventions in the situations that require them, an equilibrium develops and language learners come to conform to the conventions.

The rapid development of children's language shows the effectiveness of this transactional process. In a few short years, children are able to develop control over functional use of language systems that are still not fully understood by the scientists who study them. Through the invention, they achieve an equilibrium with the conventions of the language so that they may understand others and express themselves comprehensively. Through establishing an equilibrium between their own invention and the conventionalizing force of the social language, they appear to internalize the social language. Their inner language is now the social language, but they will continue to invent new terms, new meanings, and new rules as new experiences require them and through further transactions in new social contexts they come to control more sophisticated and more specialized conventions. Disequilibrium produces growth as the individual and the social group strive to keep language fully capable of serving their needs. Thus each individual gains access to the social language and is able to contribute to its further growth and change. They have learned how to mean and are thus empowered not only in social communication but also in reflective thinking and learning through language.

Human Learning: Perceiving, Ideating, and Presenting

In *Language and Thinking in School* our co-author, E. Brooks Smith, synthesized a view of learning which draws on Piaget and Vygotsky and on the philosophy of Suzanne Langer (Goodman, Smith, Meredith and Goodman, 1986). In this view learning involves three processes: perceiving, ideating, and presenting.

Perceiving

In the perceiving process there is focus on and engagement with aspects of the world around us as we transact with it. Attention is selective; that is, some aspects of experience are fore-grounded and hold our interest while the rest serve as background. An example might be attending to print on a wall or product package or the color scheme of a commercial logo. In each, there is not only focused attention but active engagement; that is, the individual is actively interested and not simply passively involved.

Very often what is perceived is immediately given semiotic value: it is perceived not only as having certain observable attributes but also as being representative of something else. It is placed within a semiotic system. That makes the perception process very efficient; if we know some features of what is seen we may predict and infer the others and assign significance. We see things. We perceive signs. That makes our perception quite efficient because it puts our schemas of the world at the service of our senses. Perception always therefore goes beyond simple sensory input; it is dependent on the senses—sight, sound, smell, taste, and feel—but it always goes beyond them. That's because we perceive within the process of ideation. It isn't only that we know what we see; rather we see what we know. We always seek sense in the world based on our existing schemas.

Ideating

Perception is never an end in itself. We expect to find order and sense in the world, and we are constantly bringing our existing schemas to bear on our transactions with the world. What we think we see or hear, then, is only partly the result of sensory input; it is largely the result of prediction and inference based on prior learning and on the semiotic value we assign to what we perceive. We never go to experience unprepared. We always bring a set of expectations. We have some sense of what we will see or hear and therefore we can pre-select where to attend and which aspects of a social context to engage with. In ideating we try actively to make sense—to construct meaning—of the world. In Piaget's view, we assimilate knowledge within existing schemas or we accommodate; we change the schemas to make sense of the conflicting information. In all experience there is learning; our ideas of reality are changed and we shape the world to fit our sense of it.

Problem solving is a term which is useful to describe a major type of ideating. We try to find effective means of coping with experiences that present problems to us either in what we must do or understand, or both. In the course of ideating we develop cognitive, perceptual, and problem solving strategies. In some sense these are schemas for scheme formation. They are systems for dealing with recurrent experiences and the information to be found in them.

In ideating there are cycles of perception and reflection. We reflect on experience; that is, we reconsider it often assigning alternate or enriched semiotic value to it as we seek to make sense. This may involve further need for perception with refocused attention and renewed engagement. Learning requires time to think. An experience may well be over in an instant but we have the power using our ability to think symbolically, to reflect on and reevaluate the significance of the experience. Children may not respond immediately to some significant experiences and then much later, perhaps in response to a new related experience, make it obvious that they have been reflecting on the earlier experience and have learned from it.

Reflective thought is self-mediation. The learner, in reconsidering the earlier experience, brings new insights to it. Much of the teacher's mediation in school is aimed at stimulating the reflection of pupils on their experiences, speech acts, and literacy events.

Presenting

Since we think symbolically, human learning is not complete until it has been represented in some presentational form. Usually this form is linguistic, but it may take the form of art, music, or dance. Through aesthetic language we may represent not only our ideas but also our feelings and emotions. Learning is completed when we compose what Emily Dickinson called our "letters to the world."

Very often the presentation is in the form of transactions with others: parents and family for young children and then a widening circle of contacts. But a lot of our presentation is to ourselves as we use language to represent and reflect on perception and ideation. Many teachers have discovered how trying to help others understand concepts helps themselves most as they present what they have understood.

In the process of presentation we engage in transactions that help reconstruct perceptions and ideas. We transform as we present, and then we change again as we get response in the course of social transactions. Not only are perception and ideas changed, but we also modify the language in which we are expressing them as we experience social response.

The Role of Language in Human Learning

Since language is vital to human learning and we learn language while we learn through language, it follows that both invention and convention are at work in human learning and that the equilibrium between these two forces is achieved in functional situations in which learners are trying to use language to achieve personal-social purposes. In these contexts, the social conventions are intrinsic and relate closely to the language and communicative functions. Invention will contribute strongly to the success of the transactions, but so also will the use of the social conventions. Effective and efficient communication will depend on shared social conventions. It is important to understand that there is a difference between conventions as they occur in natural social use of language and attempts to codify these conventions into rules or systems of rules to guide research and teaching. Convention develops in language as a necessary part of the language. The formal grammar and rules developed by scholars are useful ways of representing these conventions. But the real rules and systems of language only exist in the context of language use.

Invention and Convention in Perceiving

In a famous study, George Miller (1966) demonstrated that how much we can remember from an instant of visual input depends on what scheme we have for organizing our perceptions. Woodley (1984) showed that readers can recall a whole meaningful sentence from a single exposure. But they can only recall a few random numerals from a line of similar length exposed from the same brief instant. What we know controls what we perceive.

Benjamin Whorf (1956) in cross-cultural studies showed that people come to perceive the world as the people in their cultures do, using the linguistic categories that are conventional in their societies. Thus the color spectrum is divided differently according to how people in a given culture see things. That's what Halliday means when he says language learning is learning how to mean. The way the language conventionally represents meanings comes to be the way perceptions have meaning to people in the society. Personal schemes are invented for organizing perceptions meaningfully and these are tried against social schemas to achieve an equilibrium or balance. This process is easily seen in how the perceptions of young children do and don't correspond to social perceptions. Children, as Read (1971) and others have shown, perceive phonetic differences in what they hear that adults don't because the adults are more bound by phonemic and orthographic conventions: they know what they are *supposed* to hear.

The perceptual phase of learning is thus as much affected by language development as it affects language development. Since language is learned as social meaning is learned, the equilibrium between personal invention and social convention makes personal perception fit within social conventions.

Balancing Invention and Convention in Ideation

Learners make sense of the world and their experiences with it. They act like they expect the world to make sense. The schemas they form for organizing their experiences and the conceptions they build are their constructions—their own inventions. But they mediate this ideation with language, and thus the social conventions of how meaning is represented help to shape their inventions. So language mediates conceptual development and scheme formation even when it is what Vygotsky considered inner language, what we *hear* in our heads as we reflect on our experience, as an internalization of social speech. This is not to say that language development precedes ideation and conceptual development. In fact, language and thinking each depend on the other for expansion and development. The personal and social forces are at work in both.

Of course, most ideation is happening in the context of social experience. That's where the conventions of interpersonal language functions are encountered and where the grammatical and semantic conventions are situationally embedded. In the context of language use, both linguistic and ideational invention may be tested against convention to achieve equilibrium.

Presenting Invention and Linguistic Transactions

Through linguistic presentation, language mediates learning, as we express our understandings through conversation narrative, explanation, and other forms of sharing experiences. In the course of linguistic transactions in real situational contexts, our ideas are tested and refined. Presentation requires us to represent our understandings so that they may be understood by others. At the same time it requires us to relate experiences, to establish our own categories, and to choose from developing schemas. We must choose the appropriate wording and select the necessary grammatical structures. We must find language to suit the context and social genre.

Not only does language mediate personal learning but it also mediates social learning. Language makes it possible to link human minds and magnify human intelligence. Each social language situation is a complex set of transactions with each participant being affected and social meaning being stretched, tested, and modified. There is in each participant a zone of proximal development, so learning is being mediated by the situation, by the other participants, and by language. There is also a social zone of proximal development. The immediate social group also is learning and changing, and cycles of similar linguistic encounters create social ripples that affect widening social circles. There is thus a social as well as a personal balancing of the forces of invention and convention and a social equilibrium between invention and convention.

Invention and Convention in School

The basic process of human learning and the relationships of language development and general learning are the same in school as they are out of school. It is not the learning that is different in school but rather the circumstances for learning. Schools are social institutions charged by society with facilitating learning. They can, at their best, offer concentrated and enriched experiences for learners with a teacher present who is a professional at providing appropriate experiences, orchestrating social interactions, monitoring development and learning, and mediating learning to enhance and strengthen it. At their worst, unresponsive and inflexible school curricula and teachers can stifle the creative inventive energy of pupils and impose decontextualized and narrowed versions of conventions that create barriers to learning rather than mediating it.

The common notion that learning in school is different than learning outside of school comes from a confusion of school traditions with optimal school practice. School traditions coming from European education were based on common sense notions of the relationship of teaching to learning. The curriculum was a set of facts and rules. Teachers told these to learners—or administered their reading of books which told them facts and rules. Learners memorized the facts and rules or did exercises that drilled them in what they needed to know or do.

Doing well in school became something quite different than learning outside of school. But doing well in school and learning in school are quite different. The learning is much the same as it is outside of school. In sterile and controlling contexts, however, what is learned may be quite different than what the school intends. Many pupils learn to mistrust themselves as learners. They learn to think of themselves as incapable of learning, and they may learn to think of what they already know as inappropriate for school. They may also learn that not much presented in school is functional or relevant to their own worlds.

Centrifugal and Centripetal Forces Still at Play

But an optimal school curriculum is one in which students are just as involved and committed to school as they are to the real world outside of school. Individually and in groups, learners are solving problems and seeking answers to questions important to them. They are expanding their linguistic and cognitive strategies—learning language while using language to learn.

The curriculum, as they experience it, is a series of authentic speech and literacy events. With classmates they use language appropriate to functions they are performing. They chose to do so because it is appropriate to the purpose of the transactions—not because an exercise sheet requires it. They seek out resources that involve oral and written language and make sense of them as they seek to solve problems or understand phenomena. They perceive, they ideate, they present. They invent schemas and language registers to fit their needs. In the course of these transactions, they encounter social conventions of grammar, of pragmatics, and of wording and word meaning. They move to higher levels of equilibrium. In the course of this socialized learning, they form a sense of their own ownership over their thought and their language. They are increasingly empowered. All this is an extension of the learning that they've experienced before school and that they continue to experience in school.

In these authentic events, invention and convention are both at work as they always are in learning. The learners take risks, they are active participants in the events, they set their own objectives, and they evaluate themselves in the context of the situations. The teacher is a sensitive professional who knows just how much or how little to get involved. They are co-learners in the social group helping to frame questions, invent solutions to problems, and find useful resources. They demonstrate through their own strategies and their own language the social conventions appropriate to the situations. But they encourage invention and they mediate the learners' discovery of the conventions.

Inhibiting Invention and Misrepresenting Convention

Traditional schools have, by taking control of learning away from the learners, inhibited invention and risk-taking and misrepresented convention. They have made learning harder in school than outside and created a difference that doesn't need to exist and is in fact counterproductive. Sometimes this is done with the best of intentions. We think we are taking shortcuts to learning by telling the learners and not making them discover conventions for themselves. We think we can take the risk out of learning by constraining it so that non-productive invention is impossible. What we accomplish is not however what we intend. Instead of facilitating learning, we interfere with it.

Why Some Groups are Less Responsive to Schooling

Some pupils, highly motivated to do well in school, can literally play these school games. They can get satisfaction out of doing the school tasks and winning the praise of the teachers and the rewards of the system. They can then continue to learn what they can in school and integrate it with what they continue to learn outside of school. The success that many pupils have in traditional situations obscures the relationship between in-school and out-of-school learning. To understand the problems of traditional education and its failure to provide authentic learning situations, we must look to those who do not succeed in the system. What we find is that disproportionate numbers of minorities, of the poor, of boys, and of non-conformists are among the low achievers. In all of these the ability of the system to adapt to the learners is the key. Pupils succeed in traditional controlled programs to the extent that they are willing and/or able to conform and accept nonfacilitative curriculum and teaching.

Social zones of proximal development. Dewey said that schools can make pupils adjust to the schools or adjust the school to the learners. His advice was to start where the learners are. That means accepting the language, culture, and experience of the pupils. It also means understanding their motivations. There are social zones of proximal development as well as individual. Schools can accept the reality of these and provide authentic experiences that are relevant to the life experience and values of the populations they serve. That can make learning possible for all learners rather than only for those culturally motivated to put up with inauthentic school experience.

Social context is itself a powerful mediator. Classrooms are social organizations. They are necessarily different than other social groups pupils encounter since they bring numerous similarly aged people together. Their funding, staffing, and social-political status also constrain them. But it is possible to organize classrooms so that transition into the groups will be eased, social interactions will be supportive, and bridges will be provided to the cultures and social values pupils bring to school. People are well equipped to learn the conventions of new social contexts and new linguistic genres if they are given a chance. If, however, their learning in classrooms is too highly constrained, then all they will learn is the narrow set of behaviors permitted. Some pupils will find themselves permitted to fail but not to be non-conformists.

Frank Smith (1986) points out that an informal literacy club exists in North American schools, which accepts some pupils but excludes others. Social, cultural, and linguistic dues are required for membership. Those pupils who find admission to the club easy learn to read and write with little trauma. They bring the right language and experience to school, and they can accept school experience even if it is dysfunctional. Others feel unwelcome and their language and responses to school experience are interpreted as inappropriate. So they participate in a self-fulfilling prophecy: they appear to be stupid and unprepared for literacy. The school technology then classifies them as deficient and a cycle of intervention begins which eliminates all invention and most of the convention of functional language. The learners fail at this too.

All human beings are capable of learning language and learning through language. If learning in school is as authentic as learning out of school, then there are no disadvantaged groups. But not all groups are so motivated and culturally equipped for school that they can survive dysfunctional teaching and curricula. So many are excluded from the literacy club.

The Politics of Education for Language and Literacy

Things would be a lot simpler if the issues involved in schooling were only confined to how best to produce learning and support it. But schools are political institutions as well as educational ones. How we treat learners in our schools involves political as well as educational decisions, or perhaps we should say, political/educational decisions. When the pupils are minorities who are second language speakers of English or native speakers of low-status dialects of English then the political decisions have to with who they are as much as how they learn.

Even countries that have made political commitments to universal literacy may not in fact want a high level of literacy to be available to everyone. That could decrease the pool of unskilled labor and lead to a work force dissatisfied with their level of employment. In fact, even developed nations have come to accept a high level of failure or partial success in their school systems. In third world nations it is expected that a third to a half of pupils starting school will not last more than a year. If the success rate were higher, the schools would not be able to accommodate the pupils.

Freire and the pedagogy of the oppressed. Freire characterized one view of schooling as a banking view. Increments of learning are deposited in the heads of learners as if they are passive, empty vessels to be filled. In contrast, he argues that learning must be functional and relevant to the changing life-view and aspiration of oppressed people for it to be successful.

Literacy is not itself liberating. We can't take third world people or oppressed minorities in advanced countries and liberate them by first making them literate. Unemployed young black people in Detroit may be less literate than other groups in society. But even if we somehow could make them all more literate that would still not produce more jobs for them.

Written language, like oral language, is learned most easily when learners become engaged in situations in which the language is functional. Achieving new levels of literacy or learning, or coming to control new genre, must also come as the learners find themselves in situations in which their inventions may be tested and the conventions inferred. Schools can provide rich experience but there must be a real world connection before learners will respond to them.

Critical literacy education. To produce successful schooling for all people requires a curriculum and teaching that support authentic learning. But there must also be a genuine commitment to serve all people and to accept them and their culture. That means a critical view must be applied to looking at school policies and practices. Who do they really benefit? In American education, 90–95% of all elementary classrooms are dominated by basal readers. About $400 million dollars a year are spent on them. Of that, 80% is controlled by five mega-publishers. These constitute a massive block to change because the interest of the publishers stands above that of the learners excluded from the literacy club.

The Relationship of Teaching to Learning and the Role of the Teacher

Redefining learning requires us to redefine teaching. Optimal learning requires teaching that supports it and facilitates it without controlling, distorting, or thwarting it. Vygotsky's (1978) concept of mediation is a useful way to view the major component of optimal teaching. Mediation in Vygotsky's sense is a third element in a learning context. The learner is in situational context in which problems need to be solved or experience understood. The teacher is present also but in the role of mediator—supporting the learning but neither causing it to happen in any direct sense nor controlling the learning. In this way the forces of invention and convention are unfettered, and the teacher supports the learner in achieving equilibrium.

Consider these classroom episodes:

a. A group of black inner city fourth-grade pupils have read Langston Hughes poem "Mother to Son" (Hughes, 1963, p. 67). The pupils discuss the poem with the teacher, a co-discussant. The classroom procedure involves a pupil leading the discussion. The teacher wonders what they think about the mother's saying "Life for me ain't been no crystal stair." Some of the pupils point out other references to stairs in the poem. The teacher shares with them her knowledge of the author's life and political beliefs. She suggests that the stairs represent the author's view of this woman's attempt to raise herself up from her difficult conditions. One boy asks, "She talkin' 'bout climbin' up to heaven?" They decide that the mother is contrasting her hard life to the biblical idea of a beautiful crystal stair leading to heaven. In doing so they draw on their own knowledge of the likely experiences and religious beliefs of the mother. They share stories of their own mothers. "I never thought of this poem in quite that way," says the teacher.

b. An eighth-grade group in a working class suburb plans a unit on evolution. The discussion and webbing of their knowledge of the concept introduces the controversy over the biblical view of creation. Two weeks after the unit begins one boy tells the teacher his minister would like to come in and debate evolution with the teacher. The teacher declines, explaining that studying a theory is different than advocating it. The class discusses the situation and reaffirms that they are studying evolution as a theory. They decide to explore the role of theory in science and the difference between established fact and theory. The boy is encouraged by the teacher and his classmates to bring into the study literature from creationists on the subject. The ensuing study is enlivened. The pupils search avidly not only for resources on evolution but also on the history of the theory and the controversy over it. One group reads Irving Stone's adult biography of Charles Darwin (1980).

c. A third-grade class enjoys playing Hangman. In an informal conversation, some of the pupils comment that some people are better players than others. They relate this to the idea of strategies. One student comments that it pays to know which letters are most common. The teacher suggests they prepare a manual, "Rules for Hangman Players." During the course of preparing the manual, the pupils decide on studies they need to do of letter frequency, of letter sequence, and of common patterns. As they try out the rules, they become aware that if the person picking the word knows that the guessers will use sophisticated strategies, he or she can counter by picking words with uncommon letters and spellings.

In all of these examples, the teachers play a crucial but not controlling role. The teacher is not intervening in the learning but the teacher is mediating it. He or she is a co-learner, a resource, a guide and a monitor. The role of the teacher as mediator is an active one, but the teacher understands that teaching supports learning—it can't force it to happen. In areas of controversy, the teacher is not afraid to express belief but shows respect for the developing beliefs of the learners. In building comprehension the teacher knows that the pupils' development of their own strategies is more important than whether they agree with the teacher. So the teacher helps the pupils to examine the available facts, to evaluate their own beliefs, and to find more information as they need it.

Teaching as Mediating and Supporting Learning

Putting the learner at the center of education necessarily means that classrooms can't be teacher centered. That doesn't mean less of a role for the teacher in education. But it means that the teacher plays a more subtle supporting role. The teacher is not abdicating authority—rather the teacher is using the authority on behalf of the learners assuring them of the optimal conditions for learning. The teacher is not giving up power. The teacher is empowering learners. There is no one-to-one correspondence between each act of teaching and each act of learning—there never was. But if there is more learning going on in the classroom, then surely there is more effective teaching going on.

Arranging Authentic Experiences

What is common to the three examples cited above is that they represent authentic experiences. Authenticity, the extent to which school experiences correspond to real world experience, is not an absolute. In fact in any school experience what is authentic for some pupils may be inauthentic for others who lack interest or relevant background for the experience. But authenticity is a goal teachers must pursue. When school experiences are authentic then conventions are authentic and pupils will invent as they participate, infer the conventions, and establish their own equilibrium.

Teachers have known for a long time that we learn best to read by reading and to write by writing. But the reading and writing must be authentic. Similarly pupils develop problem-solving strategies by solving real problems that they recognize as important and authentic.

Detecting Zones of Proximal Development

When Vygotsky (1978) developed the concept of the zone of proximal development, he was talking about a condition of learners, their capability—in some social contexts—to learn and to perform in ways that they do not usually demonstrate. Teachers can take advantage of these zones of proximal development by:

1. Being good kid watchers, that is, being able to detect the indicators of potential *zones of proximal development.*
2. Creating the conducive social situations that will facilitate the learning.
3. Inviting and supporting the active participation of the learners in these social contexts.

4. Being effective mediators themselves, supporting self-mediation and peer mediation, and providing mediating resources (such as authentic books to read).

Teachers can't create zones of proximal development where they don't exist. Teachers need to be good kid watchers who are sensitive to the signs of learning potential even before the learning exists. What they can do is create opportunities—the conducive social contexts—to reveal the zones of proximal development. And then they need to be good at helping kids to find the courage to take the risks that learning involves.

Including Learners in the Literacy Club

Creating classroom conditions and expectations that include all learners in the literacy club is a key goal in the kind of teaching I'm describing. This means accepting all learners and the linguistic, cultural, experiential, and cognitive resources they bring to school. It means treating the learners, regardless of who they are and where they come from, as strong and well-equipped for learning. It means building on this strength without requiring the learners to change language or cultural ways of meaning. It means valuing the inventions of all the learners and involving them in experiences which are authentic for them so that they may infer the conventions. And it means being there to mediate and support the learning.

It is important for teachers to expect learning and to not be satisfied until it is happening. But it is also necessary for the pupils to expect to learn and to come to feel comfortable with the risks that learning involves. They have to see themselves as members of the literacy club.

Mediating but Not Intervening

Good teaching involves a delicate balance: knowing how much support to give without taking control of learning from the learner. That's why intervention is an inappropriate term for any kind of teaching strategy. The teacher should be aiming to give enough support to involve learners and to keep them involved in useful learning. When the teacher becomes an active intervener then the learner loses control and the nature of the learning and what is being learned changes.

Appropriate and Inappropriate Social, External Response by Teachers

The teacher's response is inappropriate when there is:

a. Substitution of authority for social convention.

b. Intervention by teachers or significant others to minimize invention and focus excessively and prematurely on the need for conventionality, and eliminate or reduce risk-taking.

c. Reward for conformity and avoidance of risk-taking.

d. Direct teaching of incorrect, decontextualized, or overly narrow conventions.

e. Punishment for failure to respond to inappropriate and inauthentic conventions, and activities designed to teach them.

The teacher's response is appropriate when there is:

a. Support for mistake making and hypothesis testing.

b. Invitations and expectations for pupils to invent within authentic situations.

c. Involvement in a rich wide range of authentic experiences.

d. Mediation to support achievement of equilibrium between invention and convention.

e. Invitation to membership in the literacy club.

References

Dewey, J., and Bentley, L. (1949) *Knowing and the Known.* Boston: Beacon.

Ferreiro, E., and Teberosky, A. (1982) *Literacy Before Schooling.* Portsmouth, NH.

Freire, P. (1982) *The Pedagogy of the Oppressed.* New York: Continuum.

Goodman, K. (1984) "Unity in Reading" in Purves, A. and O. Niles (eds) *Becoming Readers in a Complex Society.* Chicago: University of Chicago Press.

Goodman, K., Smith, E.B., Meredith, R., & Goodman, Y. (1986) *Language and Thinking in School.* New York: R. C. Owen.

Halliday, M.A.K. (1975) *Learning How to Mean.* London: Edward Arnold.

Halliday, M.A.K. (1978) *Language as Social Semiotic.* London: Edward Arnold.

Halliday, M.A.K. (1984) "Three Aspects of Children's Language Development: Learning Language, Learning through Language, and Learning about Language," in *Oral and Written Language Development Research: Implications for Instruction.* Urbana: NCTE.

Halliday, M.A.K. (1986) *Introduction to Functional Grammar.* London: Edward Arnold.

Hughes, L. (1963) *Mother to Son,* in *American Negro Poetry,* Arna Bontemps, (Ed.) New York: Hill and Wang.

Krashen, S., and Terrell, T. (1983) *The Natural Approach: Language Acquisition in the Classroom.* Los Angeles: Alemany Press.

Miller, G. (1966) "An Introduction to Psycholinguistics" in *The Genesis of Language,* Miller and F. Smith (editors) 1966. Cambridge.

Read, C. (1971) "Pre-school Children's Knowledge of English Phonology," *Harvard Educational Review* 41:1–34

Smith, F. (1986) *Insult to Intelligence.* New York: Arbor House.

Stone, I. (1980) *The Origin,* Jean Stone (editor). New York: Doubleday.

Vygotsky, L (1978) *Mind in Society,* M. Cole, V. John-Steiner, S. Scribner, and E. Souberman, (Eds). Cambridge, MA: Harvard University Press.

Whorf, B. (1956) *Language, Thought and Reality.* New York: Wiley.

Woodley, J. (1984). *Perception in a psycholinguistic model of the reading process.* Occasional Paper #11, Program in Language and Literacy. Tucson, AZ: University of Arizona.

Chapter Eighteen

Reading and Writing Relationships: Pragmatic Functions

Kenneth S. Goodman and Yetta M. Goodman
University of Arizona, 1983

Reading and writing are part of the world of children, but not in equal proportions. Children growing into literacy find people around them reading more often than they write and for more purposes. There is a world of already existing written language, including, but not confined to, books. Children see adults reading more often than they write and for more obvious purposes. Adults call the attention of children to print and invite their participation in reading. Such reading does not require the reader to assume the role of writer.

Fortunately children do play at what grown-ups do. They play at creating the aspects of their world which attract them. One function of written language which children seem to internalize in this way is labeling, perhaps their earliest attempt at writing for a general audience. Their names become part of their identity and then a way of personalizing their possessions, their rooms, their products. Logos are among the most attractive forms of print young readers encounter and one of the first forms they find meaning for. These show up in their drawings

This chapter first appeared in *Language Arts,* Vol. 60, No. 5 May 1983, pp. 590–99. Copyright (1983) by the National Council of Teachers of English. Reprinted with permission.

and in their attempts to create labels for their own environment. The following example accompanied a kindergartener's drawing of her favorite eating place.

M)c ODoALLS

One minor mystery of writing development has been why children almost universally begin writing even their own names with capital letters. It seems most likely that this reflects the influence of signs surrounding them which also have a labeling function. Children use the letter forms that they attend to in these attractive environmental labels.

This demonstrates two important influences of reading on writing. One is that children use in writing what they observe in reading. But they also must be reading like writers. They may notice characteristics of print in their environment, but it is only when they try to create written language that this observation focuses on how form serves function.

Here are some key points about the interrelationships of reading and writing from the point of view of development:

1. While both oral and written language are transactional processes in which communication between a language producer and a language receiver takes place, the interpersonal aspects of oral language are more pervasively evident than those of written language. Productive and receptive roles are much more interchangeable in a speech act of oral language than in a literacy event of written language. The contribution of listening development to speaking development is easier to identify than the similar contribution of reading to writing. One reason is that oral interaction is more easily observable than written.

2. Both reading and writing develop in relation to their specific functions and use. Again there is greater parity for functions and needs of listening and speaking than for reading and writing.

3. Most people need to read a lot more often in their daily lives than they need to write. Simply, that means they get a lot less practice in writing than reading.

4. Readers certainly must build a sense of the forms, conventions, styles, and cultural constraints of written texts as they become more proficient and flexible readers. But there is no assurance that this will carry over into writing unless they are motivated to produce themselves, as writers, similar types of texts.

5. Readers have some way of judging their effectiveness immediately. They know whether they are making sense of what they are reading. Writers must depend on feedback and response from potential readers which is often quite delayed. They may of course be their own readers, in fact it's impossible to write without reading.

6. Readers need not write during reading. But writers must read and reread during writing, particularly as texts get longer and their purposes get more complex. Furthermore, the process of writing must result in a text which is comprehensible for the intended audience. That requires that it be relatively complete, that ideas be well presented, and that appropriate forms, styles, and conventions be used. As writing proficiency improves through functional communicative use, there will certainly be a pay-off to reading since all of the schemata for predicting texts in reading are essentially the same as those used in constructing texts during writing.

7. Reading and writing do have an impact on each other, but the relationships are not simple and isomorphic. The impact on development must be seen as involving the function of reading or writing and the specific process in which reading and writing are used to perform those functions.

Basically, written language came about as a means of communicating beyond face-to-face situations over time or space or both. In most types of literacy events, writer and reader are not involved at the same time. Young readers may be only dimly aware, if at all, of an author's involvement. Most traditional school language arts programs do not help students to develop a personal functional need for being authors themselves of poems, stories, news reports, books, essays, or biographical sketches. As they progress in school they will encounter school tasks which require writing. But, too often, the purpose of such tasks from the writer's point of view is to satisfy an external demand and not an internal expressive or communicative need. Furthermore, teachers have tended to be evaluators rather than audience or respondents. Often school writing assignments involve either imaginary audiences or no explicit audience at all.

In summary then, people not only learn to read by reading and write by writing but they also learn to read by writing and write by reading. For the teacher trying to support written language development the key objective is to keep the pupils actively involved in both processes. A successful writing curriculum will be one that builds on personal writing, builds the functions of interpersonal writing, and helps pupils to find frequent real purposes for such writing with real audiences. A successful reading curriculum involves pupils in an awareness of the role of the author.

The Shopping List as a Writing Task

Consider a very mundane use of writing, the composition of a shopping list. The function of such a writing activity seems self-evident. It obviously is to create a guide in advance of a forthcoming shopping trip. But why is it needed? Is it possible to shop without a list? Of course, and most people do shop without one—at least sometimes. So why do people write them? Think about the following reasons:

1. To be sure to get what is needed.
2. To save time in shopping.
3. To avoid impulse buying.
4. To economize on expense through advance planning.
5. To guide a shopper who is not the person making up the list.
6. To follow a personal, familial, or cultural custom.

These reasons are not exhaustive and of course they may overlap and interact. Furthermore, shopping list writing may relate to other preceding or concurrent activities. The writer may first plan and write out a week's menus. Perhaps the list is related to the preparation of a particular recipe or special meal and the shopping trip is basically to obtain the needed ingredients. Or the shopper may scan the newspaper ads for special offers and bargains.

Custom often plays an important role in such an activity. People may continue a custom that their parents engaged in. So today's shopping list to take to the supermarket may be a descendent of the shopping order a prior generation handed to the corner grocer who stacked the items on a counter for the customer.

Making a shopping list may also relate to a broader personal way of organizing one's life. Some people feel more secure when aspects of their lives are planned, organized, and recorded in a visible and consultable form. Writing a list finalizes and formalizes a series of decisions made prior to shopping and assures they will not be forgotten, so it extends memory. The written record gives the writer a sense of being in control.

Why the shopping list is written also helps to determine its form. Of course, its general form as a list comes from the way it is used. The reader may scan it, but its main reading is done one item at a time to be checked off physically or mentally as it is used. The price per item may be added during the shopping in order to keep a tally of the expenditures. The list may be randomly ordered as items come to the mind of the writer. It may be systematically organized by categories such as meat, fresh fruit, and vegetables. It may be organized according to the writer's memory of the layout of the store to ease shopping and save time. It may list generic items or specific brand names and sizes, such as those on sale.

Even what it is written on and how it is written are partly related to function and use, and partly to personal characteristics of the user. It may be scrawled hurriedly on the back of a used envelope, or carefully typed on a fresh sheet of paper. It could even be checked off on a printed form for such lists with space left for personal items to be added.

Often the readers of shopping lists are also the writers; people write them to use later in their shopping. But sometimes the shopping list is written by one person to be read later by another who actually does the shopping. That makes a big difference. If the list-maker does the shopping too, then the entries on the list need only be complete enough to jog the writer's memory. But if the reader is another person then a lot more information must be included like size, brand, type, or purpose. Even so the shopper may surprise or disappoint the list-maker because important information was not explicit or because the writer made unwarranted presuppositions about knowledge the reader would bring to the task of comprehending and using the list.

We've chosen this rather special kind of reading and writing as a focus of our discussion of the relationships between reading and writing because it is one in which purpose and function are relatively easy to see, form is relatively constrained, and success or failure would be easy to judge. Careful examination of the composition of a shopping list can make clear how writer and reader relate in all kinds of written language. List-making as a kind of writing has many things in common with every type of writing:

1. Its purpose and function are usually related to communication over time and/or distance.
2. It occurs in a specific context in which the purpose or function motivates a specific writing event.
3. It has an intended audience of one or more readers.
4. Its content is relevant to the purpose and audience.
5. Its structure and format are suited to the purpose and function which will be familiar to or expected by the reader.
6. It must be so composed that it serves both the writer and the reader.

Writing shopping lists differs from other kinds of writing in that there is usually only one intended reader who is often the writer. Writing for oneself represents one end of an audience continuum. At the opposite end is writing for a totally unknown audience. Actually it would be rare indeed if a writer had no sense of the audience since he or she would, more or less consciously, have some intentions of reaching particular people or particular kinds of people. Furthermore, the content would itself help to define the potential readers. But it is not uncommon for writers to write for strangers with little personal knowledge of their backgrounds or interests.

As we suggested above, what goes in a shopping list the writer will read later while shopping need not be very complete. But writing even a shopping list for someone else to use requires a sense of audience.

A Full School Program for Reading and Writing Development

An effective school program for building both reading and writing needs to carefully consider the characteristics of literacy events in which people participate as readers and writers. Such a program needs to be built on the full range of personal uses of written language so that literacy may develop in the context of natural, functional use.

Using mundane functions of writing like shopping lists in the classroom can be helpful because all members of a literate community participate widely in the pragmatic functions of reading and writing which Michael Halliday (1975) has called the "goods and services" function of language. These are the functions of written language which help us go about the business of our daily lives—reading bus schedules, writing notes to tell family members where we are, jotting down doctor's appointments and birthdays. Children are often involved in these literacy events. In such literacy events the relationships between reader and writer are very explicit. Reader and author are more likely to be in close contact. Reading what is written is more immediate and feedback faster. Yet, too often, parents, teachers, and children themselves do not recognize these activities as legitimate reading and writing. Therefore, children are not helped to realize that they are already reading and writing, building knowledge about written language, including its various functions and forms. If children can be helped to believe they already do read and write, then school instruction does not become such a foreboding task.

As we focus on the practical functions of reading and writing, we do not minimize the significance of a language arts curriculum rich in children's literature and including recreational and informational reading as well as newspapers, magazines, and other kinds of published materials. Nor do we minimize creative and expressive composition. We want to put all of the uses of reading and writing in a complete curricular context that legitimizes the practical functions of reading and writing. We want to suggest a full developmental literacy curriculum that parallels the full development of oral language.

Building on Personal Uses of Written Language

The shopping list is one of a small number of relatively frequent writing activities that writers engage in with themselves as intended audience. Other activities in which writers are their own intended audience are: 1) Other kinds of list-making such as things to do, invitation lists, Christmas lists; 2) Information jotting such as names, phone numbers, addresses, odd bits of information, personal histories; and 3) Note taking such as during lectures and interviews or while reading or observing.

All of these writing activities have purposes which are personal, involving use of writing as a means of extending memory. Because this type of writing happens very frequently, young children see its use and develop awareness of its function quite early.

Children can be involved in making or reading lists in the classroom. Teachers may need to work with children for a while but soon they will be able to do most of the activities themselves as well as to pass on the knowledge and procedures to their peers. List-making might include: attendance taking; keeping track of which children go where during the day; grouping for centers and activities; keeping track of addresses, phones, school personnel, and birthdays; cataloging the class library; preparing lists of educational places to go after school and on weekends to send home monthly to parents; and listing children's completed assignments and accomplishments. All of these tasks eventually lead to a need for organizing, categorizing, and alphabetizing in order to involve children with a functional and personal use of written language.

Another type of personal writing is the diary, log, or journal. It differs from the other personal writing in that it is intended to be kept longer and is usually much more complete than less formal personal writing. Often, a diary takes the form of a written conversation with an imagined alter ego, sometimes addressed as "Dear Diary." It has the very personal function of recording not only events but feelings, longings, and imagined events. As it is used by teens and pre-teens it comes after other writing functions and forms have developed and shows the historical function writing can have by making possible later recall and reconsideration of the past. Like less formal personal writing it represents an extension of memory.

Teachers might capitalize on this kind of memory extension by keeping a group classroom diary to remember important classroom events. Through this experience children can be involved in jotting down information in short partial sentences for further reference. These could later be used to write a classroom letter to parents about "What I learned this week." They could also become part of a classroom newspaper.

This type of diary writing is different from the journal writing teachers encourage young children to engage in, particularly if the teachers read and respond to the pupils' entries. Those become extended written interactions. The teacher's goal may be to create a meaningful purpose for the children to write frequently so that they may have practice in using writing to communicate. The pupils use their writing to tell the teacher about their feelings, the events of their lives, and to complain or make requests. The writing does not have the immediate purpose of extending memory, nor is it personal in that the audience is not intended to be the writer. The children may enjoy reading what they have written but they are not their own intended audience.

Teachers may have begun to make extended use of school journals because they have become aware that while the personal writing children do builds a strong sense of function, it does not involve the child in the role-switching characteristic of most uses of oral language. So the writer does not have the opportunity to receive feedback from a reader and to build a sense of audience. The teacher-response journal is a kind of written language transaction in which some kind of attention to the interests, characteristics, and background of an expected audience is involved.

Teacher response journals have most recently been discussed by Milz (1980) and Staton (1980). Teachers must understand the importance of the response and must set aside time to read and respond to the journals on a regular basis. The importance of this is seen in a second grader's disappointed note to his teacher found in his journal:

I won't write no mor
til yuo write me back

Other kinds of personal reading and writing can be highlighted. The classroom can be even more of a literate environment than a supermarket, a home, or a gas station. Teachers can make the classroom a literate place in which children KNOW that they are constantly involved in reading and writing.

With function in mind, centers or special areas of the room where specific work takes place may be labeled. Restrictions related to the use of these areas may also be developed and written by the children so they know what is expected of them. Instructions about how to care for plants and animals or warnings about unsafe areas in or near the school may be composed by the children. This might emerge from a unit on animal or plant care or safety. Warning signs on drug containers, household cleaners, and so on can be used to focus on the significance and utility of such warnings and the problems in understanding their meanings.

Children can personalize their belongings, their areas of control, and their work. Mailboxes and cubbies can be labeled. If they have their own work areas such as a desk or table, the children may also label these. Children can be designated as mail carriers or box stuffers so that the labeling becomes functional in the classroom, as everyone has to learn to read all the labels in the room for some real purpose.

A unit on language or on different countries might involve learning how the children's names might be written in other languages or in other language forms such as calligraphy. Children could change their labels during the year depending on what is being studied in order to maintain interest in the activity.

When children are involved in role-playing situations, whether it is playing house or gas station in kindergarten or interviewing famous people as part of a social studies unit in upper grades, the implements and materials necessary for reading and writing should be readily available so they can easily make shopping lists, label the costs of items, write out receipts, or take notes as appropriate to the activity. These might include typewriters and calculators as well as paper, pencils, and markers.

In personal writing the writer may find out later, as a reader, how successful the writing has been and what changes are necessary to make the writing better serve its purpose. But there is not the same awareness of audience that emerges from a reader's response when the shopping list has a reader other than the writer. It is only when language is interpersonal that the writer can build a sense of how completely a message must be represented and how form must support function. Language is both personal and social, but it is its social inter-personal use which makes the user aware of how well or completely and in what form it must be expressed to be successful.

Microcomputers have recently made possible a new form of written conversation. To some extent children can hold conversations using computers with "user friendly" programs. Many owners of home computers "talk" to other computer owners through their keyboards. Some experimental use of such electronic writing has occurred in several school settings (Scollon 1982). Especially in remote communities microcomputers make writing a more immediate experience by minimizing the time of getting responses to messages. Such written conversations involve readers and writers in the role-switching characteristic of oral conversation and provide immediate response to each utterance. Deaf and hearing-impaired people have been using teletype telephones for some time in place of the usual phones, which are not very functional for them.

"Written conversations" are especially helpful for middle grade children who may need help to focus on interpersonal writing. It is literally a conversation on paper usually between two people initially including the teacher. But as the activity becomes familiar to children either the teacher's role can be taken by another child or a third member may be added to the team. For very young beginners or insecure writers, the teacher may read aloud as the message is being penned. An example of written conversation in the third grade follows:

Teacher: Pedro, how are you today?

Student: Fine how are you today?

Teacher: I feel great today. Pedro, do you have any hobbies?

Student: No. Do you?

Teacher: Yes, Pedro. I like to cook, and I like to swim. Mrs. Wendt told me you play kickball. Is that right?

Student: Yes.

Teacher: Do you like it?

Student: Yes. Do you like it too?

Teacher: Yes, I like it a lot. Are you on a team?

Student: Yes I am on bobcat. Do you like the team?

Teacher: I have never seen the bobcat play.

Student: Why don't you come and see?

Teacher: Thanks! I would like to!

But this form of written dialogue, while very useful, does not yet represent a common need in our culture. Ironically, there are not many common writing situations in which there is some kind of parity between the number of readers and writers involved.

Note and letter writing is one type of writing that most often involves a single writer with one or a small number of readers. Furthermore, this is another type of writing which children observe adults using. They also have early experiences with receiving cards, notes, and letters. So children build an early sense of the function of letter/note writing. Their early efforts are usually successful and well received because the recipients of children's notes and letters are often close relatives and friends who are willing and able to extend themselves to comprehend and respond. The more in common reader and writer have the less the writer needs to consider audience needs, the more the reader may infer, and the less complete the expression needs to be. That creates an optimal situation for language learning.

Note and letter writers learn form and purpose from receiving and reading or hearing them read and quickly adapt form to function as they write. Setting up a class or school post office has its own payoff as children develop many opportunities and reasons to send and receive messages (Cholewinski 1982; Green 1983).

Writing letters to less familiar people than classmates, teachers, and family members provides new audiences for children. Writing to a favorite author to express approval, to a company for free and inexpensive materials, to find answers to questions raised in a science or math unit, to the President, or to the editor of the local newspaper to echo agreement or disagreement with some significant policy all provide challenges for writing which often demand shifts in style and conventions.

Although the children often have the opportunity to read responses, they may also discover that important people do not always answer their mail. Paulie, a third grader, got a form postcard in answer to his plea:

Dear Mr. President,

Please help Detroit.
Do not let people carry guns.
We see you on T.V.

Our neighborhood is dirty There
is junk everywhere The windows
are busted out Please don't let
people bust out the windows.

Please make alot of houses
pretty. Not with holes, filth,
and bugs, and rats. Please
let butterflies be flying on
your hand.

                              Paulie

If all involved in literacy development can understand the strengths children have when they come to school, if they believe children have already started to read and write as they have actively participated in their literate environment, a curriculum will be developed which expands on children's knowledge. This kind of understanding is a much more supportive basis for learning than is ignoring the degree to which children come to school understanding the nature of written language.

We suggest examining the wide variety of functional writing experiences which can be turned into daily curricular experiences. Teachers can write down everything they write or read for a forty-eight hour period. The children can be asked to add to this list by observing and interviewing family members. A Friday and Saturday or Sunday and Monday are good days to choose since these include a school day and a week-end day which will expose different kinds of language functions in at least two different settings. Everything that is even scanned or glanced at quickly, such as toothpaste containers or recipes should be included. Then the teacher can sit down with the list and ask: "How can I turn each activity into a written language experience for the children in my classroom?" or "How can I relate these things to the studies I am already planning for my class?" The writing experiences can be planned so that they are done by the children alone or they can be a collaborative effort by the teacher with the children.

Many of the activities will involve both reading and writing which take place almost simultaneously. Many of the activities which begin as personal writing will become interpersonal as children expand their focus on self to a focus on communication with others.

All of these activities take time. They should not be started in a school or classroom unless teachers understand their significance, are enthusiastic about what they accomplish, and believe in the priority of such activities. If these are simply added to an already overcrowded curriculum, then both teachers and children become frustrated and the activities lose their significance. Since these activities involve the functional use of reading and writing, they include spelling, handwriting, dictionary use, and language analysis. The teacher should therefore spend less time focusing on the latter in workbooks and ditto sheets which isolate their development from use. Instead the teacher can begin to gather evidence through their daily use of reading and writing for many purposes and in all kinds of settings that children's spelling, handwriting, and grammar develop significantly through varied language use.

Through engaging in a large amount of varied reading and writing, children will develop a sense of control over them and will find a personal significance for becoming literate. Focusing on activities where reading and writing take place almost simultaneously helps children realize that one process supports the other and that they are capable of controlling them both.

We believe that development in reading and writing can only occur if people actively participate in reading and writing experiences which have significant and personal meaning for the user.

References

Cholewinski, M. "Comar Postal System." *California School Boards* 41 (December 1982).

Green, Jennifer. *The Nature and Developing of Letter Writing by Hispanic and Anglo Children Using a School Based Postal System*. NIE Final Report. Washington, D.C. 1983.

Halliday, M. A. K. *Learning How to Mean: Foundations of Language and Development*. Vol. 1, edited by Eric Lenneberg and Elizabeth Lenneberg. New York: Academic Press, 1975.

Milz, Vera. "First Graders Can Write: Focus on Communication." *Theory into Practice* (Summer 1980): 179–185.

Scollon, R., and Scollon, S. Paper presented at Literacy Before Schooling Conference, University of Victoria, Faculty of Education, British Columbia, Canada. October, 1982.

Staton, Jana. "Writing and Counseling: Using a Dialogue Journal." *Language Arts* 57 (1980): 514–518.

Chapter Nineteen

Access to Literacy: Basals and Other Barriers

Kenneth S. Goodman
University of Arizona, 1989

The good of a book lies in its being read. A book is made up of signs that speak of other signs, which in their turn speak of things. Without an eye to read, a book contains signs that produce no concepts; therefore it is dumb. This library was perhaps born to save the books it houses, but now it lives to bury them. (Eco, 1983, p. 396)

A Metaphor for Literacy

In Umberto Eco's *The Name of the Rose*, William, a detective-semiotician, becomes aware of a 14th century library with a magnificent collection of books. He learns, however, that the library exists not to make the knowledge of the ages accessible, but to keep the books it contains from the eyes and minds of those they might educate. Built in the form of a maze, the library itself is a metaphor for literacy and learning. In the end it burns down and with it is destroyed the hoarded treasure of books. But literacy itself, and not the books, is the real treasure, because literate people can create new knowledge to store in books.

This article first appeared in *Theory Into Practice*, Vol. 28, No. 4 (Autumn 1989), pp. 300–306. Reprinted by permission. Copyright 1989 by the College of Education, The Ohio State University. All rights reserved.

Access to literacy needs to be seen in this context. Literacy exists to make it possible to extend the functions of language beyond the immediate face-to-face functions that oral language serves so that communication can take place among people over time and space. In a literate society, access to literacy means access to the social knowledge and to full participation in society.

But literacy, in and of itself, is not empowering. Only when literacy is part of a general empowerment of people is its power felt. In Eco's monastery monks were assembled who were literate in most of the scholarly languages of the world. Yet their use of literacy was confined to copying "safe" manuscripts. Even the creation of new commentary on holy books was considered dangerous and undesirable. They were denied access, by those with power, to many of the books the library contained.

Of course no one even considered making literacy accessible to the Italian peasants who lived miserably in the shadows of the monastery walls. Suppose that the abbot of the monastery had decided to launch a literacy campaign among the peasants. What language would they have been taught to read and write? Certainly not Italian. The vernacular languages of Europe were considered unworthy of literacy at that time. No, most certainly it would have been Latin. What materials would he have used? What would they have been permitted to read while they learned if even the holy monks were so constrained in their reading? And what methods would have been employed? Were the methods for teaching the monks suitable for the peasants? What uses would the peasants have found for their literacy if they attained some degree of competence? What was there, in their lives at the time, for them to read? How would the power groups of the time, the nobles of the church and state, have viewed an attempt to make their peasants literate? Who would have profited and who would have something to lose in their becoming literate?

Never mind. It could not have happened anyway. What we now understand is that literacy is hard to learn if the skills of literacy are separated from the functional use of literacy. The peasants would not have responded to the instruction without a radical redistribution of power that would have changed their lives and made literacy functional for them.

Modern American Literacy

Life in 20th century America is certainly quite different from that of 14th century Italy. Written language is not confined to a select few in monasteries. It is visible in the environment in which we live. The

United States has a national commitment to make everyone literate as a means to education and full participation in society. But the issue of access and the relationship of literacy to the power to use it still exists. How else can we explain the strong correlations between family income and success in literacy and schooling? How else can we explain the gap between the achievement of low status populations (e.g., economically poor Whites, Blacks, Latinos, and Native Americans) and more privileged groups?

We can, of course, find an alternate explanation. We can conclude that it is the fault of the learners, that they are intrinsically inferior as groups. Science, however, is making such a view less and less viable and ethnographic studies are demonstrating the gap between home and school. Schools, moreover, are failing to build on the literacy experiences and functions in the home and community while requiring pupils to adapt to a technology of basal texts and standardized tests (Bloome, 1987).

The societal need for widespread literacy is a recent phenomenon. Long after the invention of the printing press, industrial societies needed only a minority of literates to carry forth their literacy functions. Even as commerce developed and the need for literate clerks grew, it was sufficient to provide most people with the minimal competencies in reading, writing, and arithmetic. If large numbers of pupils did not succeed in school, society did not need that many clerks anyway. Beginning industrial societies needed cheap, unskilled labor.

Modern literacy education grew out of the view that we could expect large numbers of people to fail in school. If children failed they simply left school within a few years. That is still true today in poorer countries. For example, I have been told that in Mexico one third of those who start first grade do not go on to second grade, primarily because they do not succeed in learning to read and write.

In the United States, however, and in other developed countries more recently, we have been faced with a contradiction. We have made the societal and then legal commitment to universal education and universal literacy. Yet we have not dealt sufficiently with how to adapt schools to the full range of learners so that literacy is accessible and functional for them.

Success or lack of success in acquiring literacy is broadly related to how schools treat different learners and whether schools are willing and able to accept all learners and provide appropriate curricula to support their learning. The basal, which began as a technological attempt to adapt schools to mass education, has become the principal barrier in the way of many people becoming literate. As a proprietary technology, used in the invariant and pervasive way it is in most American schools, it becomes an effective screen for keeping large numbers of the poor, minorities, and nonconformists out of what Smith (1988) calls "the literacy club."

Two Kinds of Science

At the time American society was ready to support universal, free, and mandatory public education there were those who argued that this required a "new education." This meant an education adaptable to the full range of social, cultural, and individual differences found in the schools. As early as 1893 successful examples could be found of schools that, according to an account by Rice (1893), were scientific and progressive in making literacy and education available to the widening range of pupils. A "science of education" was emerging based on the concepts of Rousseau, Pestalozzi, Froebel, and Herbart. "This science focused on the study of children's needs and unification of subjects within a curriculum" (Goodman, Shannon, Freeman, & Murphy, 1988, p. 9). Later, Dewey and his followers would transform this into the "progressive education" movement (Cremin, 1961).

Rice (1893) described reading instruction in the "new education":

> In schools conducted upon the principles of unification, language is regarded simply as a means of expression and not as a thing apart from ideas. Instruction in almost every branch now partakes of the nature of a language-lesson. The child being led is to learn the various phases of language in large part incidentally while acquiring and expressing ideas (p. 223). ... Strange as it may seem, it is nevertheless true that the results in reading and expression of ideas in writing are, at least in the primary grades, by far the best in those schools where language, in all its phases, is taught incidentally. (p. 224)

But there is more than one kind of science. A split developed in American education between the humanistic learner-centered science of the new education and a technology-centered science (Dewey, 1928/1964). It should not be a surprise that Americans, faced with the realities of educating the masses, turned to industrial "scientific management" approaches rather than the scientific humanism of the new education. Psychology was producing a measurement-management oriented experimental science of education easily implemented by industrial technology. "In this ethos of business, science, and psychology, the radical changes required to implement the new education seemed inefficient, sentimental, and overly optimistic concerning human learning" (Goodman et al., 1988, p. 13).

Learner-centered education required highly knowledgeable professional teachers. At the time when this split took place teachers, particularly in elementary schools, were meagerly educated. Technology-centered education promised to minimize the importance of the teacher by tightly controlling what they did and how they did it. By controlling teachers, learners would be controlled. Furthermore, what they read would also be safely controlled.

In 1911, leading educators formed the Committee on the Economy of Time (Horn, 1918; Seashore, 1919). Its charge was to produce an efficient curriculum with optimal methods and to set minimal standards. This committee laid out the framework of a technology of reading instruction that was published in a series of four reports between 1915 and 1919 (see Gray, 1919; Horn, 1918; Seashore, 1919; Wilson, 1917). The final report included the "Principles of Method in Teaching Reading, as Derived From Scientific Investigation" (Seashore, 1919), which enunciated the key criteria on which basals have been constructed ever since (Goodman et al., 1988).

Basal Readers: The Embodiment of the Technology[1]

The basal reader thus began on a strong wave of technological optimism. Although some of the rhetoric of the new education was retained, the focus was on carefully managed sequential development of reading as a skill. There was some controversy over whether to teach skills synthetically (first the skill and then the word) or analytically (first the word and then the skill). In both views, however, pupils were to be taught the skill of reading before they were allowed to use reading functionally.

Emphasis on tightly controlling the introduction of words to conform to Thorndyke's laws of learning (Thorndyke & Woodworth, 1901) meant that a new genre of primerese was created, since primers could only contain words already introduced plus a very small number of new words. The first experiences children have in school are with these synthetic texts that make no sense and bear little relationship to the real written language children encounter outside of school.

As the technology developed it expanded at both ends. Preprimers with even fewer words were introduced to precede the primers, followed by readiness materials to precede the preprimers. Initial experiences with reading in school made less and less sense. The series of graded readers was extended to sixth and sometimes to eighth grade, with the rationale that the hierarchy of the technology has so many skills that many are still not known years after initial literacy is achieved. Even in upper grades pupils believe the stories they read are for the purpose of practicing skills and learning words. In fact, the stories are carefully prepared or rewritten to serve those ends (Graham, 1978, p. 100). Readers who are capable of reading a wide range of written genre including literature written for young people are treated as non-readers who must be taught skills and vocabulary right through to sixth or eighth grade.

Before the turn of the century the new education had already demonstrated that reading and writing are learned best in the context of their use. Contemporary research and theory has made clear that this is true because language processes are transactions in which meaning is expressed or understood. Reading and writing are constructive. Writers construct texts to express their meaning and readers construct their own meaning based on their own experiential schemes (Goodman, 1984).

The logic of the basal technology is that learning to read is acquiring a complex hierarchy of skills and an increasing vocabulary of words recognized at sight (Goodman et al., 1988). It is considered essentially the same for all learners. The gap between focus on the skill of reading and its functional use has widened over the decades of basal development. This decontextualization and the use of uniform mass methods has led to widespread failures of pupils who are unable to make the adjustment to the system. The toll is heaviest on minorities and the poor.

Since technology has not been identified as the problem, "objective" empirical research focuses on the deficiencies of the learners. Psychometric instruments have been developed and remediation has been added to the technology. Students who are failed by the basal technology are labeled dyslexic, alexic, disabled, etc. Rather than adapting the technology to the learners, the students' deficiencies are identified and reified, so they can then be recycled back through an even more decontextualized version of the skill sequence.

The contemporary basal program puts so much more emphasis on learning reading skills rather than functional reading that only about 10 percent of the basal lesson sequence is devoted to reading (Goodman et al., 1988, p. 85). That reading, moreover, tends to be of synthetic or adapted texts interrupted with skill prompts and "comprehension" questions.

Learning to read has become identified with progress through the basal reader (Shannon, 1989). Though the original intent of technology-centered science was to produce detailed sequential materials in every aspect of education, reading is the only field in which they appeared to be successful. As a result a disproportionate amount of elementary school time has gone to the teaching of reading, while writing, oral language, social studies, science, and the arts have been crowded out. So much faith was put in the scientific nature of the basal that when schools in the '60s misunderstood the call of Goodlad and Anderson (1959/1987) for doing away with lockstep graded schools, many of them substituted levels in basal readers for grades instead of moving toward nongraded organization. End-of-level tests in basals thus became the criteria for promotion.

Maintaining Basal Power

Understanding the basal reader requires peeling away the aura surrounding basals after years of almost universal use. It requires separating fact from myth. In the Report Card on Basal Readers (Goodman et al., 1988), we found that the basal is (a) an industrial product designed and marketed to maximize corporate profits and (b) an expanding technology that promises to teach every child efficiently and well if teachers follow the imperatives in the manuals explicitly. When the program is less than fully successful, more components are added to remediate the failures.

From the beginning the basal reader has been a proprietary technology. Mass education created a huge market controlled for almost 60 years by a handful of major school publishers. Corporate mergers have concentrated control of the market. Today six programs published by five companies control 80 percent of a $400,000,000 a year market. A recent program cost $40,000,000 to develop.[2] Basals are big business.

While publishers often list recognized researchers as authors or consultants and quote research in their marketing efforts, the basal industry does not itself engage in or support research. Experimental technology-centered science produced the basals and continues to sustain them. But the publishers are not motivated by the need for new concepts to produce more effective materials. Control of the basals, their content, and their methodology is firmly in the hands of the publishers. It is a fact of corporate life that products are designed to maximize profits (Apple, 1989).

The basal study (Goodman et al., 1988) also found that the quality of basals is not controlled through competition, since the products are very similar. Those most affected by the basal programs, the teachers and learners who must use them, have no power to influence decisions. Although some teachers serve on selection committees, their role is confined to using checklists based on the same criteria that underlie the basal technology. Basal decisions are usually made by committees at the state or local levels whose choices are restricted to choosing among the basals submitted. In a study of the basal selection process, Farr and his associates made this observation:

> Indeed, in some of our interviews with textbook adoption committee members, many individuals could not tell one (basal) program from

another when they examined instructional materials without seeing the name of the program, even though these interviews took place immediately after the committee members had completed a several month review of the materials and had selected the program that they believed was best for their school or district. (Farr, Tulley, & Powell, 1987, p. 268)

One reason selection committees are not surprised at how similar competing programs are is that they assume that they all derive from the same unseen scientific authority. Like many teachers and administrators, they believe the basals are constructed by teams of experienced editors working with scientists and educators to craft each lesson and fit it like clockwork into an all-inclusive scope and sequence plan.

The basal study (Goodman et al., 1988) found that the process of producing a basal program is quite different. Market decisions are more likely to dominate basal production than science. The authors have little to do with the writing of specific lessons. These are usually written by junior editors who sit in cubicles in publishing houses producing them by following rigid specifications. These junior editors could be considered the modern day equivalents of the monks who copied manuscripts in Eco's monastery. They are equally restricted in the use of their own knowledge.

In the epoch Eco evoked in *The Name of the Rose*, the monastery was, at the same time, the publishing industry, expert authority, and instrument of divine authority (fused with political authority). It was both authoritative and authoritarian since it could, in the name of God and king, determine who would read, what they would read, and what they would understand from what they read.

Today's basal publishers exercise their hegemony by substituting scientific technology for the authority of Eco's monastery, and they are equally authoritarian. The message to teachers, expressed in the teachers' manuals in imperatives, is this: You must follow precisely what we tell you because we have the authority of science and you do not.

Thus, the publishers can make superficial modifications in their programs, particularly cosmetic ones, but they cannot risk fundamental changes because that would suggest that the truth is not monolithic. In turn faith in the basals might waiver and all might collapse. If the old program is selling well, why change it? If it isn't then make it as much like the best selling program as possible. In both cases publishers avoid risky innovation.

People in the publishing industry who would like to make basic changes in basals also lack the power to do so. The publishing industry is in a position where faith in their product and not the quality of the product is what is crucial to sales and maintenance of its market.

The marketplace does not operate to produce better reading programs. Rather, maintaining the market for their materials is the major concern of publishers. A large part of the cost of producing a basal is the cost of selling it.

Keeping control in the basal means denying any power over literacy development to the teacher or the learner. The key sales message of the basal publishers is that if the basals are used as the manuals dictate, children will learn to read; and if not, they will not. Also, control over teachers' use of basals keeps them dependent on the program. If teachers took charge of the use of basals, they might discover reading can be taught without them. Thus, the sales pitch for school decision makers is trust the program, not the teachers.

The *Report Card on Basal Readers* (Goodman et al., 1988) concludes:

> Their major strength is also their major weakness, because the essential elements of the organization and sequence do not easily permit modification in any but superficial ways. New understandings of the reading process ... find their way into the language of the manuals and even into how the system is described but they do not change the essential nature of the basal or how learners and teachers experience it. They remain locked to the notion that the learning of reading can happen skill-by-skill and word-by-word and that learning is the direct result of teaching. ...
>
> More than anything else the basals are built around control: they control reading; they control language; they control learners; they control teachers. And this control becomes essential to the tight organization and sequence. (pp. 124–125)

Research and the Basal

Knowledge about language processes, language learning, and teaching literacy has been growing steadily. Publishers and the editors who produce the basals for them do a good job of keeping up with this knowledge. They are quick to pick up the catch phrases of new theories and new concepts. However, even if editors and publishers want to act on this new knowledge they are severely constrained by the overriding concern for avoiding risks to profits.

What makes it easier for publishers to resist accommodating new knowledge is that a body of research can be drawn on that continues in the technology-centered experimental traditions. Many researchers in this tradition can fit within the view that the basic technology and authority of the basals must not be challenged. They produce research that sustains the image of an unseen authority. A strong attempt is made to be objective, that is, to carefully avoid a point of view. The research questions asked are safe ones that fit neatly within the technology but do not commit the heresy of challenging its premises. All this makes it possible to avoid responsibility for who gains and who loses from the basal programs. Objectivity makes it possible to see learner deficiencies rather than program deficiencies as the cause of lack of success of pupils in the programs.

Such research is also reductionist. Experimental designs require that the world be orderly, reduced, and controlled to make it possible to study it rigorously. So experimental researchers equate gain scores on norm-referenced tests with reading achievement. They can do studies to compare controlled and experimental ways of presenting skill lessons from specific basals.

Experimental researchers' arguments can be as self-contained as those of the medieval clerical scholars who argued the number of angels who could stand on the head of a pin. They focus on studying smaller units of language (words and skills) so the results can be used to justify the basal focus on words and skills. All "skills" are of equal value. Knowing the "main idea of a paragraph" will be treated as no more important than knowing "the sound of the letter *b*."

Research cannot be separated from political reality. It is a political reality that some groups in our society have power and some do not. At the same time, all researchers have social class, ethnicity, vested interests, and prejudices. They have values they bring to their choice of topics, their interpretive judgments, and more basically their choice of research models. Choosing a research model is taking a political stance, even if that stance appears to be studiously apolitical.

The issue of power may be treated as central to the issues in school literacy programs. Whether by design or not children from less powerful groups do less well in school literacy programs. The basal methodology is not part of the solution to this problem; it is part of the problem. If researchers treat that as a central issue, they will center their studies around finding the connections and determining how the process of discrimination works.

Flawed Products of a Flawed Technology

In the research for the basal report (Goodman et al., 1988), my colleagues and I became aware that the technology of the basals is flawed in its execution:

> At each point where the apparently tight system and goal-orientation of the basal is carefully examined, there appear to be misconceptions, inconsistency, misdirection, and misapplication. Lessons and

test elements do not do what they claim to do. Labels are used inconsistently. And poor execution is found throughout the program: Mismatching of questions and content, incoherent texts, awkward grammar and phrasing, unreadable text, unanswerable questions. The basals are not in reality what they appear to be. They are not consistent with their own design criteria. (p. 125)

This pervasive flawing of the basals is not the result of carelessness on the part of those who have produced it. Every word, line, picture, and page of the basals is reviewed by scores of people involved in the process. The flaws result from the internal inconsistency of the technology itself. When a junior editor is using a framework to generate "comprehension questions," for example, labels such as literal and inferential are applied, but inconsistently, because the categories are not mutually exclusive ones. The questions trivialize the text because the requirement to produce as many questions as lines in the text lowers the focus.

Stories are incoherent and noncohesive because they are basically treated as vehicles for presenting and practicing a sequence of words and skills. A basal version of *Little Red Riding Hood* ends with the child who has just been saved from a horrible death saying, "I like you woodcutter. Come have some apples. I put red apples into my basket. I put big red apples into my basket" (*Scott Foresman Focus*, 1985, p. 32). Even when a story survives reasonably intact, the process of directing attention to words, attending to minor aspects of the texts, and answering trivializing questions seriously constrains any personal aesthetic experiences readers may have with the story.

Conclusion

As long as the public and profession accept the basals as the technological triumph of science and are willing to pass on the failures of the basals to teachers and pupils, any major change is unlikely. The resistance to change in basals may eventually become their own undoing. Teachers who refuse to be controlled find that there is no compromise:

There is no easily identifiable pattern to modify either content or design of what the "master developers" prescribed in the basal. As one of our teachers said, "You can't understand it; you can only follow it." (Duffy, Roehler, & Putnam, 1987, p. 362)

Those teachers who will not follow are rejecting the basal and wondering why they ever thought they needed it.

Concern is developing among the public and the profession with the quality and integrity of the literature the basals present. Basal publishers have responded by pointing to increased representation of well-known children's authors. But the publishers have always rewritten children's literature to fit the skill sequence and readability formulas and to avoid antagonizing critics. If they stop censoring they will be in trouble with pressure groups. Ironically, it is because every selection in the basal is required reading that judges have been able to support parents who object to their children reading certain stories. If children chose their own books, there would be less justification for complaints that family values are being violated.

It may well be the teachers who bring about the revolution that overthrows the basal dominance. Teachers have the potential power to change, mollify, or eliminate the discriminatory effect of the current basals, but they have thus far been effectively controlled by the manuals and administrative restrictions. In short, teachers have been deprofessionalized. However, professional teachers and administrators are becoming aware that the knowledge exists to make literacy universally accessible if schools are able to adapt to the learners rather than requiring learners to fit the rigid system.

Teachers are also recognizing that children learn language, including written language, easily when it is authentic and functional for them. In other words, learning to read and write occurs when reading and writing are used to learn, not as separate, discrete skills. These professionals are revitalizing the learner-centered science and creating the whole language movement. They are rejecting the basal technology that has failed the poor, the minorities, and the nonconformists among their pupils. They are aware that there is no place in learner-centered schools for technology-centered basals. If this movement spreads and publishers are forced to change, what they offer it will have to be something very different from today's basal.

Eco's library was born to save books but came to be a place to bury them. The basal was born to bring literacy to the masses. It now exists to limit who will be literate and to limit access to the modern day storehouse of literate works.

Notes

1. The historical material that follows is based on Goodman, Shannon, Freeman, & Murphy et al. (1988), and Shannon (1989).

2. The patterns of mergers among publishers have been so active lately that the figures cited here update information in Goodman et al. (1988). Estimates of market size come from Squire (1987). Publishers do not reveal their production costs, so the $40,000,000 figure is obtained from personal communications with reliable sources in the publishing industry.

References

Apple, M. (1989). Textbook Publishing: The Political and Economic Influences. *Theory into Practice, 28:4*, 282–87.

Bloome, D. (1987). *Literacy in schooling.* Norwood, NJ: Ablex.

Cremin, L.A. (1961). *The transformation of the school: Progressivism in American education,* 1876–1957. New York: Knopf.

Dewey, J. (1964). Progressive education and the science of education. In D. Archambault (Ed.), *John Dewey on education* (pp. 169–181). Chicago: University of Chicago Press. (Original work published in 1928)

Duffy, G.G., Roehler, L.R., & Putnam, J. (1987). Putting the teacher in control: Basal reading textbooks and instructional decision-making. *Elementary School Journal, 87,* 357–366.

Eco, U. (1983). *The name of the rose.* London: Pan Books.

Farr, R., Tulley, M.A., & Powell, D. (1987). The evaluation and selection of basal readers. *Elementary School Journal. 87,* 267–281.

Goodlad, J., & Anderson, R. (1987). *The nongraded elementary school* (2nd ed.). New York: Teachers College Press. (Original work published 1959)

Goodman, K. (1984). Unity in reading. In A. Purves & O. Niles (Ed.), *Becoming readers in a complex society* (83rd yearbook of the National Society for the Study of Education) (pp. 79–114). Chicago: National Society for the Study of Education.

Goodman, K., Shannon, P., Freeman, Y., & Murphy, S. (1988). *Report card on basal readers.* Katonah, NY: Richard C. Owen.

Graham, G. (1978). *A present and historical analysis of basal reader series.* Unpublished doctoral dissertation, University of Virginia.

Gray, W.S. (1919). Principles of method in teaching reading, as derived from scientific investigation. In E. Horn (Ed.), *Report of the committee on the economy of time in learning* (18th yearbook of the National Society for the Study of Education, Part II) (pp. 29–43). Bloomington, IL: Public School Publishing.

Horn, E. (Ed.). (1918). *Third report of the committee on the economy of time in education* (17th yearbook of The National Society for the Study of Education, Part I). Chicago: University of Chicago Press.

Rice, J.M. (1893). *The public-school system of the United States.* New York: Century.

Scott Foresman focus: I can read. (1985). Glenview, IL: Scott, Foresman.

Seashore, C.E. (Ed.). (1919). *Fourth report of the committee on the economy of time in education* (18th yearbook of The National Society for the Study of Education, Part II). Chicago: University of Chicago Press.

Shannon, P. (1989). *Broken promises: Reading instruction in 20th century America.* Granby, MA: Bergin & Garvey.

Smith, F. (1988). *Joining the literacy club.* New York: Heinemann.

Squire, J.R. (1987, November). *A publisher reports on the basal report card.* Paper presented at the National Council of Teachers of English Conference on the Basal Reader, Los Angeles.

Thorndyke, E., & Woodworth, R. (1901). The influence of improvement in one mental function upon the efficiency of other functions. *Psychological Review, 8,* 247–261, 384–395, 553–564.

Wilson, H.B. (Ed.). (1917). *Second report of the committee on minimum essentials in elementary school subjects* (16th yearbook of The National Society for the Study of Education, Part I). Chicago: University of Chicago Press.

Chapter Twenty

Learning to Read Is Natural

Kenneth S. Goodman and Yetta M. Goodman
University of Arizona, 1979

When a human society experiences the need for communication over time and space, then written language is developed. Until that time, language is used in face-to-face, here-and-now contexts, and oral/ aural language suffices. But when a society is literate, written language is functional for the society, and the members of that society must learn the written form. We believe they learn it and oral/ aural language in similar fashions. Written language includes two of the four language processes. Reading is the receptive and writing is the productive form.

Children are born into a family, a community, and a society in which language is used. Children are born dependent. Furthermore, humans are social animals; they need to interact linguistically and to communicate in order to survive and to participate. Because of this need, almost all children develop language easily and naturally. They do so within the "noisy" situations in which they interact with parents, siblings, and others. Strongly motivated by the need to understand and be understood, they sort out and relate language to nonlanguage, acquire control of symbol and rule systems, use appropriate language for appropriate purposes, build an impressive, even precocious, repertoire of utterances, and become able both to understand and produce language they have never heard before.

This chapter first appeared in L.B. Resnick and P.A. Weaver, (eds.), *Theory and Practice of Early Reading*, Hillsdale, NJ: Erlbaum, 1979, pp. 137–54. Copyright (1979) by Lawrence Erlbaum Associates. Reprinted with permission.

Their language moves rapidly toward the familiolect and dialect that surrounds them, so rapidly that some scholars have come to view language as innate, while others have seen it as an example of conditioning through stimulus and response. Our view is that language is both personal and social invention. Both the individual and the society never lose the ability to create language. We believe, as does Halliday (1975), that function precedes form in language development. The ability to create language makes it possible for individuals to express original thought in original, yet understandable, language and for society to cope with new situations, new circumstances, new insights. It is communicative purpose that motivates language development and moves children toward the language around them.

Children growing up in a literate society begin to encounter written language before they personally experience the need to communicate beyond face-to-face situations. All of them become aware of and able to use written language to some extent. They become aware of books, signs, captions, printed containers, logos, and handwriting in their day-to-day experiences. They recognize stop signs, read cereal boxes, scribble letters, write their names, and follow and join in the reading of familiar stories.

For some children, their awareness of written language and its uses leads so naturally to participation that they are reading and writing, even inventing their own spelling rules, before they or their parents are aware that they are becoming literate. For such children, the process of developing written language parallels that of developing oral language.

Our contention is that acquisition of literacy is an extension of natural language learning for all children. Instruction consistent with this process will facilitate learning. Instruction that does not build on the process of natural language learning will, in some respects, be at cross-purposes with learners' natural tendencies, will neutralize or blunt the force of their language learning strengths, and may become counterproductive. To become literate, learners may then have to overcome barriers placed in their way.

Natural Language Learning

We believe that children learn to read and write in the same way and for the same reason that they learn to speak and listen. That way is to encounter language in use as a vehicle of communicating meaning. The reason is need. Language learning, whether oral or written, is motivated by the need to communicate, to understand and be understood.

Natural, Not Innate

Our view of the development of literacy as natural is not the same as the view held by those who regard language as not learned but innate. Many of those who espouse such a position have tended, reasoning back from the apparent lack of universality in acquisition of literacy, to treat oral language as innate and written language as acquired. Mattingly (1972) summarized such a view:

> The possible forms of natural language are very restricted; its acquisition and function are biologically determined. . . . special neural machinery is intricately linked to the vocal tract and the ear, the output and input devices used by all *normal* human beings for linguistic communication. . . . My view is that . . . speaking and listening are primary linguistic activities; reading is secondary and rather special sort of activity that relies critically upon the reader's awareness of these primary activities [p. 133; italics added].

That leaves Mattingly by his own admission rather surprised "that a substantial number of human beings can also perform linguistic functions by means of the hand and the eye. If we had never observed actual reading or writing we would probably not believe these activities possible [p. 133]."

Mattingly's use of *awareness* in describing reading is a focal point. Oral language is a "synthetic," creative process that is not "in great part deliberately and consciously learned behavior like playing a piano . . . [p. 139]." "Synthesis of an utterance is one thing; the awareness of the process of synthesis quite another [p. 140]." Mattingly is led then to conclude that reading, unlike speech, requires very deliberate awareness of the linguistic process. This view makes the learning of oral and written language very different. Learning to read is seen, not as natural like learning to listen, but as a deliberate, conscious, academic achievement, dependent on awareness of certain aspects of oral language.

Since we view language as a personal-social invention, we see both oral and written language as learned in the same way. In neither case is the user required by the nature of the task to have a high level of conscious awareness of the units and system. In both cases control over language comes through the preoccupation with communicative use. Awareness of the uses of language is needed, but in neither case is it possible or profitable for the competent language user to be linguistically aware in Mattingly's sense. In reading, as in listening, preoccupation with language itself detracts from meaning and produces inefficient and ineffective language use.

Not a Garden of Print Either

When we use the term *natural learning,* we do not regard the process as an unfolding in an environment free of obstructive intrusions. Teaching children to read is not putting them into a garden of print and leaving them unmolested.

Readers are active participants in communication with unseen writers. They are seekers of meaning, motivated by the need to comprehend, aware of the functions of print, and adaptive to the characteristics of print. The environment for reading development must certainly be rich in print, a literate one. But reading instruction, particularly beginning instruction, has a vital role to play in creating and enhancing the conditions that will bring the reader's natural language-learning competence into play. Children must be among people who talk in order to learn to speak and listen. But that's not enough. Their need to communicate must also be present for learning to take place. This is also the case in acquiring literacy.

Instruction does not teach children to read. Children are in no more need of being taught to read than they are of being taught to listen. What reading instruction does is help children to learn.

This distinction between learning and teaching is a vital one. Helping children learn to read is, as Smith (1973) has put it, "responding to what the child is trying to do [p. 95]." That's possible, given children's language competence, language-learning competence, and the social function of written language. Teaching children to read has often meant simplifying and fractionating reading into sequenced component skills to be learned and used. With the focus on learning, the teacher must understand and deal with language and language learning. The learners keep their minds on meaning; they learn language through using it to communicate meaning. With the focus on teaching, both teachers and learners are dealing with language, often in abstract bits and pieces. The need of the learners for making sense may help them to use their language-learning competence to circumvent such instruction. But that demonstrates how we have tended, as Smith (1973) has said, to find easy ways to make learning to read hard.

Halliday (1973) has stated a position we can agree with:

> There is no doubt that many of our problems in literacy education are of our own making; not just ourselves as individuals, or even educators as a profession, but ourselves as a whole—society, if you like. In part the problems stem from our cultural attitudes to language. We take language all too solemnly—and yet not seriously enough. If we (and this includes teachers) can learn to be a lot more serious about language, and at the same time a great deal less solemn about it (on

both sides of the Atlantic, in our different ways), then we might be more ready to recognize linguistic success for what it is when we see it, and so do more to bring it about where it would otherwise fail to appear [p. viii].

We have been solemnly teaching letters, phonics, words, and word attacks, hoping to make children aware of linguistic abstractions, while failing to take seriously their constantly demonstrated competence in using and learning functional language.

The Functions of Language and the Differences Between Oral and Written Language

According to Halliday (1969), "What is common to every use of language is that it is meaningful, contextualized, and in the broadest sense social" [p. 26]. Modern linguistics correctly shifted the main focus of linguistic concern from written to oral language several decades ago. It is unfortunate, however, that many linguists began to equate speech with language to such an extent that written language came to be treated as something other than language. Such a view is unscientific since it is largely unexamined and illogical: If written language can perform the functions of language, it must be language. Rather than being surprised that people can perform linguistic functions by means of hand and eye, we must be prepared to abandon a view of language that would make such linguistic reality surprising. Written language in use is also "meaningful, contexualized, and social."

For literate users of language, linguistic effectiveness is expanded and extended. They have alternate language forms, oral and written, that overlap in functions but that have characteristics that make each better suited to performing certain functions than the other. Table 20.1 shows the basic characteristics of the alternate language forms.

Speech lends itself easily to here-and-now, face-to-face uses. Writing is best suited for use over time and space. Certainly the need for extending communication between people separated by time and distance was historically the social, cultural reason for development of literacy. In some early societies, this social need required literacy from only a few people who functioned either as a kind of signal corps or as the archivists of the communities. The Persians used a small corps of literate Hebrew slaves to handle communication across their empire. In other societies, the need for and uses of written language become more pervasive. Religious communities that hold the belief that each individual must share in a body of knowledge stored in printed documents will develop widespread literacy.

Table 20–1

Basic Characteristics of Alternate Language Forms

Characteristics	Oral Language	Written Language
Input-output medium	Ear/voice	Eye/hand
Symbolic units	Sounds and sound patterns	Print and print patterns
Display	Over time	Over space
Permanence	Instantly perishable unless electronically recorded	As permanent as desired
Distance limits	Distance between encoder and decoder limited unless amplified or electronically transmitted	Distance between encoder and decoder unlimited
Structure	Phonological surface representation of deep structure and meaning	Orthographic surface representation of deep structure and meaning

Oral language is, of course, the first language form used by most individuals, even in literate societies. This means that for a period of their lives, children will use oral language as a primary means of dealing with all the language functions. Evidence exists, however, that very young children have some awareness and make some use of both the form and function of written language long before their control of oral language has become fully functional.

Our contention is that acquisition and lack of acquisition of literacy can be explained in terms of the internalization of the social-personal functions of written language by children. Let's start with a simple example: Children in a developing nation go off to a village or boarding school where they are taught basic literacy, among other things. The functions of written language they encounter in school may have no parallels in their homes. Instruction may deal with the mechanics of reading and writing and not even attempt to establish need or linguistic function. Instruction, literacy, and materials may even be in an unknown language. Success in initial acquisition of literacy will certainly be limited in any sense. If any mechanical skill is achieved, it is unlikely to become functional. Furthermore, when the pupils leave school, there will be little or no use to be made of written language. The village culture is one with little use for print. Literacy is not required because the functions have not been culturally sustained or personally internalized. Since there are strong patterns in many countries of early school drop out before the third or fourth grade, progress in developing literacy is unlikely.

Halliday (1969) has presented a view of children's models of language that we wish to apply to written language. In his view children create a model of each function, a "positive impression of ... what language is and what it is for [p. 28]." Halliday stated that "the child knows what language is because he knows what language does [p. 27]" Children in literate societies use written language to various degrees and for various social or personal purposes. Halliday says that these functions appear in approximate order, and he believes that they develop before children learn the adult language. In building initial literacy it is important to understand that function precedes form in language development and that children have acquired all functions before they go to school. Halliday's functions of language and the sequence in which children become aware of them are as follows (1975, p. 244):

Instrumental: I want

Regulatory: Do as I tell you

Interactional: Me and you

Personal: Here I come

Heuristic: Tell me why

Imaginative: Let's pretend

Informative: I've got something to tell you

The extent to which children become aware of each function in written language depends on which ones are most commonly served by print and which continue to be best served by speech in their cultures and communities.

The people who write the advertising copy for the Saturday morning TV cartoon shows work hard at establishing the I want function so that millions of preschoolers will be able to spot the Count Chocula box and say, "I want Count Chocula."

Children in literate societies are aware early of the regulatory function. For example, they become aware of the function of stop signs quickly. When a 6-year-old was asked why she thought it was important to read, she said, "You might be out driving. And you might want to park. And there might be a sign that says 'No Parking.' And a man might come out and say, 'Can't you read?'"

Letter and note writing represent the interactional function of language. Many children become aware of letters, enjoy receiving them, dictate letters to be sent to grandparents, and begin to play at writing or actually produce letters. Parents often leave notes for children.

At this point it should be noticed that the interactional function illustrates important differences between the oral and written forms of language in use. Conversation is oral interaction. Usually, it is strongly situationally supported. Speaker and listener are together, responses are quick, and topics usually relate to the situational context itself. Pointing, facial expressions, and body movements support successful communication. Interacting through print is not situationally supported (the context is more abstract). Telephone use also lacks situational support; the extension of oral interaction to telephone conversation causes children to refine and extend the function. But telephones provide immediate response, whereas written letters result in delayed responses. Another difference between oral and written interaction is that the writer, the partner in communication with the reader, is most often unseen and unknown. The young reader may be aware of the message but not its source. This difference also shows in other written language. Signs tell you to "keep off the grass." Who wrote and put them there may not be something children have considered. Children may be no more concerned with who puts stories in books than they are with who puts milk in bottles. In fact, the message may appear to come from the language itself (or from its context in the case of signs).

Some children may become aware of the personal function of written language earlier than others. They may be in a very egocentric stage when they become aware that they have their own written names. This written representation of self becomes a way of identifying what is "mine." One of our graduate students recently reported an experience of a 10-year-old fifth grader who was considered learning disabled. Reading is so far from having a personal function for him that he encountered the name *Miguel* four times in a story before he recognized it as his own name. Then he was amazed to find it in print. On the other hand, a 3-year-old, asked to write his own name, scrawled an *A*. "That's Ali," he said. Then he drew a picture with an *A* discernible in its center and said, "That's Ali on his bike." His graphic name was his image.

If Halliday is right about the sequence in development of language functions, then it is interesting that the last three—heuristic, imaginative, and informative—are the functions for which written language is most heavily used in literate societies. As language functions are extended beyond immediate concerns, needs, and interactions of children to exploration of the real world, the world of ideas, and the world of what might be, language expands, takes on new textures, and begins to transcend the immediate contexts in which it occurs. Similarly, the language of children expands to serve their needs as they become fully interactive with their communities.

Halliday (1969) suggested that the informative (or representational) function of language, which is the abstract use of language to talk about ideas, may be the only function of language that adults articulate, but that it is a "very inadequate model from the point of view of the child [p. 33]." He indicated that if our concept of language is to be helpful to children, it must be exhaustive. It must take into account all the things language can do for children. In reading, that means using street signs, buying favorite toys and foods, finding favorite TV programs, writing and reading notes from parents left under magnetic markers on the refrigerator, reading stories that expand the creative and fanciful world of play, using books to discover how to make a sock puppet, or reading a recipe from the box to find out how to make marshmallow Rice Krispy crunch.

Readers in our society who are the readers who do read, as opposed to the readers who can read, use reading for all its varied purposes. We must focus more and more attention on how written language is used in society, because it is through the relevant use of language that children learn it. They learn it because it has meaning and purpose for them. Written language, too, can then fit into Halliday's statement that what is common to every use of language is that it is meaningful, contextualized, and social.

When and How Does Reading Begin?

Reading begins when children respond to meaningful printed symbols in a situational context with which they are familiar. The onset of this process probably goes as unnoticed as the time when children begin listening. Yet there is lots of evidence in the literature that suggests that children develop some kind of print awareness at a very early age without formal instruction.

Smith (1976) makes several points relating to the onset of reading:

> The first is that children probably begin to read from the moment they become aware of print in any meaningful way, and the second is that the roots of reading are discernible whenever children strive to make sense of print before they are able to recognize many of the actual words....
>
> Third, not only are the formal mechanics of reading unnecessary in these initial stages, they may well be a hindrance. It is the ability of children to make sense ... that will enable them to make use of the mechanics.... Fourth, words do not need to be in sentences to be meaningful, they just have to be in a meaningful context... [pp. 297–299].

The awareness of print seems to develop as children learn to categorize the large amount of print information surrounding them in a literate society. As they drive down a highway, walk down a street or through a shopping center, or watch television, they are bombarded with print. Children learn to organize their world and make sense out of it. When printed language is part of that world, they use that aspect of the environment if it is functional and significant·to their life and culture. Gibson (1970) reported on 4-year-old children who not only could "separate pictures from writing and scribbles ... [but who could also] separate scribbles from writing [p. 137]."

After becoming aware of print as being different from other graphic information, children begin to assign meaning to the print in their environment. Ylisto (1968) studied preschoolers who, with no formal instruction, responded to signs in a situational context. Ylisto concluded, "In reading as the child interacts in a print culture his awareness and recognition of printed word symbols become more and more autonomous. He abstracts the printed word symbol from the contextual setting, classifies and orders it and systematizes or assimilates it in a language system he knows [p. 35]."

Our current pilot research substantiates this movement from learning to read printed symbols in familiar situational contexts toward more reliance on language contexts. Children from age 3 on are asked to respond to common signs in their environment. Certain signs are recognized in the situational context only. The logo *Circle K Market* may be recognized when the family drives by the store, but the same logo may not be recognized on a matchbook cover. However, certain logos such as those of McDonald's and Coca Cola are recognized as long as the print retains its distinctive form, even when away from the golden arches or the sexy bottle.

Children's responses to signs suggest that they are more concerned with the meaning of the graphic unit than with the representation of the name itself. When some children see *Chicken and Stars* in white block letters similar to those printed on the can, they will say, "That's Campbell Soup"; and they respond to the Campbell logo the same way. One 3-year-old called signs of Burger Chef, Burger King, and McDonald's all McDonald's. But when the child was shown the sign of a local hamburger place that was more distinctly a sit-down, as opposed to a take-out, place, the child said, "That's a restaurant." Children categorize using associations other than significant graphic features to read. One 2 1/2-year-old says *mother* when she sees the words *Myna* and *Mother*. Myna is her mother's name. Her father's name is Mark. When *Myna, Mark, Daddy,* and *Mother* are all presented to her, she interchanges *Daddy* and *Mark* but never confuses *Mark* with *Mother* or *Myna*. In the beginning of reading, children may relate a concept of meaning to a graphic unit and not be concerned with an exact oral representation. It is not surprising, therefore, when a kindergartner responds to each graphic alternative of his name by saying, "That says Jimmy," whether the name is written *Jimmy, Jim, James,* or *James Jones, Junior.*

Just as oral language meanings are developed and used in ongoing everyday experiences, so written language is learned through functional use. Clay (1972a) studied 5-year-old entrants to New Zealand's schools. She suggested that children are print aware when they ask, "What's that say?" in response to a TV advertisement, or when, in telling a story from a picture storybook, they might sigh and say, "I can't read all the words but I know what they say [p. 28]." She described children who are reading a book, obviously not following the print, but using a book-like pattern such as "Once upon a time ... " or "Mother said, 'Do you want a piece of cake?'" Instead of the familiar "Reading is Talk Written Down," these children indicate that "Books Talk in a Special Way" (Clay, 1972a, p. 29).

As children respond to written language in its contextual setting, they begin to respond to significant features and may even use metalinguistic terminology to suggest their developing rule structures. In our own pilot research, for example, one child named Roberta suggested, "Revco has the same face as my name." But for the most part, children use language. They become interested in signs that help them to control their lives. The Men, Boys, and Senors signs are all important signs to learn to read. Exit signs are important, and many preschoolers respond to them appropriately (although a doctor's son at age 4 responded to one by saying, "I know that's not X-ray").

Read and others have made us aware of the children who seem to be developing rules of written language through their invented spellings. According to Read (1975):

> Certain pre-school children print messages, employing an orthography that is partly of their own invention. They represent English words with the standard alphabet and are thus compelled to classify distinct phones in some way. They do so according to articulatory features, making judgments of similarity that are quite different from those that most parents or teachers might make [p. 329].

Clay (1972a) suggested her own model of beginning reading and how children begin to develop rules about written languages:

> Beginning reading is a communication system in a formative stage. At first the child is producing a message from his oral language experience and a context of past associations. He verifies it as probable or improbable in terms of these past experiences and changes the response if the check produces uncertainty.
>
> At some time during the first year at school visual perception begins to provide cues but for a long period these are piecemeal,

unreliable and unstable. This is largely because the child must learn where and how to attend to print [pp. 161–162].

Clay (1976) suggested that the way children view the significance and function of written language in their own particular culture may provide the basis for success in reading. She studied Pakeha, Maori, and Samoan children in New Zealand. Statistics indicated that "the English language skills did not relate closely to progress in reading. While every Samoan group had the poorest average scores on each language test at every age, the Maoris had the poorest reading averages [p. 337]." She suggested these reasons: The Maories had little contact with printed material prior to entry into school and had few opportunities to learn concepts about print. The Samoan children do not have homes filled with books, but their culture provides oral Bible reading in the home. A Sunday School teacher reported (Clay, 1976) that "...four year old Samoan children who came to Sunday School all want to write. They take the pencils and paper and write [p. 341]." This teacher described back-home relatives involved in selling various crafts at the market place to tourists on Boat Day. While working, they are "reading their mail from New Zealand and frantically writing their answers so that the boat which only stays a few hours can take the letters back to New Zealand. ... Children would see high value placed on written messages [p. 341]." Clay (1976) said:

> The Samoan child, who speaks two languages, who is introduced to a book and to written messages in his home, who is urged to partici-pate fully in schooling and is generally supported by a proud ethnic group with firm child-rearing practices, manages to progress well in the early years of his school without handicap from his low scores on oral English tests [p. 341].

Readers know how to use written language long before they can talk about it. Downing and Oliver (1974), Clay (1975), and Read (1975) have all reported that 5- and 6-year-old children cannot respond ap-propriately with terms such as *word, letter,* and *number.* However, it is important to consider that the ability to apply the labels may follow the grasp of the concepts.

How Beginners Differ from Proficient Readers

In our research on the reading process in readers with widely different levels of proficiency we (Goodman & Burke, 1973) reached certain key conclusions:

1. There is only one reading process. Readers may differ in the control of this process but not in the process they use.

2. Nonproficient readers show problems in getting it all together. They tend to bog down in preoccupation with letters and words and lose meaning.

3. The major difference among readers of varying proficiency is their ability to comprehend what they read.

4. Older, nonproficient readers seem to have acquired a nonfunctional skill. They can produce phonic matched or near-misses for words. They can handle short phrases. But they don't get much sense from what they read and seem not to expect sense.

In fact, it appears that a gap develops for some children between the skills of reading and any useful function of language. So much focus has been placed on form and those functions explored through reading have been so removed from the functional needs of the learner that reading becomes a school subject, not a useful language process. Even when some degree of functional reading competence is achieved through such instruction, it often leaves people with so strong a distaste for reading that they read only what they must, particularly avoiding literature and educational materials, the most common school-related written language.

Beginners may follow four basic paths in moving into literacy:

1. They may move forward from the natural beginning they have made, gaining flexibility and control of the process as they expand the functions of written language they control.

2. They may be distracted from function by instruction and come to regard reading as an essentially nonfunctional, nonlinguistic school activity.

3. They may, themselves, bring their natural growth and school instruction together, choosing from instruction that which facilitates learning.

4. They may develop functional literacy outside school, while developing a school behavior that is nonfunctional but which satisfies school and teacher demands.

The key to these different results lies in reader's perceptions of the functions of reading, the extent to which reading is functional in their culture, the extent to which instruction is facilitative, building on natural development, and the extent to which school experiences are relevant to the functional needs of the learners.

Beginners have a sense of function that leads to some beginning of literacy before instruction. Shifting their focus to the forms of written language does not make them like proficient readers since the latter never sacrifice function to form, even when they encounter misprints. That people can achieve literacy under less than optimal conditions, even in very unlikely circumstances, is more a tribute to the universal human ability to acquire and use language than it is proof that educators can afford to be unconcerned about building programs that create optimal conditions.

How Does Proficient Reading Work?

Our research (Goodman, 1976) on reading miscues has been primarily concerned with developing and testing against reality a theory and model of proficient reading. We have come to view proficient reading as a process in which readers integrate grapho-phonic, syntactic, and semantic information as they strive to construct meaning. Reading consists of optical, perceptual, syntactic, and semantic cycles, each melting into the next as readers try to get to meaning as efficiently as possible using minimal time and energy. That involves sampling from available cues, predicting syntactic structures and subsequent graphic cues, confirming or disconfirming predictions, correcting when necessary, and accommodating the developing sense as new information is decoded.

Efficiency (using minimal cues) and effectiveness (constructing meaning) depend on the reader's ability to maintain focus on meaning. For that to be true, the material being read must be meaningful, comprehensible, and functional to the reader. We are not surprised by the facility readers develop or by the fact that reading actually becomes more efficient than listening. This difference in efficiency is due, not to a basic distinction in the two receptive processes, but to differences in the conditions of use. Listening need happen only as rapidly as speech is produced; reading has no such constraint, so it happens more rapidly with no loss of comprehension. We could listen as efficiently as we read; we just don't need to.

Proficient reading and listening processes are parallel except for the form of the input, their speed, and the special uses we make of each. Proficient readers do not recode print as speech before decoding it. Why should they depend on less efficient process, and how could they, given the greater efficiency of reading? It is not their ability to listen but their underlying ability to process language to get to meaning that beginning readers rely on to develop reading competence. The strategies we have described proficient readers as using are already used effectively and efficiently by children beginning to read their native language. Within meaningful, functional use of written language, children naturally, quickly, and easily learn to use these same strategies with the new graphic inputs in the new contexts.

The Natural Sequence: A Theory and Some Premises

We believe that motivation is inseparable from learning. Recognition of function, the need for language, precedes and is a prerequisite for acquisition. The crucial relationships of language with meaning and with the context that makes language meaningful is also vital. Learners build from whole to part and build a sense of form and structure within their functional, meaningful experiences with language.

Written language development draws on competence in oral language, since both written and oral language share underlying structures and since, for most learners, oral language competence reaches a high level earlier. As children become literate, the two systems become interactive, and children use each to support the other when they need to.

We believe that it helps educators in understanding the reading process to study what proficient readers do when they read. But it is a serious mistake to create curricula based on artificial skill sequences and hierarchies derived from such studies. To build facilitative instruction, we must understand not only how language processes work but also how and why they are learned. Our research has convinced us that the skills displayed by the proficient reader derive from the meaningful use of written language and that sequential instruction in those skills is as pointless and fruitless as instruction in the skills of a proficient listener would be to teach infants to comprehend speech.

Methodology and Motivating

We take as our principle premise in designing initial reading instruction that our goal is to create conditions that help all students to learn as naturally as some do. In this chapter we focus on instruction for children growing up in a highly literate society. But we must, in passing, reiterate our premise that literacy will not be acquired if the community and society do not use literacy to any significant degree for any significant purpose.

Our initial instructional concerns are twofold: (1) to determine and expand on the literacy learners have already achieved, and (2) to establish and expand children's awareness of the function of literacy.

An old but essential educational premise is that education takes the learners where they are and helps them grow in whatever directions are legitimate for them. That turns out to be essential in building literacy. In the balance with this chapter we explore some in-school activities that school and teachers can include in initial reading instruction. What we propose are elements in a program; it is not yet a full program.

Finding out what they can read. If teachers take children for a walk around the school, the neighborhood, or a supermarket, they can get quick insights into the literacy kids have already attained. With a Polaroid camera, a pictorial record can be brought back to the classroom. The teacher needs only to say, "Show me anything you can read, and I'll take a picture of it." Developing this sense of what children are reading is important for the teacher, but the activity is also important for the kids, who will discover that reading isn't new, it's already part of their experience.

Clay's (1972b) Sand test gets at kids' concepts about print. The tests relate to Clay's concept that careful observation of children is a basic requisite to facilitative instruction. However, noting how children handle books, how they respond to print, and how they relate print to meaning are things teachers can do with or without the test. The teachers must be informed monitors, able to see where the kids are and able to help them to find function in printed language and build competence.

Creating a literate environment. The classroom and school must become an environment rich in functional use of written language. That means that there must be lots of written language pupils will need and want to read. It does not mean that every chair, table, or window should be labeled. The uses of written language must be both natural and functional. Furthermore, it will be helpful if the kids are involved in creating the literate environment to give them some sense of where written language comes from. Dictating a set of "Rules for Taking Care of Our Hamster" is an example of this kind of participation.

Work, play, and living. Play is the child's equivalent of the work world of the adult. In language development, play forms a valuable adjunct to the real-life experiences of children. They can read real letters, but they can also create a classroom post office that delivers letters and notes between class members. We need to bring back into kindergartens and primary classrooms the stores, kitchens, gas stations, playhouses, and other centers for dramatic play.

Reading something. Language, reading included, is always a means and never an end. Reading is best learned when the learners are using it to get something else: a message, a story, or other needed information. Literacy development, therefore, must be integrated with science, social

Table 20–2

Language Functions and Learning Experiences

Function	Experiences and Activities
Instrumental (I want)	Sign-ups for activities or interest centers Picture collages with captions: *Things I Want* Play stores and gas stations Orders for supplies: *Things I Need*
Regulatory (Do as I tell you)	Signs Directions Rules for care of class pets, plants, materials Instructions to make things
Interactional (Me and you)	Message board for notes from teacher to children Class post office Games involving reading
Personal (Here I come)	Books about self and family with captioned pictures Individual language-experience stories
Heuristic (Tell me why)	Question box Single concept books Science experiments
Imaginative (Let's pretend)	Storytelling Picture–story sessions with class participation Creative dramatics activities Read-along books and records Comic strips
Informative (I've got something to tell you)	Message boards and bulletin boards Notes to pupils paralleling school messages to parents Class newspaper Community newspaper and *TV Guide* Content textbooks Resource books

studies, math, arts, and other concerns of the classroom. In isolation reading becomes nonlanguage and nonfunctional.

Reading and writing. Reading needs to be related constantly to writing. Wherever possible, composition in written language should be related to reading activities.

Using all functions. Halliday's (1975) seven functions make a good guide for generating learning experiences for initial and continuing reading instruction. Since most forms of writing are almost completely outside a situational context, it is important to begin in school with those situationally supported functions that children have already begun using: the instrumental, regulatory, and personal.

Teachers

In all that we have said, we see the teacher as making the crucial difference in whether some or all children will learn to read. The teacher's role, in our view, is a complex one. It includes the following.

Kid-watching. To build on what kids have learned and to facilitate natural acquisition of reading, teachers must be insightful kid-watchers. They must know what to look for, how to look, and how to interpret what they see. As children progress, teachers must be able to monitor progress, build on strengths, and help them over the hang-ups.

Environment-arranging. Teachers must be able to create the literate environment that will facilitate learning. They must constantly be bringing kids in contact with relevant, functional print.

Interacting. The teachers will be the literate adult using print in functional ways to interact with the learners.

Motivating, stimulating, and encouraging. Teachers have major roles to play in helping children to recognize functional need, stimulating children's interests, and encouraging and responding to their efforts.

Summary

We have argued that learning to read, like learning to listen, is a natural process for children in a literate society. We have argued that instruction facilitates children's development of literacy only if it is based on understanding the following:

1. How language functions in conveying meaning.
2. How communication of meaning functions as the context in which language is used and learned.
3. The subtle differences and similarities of oral and written language in use.
4. The personal and social motivations that led children to learn or not learn language.
5. The social, cultural factors that make the acquisition of literacy of more or less personal importance to children of differing backgrounds.

6. The natural process by which some children achieve literacy.

7. All children's self-initiation of literacy in literate societies.

8. How programs and environments that enhance children's natural motivations, awareness, experiences, and cultural backgrounds can be created so that reading is learned naturally by all children.

9. The roles teachers must play as guides, monitors, environmental arrangers, and stimulators to facilitate the process.

Acknowledgments

Some of the research reported in this paper was supported by the United States Office of Education and The National Institute of Education, Department of Health, Education, and Welfare. The opinions expressed do not necessarily reflect the position or policy of the Office of Education or the NIE and no official endorsement should be inferred. Other research was supported by The Center for Expansion of Language and Thinking.

References

Clay, M. M. *Reading: The patterning of complex behavior.* Auckland, New Zealand: Heinemann Educational Books, 1972. (a)

Clay, M. M. *Sand—the concepts about print test.* Auckland, New Zealand: Heinemann Educational Books, 1972. (b)

Clay, M. M. *What did I write?* Auckland, New Zealand: Heinemann Educational Books, 1975.

Clay, M. M. Early childhood and cultural diversity in New Zealand. *Reading Teacher,* 1976, *29,* 333–342.

Downing, J., & Oliver, P. The child's conception of a word. *Reading Research Quarterly,* 1974, *4,* 568–582.

Gibson, E. J. The ontogeny of reading. *American Psychologist,* 1970, *25,* 136–143.

Goodman, K. S. Reading: A psycholinguistic guessing game. In H. Singer & R. Ruddell (Eds.), *Theoretical models and processing of reading* (2nd ed.). Newark, Del.: International Reading Association, 1976.

Goodman, K. S., & Burke, C. L. *Theoretically based studies of patterns of miscues in oral reading performance* (U.S. Office of Education Project No. 9-0375). Washington, D. C.: U.S. Government Printing Office, 1973. (ERIC Document Reproduction Service No. ED 079 708)

Halliday, M. A. K. Relevant models of language. *Educational Review,* 1969, *22,* 1–128.

Halliday, M. A. K. Foreword to *Breakthrough to literacy* by D. Mackay, B. Thompson, & P. Schaub. Glendale, Cal.: Bowmar, 1973.

Halliday, M. A. K. Learning how to mean. In E. H. Lenneberg & E. Lenneberg (Eds.), *Foundations of language development: A multidisciplinary approach* (Vol. 1). New York: Academic Press, 1975.

Mattingly, I. G. Reading, the linguistic process, and linguistic awareness. In J. F. Kavanagh & I. G. Mattingly (Eds.), *Language by ear and by eye: The relationship between speaking and reading*. Cambridge, Mass.: MIT Press, 1972.

Read, C. Lessons to be learned from the pre-school orthographers. In E. H. Lenneberg & E. Lenneberg (Eds.), *Foundations of language development: A multidisciplinary approach* (Vol. 2). New York: Academic Press, 1975.

Smith, F. Twelve easy ways to make learning to read difficult. In F. Smith (Ed.), *Psycholinguistics and reading*. New York: Holt, Rinehart, & Winston, 1973.

Smith, F. Learning to read by reading. *Language Arts*, 1976, *53*, 297–299; 322.

Ylisto, I. P. *An empirical investigation of early reading responses of young children.* Unpublished doctoral dissertation, University of Michigan, 1968.

Part Six

Teaching and Curriculum

In the 1960s Kenneth Goodman began with a theory of reading that was unlike any of his predecessors. In the twenty years that followed, the insights about language, language learning and language learners that were made available by the theory laid the groundwork for a major educational innovation: whole language. Teachers have applied Goodman's theory to their own practices and have conducted their own research into the nature of reading and learning. The result has been the development of progressive practices that are grounded in articulated theories of teaching and curriculum. These theories have given rise to practices that include the expanded use of literature, decreased dependency on basal series and other programmed materials, curriculum-as-inquiry, authentic classroom language studies that include retrospective miscue analysis and incorporate reading strategy lessons, and teaching for social justice.

The chapters in this part address various aspects of teaching and curriculum ranging from discussions of fine points about reading, language, and learning (*Decoding: From Code to What?*) to treatises on classroom practices and environments that support literacy learning (*Teachers Supporting Learners: A Transactional View, Orthography in a Theory of Reading Instruction* and *Strategies for Increasing Comprehension in Reading*). Each chapter demonstrates how insights from Goodman's theory contributes to and underpins progressive developments in teaching and curriculum.

The chapters also speak to the wholly positive and humanistic nature of Goodman's vision of education culminating with *Revaluing Readers and Reading*. "Revaluing" is Goodman's term for identifying and valuing the linguistic strengths and productive strategies that all language users possess as they learn and use language. "All children seem to be remarkable language learners outside of school," Goodman writes. "If they appear less successful in school it is because learning language has been made too hard for them in the quest of making it easier" (p. 423). Goodman describes how schools fail to help students who need help the most. He also offers an alternative—patient support in the form of a caring teacher who helps the reader shift the focus from non-productive strategies aimed at sounding out and identifying words to taking risks and self-monitoring by continually asking: *Does that make sense?*

This is the key test, whether it is about reading as a process of meaning construction, a teacher coming to understand how to support literacy development, or a child working to understand how to make written language work. For Goodman, it is all about making sense.

Chapter Twenty-One

Teachers Supporting Learners: A Transactional View

Kenneth S. Goodman and Yetta M. Goodman
University of Arizona, 1989

In *Crow Boy* by Taro Yashima, one of the finest authors and illustrators of children's books, we are introduced to Mr. Isobe, a new teacher to the village school who is "a friendly man with a kind smile." Things are very different with Mr. Isobe as teacher. He often "took his class to the hilltop behind the school." He responds to Chibi, the tiny boy in the class who has been an isolate for six years, a "forlorn little tag along."

- He (Mr. Isobe) was pleased to learn that Chibi knew all the places where the wild grapes and wild potatoes grew ...

- He was amazed to find how much Chibi knew about all the flowers in our class garden ...

- He liked Chibi's black and white drawings and tacked them up on the wall to be admired ...

- He liked Chibi's own handwriting, which no one but Chibi could read, and he tacked that upon the wall.

- And he often spent time talking with Chibi when no one was around.

This chapter first appeared in the *Australian Journal of Remedial Education*, Vol. 21, No. 2, 1989, pp. 14–19. Copyright (1989). Reprinted from the *Australian Journal of Remedial Education* with the kind permission of the Editor.

- But when Chibi appeared on the stage at the talent show of that year, no one could believe his eyes. "Who is that?" "What can that stupid boy do up there?"

Until Mr. Isobe announced that Chibi was going to imitate the voices of the crows. "Voices?" "Voices of crows?" "Voices of crows!" Taro Yashima's Chibi was a whole language learner. He learned from staring at ceilings, gazing out of windows, wandering the hills, and listening with great attention and interest to birds. But it wasn't until Mr. Isobe appeared in his sixth year of school that he found out that he could also learn in school and that what he had learned outside of school was important, valuable and of interest to others. Mr. Isobe, like so many teachers, saw no clear distinction between teachers and learners. He saw himself as a learner and suspected that even the least of his pupils knew a lot and had a lot to teach him. He was a kid-watcher who evaluated his pupils by talking with them, observing them and transacting with them. Like Chibi, all children are whole language learners. Unfortunately, also like Chibi, they don't always encounter whole language teachers.

This paper explores teaching and learning as transactional processes. We take the term transaction from John Dewey's use of it. In interactions the elements may affect each other but they remain the same. But in transaction all the elements are changed in the process. In our work we have explored literacy processes, reading and writing, transaction between a reader or writer and a text. Writers are transformed as they write and readers as they read. They know and feel differently after the transactions. The text in the writer's mind is not the same as the one created through writing and the published text is not the same as the one the reader constructs during reading: beliefs, attitudes, and prior knowledge all enter into these transactions.

So in classroom transactions teachers and learners are changed. The idea that teaching can control learning or that each act of teaching results in an act of learning in each learner is too simplistic. Teachers learn and learners teach and as they transact each is changed. Both can resist this change by not committing themselves to the transactions. Whole language teachers recognize the power of classroom transactions and plan for them. One key to their success is building an atmosphere of mutual respect in their classrooms where they value each learner, help the learners to value themselves and teach others and win the respect of their pupils.

Collaboration in Whole Language Classrooms

Classroom teachers lead by virtue of their greater experience and knowledge in their classrooms. They know that their pupils monitor their learning and provide support and resources as they are needed.

But they recognize that there must be collaboration between themselves and their pupils if an optimal learning atmosphere is to be created. Experiences and literacy events must be authentic in the classroom as they are outside of it. Pupils feel a sense of purpose, of choice, of utility, or participation and of shared ownership in their classrooms and in what happens there. Even as young beginners they need to participate in decision-making and see relevance in what they are doing. The tenor of relationships between teachers and learners becomes one of trust and collaboration rather than conflict and domination.

Classroom as Communities of Learners

In our research from the Tohono O'odham Indian reservation we become aware of the complexity of the community of learners in the classroom. We concluded our research by showing that in every language event in which a learner is involved he or she is impacted and constrained by an overlapping group of influences. The language user in the classroom setting is influenced by all the members of the community including the parents outside of the classroom as well as by the teacher and students within the classroom. Attitudes about school, about the ability of the students to succeed in school, views about literacy and the values parents and teachers have about the students and their schooling are all aspects of how students choose to make meaning in classroom settings.

The language and dialects used by the adults and the young people and the values they ascribe to their own language variations as well as language variations within the school setting and the community also influence meaning making. The organization of the classroom and the degree to which the teacher involves the students in their own planning and evaluation has impact on the use of language in the classroom. The student's history, background knowledge, personal experiences and language knowledge are major influences on the ways in which students use language to make meaning. Finally the text being used by the students influences the ways in which they choose to use language to express their own meanings.

The role of the teacher and teacher's attitudes towards the place of the students in the learning community become crucial elements in whether the language experiences in the classroom will have a positive or negative effect on the language learning of the students.

Sharing Power

In whole language classrooms, teachers are empowered. They are not reduced to powerless technicians administrating someone else's worksheets, skill drills and reading schemes to powerless pupils. In turn they empower learners by valuing who they are, and what they know, do and believe. They support the learners in solving their problems and pursuing knowledge. The learners are involved and committed to the on-going learning events in their classrooms because they are empowered participants, not passive inmates.

The Role of the Learner

With this view, learners are strong not weak, independent not dependent, active not passive. They are capable of learning relatively easily, what is relevant and functional for them. So the purpose of schools is to help learners to expand on what they know, to build on what they can do, to support them in identifying needs and interests and in coping with old and new experience. John Dewey provided considerable insight into the relationship between learning in school and learning outside of school. We learn by doing, he showed us. It becomes important then that students are involved in functional authentic activities in school. School is not preparation for life; it is part of life. Children can learn much more easily, therefore, when the knowledge is immediately useful; learning is more difficult if it has a more distant purpose. In Dewey's pragmatic philosophy there is no useful separation between ends and means in learning; what we learn today is the means of further learning tomorrow. There are no end products, no mastery goals; rather each goal is part of the means to a new schema, a new concept, a new view of the world. The transactional view of learners in whole language classrooms owes much therefore to Dewey's progressive view of education. He recognized the importance of integrating language, thought, and content in thematic solving of problems. Learning by doing means that we learn to read by reading and to write by writing as we are using literacy for purposes that are important to ourselves. Skills cannot be isolated from their use but in fact they develop most easily in the context of their use.

Dewey, like Piaget, also understood the relationship of play to learning. They considered play the work of children. In play children exercise their imaginations but they also explore the roles of adults in the common experiences children observe their parents and neighbors having.

Play often involves fantasizing. When it does, children draw on their experiences with hearing stories and books, on their television and film watching, and on the special folklore that is passed on from each generation of children to the next. When our daughter Debra drove from Detroit to Tucson with her then three year old son Reuben, she planned to stop at parks along the way for him to run and play to relieve the long stretches of sitting on the trip. She carefully packed toys and supplies for him to occupy himself with on the trip. At the time his favorite playthings were the plastic figures from Masters of the Universe which he also watched on television. Within minutes of arriving at a park he and other pre-schoolers were actively involved in imaginative play easily fitting into the roles of He-man and Shera as they opposed the imaginary forces of evil. They quickly lost any shyness and found common images and language to share their play.

At other times the play appears more realistic as children play house or school or store or office. They pretend to be parents and children, teachers and pupils, petrol dispensers, doctors and nurses, bus drivers, pilots, police officers, store clerks. As they do they adopt the appropriate language and engage in the relevant activities.

It was in the context of observing children at play that Vygotsky, the brilliant Russian psychologist, became aware of what he called the zone of proximal development. Play creates a zone of proximal development of the child. In play a child always behaves beyond his average age, above his daily behavior; in play it is as though he were a head taller than himself. As in the focus of a magnifying glass, play contains all developmental tendencies in a condensed form and is itself a major source of development.

Play itself mediates the learning of children. They are free to risk doing things they are not yet confident they can do well because they are "only" playing. In social play children transact with each other mediating each other's learning.

In our graduate classes we often ask teachers to collect samples of children's writing. Pre-school and kindergarten teachers sometimes say, "My children can't write yet." "Ask them to pretend they can," we advise them. Usually they are quite surprised at how sophisticated and orderly the early writing of young children is, how much knowledge it reveals when they are playing at writing.

Vygotsky helps us understand that as children transact with their world they are capable of doing more than they superficially appear to be and that they can get much more out of an activity or experience if there is an adult or more experienced playmate to mediate the experience for them. Language development in Vygotsky's view involves an internalization of the social language which then becomes inner speech. Though language and thinking develop independently, each depends on the other.

The zones of proximal development are created within the learners in the context of activities. Caring adults are sensitive to the directions children's curiosity takes them, their attempts to express needs or understandings, and the meanings they are creating. These adults track the development of the learners and they are eager to help them learn, in fact they take delight in the learning and in the half formed ideas and invented language of the children. Teachers, as professionals, but still caring adults, can be insightful kid watchers who sense from what kids are doing what they are capable of doing. They are able to involve learners in relevant functional activities and experiences which will stretch their capabilities and they mediate the learners' transactions with the world in minimally intrusive ways supporting learning without controlling it.

Both John Dewey and Vygotsky and the other Russian psychologists who built on Vygotsky emphasized the importance of activity and learning in the process of doing. In whole language the importance of authentic activities, in which language, both oral and written serves in real and functional ways is always stressed. In fact the popular term 'whole language' derives at least partly from a concern for keeping language whole and in the context for functional use.

Piaget has demonstrated that children are active and intelligent learners. They expect the world to make sense so they continually seek order in the world as they transact with it. In coping with the physical world they shape the world and are shaped by it, in processes of assimilation and accommodation. Learners adapt to the physical world by building schemes to which they assimilate new knowledge. If there is a disequilibrium, if they cannot assimilate because of contradictions between existing schema and new experience, then they must accommodate by modifying existing schemas or developing new ones. This process of adaptation is one which can be supported by caring and insightful teachers. But it cannot be forced or controlled by the teachers. In fact teachers must be careful that they support real learning rather than forcing superficial behavior which may satisfy school requirements without real learning. David Bloome, in his ethnographic studies calls this superficial behavior "procedural display." School becomes a place where you display the expected behavior by acting in acceptable ways without any real adaptation, without any real learning.

Learning Language and Learning Through Language

In his study of language development, Michael Halliday uses the phrase "learning how to mean." He helps us see the development of range of personal-social functions which then stimulate the development of the forms of language. In the process, children internalize the way their society uses language to represent meaning. So they are learning language at the same time they are using language to learn. They also are learning about language. But all three kinds of language learning must be simultaneous. A mistake schools often make is thinking that we can teach the forms of language as prerequisite to their use.

Halliday puts language in a social context. The very form that language takes derives from the fact that it is used socially and that through its use language users, including children, create and learn the language conventions, or social rules of language, to make communication easy and effective.

It's equally important to recognize the central role that language plays in human learning. Language makes it possible to share experience, to link our minds and produce a social intelligence far superior to that of any individual. We can learn from shared vicarious experience through language. So language, oral and written, can never be simply a school subject. Every school experience depends on and produces language development.

The Politics of Learning

Paolo Freire contrasts "banking" views to pedagogy with liberating views. The banking view treats learners as empty vessels. Teachers deposit bits of learning into their heads. They have no control over the process nor are their needs or interests considered. Liberating pedagogy sees learners in a power relationship to society. If education is to help them to liberate themselves it must empower. The learners must own the process of their learning. They must see learning including literacy and language development as part of a process of liberation. Freire was successful in helping Brazilian peasants to become literate by using the ideas and concepts of their political movement in the texts they used in learning to read. In a broader sense Freire was recognizing that learners learn best when they control their own learning.

The Role of the Teacher

If we understand teaching as transacting with learners, then the role of the teacher is one of mediating shared experiences. Teachers are professionals who bring to their classrooms knowledge of learning, development and language. They know their pupils and the strengths and needs they bring to the classroom. They plan experiences with their pupils and invite their pupils to participate, supporting and encouraging them and responding to their needs. Mediation, as Vygotsky uses it, is acting as a catalyst in the transactions pupils have with the world. The teacher is a knowledgeable kid-watcher who knows just how much support to give to learners without overwhelming them or doing the learning for them.

Teachers who have no power because they are locked into highly structured textbook series or curricula driven by standardized tests can't function as professionals. At best they can only slightly soften a rigid and invariant school experience. But if teachers have no power they must carefully exercise that power so that it liberates and empowers their learners. There is no necessary conflict between the purposes and the roles of teachers and learners in the classrooms. Teachers who work in support of learners find that they are releasing reservoirs of energy and creativity and that the learners develop a pride in the classrooms which they feel belong to them. The teacher is respected and seen by the pupils as guide, mentor, and collaborator rather than as taskmaster or disciplinarian.

The Role of the Text in Language Learning

It's been apparent to teachers for a long time that basically we learn to read by reading and to write by writing. In our miscue research we became aware that every time we analyzed a reader's miscues in reading a whole story we saw learning and development. Readers were developing new strategies, new vocabulary, new confidence in their ability to read. In authentic literacy events there are transactions between the reader and the text in which the reader is continuously solving new problems and building and extending psycholinguistic strategies. In our studies of children's writing we also saw the developing written text mediating the learning. So there is a continuously moving zone of proximal development in every authentic literacy event. Text itself becomes mediator of reading and writing development as the language user seeks actively to make sense of and through the text. For this self-development to take place the text must be authentic, that is it must be whole with all the characteristics of real texts in real contexts. Vygotsky recognized reading as a "complex cultural activity." In his view, "Writing must be 'relevant to life'. . . " Writing should be meaningful for children, that an intrinsic need should be aroused in them and that writing should be incorporated into a task that is necessary and relevant for life. Only then can we be certain that it will develop not as a matter of hand and finger habits but as a really new and complex form of speech." In our miscue research, John, a second grader, was reading a story in which the word oxygen occurred a number of times. Each time he came to the word in his oral reading he omitted it but commented "There's that word again" or "I think I'll skip that word." Later, during his retelling of the story, he was relating that the men in the space station were feeling sleepy because the air was bad. He said, "They didn't have enough . . . oxygen! That's that word I didn't know! Oxygen!" Given the opportunity to think through the text while retelling the story the meaning came together for him and he was able to identify a word that he thought he didn't know while he was reading earlier. At no time did the researcher give John specific information. So he solved his own problem and learned. The same kind of use of the texts mediator can be seen in this example of a child's writing development. Gabriel, a third grade native-American child decided that foot and ball needed to be placed closer together in the word football than the normal spacing between words. Observing him in the act of composing over two years, we saw him deal with spacing and hyphenation as he gained control over the features of how compound words are represented in written English. Once he whistled as he used a hyphen to call the attention of the researcher to the feat he was pleased with.

Centrifugal Force and Centripetal Force: Personal Invention and Social Convention

We believe that there are two opposing forces that shape the development of language in individuals and in communities. Although they are opposing in a sense, they operate in an integral fashion. The metaphor we use to describe these forces comes from the concept of the centrifugal and centripetal forces of physics. If a ball is twirled on a string there is a centrifugal force pulling it away from the center. If the twirler lets go, the ball flies off in a straight line. The string is an opposing, centripetal force pulling it back toward the middle. As long as these are in balance, the ball will orbit the center.

In language, the centrifugal force is the ability of people individually and collectively to invent new language to deal with new experience, feelings and ideas. This force produces change and makes it possible for language continuously to meet the developing and changing needs of its users. If language were static and unchanging it would quickly inhibit its users in learning and in communicating their responses to new experiences. But if this force were unchecked language would expand so rapidly that it would lose its social utility. People would soon be unable to understand each other at all.

The centripetal force that provides the counterbalance and relative stability is the social nature of language. Change in language, whether temporary or permanent, may be initiated by individuals, but it must be understood and accepted by others in order for language to be effective. To serve its functions it must be comprehensible by others, not just by the speaker or the writer. When language changes there is always balance between the creative force and the need to communicate. Every language must have within it devices for change but innovators must use the devices for change the language provides, or risk not being understood.

Language development in children then can be viewed as being shaped by these two forces. There is an almost explosive force from within the children that propels them to express themselves, and at the same time there is a strong need to communicate that pushes the direction of growth and development toward the language of family and community. This shaping is accomplished through the myriad language transactions that involve children with others. The language is generated by the child, but it is changed in transactions with others by their comprehension or lack of comprehension and by their responses. Thus parents, caregivers, siblings, peers and significant others play vital roles in their language development. They are less teachers than essential communicative partners, less role models than respondents, less to be imitated than to be understood and understanding.

Another way to view these two opposing forces shaping language is a balance between invention and convention. Both invention, personal creation of language and convention, the socially established system are necessary for learning. Language is not learned by imitating adults or learning rules out of the context of language use. It is invented by each individual and in the context of its social use it is adapted to the social conventions.

The Teacher's Role in Balancing Invention and Convention

Teachers have traditionally been seen as agents of conformity in the language use of their pupils. This role must be reconsidered to give sufficient room for invention and to let learners become aware of convention as it exists in the social language rather than as a set of arbitrary rules established by texts or teachers.

Too often teachers have rewarded conformity, punished experimentation and risk-taking, and confused learners about conventions just as they were building some sense of them. Often, in fact, the rules taught in school were based on authority and not on study of the language in use so that learners often found it hard to apply the rules or confirm them in their own language experiences. For example, teachers have sometimes taught pupils that 'and' and 'but' may not be used to start sentences. But pupils often found examples of sentences that did start with these words in their reading.

Too much intervention and direction by significant others, particularly teachers, can minimize invention and focus excessively and prematurely on the need for conventionality. Instead of facilitating language development the whole process can be distorted and children can lose their ability to learn and use language.

Everything people learn involves imperfection and error as we gain competence. Support for mistake making and hypothesis testing is one way teachers can mediate the balancing of invention and convention. "To err is human" is an old saying which illustrates how long people have been aware that error is a normal part of human learning. If language learning were purely imitative or purely innate it would be hard to explain the pervasiveness of error. But if we understand the role of invention then we can understand that as people move into equilibrium between invention and convention their errors reflect their progress. The two year old who says "I taked it" has moved to a rule for the past tense which is part way between his early inventions and the convention of adult grammar, with its exceptions and limitations. The six year old who invents the spelling "WAT" for went has invented the alphabetic system whereby letter sequences represent sound sequences. Her spelling represents what she hears and her own articulatory system. The /n/ in went is nasalized, a feature which does not fit the phoneme she represents with <n>. But spelling conventions in English are the same across dialects and therefore standard spellings cannot be dependably generalized. For the sake of standardized spellings across dialects the system sacrifices conformity to rules. The invented spellings represent the control over the basic principles of the orthography but not the many exceptions.

If the teacher treats all non-standard spellings as equally wrong the insight into the learner's control of English spelling is lost. If the teacher insists on conventional language at all stages of development and during every phase of the composing process, then the whole balance between invention and convention is destroyed and the strength of the pupils in language learning is neutralized.

Children encounter the conventions of language in the course of using it in authentic speech acts and literacy events. So whole language teachers concentrate on inviting children to participate in rich experiences in which language is used authentically in all forms. Teachers then closely monitor the children's transactions with the texts and mediate them when it is appropriate to do so. There is a difference between supportive mediation and overbearing intervention. In mediation the ownership of the use and learning of language is the learner's. In intervention, control is taken over by the teacher and the creative inventive force is suppressed. School language learning then becomes quite different than language learning outside school.

Invitations to Belong to the Literacy Club

Frank Smith has used the metaphor of the "literacy club" to explain why some pupils expect to and are expected to learn to read and write and do learn while others are not expected to do and do not. There is in school, he argues, a literacy club of people who use language easily and well. The school is organized to induct some pupils into the club while others are kept out.

We believe that maintaining the balance between invention and convention in developing reading and writing is a major factor in whether pupils come to consider themselves as insiders, members of the club, or outsiders excluded from the club benefits. If all students are subjected to the same rigid curricula and interventionist teaching some will survive and make their way into the club anyway. As they do they will be permitted more latitude in their reading and writing and will be able to balance their inventive energy against conventions they find in their authentic literary events. Other pupils will be confused and defeated by the rejection of their inventions of textbooks and the inflexibility of prescriptive language rules. So these pupils will be excluded from the literacy club. The less they succeed the less authentic will be their experiences and the less control they will be permitted. Ironically, the interventionist program is given credit for those who make it into the literacy club while the pupils who do not make it are blamed for their failure.

Society in general values the inventions of some but not others. Established artists, writers and scientists are supported. Art shows, books, drama and concert reviews often praise the creative aspects of artistic works and performances. New discoveries of scientists are extolled on the front page of newspapers. But a scientist whose discovery breaks with the dominant paradigm will not be easily accepted by his or her peers. Consider how long it took Darwin to establish biology as a science.

Even established artists are often harshly reviewed when they break with convention or appear to do so. The French impressionists were vilified and unappreciated because they broke with the conventions of their time. Eventually their inventive energy was so strong, and they themselves so persistent, that the new conventions emerged. The fact that these artistic non-conformists were also non-conformists in their lifestyle did not help their acceptance.

In society in general and in our schools in particular, we are likely to reject and minimize the creative invention of some groups more than others. Poor people, minorities, those from sub-cultures outside the mainstream, and non-conformists in general are not expected to contribute in valued ways. Their lack of conformity to social conventions defined by the reference to the dominant culture is interpreted as ignorance and incompetence. The inventive abilities of young people of all ages are often treated as disruptive and anti-social. So school practice in all respects has tended to treat difference as deficiency, and inventive strength as random weakness. Instead of understanding the ability of all pupils to learn and the need for them to make their own way to an equilibrium between invention and convention, we treat some as lacking in qualification for entry to the literacy club and use interventionist strategies that become self-fulfilling prophecies: eventually they accept the view of themselves as incapable.

Invention and Convention in Whole Language Classrooms

With the focus in whole language classrooms on authentic experiences, learners are engaged in purposeful and meaningful use of language, both oral and written. There is no artificial breaking down of language learning into sequences of abstract skills and no synthetic language designed to control vocabulary or focus on the form of written language out of the context of its functional use. Teachers are knowledgeable empowered individuals who are not afraid to empower their pupils. Because of the emphasis on whole language in situational contexts there is no disruption of the two forces, personal and social, which shape language and facilitate learning. Teachers are free to learn collaboratively with their pupils and are there to support and mediate the learning. There are no official limits on what can be learned nor any school imposed barriers to the literacy club.

Long before teachers began to use the term whole language there were whole language teachers like Mr. Isobe. These were teachers who understood that schools existed for the students that were in them. They realized that their role was to discover the strengths and knowledge that their students had and to build on the base to support their growth language, thinking and knowledge.

Largely these teachers were successful because they cared about their pupils and knew them well. Their empathy provided them with all the intuitive sense of what sort of support their pupils needed. What whole language adds is a scientific base of knowledge about language, learning and teaching amassed over several decades. Teachers no longer have to depend on their intuitions alone. But this base would not be enough without teachers like Mr. Isobe.

References

Dewey, John (1978) *The Middle Works 1899–1924*, Jo Ann Boydstom, Editor. Carbondale: Southern Illinois University Press.

Freire, Paolo (1972) *Pedagogy of the Oppressed*. New York: Herder and Herder.

Goodman, Kenneth, E.B. Smith, R. Meredith, and Yetta Goodman (1987) *Language and Thinking in School*. 3rd Edition, New York: R.C. Owen

Halliday, Michael (1975) *Learning How to Mean*. London: Edward Arnold.

Piaget, Jean, and B. Imhelder (1969). *The Psychology of the Child*. New York: Basic Books.

Smith, Frank (1986) *Insult to Intelligence*. New York: Arbor House.

Vygotsky, Lev (1978) *Mind and Society*, M. Cole et al (editors). Cambridge, MA: Harvard University Press.

Yashima, Taro (1955) *Crow Boy*. New York: Viking Press.

Chapter Twenty-Two

Orthography in a Theory of Reading Instruction

Kenneth S. Goodman
Wayne State University, 1972

Orthography must be considered in its relation to a theory of reading instruction because the teaching of reading has come to the point now where it must be soundly based on an instructional theory.

The knowledge is available to answer the crucial questions of reading instruction. It cannot continue simply to be based on traditions that have accumulated over the past, or on unexamined theories which are not fully articulated.

Even when people don't state an instructional theory in building programs for teaching reading or materials for teaching reading they are likely to have one. One of the major problems of reading instruction is the failure on the part of people who are developing and promoting such programs to examine their theories of instruction.

Requisites for an Instructional Theory

A viable theory of reading instruction has to be based on an articulated theory of the reading process. Simply speaking, we have to have some understanding of what it is we're trying to teach people in order to

This chapter first appeared in *Elementary English*, December, 1972, Vol. 49, No. 8, pp. 1254–1261. Copyright (1972) by the National Council of Teachers of English. Reprinted with permission.

develop an instructional theory that relates to it. There is a remarkable belief among many people who've spent time working on reading that the process is self evident and easily understood. Linguistic scholars have always been faced with that problem. As knowledge accumulates about how language works people tend to reject it by saying "But language can't be that complex because I use it all the time."

There also must be a learning theory built into the reading instruction theory. And that learning theory has to be appropriate to human language learning. Regardless of recent work with chimpanzees and porpoises, no species yet found does, in fact, develop language in any sense like humans do.

Third, there has to be a sound pedagogy built into this instructional theory. It has to assign a practical functional role to the teacher and to any other professionals that are involved. It has to incorporate some rules for the production of materials and it has to begin to produce a methodology which is sound from a pedagogical point of view. As a teacher would put it, it has to be teachable.

It also has to incorporate scientific knowledge of child language development. Considerable knowledge is developing in this area, not all of which has been applied in the teaching of reading. Besides that, flexibility has to be built into the theory to allow for the characteristics of the specific learners involved.

There has to be a differentiation in instructional theory between language competence, what a person is capable of doing, and language behavior, what he, in fact, is observed to do. Those are not the same thing. They must not be confused in building instructional theories.

We have to take into account cultural and social backgrounds in reading instruction. We have to take into account the legitimate differences in interest between children. Boys, in general, may be interested in adventure stories. That doesn't mean that any particular boy has to be interested. And theories must, of course, allow for the physical and mental variables that exist among children.

Where do the inputs come from for instructional theory? Obviously we've been seeking input for instructional theory in reading from psychology for some time. There are shelves of books on the psychology of reading. Probably one of the best is the one that Huey wrote in 1908 (Huey 1908, 1968). Somehow we got away from some of the things that he, and other psychologists were moving toward at that point. Input also has to come from education, from the classroom, from theoretical work, from dealing with teaching-learning issues. It has to come from linguistics because reading, after all, is one of the language processes. It has to come from psycholinguistics, the intersection between psychology and linguistics.

Other important input comes from sociology, social linguistics, and communication theory. Input must come from social-psychology for a number of reasons, not the least of which is that language is, after all, largely a phenomenon of human interaction. Physiology and neurology are also important.

As obvious as these areas are we have usually failed to touch all the bases, to examine all the questions that are relevant and to seek the answers from all of these relevant inputs. The task is a difficult one because it's not sufficient to add everything, to pile it into one bag, shake it up and pour out an instructional theory. The knowledge must be integrated. Educationists must take on this task.

Dangers of Narrow Bases

The people providing the input are going to stop short of instructional theory; they're going to say, "This is knowledge that you need. You decide how to use it." And particularly when every question involves psychological, linguistic, social, child development, and educational input it becomes a complex but vital function to integrate this knowledge and to make decisions that are as sound as possible in all respects. Legitimately a scholar from one of the academic disciplines ought to stop short unless of course, he's going to make himself an educationist. There are many risks involved in operating on narrow bases which characterize almost all current reading programs and fragmentary instructional theories.

One such risk is a tendency to make leaps from research and from key concepts emerging from research directly to instruction. A good example of that is what Bloomfield (1961) and Fries (1968) did as linguists. As soon as they got some interesting notions about reading they immediately moved to developing programs for teaching reading. Both took key linguistic concepts, such as minimal contrasts, and built narrow instructional materials on them. They didn't consider appropriate learning theory or even other aspects of linguistics such as grammar and intonation.

There also is a tendency to work backward from output. That's very tempting, particularly with the preoccupation now with behaviorally stated goals. It's tempting to say "we're going to get this many children to read at this level by this point in time." Some have suggested that input is unimportant, that the only important thing is output. Such a view says that ends justify means and that desirable products can result even if processes are not understood or have negative, undesirable features.

Too much available knowledge is going to be ignored if there is only concern for output. Too much unplanned incidental learning will result.

One of the problems with operating from narrow bases is that they provide distorted views of the very elements that are looked at most clearly. For instance, take the relationship between letters and sounds.

If that's the only thing that is looked at then one may come to the conclusion that the relationship of any letter to any sound is equally important with all others, that it's the same in a list of words as it is in a text, or that it's the same in all contexts. But it's very easy to demonstrate that, in fact, what's vitally important in one situation is quite unimportant in another.

Consider that contrast which distinguishes two entirely different chemical compounds as in *sulfate* and *sulfite* in the sentence *"Add 20 grams of calcium sulfate."* The contrast in the *ite* and *ate* suffixes is crucial. But if you know something about chemistry (and if you're going to read something about chemistry you're going to have to know something about it) then you operate within a framework which makes it easy to know when you've miscued. That vowel contrast is very unlikely to be of similar importance even in words of the same sentence that it's found in, so that at any point the value of any particular element varies depending on all other available cues. "Add 20 grims" is not a contextual possibility. When one operates from a narrow base such information is lost. Particular information is exaggerated out of its relative importance and then learning problems are created where they didn't need to exist.

People can think they teach reading without an articulate instructional theory. Some will say, "I teach phonics; never mind the learning theory that's involved" for example. Since such practice really has a theory underlying it, the user is constantly making implicit decisions about unconsidered variables. Every time one decision is made a whole set of other decisions follow and the fact that the other inputs are ignored doesn't mean that decisions in relationship to them haven't been made.

ITA pushes one into ignoring dialect differences or making unknowing decisions about their relative importance in the reading process. If one shifts to looking at dialect differences it may cause one to make some different decisions about the use of the ITA. That is, once one does add additional input it changes the values of everything else.

So called "linguistic programs" which emphasize phoneme-grapheme correspondences a la Bloomfield and Fries are still emerging, perhaps five or ten years beyond that point where there was any justification at all. But even from a linguistic point of view if they only concentrate on letter sound relationships they lose the significance of syntax and also the significance of semantic context. Furthermore, of course, one tends to violate psychological principles by ignoring them and making implicit psychological decisions. In the Southwest lab program this writer found inadequate the decisions that were implicit in the ordering of the things that were being taught since no psychological principles were consciously used in determining sequence (Cronnell, 1971).

Word recognition programs, those based on expanding vocabulary as a concept, have tended to ignore all other language variables, except as they contribute to word recognition. Sentences are created that are composed of frequent words but that are hard to read, with extremely complex or unnatural kinds of syntax and sequence.

Programmed learning is another example of what happens with a narrow base. Programmed learning forces everything through the narrow bottleneck of highly systematic sequencing. It elevates sequencing to the primary consideration and then says, "Let's find something we can sequence." It appears that that's exactly what the Southwest Regional Laboratory has done. They didn't decide phonics was a good way to teach reading. They decided it was a good thing for sequencing in order to get the kind of programming they could control so that they could now give the teacher daily feedback on the child's progress. Once that decision is made then a whole series of other decisions follow which are not really examined since they would require the developers to go back and look at the initial key decision.

The part-whole relationship is certainly distorted, perhaps destroyed in that kind of programming. Questions relating to whether, in fact, language can be learned sequentially are ignored. That brings one into the position of having to ignore a whole body of research from the last decade on child language development.

Concentration on behavioral objectives forces one to abandon much that can't be measured. One may say, "If you can't measure it, it's not important," except that there's neither logic nor substance to the statement. And, unfortunately almost any teacher knows that most of what's important that's happening any day can't be measured at that point. Results show at later points in the child's progress.

Now, a hypothesis may be stated: *No program of reading instruction can be sound if it is not based on consideration of all areas of decision making, no matter how sound particular aspects are.*

The worst part of building narrow programs that don't examine all the relevant areas is that it leaves it to the learner to make up for the deficiencies of the program. It's been obvious in research, including ours, that much of learning to read at the present state of the art of teaching reading is learning to overcome that which is taught. The learner must do things specifically against the advice of the program that's teaching him. That learners can do that is obvious. Many children are going to have the capacity to overcome the deficiencies in programs and learn anyway. No program, no matter how silly, didn't wind up with somebody saying in answer to questions, "But the children learned." Some learn with the family Bible or the Sears Roebuck catalogue.

Teachers don't have the right, however, to constantly shift the burden to the learner and say never mind the deficiencies of the program, the kids will learn. Obviously some of them have trouble doing that, precisely because of the programs' deficiencies. The non-learners are those unable to ignore bad advice, screen out misconceptions, fill in the gaps and learn anyway.

Neither is it enough to validate a program simply by field testing it. Its basic soundness must also be examined theoretically in terms of the knowledge available and the areas of decision making that go into building a program based on sound instructional theory. The basis does exist for judging programs now in terms of their validity on a number of grounds. Educators have a right to evaluate them on those bases even if they don't have better programs to offer. Maybe in the process of tearing down existing programs the means of building better ones can be found.

With this background we can examine orthography, in relationship to a number of aspects of reading and ask two questions: How is orthography used in reading? And what other kinds of decisions must constantly be played against those involving orthography?

A series of key concepts have emerged from recent theoretical research. *First,* alphabetic systems don't simply operate on a letter-sound basis. If there are relationships that can be described between written and oral language they involve looking at patterned relationships. Sequences of sounds seem to have relationships to sequences of letters, not simply because of the alphabetic principle on which the system was produced originally, but also because there is a common base underlying both of these. For the user of language, surface oral language and surface written language are related through a common underlying structure. As a language user generates a sentence, his thoughts bring him to a point at which he can apply a set of orthographic rules and write it.

The *second* key concept is that regularity ought not to be confused with complexity; an orthographic system can be regular and very complex. That shouldn't surprise us because phonology isn't simple either. This regularity can involve many rules and subrules and exceptions to rules that kids learn through writing. These rules are learned by considerable exposure to written language. They cannot be taught to one who lacks such exposure. But that's a lesson we've learned in many fields of instruction, not just reading. It's always very tempting to take an adult conclusion and plug it into a child and say, "Now you know what I know." Obviously learning doesn't work that way, particularly language learning.

A *third* key concept involves the relationship of grapheme and allograph.

A reader has to be able to equate several very different graphic squiggles with the same abstract name or idea. That is, he must be able to say A̲ and a and A̲ and a̲ are the same but A̲ and H̲ are different even though these last two have the most common features as compared to the others. There are perceptual categories that operate and it's the establishment of these perceptual categories that influences the ability to process graphic input. One must use some distinctive features to do so but those distinctive features are going to shift depending on which allographic system is in operation. Differentiating *All* and *Hall* does not use the same features as *all* and *hall*. Fortunately, of course, we don't mix those systems very often, except for special effects. When we do they cause trouble in reading.

A *fourth* basic principle is that the spelling system is standardized across dialects. That makes it possible for people who have phonological differences to be unencumbered with them in communicating with each other because they share common spellings. Each may not understand the way the other says a word but when they write it they write it with the same spelling.

Spelling reform has to take into account this positive characteristic of traditional orthography. Different dialects will of course have different homophones though homographs are the same for all.

Those are some key concepts. They're not inclusive but they're ones that have to be dealt with, and they are somewhat at variance to some old commonplace notions about orthography.

Let's look at the question of recognition and identification. Smith builds an incontestable case for the proposition that readers don't identify letters (Smith, 1971). Rather, they use the minimal distinctive features to get where they're going. He demonstrates that if they're going to work at identifying letters they need a lot more information than if they're going to identify words. And, of course, one must go beyond words to get at meaning. In fact, if the reader is preoccupied with identifying words it not only is an inefficient process because he's using too much information, but it's ineffective as well because it gets in the way of getting at the meaning and clutters up the short term memory function.

That raises some real questions about our tendency to teach kids to be careful readers, with all that that implies. A careful reader may use entirely wrong strategies. He may use far more information and not develop the kinds of selectivity that he has to develop to read effectively and efficiently.

Smith uses the term "reduction of uncertainty" to describe how a reader uses a minimal amount of information to reduce uncertainty as he proceeds. How letters get recognized or perceived becomes unimportant. The question now becomes how little is the amount of information that's required to get to the meaning. That requires some very different kinds of decisions in building programs and instructional practices.

The literature is cluttered with studies based on the idea that one could learn something about language learning or reading by studying lists of words or lists of nonsense syllables, or even unpronounceable strings. There may be some interesting things that can be learned from such research but they have to be carefully evaluated before one draws any conclusions at all about their applicability to learning language including reading. Such research treats language as a string of sounds, letters or words; it assumes that language is like a salami that you can slice as thin as you want, each slice still retaining the characteristics of the whole. That simply is not true. Language can't be broken into pieces without qualitatively changing it.

A reader, like a listener, has to get from some surface information to an underlying structure at which point he can assign meaning. A sentence that illustrates this is "See Spot run." The understood subject is not present. The reader has to, somehow, induce it. He has to somehow induce a relationship between an imbedded clause *Spot run* to another, *You (understood) see (something)*. There are a whole set of relationships that he has to get at and through to get from *See Spot run* to an understanding of what meaning is involved. The task of the reader is to get from surface structure to deep structure to meaning, not to get from written language to oral language to meaning which implies a wholly different direction and one, in fact, that is quite unproductive.

The reader has to use the graphic input, but he has to constantly process grammatical and semantic information as well. The value of the graphic input, then, is entirely dependent on the amount of syntactic and semantic information that he can process. One can show this in many ways including some rather traditional ones, like how many words can be remembered if they're meaningful and grammatically sequenced as compared to if they're nonsense or simply strings of unrelated letters. Obviously much more information is being processed and therefore much less of the graphic information must be used when the other information is available.

Readers are able to make predictions. A prediction is based on minimal kinds of information and the linguistic competence that the reader brings to the task. As soon as he recognizes a graphic display as a written language form that has some kind of familiarity to him he starts to predict its patterns. Punctuation appears to be an unimportant part of the reader's cues because it comes at the wrong end of the sentence. The reader has to predict a question pattern long before he gets to the question mark. The exclamation point only confirms what he already should have known if he's going to read successfully. So at the best punctuation is a system of checks against the reader's predictions. Intonation is largely a function of syntax in oral reading. Once the reader has a pattern, he assigns an intonation. He doesn't use the intonation to predict the pattern.

Readers can leap over steps. The writer must go completely through a generative process resulting in a more complete product than oral language requires. But the reader can sample from that and make leaps to his own underlying structure and then to meaning. What becomes important is that he sample just enough additional graphic information that he can confirm or contradict what he has predicted. The reader samples, guesses and then tests. The tests are primarily semantic and syntactic. If those don't work then the reader takes another look at the graphic information so he may have a double cycle where he samples certain graphic information and then comes back for more if he needs it. He uses the most useful cues the first time. The second time through he needs to use some cues that are normally less useful or reprocess the same cues and try it another way.

The reader is selecting (even in the beginning) the graphic information he uses on the basis of what he expects to be there. An efficient reader then uses the minimum amount of information that he needs.

There are a series of strategies the reader must develop. Let's examine them and ask what the significance of orthographic input is in each.

Prediction is largely based on the syntactic competence of the learner and the experiential-conceptual background that he brings to the particular task. If he's reading something where he lacks background he has a hard time predicting its meaning or handling it, for that matter, when he gets through to it. In terms of sampling strategies the graphic input is very important. But what is most important is what the reader knows about the relative amount of information that particular graphic cues carry and therefore which distinctive features he ought to be looking for. It's this search for cues that is missing from many earlier notions of the use of graphic information. It's commonly assumed that the reader must pull in all graphic information, stir it around and then start to process it. But the processing actually starts before he has used any input and influences what he collects, how he perceives it, and how he uses it.

In the *testing* strategies there is a sequence in which the reader decides whether his guesses are right by asking a series of questions of himself. First he uses meaning asking, "Does it make sense?" Second he uses syntactic information: Is that something that really fits there? Only then does he say, "How does it start? How does it end? What do I think the word might be?", using graphic information. For *confirmation,* graphic cues only become important after he's already made a decision that there's something wrong. Then, he may take a second look. Readers may of course have been taught to be very careful and to read accurately. Then they may be operating in a very ineffective reverse sequence, processing too much graphic information with accuracy, not comprehension, the goal. *Correction,* of course, is vital. Correction strategies provide the ability to do something about it when a reader realizes that he's gone wrong. That does depend on some rather sophisticated ability to reprocess graphic input and to get at some of the graphic input that gives less reliable information.

The significance of semantic input in reading must be understood. Every person is functionally illiterate to some extent. No one can possibly read and understand everything that is written in his native language. The ability to read and understand is totally a function, beyond a certain minimal point, of the amount of background the particular reader brings to each task. That contradicts a wide spread commonsense notion built into many achievement tests that there is some kind of reading achievement level that cuts across everything within a single individual no matter what he's asked to read.

Phonics isn't necessary to the reading process. In fact, in a proficient reader any kind of going from print to oral language to meaning is an extremely ineffective and inefficient strategy. By inefficient is meant that it's not the best way to do it and by ineffective is meant that the reader doesn't get the results that he's after.

The question, of course, is whether in beginning stages of acquisition phonics has any function. This writer believes that excessive concern for phonics induces short circuits in reading. Instead of teaching the processing of language to get to meaning, phonics instruction teaches the processing of language to get to sounds or to get to words. Such instruction at best introduces many strategies which either have to be subsequently unlearned or which will interfere with the effectiveness of the reading process. Maybe the success of speed reading courses is simply that they force people to abandon these ineffective processes that they've learned in school and to move to a more rational, more productive way of reading. Those short circuits are evident in a number of ways. But the most alarming evidence is the lack of comprehension in upper grade and secondary pupils who score well on skill tests.

In current reading miscue studies at Wayne State, using four different ability groups of 10th graders, all but the lowest group could read, for research purposes, the same story. Such readers vary in the kinds of miscues and the extent to which they correct more than they do in the number of miscues. But most particularly, what varies is their comprehension. Schools may be teaching kids not to comprehend. They may be teaching them to match oral language with written language, which is very different from comprehending.

Reading materials used in instruction must be relevant. Irrelevant materials are not only bad from a humanistic point of view but they're bad instructional materials since background determines comprehension. Some Hawaiian kids reading a story about the first robin of spring are having an irrelevant experience but it is also impossible for them to know whether they have understood. They lack the background experience to know whether they have understood. They lack the background experience to know what the heck a robin is and what's spring, and what a robin has to do with spring. Teaching must be directed toward developing ability to sample for distinctive features.

Perhaps all this discussion has provided is a new set of questions to ask, a new focus. If so, the most crucial concept is that language is always a means and never an end. And teaching kids to match letters to sounds is not related to the end which is comprehension. Teaching them to read nonsense is as bad because they can't tell, when they're done, whether they've been successful since what they read makes no sense. The orientation toward meaning is intrinsic in the process that the child has to master and basic to the mastery of the reading process. It isn't something that comes later. It isn't possible to break reading into code and meaning because the code has no existence and certainly no use apart from meaning.

References

Bloomfield, L., & Barnhart, C. 1961. *Let's read, a linguistic approach.* Detroit: Wayne State University Press.

Cronnell, B. 1971. Designing a Reading Program Based on Research Findings in Orthography. *Southwest Regional Educational Lab., Inglewood, CA.* Washington, DC: Office of Education (DHEW).

Fries, C. 1963. *Linguistics and reading.* New York: Holt, Rinehart and Winston.

Huey, E. B. 1908, 1968. *The psychology and pedagogy of reading.* Cambridge, MA, The M.I.T. Press.

Smith, F., & Holmes-Lott, D. 1971. The Independence of Letter, Word, and Meaning Identification in Reading. *Reading-Research Quarterly, 6(3),* 394–415, Spr 71.

Chapter Twenty-Three

Strategies for Increasing Comprehension in Reading

Kenneth S. Goodman
Wayne State University, 1973

Reading teachers in past decades have been so close to reading and so anxious to help children develop into good readers that they have sometimes lost sight of the essential nature and purpose of reading. Sometimes we have even let ourselves slip into thinking of reading as the score on a test or the ability to deal with skill exercises. We must remind ourselves that reading is a language process. It is a receptive process similar and parallel to listening. Its purpose is to construct, from language in written form, a message which will match to a high degree the one the author intended to convey. *We read to get the meaning.*

A reader, then, is a user of language who constantly seeks sense from what he reads. His success in any reading task can be judged primarily on the basis of what he has understood. Teaching someone to read is a matter of helping him become competent in getting meaning from written language. Reading is not matching sounds to letters or sound patterns to spelling patterns, or naming, recognizing, or perceiving words, though in the process of reading a reader may do any or all of these things. Yet he may do them all with relative success but not get

This chapter first appeared in H. Robinson, (ed.), *Improving Reading in the Intermediate Years*, Glenview, IL: Scott Foresman and Co., 1973, pp. 59–71. Reprinted with permission of the author.

the meaning. Only getting intended meaning is the test of the success of reading instruction.

The ability of a reader to get the meaning from written language is his effectiveness as a reader. This is not a matter of exact agreement with the author. In fact, exact agreement is unlikely many times because of the differences in attitudes, concepts, and backgrounds of the reader and the writer. Furthermore, much written language presents complex multi-layered meanings. One may understand the basic theme of a story while missing some of its fine details because of an unfamiliarity with the settings or some of the activities in which the characters engage. Or one may gain a superficial understanding without grasping the theme because it involves subtleties and concepts which the reader does not have in his background. If teachers expect and only accept exact agreement with the way they understand the author's message, they are expecting an impossibility. At the same time teachers may impose a convergent view of meaning in which creative and divergent views are discouraged. If meaning is viewed as absolute, then critical reading will be discouraged.

Effective and Efficient Reading

Efficient reading gets to the meaning with the least amount of effort necessary. This efficiency is gained by using the fewest number of graphic cues and making the best possible predictions on the basis of what the reader knows about language and the content of what he is reading, without sacrificing meaning. Slow, plodding, careful reading may be effective, but it is likely to be inefficient if only because of the time and fatigue involved. It may well be ineffective, too, because of the load it imposes on the memory of the reader who is attempting to store too much information and delay making decisions about meaning until he has all the information. By the time he is ready to make a decision, he may have lost some of the information he needs. As a result some rapid readers may have higher levels of comprehension. Speed in itself is of no particular significance in reading comprehension. But increasing speed often requires the reader to use more efficient strategies and to be more selective in the information he uses as he reads.

The word *strategy*, which has been used here, grows out of research and theories of reading. As one reads, one must have means to get from print to meaning which are flexible enough and varied enough to deal with a wide range of demands. These general approaches for using available information are called strategies.

Scanning Strategies

Written English progresses from left to right. Consequently a reader must develop *scanning strategies* which respond to this characteristic of the language. However, some graphic information encountered later has important effects on the value of that which precedes it. A final "e," for example, marks the preceding vowel letter's relationship to a vowel sound. The reader, then, must accommodate his use of scanning strategies and the information they provide, so that he anticipates or seeks out information which may not be in a simple left-to-right sequence. To get to the meaning of a passage, a reader must assign a grammatical structure. He knows then how the elements fit together and anticipates what to expect as he gathers more graphic information. He seeks cues early in the sentence to help him identify a first element in a pattern and predict what follows. He may identify a common statement pattern (subject, verb, object) by finding that the sentence starts with a noun phrase: "*Franklin* had a marvelous sense of humor. *His brother* printed a newspaper." Or he may predict a question if the sentence starts with a question marker like *what:* "What good could a balloon be?" Or his cue that it is a question may be that it starts with a verb marker: "*Do* you know what my favorite is?" Punctuation which comes at the ends of sentences can confirm a prediction about the grammatical pattern of the sentence, but it is of little help in formulating one.

Selection Strategies

The efficient reader selects graphic cues, letters or letter parts, or configurations of letters, which will identify for him most directly a grammatical structure resulting in meaning. The brain can only handle a limited amount of information at a given time. One may think of one's eye as transmitting visual information to a tiny television screen which can hold a small picture for only a very short time before it is replaced by a new image. Therefore the reader must select carefully what is to be fed into that screen, or he will waste a great deal of effort and be inefficient. He has *selection strategies* which draw on his familiarity with language structure, his expectations as he reads, and his ultimate concern for meaning. Meaning is very important because if the reader is concerned with correctly identifying letters one at a time, he will use more graphic cues than he needs and use them differently. For example, try to read this sequence of letters: tygizdziezagizdozony. Since it has no apparent pattern, one is forced to concentrate on letters. Even when word spaces are inserted, a great deal of graphic information is required to say, remember, and reproduce it: Ty gizdzie zagizdozony. On the other hand a native speaker of Polish will be able to not only remember and reproduce it with ease, but will know what this line from a fifth-grade Polish reading text means. The difference is basic competence in the language. A native speaker of English can go directly from minimal graphic cues to meaningful grammatical structures when he reads English, and he has no need to inefficiently identify every letter or word to do so. In fact, even what he thinks he sees is largely what he expects to see.

Prediction or *expectation strategies* are used in close harmony with selection strategies. Simply speaking, the reader uses minimal cues, graphic as well as grammatical and semantic (meaning), and guesses at what is coming. How good his guesses are is dependent on how efficient he has been in using his selection and prediction strategies. Again the most important factor in his success is his concern for meaning.

Confirmation Strategies

Having made predictions, the reader must use *confirmation strategies* to check on the consistency of his expectations with the cues he is encountering as he reads on. He must ask himself whether it is making sense and whether the grammatical pattern he had predicted is the one he is finding. The same graphic cues which he uses to make subsequent predictions are used to confirm or reject prior predictions.

Two contexts are created as the reader checks his guesses. One is a semantic or meaning context as he looks for sense. The other is the syntactic, sentence-pattern context which relates elements to clauses and clauses to each other. Efficient and effective reading requires that the reader closely monitor his reading through these confirmation strategies. Knowing when and where he has lost the meaning is as vital to successful reading as making strong predictions in the first place. The reader uses correction strategies to reprocess information when he needs to do so, in order to recover from miscues which have resulted in meaning loss. Sometimes he can rethink the significance of the information he has and try an alternate prediction consistent with the cues he has. At other times he will need to regress with his eyes to the left and up the page, seeking more information and additional cues showing where he got off the track. Knowing what to do when one has lost the meaning is a vital part of learning to read. All readers make miscues. Efficient, effective readers know what to do when they need to correct them.

It is also necessary for an efficient reader not to waste his energies and time correcting miscues which do not result in loss of meaning. Preoccupation with accuracy in word identification for its own sake requires the reader to use more information than he needs and to use inefficient selection strategies. This view of efficient reading contradicts the commonsense notion that there is value in being careful and accurate in all reading situations. But it is not difficult to see that if the reader makes confident predictions, keeps his concern for meaning constant, recognizes when he has lost the meaning, and corrects to recover the meaning, then that correction only for the sake of accuracy alone is more of a distraction than an aid.

There is also a time in reading when correction will not be of value. The reader is aware that he has not understood the author's meaning and checks to make sure that his lack of meaning is not because of miscues. He rereads to see if he can make more sense of what he has read, but cannot make any sense of it. He can read ahead, hoping that subsequent reading will make the meaning clear. If that does not help, he may have to conclude, as even proficient adult readers often do, that he lacks the background necessary to read the particular selection. He must either get the experience or find a more relevant selection.

Research on the reading process has shown that in children's oral reading, the most important indicator of their basic reading competence is the extent to which they retain meaning even when they produce miscues. Teachers should be concerned with the effect of miscues and not with their quantity. If the miscues do not disrupt the meaning, then the reader is being effective. If he corrects when his miscues do disrupt meaning, he is indicating his pervading concern for meaning.

Here is an example of a miscue that does not affect meaning:

in
"How come everybody is zonked out ~~on~~ the living room floor?"
Brian asked.

Here is one that did disturb the meaning and grammar but was corrected:

Ⓒ
"You can be@nutseller!"

Note "a" is omitted but the reader realizes as he starts the next word and goes back to correct. He is using confirming strategies to check himself out.

Teachers can help developing readers to build the strategies they need for effective and efficient reading. In doing so the teacher helps the pupil build on his strength and fill in his areas of weakness. Thus the teacher is working with the learner rather than at cross-purposes with him. The teacher is not so much a source of wisdom in sound reading instruction as a guide and aid, monitoring the learner's progress, offering help when a hang-up is detected, stimulating interest in reading, helping him find relevant, worthwhile materials to read, and offering continuous encouragement.

Everything that the teacher does for and with the learner must be thought through in terms of how it contributes to his attainment of meaning. Perhaps the most important question a teacher can ask a pupil is "Does that make sense to *you?*" The teacher must help the learner at all times keep in mind that he is seeking meaning.

It is also very important that the teacher build up the learner's confidence in himself as a user of language. Every child who speaks a dialect of English has the language competence necessary to predict English sentence structures and get meaning from them. But the developing reader must come to trust his own judgment and linguistic intuition. He needs to be assured that what has worked for him in listening can work in reading, too, if he approaches reading with ease and confidence.

It is doubly important that the teacher does not confuse teaching pupils to speak a high status dialect of English with teaching them to read. If the teacher "corrects" a reader's pronunciation from what sounds right in his dialect to what sounds right in the teacher's, the reader may become confused and think that he is not a successful reader. Furthermore the information the teacher is providing him by such a correction does not help him relate print to speech as *he* knows it, but rather to relate it to another sound system he does not control. A rule of thumb for teachers in cases where they are doubtful is that if the pupil reads the way he speaks, he is not having a reading problem.

It is very important that the teacher help the developing reader to use his own resources, to build his own strategies. When a reader pauses, many teachers assume it is because the reader doesn't know the next word, so they tell him what it is. But he may have a very different problem. He may know what it is but not be able to figure out how it relates to the pattern or meaning of the sentence. Telling him the word is like saying "Even if it doesn't make sense, say it anyway." Rather, the teacher should probe to find out what the reader considers his problem to be. Even if he says "What's that word?" a perceptive teacher might say "What do you think it is?" The pupil's response may contain some surprises such as: "I think I know, but that doesn't fit" or "I know all the words, but I can't get any sense out of it."

The teacher can be very helpful at times when the reader is groping for meaning to help him crystallize his strategies. "What would make sense here?" is a good first question. It puts everything in the context of a search for meaning. "What would sound right or fit here?" is a good next question if further help is needed. Such a question directs the reader to use his sense of English grammar. Having established these meaning and grammar limits, if help is still needed then one might add "What looks like this word that could fit and make sense here?" The teacher must remember, however, that the goal is to help the reader get to meaning, and that is more important than getting each word exactly right.

Correction Strategies

When the reader knows he has lost the meaning, the teacher can help him develop correction strategies. Some suggestions a teacher might make are:

1. Go back and see if you can find a place where you might have gotten off the track.
2. Think about what you think the page should be saying. That may help you find where you got off.
3. Read ahead and see how things work out.

Sometimes readers indicate a kind of inefficiency by correcting themselves when they do not need to do so. Only when the meaning is disrupted is there any real need for correction. If the teacher is relaxed and at ease about deviations that do not upset meaning, the pupils are likely to be more relaxed as well.

When the problem the reader faces is an unfamiliar word, phrase, or word usage, the teacher can help the child understand that:

1. The way the word or phrase is used is a good clue to its meaning in the particular passage.
2. Authors frequently provide simple definitions right in the text: "To measure wind speed, meteorologists use an anemometer."
3. If the word is important it will occur several times. Each subsequent occurrence will provide a new context to help the reader zero in on its meaning.
4. If the word is unimportant to the reader's comprehension, he will need only a vague notion of its meaning to go on. Usually its context provides that. Most proficient readers have learned to be undisturbed by a few unimportant words, the meanings of which are uncertain.
5. Dictionaries are most useful for confirmation when the reader has formed a fairly strong notion of a word's meaning from the context.
6. If the word or phrase is a name difficult to pronounce or a foreign word, it may be sufficient to use a placeholder to facilitate reading. Calling the character with the Slavic name Ivan may be good enough—and save a lot of time while avoiding distraction.

7. One need not be able to pronounce every word to get its meaning. Most proficient readers have many words in their reading vocabularies they do not use or have not heard used orally.

Our research has shown that less proficient readers dissipate a lot of energy working at every word while more proficient readers have the confidence that they can get the meaning without word-by-word accuracy.

Teacher Analysis of Miscues

Teachers can learn to infer from the miscues a learner makes, what his strengths and weaknesses are. This may be facilitated by having a pupil read orally to a tape recorder. The teacher can then analyze his miscues at a later time, using the steps listed below:

Consider whether the reader's response is simply an evidence of his own dialect. If so, then it is not a miscue to be concerned about since the reader has shifted to his own dialect while getting to meaning. Most dialect miscues are phonological. In oral reading the reader says the words as he does in his speech: "help" may be "he'p," "pumpkin" may be "punkin." There are four ways that "almond" is pronounced in various parts of this country, two with "l" and two without. Clearly, if the reader uses his preferred pronunciation, he shows he knows the meaning. If a teacher insists on a preferred or standard pronunciation, it is likely only to confuse the reader. Other forms of dialect related miscues may involve inflectional suffixes; the "s" or "ed" endings in the speech of many black youngsters are dropped. Appalachian pupils may not use "s" forms after numbers: "two miles" becomes "two mile." Sometimes readers may switch to a different grammatical form as they go to meaning. They may, for example, use a different form of "be": "There was lots of goats." Again these are shifts to the reader's own dialect and show that he has understood. Readers will even, at times, substitute a preferred word in their own dialect, "minute" for "moment," for example.

If teachers make themselves aware by listening objectively to how the dialects found in their classrooms are used, they will easily be able to separate miscues that matter from these dialect shifts.

Consider the effect of the miscues on meaning. The best indication of the strength the reader brings to any reading task is the extent to which his miscues still result in acceptable meaning. Such miscues show the basic preoccupation of the reader with meaning. If upwards of forty percent of the reader's miscues produce acceptable meaning (before any correction takes place), the reader shows this vital ability to get to meaning. There is no need for teachers to be concerned about correcting miscues that produce acceptable meaning. Such miscues may produce changes in meaning even if they make sense, however. The teacher should consider how the meaning is modified in judging whether the pupil is showing strength or weakness. Often the change is more an indication of a conceptual problem than difficulty with reading.

Consider the ability of the reader to handle the grammar. Often, even when the reader loses meaning, he stays with the grammatical pattern of the author or produces another acceptable pattern. Even when pupils produce non-words they may preserve the affixes of the original word, showing their sense of its grammatical function. In word substitutions pupils who are operating with reading as language may substitute only nouns for nouns, verbs for verbs, and the like.

Among intermediate-grade readers a strong disparity between the percent of their miscues which produce acceptable grammar and those which produce acceptable meaning may indicate that the conceptual load is heavy for the readers. If they are not able to comprehend, they may treat what they read as grammatical nonsense, manipulating the English structures effectively even though they cannot understand. Even proficient adults behave this way with difficult texts, such as legal documents.

Consider the relationship between the miscue and the text in terms of sounds and shapes. The reader's miscues, when they are word substitutions, may be considered on the basis of how much they look or sound like what was expected. Ironically, teachers have often assumed that when pupils produce a number of substitutions that vary in minor aspects from what was expected, the pupil is showing evidence of a phonics problem. In fact such miscues show the opposite. They show the reader is able to use phonics to get close to the right pronunciation. If the miscues also produce sense, then the reader has no serious problem. If, on the other hand, his phonic "near-misses" produce nonsense, his problem is not phonics but may even be the result of preoccupation with letter accuracy and too little concern for meaning. In that case the teacher will try to help the reader develop his ability to use meaning and grammar contexts and temper his use of phonics strategies.

Consider when the reader corrects. Effective readers know that when meaning is disrupted, when they cannot get sense from their reading, they must correct; that is, go back over what they have read to make sense out of it.

Correction in reading is a complex phenomenon, however, because the reader who is proficient produces a majority of miscues which have acceptable meaning and do not need correction. Less effective readers may correct by persevering on individual words until they get them right while they do not correct on other types of miscues which produce nonsense. The teacher, then, must observe whether pupils correct miscues where the meaning is affected.

Helping pupils to build sound, useful correction strategies requires that they learn to detect miscues that need correction. Teachers must resist the temptation to tell the pupil when and why he needs to correct; furthermore the teacher must help the reader use his own resources in correcting. Rarely is it ever desirable for the teacher to tell the pupil what he should have said. If the pupil develops his own correction strategies, it will not only build his confidence and success in getting to the meaning but will lead to his producing fewer miscues that need correction as he becomes more aware of the importance of keeping meaning his main concern.

Different Strategies for Different Tasks

Though general reading strategies are essential for all kinds of reading, different materials may vary in ways which require the reader to employ special strategies.

The language of literature, for example, has the general characteristic of being less predictable than everyday conversation. Authors avoid using common, repetitious vocabulary. This rich language full of surprises adds to the pleasure of reading but it creates problems for a reader for which he must have flexible strategies to apply. Consider this passage:

> A feeling of panic surged through Stan as he tried to wriggle free. Then he fought back the terror, realizing that panic was as big an enemy as the current which held him fast.[1]

Suppose the author had written it this way:

> Stan was scared. He tried to get loose. Then he knew he shouldn't get scared because that was as bad as the current that kept him from getting loose. So he tried not to be scared.

Both passages mean the same thing, but the original will be less predictable and harder to read and understand. The more predictable language is dull and flat-sounding. The teacher must help the children develop strategies for dealing with the language of literature.

In contrast, the language of the content areas may be expository, designed to present new concepts and ideas. It employs a technical vocabulary and uses some common terms in specialized ways. Teachers must provide relevant experiences and must help pupils acquire the necessary concepts so that the technical vocabulary will become useful and easily handled. Language and concepts depend on each other. Moreover, most content-area texts are heavily laden with concepts. Thus they are written with an economy of words to express complex ideas. In these areas it is more difficult for pupils to comprehend unless the teacher builds concepts through advance preparation for reading, even if the author is careful to define his terms.

The language of literature provides central characters, plot, and mood around which rich and continuous context is developed. In contrast, continuity in social studies or science may be weak as the text moves from idea to idea and may be interrupted by reference to maps, charts, graphs and tables. The child must build comprehension strategies to learn these aids.

The language of mathematics has a special logic and grammar. There is less redundancy so that the omission of a word may change the meaning entirely. These special comprehension strategies are most readily learned in the materials and situation that approximate their use. Thus the social studies strategies are learned most easily in social studies materials. The quantitative language of mathematics calls for more careful concern for detail within a search to determine the problem-solving steps and the relationships between the quantities.

Checking Comprehension

All of the foregoing strategies help make pupils independent and effective readers. In most instances they will approach the meaning that the author intended, although special features of the author's style may complicate this. For example, some authors use exaggeration or analogous statements to emphasize a point. It is important for teachers to help pupils develop strategies to comprehend particular features of literary style. Moreover, there are times when pupils achieve a meaning which is quite far from the one the author started with. It is important for the teacher to be aware of how much the pupils have understood.

Comprehension of subtle and implied meanings, as pupils encounter complex materials, develops gradually. A good story almost always has more than any one reader can find in it. Teachers, with patience, can help pupils find this richness.

Conclusion

Pupils in the intermediate years can be helped to analyze their own strengths and difficulties in reading. After a pupil has read to a tape recorder, the teacher may find it useful to analyze his reading with him, encouraging him to consider what he is doing as he reads and perhaps helping him gain insights into how he can become more proficient. Together they may find that the pupil is either too cautious or too impetuous, too much concerned with accuracy when it is not essential, or too quick to leap to a conclusion. He may be helped to think through what information he could have used, or what strategy would have helped handle a particular problem. Such a joint analysis may provide the teacher with additional insights into the reader's strengths and weaknesses, so that the teacher can design productive learning activities.

Any help a teacher provides is most useful if it builds confidence and independence in the learner. Help that builds dependence on the teacher will not serve the pupil in the situations in which he reads, without the teacher there to guide him. Teachers must help the pupil expand, on his own, language and cognitive resources. Teachers who work *with* children will find that in the process of helping them build strategies for comprehension, they have helped them become efficient and effective readers.

Note

1. From "Danger in the Deep" by Charles Coombs from *Young Readers Water Sports*, Lantern Press, Inc., Mt Vernon, NY, 1952.

Chapter Twenty-Four

Decoding—From Code to What?

Kenneth S. Goodman
Wayne State University, 1971

"Anything short of meaning, anything that doesn't, in fact, go from code to meaning is not decoding."

The concept that underlies the use of the term *decoding* has become so distorted that we need to carefully re-examine it. It has crept very rapidly into our literature and into our terminology, and has been substituted for some earlier terms that fell into disrepute, such as "sounding-out."

Both oral language and written language are codes. There is nothing less a code about the noises a speaker makes and a listener reacts to than there is about those ink blotches on the page or chalk marks on a board. Both are code forms of language. Language has the capability, in the hands of people who know how to use it, of communicating meaning. Like any code it has no intrinsic meaning of its own. For literate people

This chapter first appeared in the *Journal of Reading*, April, 1971, Vol 14, No. 7, pp. 455–462. It is based on a paper presented at the convention of the National Council of Teachers of English, November 1970, in Atlanta, Georgia. Copyright (1971) by the International Reading Association. Reprinted with permission.

there are two code forms that complement each other, a written code and an oral code.

But if you look carefully at the term *decode,* that term implies that one is going from code to something other than code. If, in decoding, we go from code to something else, what else is that something else? An immediate answer is that if the reader moves from code to code, no decoding has taken place. If he moves from written language to oral language in some form, however distorted or complete, he has not decoded anything. In a similar manner the army signal corps operator receives a coded message that comes to him as a dot-dash signal over a radio. He then transcribes that into letter sequences. But he can't take that piece of paper with the letter sequences and say "Here, I've decoded the message." In fact, he has to get a code book out and somehow reconstruct the message which has been carefully obscured through several different encodings in order to keep other people from getting the message.

It isn't until he gets the message that any decoding has taken place. Anything short of meaning, anything that doesn't, in fact, go from code to meaning is not decoding.

There are some non-decoding kinds of things that happen in reading. These are short circuits that can develop and that unfortunately are apparently taught, and which kids unfortunately then learn. Kids have a nasty habit of learning what they are taught. Then teachers become very unhappy about the fact that they did, not realizing what brought the learning about. These short-circuits will be discussed more fully later.

Decoding must move the language user from language to meaning. But there isn't any intrinsic meaning in language. If we ask any physicist to describe from a physical point of view what, in fact, is going on when language is spoken, he would not find any property of that sound that had any intrinsic meaning. Even the quaint notion that maybe people started to learn to talk by imitating the sounds around them and using them as symbols is a pretty thin theory to explain language development. Obviously, very few noises any speaker makes have anything to do with the meaning he's trying to produce. As users of language we've gotten so used to thinking of ourselves as dealing directly with meaning we very often lose sight of the fact that the speaker cannot be projecting meaning into his listener's brain. He's broadcasting, taking his message and encoding it, and what the listener is doing, on the basis of what he's learned about language is taking that sound signal, the noises that the speaker has made, and decoding for meaning. The listener reconstructs the message or attempts to reconstruct the message that the speaker was broadcasting. There's no direct pipeline from mind to mind. There's no way of the speaker insuring, short of doing the best job he can of encoding, that decoding is going to be successful.

The speaker can try to think about what the listener brings to the task. That is, he can be "audience minded," as any speaker or writer tries to be. But all he can do is broadcast. From that point on it's the listener's job. The meaning is always in the speaker and the listener or in the writer and the reader.

Literate users of language, as listeners, can reconstruct the meaning from spoken language. As readers they can take written language and reconstruct the meaning. There are obviously some differences in the way the forms are used. Listeners can usually see speakers. They make motions with their hands. They make facial gestures and body movements. They may point to things. If speakers are conversing, they might show each other something or hold something or exchange something. There's a situational context that operates. Written language is always more removed from that which it refers to. It's most frequently out of any situational context. But an exit sign over the door is in a context. It has meaning partly because of its location. Even if you didn't know what it said, if it were in a foreign language, you'd be able to know what it must mean because of the context in which you find it.

At international airports, besides the words for men and women there are also picture clues to help get the meaning across.

To understand how language is decoded for meaning, psycholinguistic theory is needed. This theory has not grown out of a desire to promote a particular theory of language and a particular grammar, but rather from research on what people do when they read and when they listen.

The listener must cope with a stream of sounds which he has learned to organize according to certain perceptual categories that he has, the kinds of things that certain linguists call phonemes. In terms of certain contrastive features of the sounds, he's learned two very important things as he learned the language: what to pay attention to and what not to pay attention to. If he didn't know what not to pay attention to, it wouldn't do him much good to know what to pay attention to. He'd be constantly distracted.

But what's more important, the listener has to be able to take what's coming at him and from it induce its underlying structure. He has to be able to plot it into structural units and be able to handle the interrelationships of those units. If the speaker produces a statement which is a series of clauses, joined and interrelated and embedded in each other, the listener has to sort out those interrelationships, organize the clauses and assign meaning once he has the underlying, or deep, structure. That's the way the message is recreated. Listeners can't go directly from the signal, that stream of sounds, to meaning. There is no way of explaining how one could unless he has dealt with its structure. Everybody has the experience both in listening and in reading of finding that he's assumed the wrong underlying structure, one that doesn't make sense. So the listener has to reorganize, reprocess, and try a different underlying structure and then get the meaning.

Whether one starts with speech or with print, the task is to determine what the underlying grammatical structure is and then assign meaning. This sequence is virtually simultaneous. The language user is immediately getting some meaning sense. If language is anything, it is a meaning-seeking process. And it's only when the user of language is actively seeking meaning that, in fact, it operates as language.

If teachers doctor up language, if they select it in such a way that it turns out not to be language which is meaningful, or acts like language, then both the attempt to reconstruct the underlying language structure and the attempt to get at the meaning are frustrated and it becomes an experience in nonsense. Psychologists should have recognized in their own research, year after year after year, that whenever they used a language-learning task which was meaningful it was easier to learn than something that was nonsense. Whenever they tried something that had the grammatical sequence of natural language, even if it wasn't meaningful, that was easier to handle than unstructured nonsense. That's because a language user engages in the process of seeking meaning through the grammatical structures. He uses the surface structure, the sequences of sounds or the letters, only as signals or means of getting at, or inducing or recreating, the deep structure.

Because of the way language works, language users in decoding have to go from a surface structure to an underlying structure and then to meaning.

Now let's contrast speaking and writing with how listening and reading work. The contrast is between the encoding part of language and the decoding part of language. By this time the reader should understand that decoding is not being used here in any sense as a letter-to-sound shift. Decoding here means going from language to meaning and contrasts with encoding: from meaning to language. It doesn't even quite matter whether the person is successful. What's most important is that the activity he's engaged in is one in which he is seeking meaning or moving from meaning.

Encoding starts with meaning. The language uses a message to communicate a need, a feeling, an idea, a reaction to the world. When you turn to somebody and say something and he's standing on your foot, you hope he'll get off your foot. If he doesn't understand, he may continue to stand on it for a while. So, you start out with a message; then you assign a deep structure. As a language user you're not quite aware of the process because it's become so well learned, but you could not call this an unconscious process because you obviously control it.

One of the evidences that the process is controlled is that it sometimes comes out not quite the way we intended it to. It's not a totally unconscious process but language users are so agile that they're not quite aware of how it works. Users assign a deep structure, then they use a set of rules that they learned as youngsters. While learning the language, language users induced the set of rules for generating it and got to the point where they could use them almost automatically. In the meantime as they learned to use them they produced some funny sounding kinds of things like "I taked it" instead of "I took it." They tried to overgeneralize the rule and had to learn its exceptions. As they learned to use the rules they produced language, not on the basis of imitating what they heard, but on the basis of this set of rules that move language toward a surface representation.

It would appear at first that reading and listening are mirror images of speaking and writing. However, we have to be aware of the way the human mind works and what is possible in the language situation. The human mind finds it possible to make receptive language a different process, not a mirror image.

Receptive language use is not the directly opposite sequence of language encoding. The receptive language user does have to get to the deep structure in order to get to the meaning, but he doesn't have to use all the surface structure; that is, he doesn't have to use every feature of every sound and every relationship of every sound. He doesn't have to perceive it all. He doesn't have to hear it all accurately. He can hear partially, in fact, and still handle the situation just as he can read a text that has smudged print. The reason for that is that in getting at that deep structure he can make giant leaps, can interpret a few key clues or cues (either one applies here) and on that basis make a quick guess, a quick prediction, of what the structure is. Once he has predicted the structure, then all he has to do is sample from the subsequent signal, sounds or letters, in order to confirm what he has already predicted. He makes a giant leap. What's very important in the effectiveness of his guessing or predicting are the tactics or strategies that he's developed for knowing, before he sees them, which are the most important cues to look for. A reader, like a listener, develops strategies for picking out the most productive cues before he encounters them. It's been known for years that all the letters in a word are not equally important; the initial consonant is quite important. From an information theory point of view, the initial consonant carries more information; therefore, the reader learns to zero in on it, search for it, even before he sees it.

What a reader thinks he sees, just as what a listener thinks he hears is only partly what he actually processed, and mostly what he expected. The language user knows what to expect so that there's a process of guessing, of using minimal cues, of selecting the cues that carry the most information. Beginning cues in reading are graphic, obviously. Language users may attach, because they're listeners before they're readers, some generalizations about the relationship between the writing system and the speech system and use some phonological cues then. But there has been an exaggeration of the importance of these cues. They are misused when taught out of language context, because they are of value only in language contexts. The reader, like the listener, brings to the task his knowledge of the way the language works. His knowledge of the grammatical system makes it possible for him to predict from key graphic symbols what, in fact, the structure could be. Of course, the more complex it is the more processing he has to do, and the more interrelationships there are. A series of short simple sentences is easier to process than one sentence that contains several clauses embedded and conjoined. But the reader has to get the underlying structure. That's what he moves toward. As he brings his knowledge of grammar into play, he may be much more interested in the grammatical functioning of *the* than in its graphic qualities. Equally important, though, since this is a meaning-seeking process, the reader has anticipated, and is setting up, an expectation semantically. He builds a semantic context in which he tries things out, and he keeps saying to himself as he processes and guesses, "Does it make sense?" In language, meaning always is both input and output. One can't read and understand something that one doesn't have the conceptual development to handle. If, when he's done, a reader doesn't know if something makes sense, he doesn't know whether he's been successful or not. And if he doesn't know whether he's been successful he can't judge whether the strategies he used are ones that he should keep on using or ineffective ones that he should drop.

This need to confirm the guess on the basis of one's knowledge of the language and of the meaning that one brings to it is perhaps the strongest argument for why kids from the very beginning have to encounter meaningful natural language in their reading materials. It's an old cliché in education: "First you learn to read and then you read to learn." Essentially that's true but we have to put it into context of saying that the meanings that the reader gets from early reading experiences have to be broadly within his experience already, and broadly within his conceptual grasp. If there are new ideas that he's not yet able to handle, then the task is self-defeating right from the beginning.

The relationships between oral and written English have to be understood in a couple of contexts. Everybody knows we have an alphabetic system. An alphabetic system means that at least in origin there's an attempt to represent not simply the meanings graphically as idiographic writing systems do, but to actually represent the oral language so that there is in fact a set of relationships between oral and alphabetically written languages. Language changes over time. The fit between the oral and written language tends to change, not just for English but for all languages. Some languages have less complex relationships than English, but there is no such thing (and can never be any such thing) as a written system that is a perfect representation on a one-to-one basis of the oral languages. Language changes; dialects drift apart, the sound systems of all dialects are not the same. Scottish speakers, for instance, have a closer correspondence in those *night, light* words than we do. The *gh* was taught to me as silent letters, because they don't relate to anything in my sound system. To Scottish speakers they do relate to something in their sound system, and a spelling shift to accommodate my sound system would be a shift away from theirs. The correspondences in alphabetic writing systems turn out not to be between letters and sounds but between patterns of letters and patterns of sounds. And those are necessarily complex. Sounds shift in relationships to the sounds around them as affixes are combined with bases to achieve certain meaning sequences, certain grammatical interrelationships. In the word *situation,* for instance, neither *t* represents the phoneme that is most frequently associated with the letter *t*.

Because the child is a listener before he's a reader, the complexity illustrated by *situation* turns out never to be a reading problem. Systems of teaching reading that have treated it as a problem have created more difficulties than they've solved. A child normally would have no tendency to read *situation* as *sit u a ti on,* unless someone had taught him an inappropriate rule, one that didn't fit with the phonological rules he had already learned. As soon as he tries to say a word sequence, the rules that he's applying in producing that language take over, and it comes out a certain way. In fact, it's very difficult for him to say it any other way.

Having dealt to some extent with the relationship of reading and listening and the relationship of writing to speech in English, let's consider just what breaks down in the reading process that might cause concern as we look at the ways reading has been taught and the kinds of problems that result. The listener has already learned a very efficient language process. He has become competent with the oral language to the point where he can go from that oral signal to the underlying structure, to meaning, efficiently and rapidly. He knows which cues to select and knows how to plug in to the grammatical system to pick up grammatical cues and get at the underlying structures. He can plug in the meaning from his experiences and from concepts that he has developed. All that is working already. Now if the difference between reading and listening is a matter of going from a written signal rather than an oral signal what, in fact, he has to learn is not how to match

letters to sounds but how to get from that written signal to the underlying structure in much the way that he has learned to get from the
oral signal to the underlying structure.

The task in reading is not to hear the word or recognize the word
or name it. The task is to get the underlying structure, to get at the
meaning, and to constantly keep the meaning in mind. And that means
that even when teachers set out to teach the relationships between
oral and written language they turn them into a set of abstractions
unless they keep these relationships within the context of language as
it functions. The task in reading is to get at that underlying structure;
teaching reading often turns into an unrelated task, one that can now
be labeled *recoding*, going from the graphic code to an oral code. At
that, the oral code is fragmentary, because in order to do a real job of
encoding orally I have to already have the meaning.

Readers, as we said earlier, can be taught to have short circuits.
Instead of going from print to meaning, they wind up with something
that isn't meaning at all.

Grunting sounds in response to print is one kind of short circuit.
Among early readers in some instructional programs there's a strong
tendency to go through an unfamiliar text and name the words they
know and then sit back complacently. Or they'll point to a word and
they'll say, "We haven't had that word yet." The task for them is to
produce an oral name for the word and the notion that this is supposed to be a language process and a meaning-seeking one hasn't come
through to them. Kids who have learned the whole galaxy of word attacks can come up with very close correspondence in oral reading. As
a matter of fact, if you listen superficially to their reading you would
think they must understand because they're so accurate. And then you
discover that all that they were doing was efficiently attacking words;
that is, they have achieved a complex kind of recoding that functions
extremely well but short-circuits the meaning-seeking process.

In our research there are subjects that recode so effectively that
they even handle the syntactic structures. They go from the print to a
kind of non-semantic underlying structure and then right back to oral
language, still without understanding. Much in-school activities teach
them to do that, by the way. Pupils are given a chapter in a book on
Brazil, for example. Then they are asked the question, "What are the
principal products of Brazil?" The readers go back through and find a
line that starts out "The principal products of Brazil are..." and copy
it, knowing that the end of that sentence is the answer. What they
have done is a complex kind of recoding, but still really recoding, in the
sense that the child has not sought meaning. In fact, some readers may
have come to the conclusion that for them reading doesn't really yield
sense.

Summary

Simply speaking, reading is a meaning-seeking process. Listeners have learned to handle listening as a meaning-seeking process. What a reader has to do is to get from print to that same underlying structure, from which he can get to meaning. And he always has to keep in mind that language has as its purpose to get the meaning. It's not an end in itself but always a means to an end.

To summarize in one short statement: there should never be an argument between whether to start with code or with meaning because the code only operates in relationship to meaning.

Chapter Twenty-Five

Revaluing Readers and Reading

Kenneth S. Goodman
University of Arizona, 1982

The use of the term *readers in trouble* will be used here by the author for all those who are not doing as well as they think (or someone else thinks) they should do in the development of reading proficiency. The common denominator among such readers is that they have become their own worst enemies. They have acquired a view that the world is populated by two kinds of people: those who can read and those who cannot, those who can learn and those who cannot. They believe that if they could just learn the phonics rules, just get enough word attacks, just master the skills, then they could do what good readers do easily and well. However, they know they cannot because something is wrong with them; they just do not learn like "normal" people.

The key to helping readers in trouble is to help them revalue themselves as language users and learners, and revalue the reading process as an interactive, constructive language process. They must set aside the pathological view of themselves, cast off the labels, and operate to construct meaning through written language using the strengths they have built and used in making sense of oral language or sign. To do that, they need support and help.

This chapter first appeared in *Topics in Learning and Learning Disabilities*, Vol. 1, No. 4, January 1982, pp. 87–93. Copyright (1982) by PRO-ED, Inc. Adapted with permission.

Reading: A Unitary Psycholinguistic Process

Unfortunately, many educators have come to view reading as performance on tests, exercises, and workbooks. Teachers must put aside the instructional technology they have equated with reading, and see reading instead as a process of making sense of written language, a receptive language process parallel to listening. In reading there is interaction between a reader and a written text and through it with a writer. What the reader brings to the text—experience, attitudes, concepts, cognitive schemes—is as important as what the author brought to it in creating it. The reader's act is creative too; meaning is created in response to the text.

Reading is a psycholinguistic process in which thought and language interact as the reader builds meaning. Readers are not the prisoners of their eyes. They have brains with which they seek sense as they read—they predict and infer where the meaning is going, what sentence patterns are coming, what words and phrases are expected, and what the text will look like.

Within the continuous preoccupation with meaning, the reader selects from the available cues only those that are most useful, predicts on the basis of knowledge of language and the world, monitors his or her own success, and corrects when necessary to make sense. The reader is always tentative but confident. He or she is self-monitoring to make sure predictions are confirmed, but he or she is willing to take the risks necessary to move to meaning. Risk-taking, self-monitoring, and self-confidence are the essence of a revaluing program.

How Is Reading Learned?

Learning language is largely a matter of finding its underlying system, inferring its rules, and then being able to use them to express meaning and to understand it. Language is easiest to learn when it is whole, relevant, real, in context, and functional for the user. In this respect, written language is no different from oral language.

One need not be unusually clever to learn to read and write any more than to learn oral language. Only when learners are distracted from meaning by instruction or confronted by materials full of abstract nonsense is a disadvantage created for those who may have mental or physical impairments. Learning letters is more difficult than learning words, which is more difficult than learning to remember or comprehend sentences. Understanding sets of unrelated sentences is more difficult than comprehending coherent stories or other meaningful texts.

Recent studies have demonstrated that children make a strong beginning as readers and writers as they encounter print in their environment and learn to understand its functions (Goodman, 1980). As they see print used, they come to know what it is for and what it means. The key to the learning is the universal search for order and comprehensibility that is characteristic of all humans. If educators can grasp that, then they can understand the tremendous strength that all pupils bring to learning to read and write. That understanding can help teachers to revalue nonachieving pupils and to understand that their failure is educators' failure to help them use the strengths they have. All children seem to be remarkable language learners outside of school. If they appear less successful in school it is because learning language has been made too hard for them in the quest to make it easier.

Overemphasis on Skills and Teachers

Skills have been the focus of the instructional programs troubled readers have repeatedly experienced. At the same time these pupils are trying to make sense of print they are also trying to read by the numbers: sounding out, attacking words, using skills. Getting the words right becomes more important, for them, than making sense. Every unfamiliar word becomes a major obstacle to be identified before going on. The reader suffers from the "next word syndrome"; each unconquered word is a symbol of defeat.

Readers in trouble are more likely to be the victims of too much skill use than not enough. They persevere on a single word, producing many nonword attempts before giving up. Many of them have had intensive instruction in phonics and word attacks over and over as they moved through remediation programs. Although the effect of this training shows in their phonic near misses, their miscues are often interpreted by diagnosticians as proof that more phonics is needed.

Readers in trouble also tend to look to the teacher to tell them what to do next. The pattern is to wait for a few seconds each time a problem word or phrase is encountered; then the teacher will supply the next word or an admonition to sound out the next word. The teacher may think he or she has helped by supplying the next word, but such repeated experiences only sustain the next-word syndrome and the basic feeling of defeat and inadequacy of the reader in trouble.

Scenario for Failure

Readers in trouble in literate societies with schools universally available have experienced repeated cycles of failure. The natural history of each cycle is something like this: The students are not doing well in school.

The less well they do, the more intensively the teacher applies the program. If pupils are not doing well on worksheets, flash cards, skill drills, and remedial exercises, then the teacher repeats the same ones or provides supplementary, similar ones. If the usual amount of time spent on such activities is not paying off, then more time is provided for them, either at the expense of other, more meaningful aspects of the reading period such as free reading time, or of other aspects of the curriculum such as social studies, science, music, or art. If there is an aide available then the aide is assigned to review and repeat with the readers in trouble what has not worked when the teacher did it. Recesses, lunch periods, after school time, even vacation periods are invaded in the name of helping the readers in trouble to overcome their deficits.

Soon the classroom teacher gives up and the child is referred for remediation. Remediation usually begins with a heavy battery of tests that confirm that the pupil is inadequately responding to skill instruction. The tests reveal patterns of weakness and deficiency. Remedial exercises are prescribed to eliminate the weaknesses. The exercises will tend to be more abstract and fragmented versions of what did not work in the classroom.

Sometimes at the beginning of remediation there appears to be an upsurge of achievement and a flicker of hope and enthusiasm on the part of the learner. The pupil enjoys the special attention, particularly if the remedial teacher is warm and encouraging. Somewhat improved scores are achieved. As the remediation continues, however, the learner sinks once more into despair. The abstractness of the fragmented skill drills leads to frustration. What was fresh and new is recognized as the same, dull, repetitious, and tedious exercises that have not worked before. Pep talks and admonishments to try harder build personal guilt. Furthermore, the teacher shows resentment at the ingratitude of the learner for all the personal care and attention.

Meanwhile, back in the class, the remedial pupil is missing important learning opportunities; the time spent on remediation is the time classmates are spending building concepts, reading, writing, doing. So the learner in trouble, in the name of building basic skill competence, is deprived of rich school experience. Ironically, the pupil who rebels and acts out may be showing a healthier reaction than the pupil who withdraws or submits meekly to all this. At least such a rebel is showing a resistance to accepting full responsibility for failure.

Need for Revaluing

The answer to this dismal scenario is *revaluing*. The pupils must be helped to revalue themselves as learners. They must revalue the process of reading as the construction of meaning in response to print. They must come to be able to appreciate their own strengths, to recognize the productive strategies they already can use, and to build positively on those. They must come to put in perspective the interaction of themselves with an author through a text. Then they can put proper value on themselves, understand that no one can easily read and comprehend everything, and that what one knows before reading constrains what one can know after reading. They need to know that some texts are difficult to read because they are poorly written, and others because they contain new, complex ideas. They need to know that while everybody can find interesting, entertaining, or useful things in print, not everybody has to like everything they read. Finally, they need to realize that the easiest things for them to read are going to be the very ones they have the most interest in, the most background for, and that they get the most pleasure from.

Methods and Materials for Revaluing

Revaluing is not going to happen simply, easily, or quickly. It requires great patience and gentle support from teachers to help pupils in a long, slow rebuilding of the sense of self and sense of reading. Essentially, a revaluing program involves getting readers to read real meaningful texts, to strengthen and gain new appreciation of the productive strategies that lead to comprehension, and to drop the nonproductive strategies.

Teachers can turn the conflict that readers in trouble experience every time they attempt to read into a positive force to achieve the revalued reading. Piaget (1971) talks about disequilibrium, a point in learning where the learner has unresolved conflicts and has not yet accommodated. Readers in trouble have been in this unbalanced state for so long that it has *become* reading for them.

From Skills to Meaning

However, the very conditions of their discomfort contain the seeds of productive resolution: Here is a written text created by an author to coherently represent a message. Here is a reader trying to make sense of the text no matter what else he or she is doing. Patiently, in the context of supporting the reader's search for meaning, the teacher helps the reader to shift away from word identification, from sounding out, from teacher dependence. Patiently, the teacher helps the troubled reader to trust his or her own linguistic judgment, to have faith in the predictions and inferences that are coming to mind, to take risks, to self-monitor by constantly applying the key test: Does that make sense? Gradually the reader finds that the text is making sense. An accommodation takes shape in which graphophonic, syntactic, and semantic cues are used selectively to the extent that they are useful. Any exaggerated value attached to any one cue, cue system, or strategy gives way to putting each in its proper perspective.

Teacher as Catalyst

The teacher, carefully monitoring this conflict between productive and nonproductive strategies, between getting the next word and making sense, can be a catalyst. The teacher tips the balance by supporting the troubled readers' intuitions, by appreciating when something has worked or by asking a timely question at a point where the reader falters: *What's happening in the story? What do you already know about—? Did that make sense? Why not?* (See Altwerger & Bird, 1982.)

The teacher starts by learning about the learner. That does not mean diagnostic tests. It means asking learners what they read. It means inviting them to read a variety of things that vary in content, function, and complexity. It may mean, if the student has made some kind of start at becoming a reader, using some variation of miscue analysis (Goodman & Burke, 1980). The teacher moves slowly and supportively to overcome the fear and despair. Often, as pupils relax, they reveal themselves to be much more capable than either they or the teacher had supposed.

One problem that may be faced at the beginning of a revaluing program is that the learners have so strongly internalized an expectation of how reading will be taught that they reject anything else. The pupil must come to trust the teacher and learn new ways of evaluating his or her own progress. The teacher must let the learner see how progress comes through a focus on trying to make sense of meaningful texts. This focus, of course, is near the center of revaluing.

Building Self–Confidence

In starting to work with any reader in trouble, the teacher must take care not to assume that the pupil is devoid of reading ability. Thus group or individual tests are untrustworthy: All they may reveal is the pupils' great fear of failure and the ease with which they become discouraged and give up. It is only after the pupil has relaxed and begun to fully participate that any trustworthy insights may be drawn. At the beginning the instructional situation must be made completely nonthreatening. For some readers who are in serious trouble, it will be sufficient, as a beginning, to encourage them to follow as the teacher or aide reads. (See Bos, 1982.)

As the reader gains confidence and begins to reveal interests, focus may shift to a variety of kinds of reading: signs, catalogues, manuals, menus, *TV Guides,* and the like. The teacher will seek evidence of particular pupil interest and supply materials, either narrative or expository, that will be highly motivating—materials that are interesting and will help build the reader's self-confidence.

To be successful in helping troubled readers, teachers must take their lead from the pupils. The teacher monitors the learner, letting the learner set the pace and direction, but offering the right help at the right time. This process is not unlike what parents do intuitively as they support the oral language development of preschool children.

Difficult Textbooks

Coping with school texts, especially in upper elementary and secondary grades, is a problem that most troubled readers face even as they are improving in their ability and self-confidence. In fact, it is often discouraging for pupils to realize that although they know they are reading much better, they still cannot handle grade level texts. In dealing with this problem, as in all aspects of working with troubled readers, it is necessary for the teacher to be absolutely honest with the students. However, the pupils need to understand that it is not simply because they are ineffective readers that this problem occurs. Texts are difficult to read for many reasons:

1. The texts may be poorly written. Too many subject matter texts are still written by authors who do not write clearly and concisely with the nature of the intended readers in mind. Often vocabulary is used that is unnecessarily technical and obscure or not properly developed, illustrated, and defined.

2. The texts may present too much information too superficially and too rapidly. This is, of course, a problem that will vary with the background and interest of the learner, and the skill of the teacher in providing experiences to help the pupils read and understand the text. The problem may not be a general weakness in reading but rather too little background for the concepts presented.

Helping pupils realize that it is not always their fault as readers that they have trouble learning from textbooks is itself an important part of revaluing. Readers in trouble often think that good readers understand everything they read the first time they read it. Even when readers in trouble have had reasonably good comprehension, they think they have failed because they cannot remember every little detail.

Strategies

Readers in trouble also need other kinds of coping strategies:

a. knowing how to read for the gist of a text rather than every detail and knowing how to skim and survey materials to decide whether they are worth pursuing;

b. knowing how to reread to focus on what is important in difficult materials;

c. knowing how to frame questions to ask the teacher when they do not understand;

d. knowing how to find information in simpler, easier to read reference books; and

e. knowing how to get information from sources other than books.

Part of the solution for dealing with difficult school texts lies with teachers understanding why pupils have difficulty with them. Misuse of texts by teachers (expecting pupils to learn from them without the teacher's help) is at least as important a cause of difficulty as ineffective reading.

Writing

Teachers of readers in trouble often find that as their pupils improve in reading, they become enthusiastic writers. Troubled readers are seldom expected to write much, so they have usually had little experience in writing. Their first efforts will look like those of near beginners, full of invented spelling and shaky mechanics and punctuation. Encouraging pupils to keep journals will create a nonpressured opportunity to write without worrying about accuracy. Pupils can then move on to a variety of other expository and creative writing. The key to writing development for troubled readers is to create a sense of *function* by focusing on the most useful and meaningful forms of writing.

Challenge for Educators

It will not be enough to turn troubled readers into reluctant readers. Schools have produced too many people already who can read but do not choose to. Reading for troubled readers has been difficult, tedious, and nonproductive, and its acquisition has been associated with much embarrassment and pain. Teachers must patiently help such students to find reading materials that give them personal satisfaction and pleasure. They must help them realize that reading is something they can do when traveling, when waiting, when there is some time available for a quiet, personal activity, when there is nothing interesting on television or nobody to talk to. Pupils must reach the point where they choose to read when there is nobody to make them do it, before educators can really claim success.

Teachers can make the difference in whether readers in trouble find their way out or not. However, to be successful they will need the help of parents, colleagues less directly concerned with literacy, and the pupils themselves. All must come to revalue the readers and the reading process.

References

Altwerger, B., & Bird, L. "Disabled: The learner or the curriculum?" *Topics In Learning & Learning Disabilities 1(4):* 69–78, 1982.

Bos, C. "Getting past decoding: Assisted and repeated readings as remedial methods for learning disabled students." *Topics In Learning & Learning Disabilities 1(4):* 59–68, 1982.

Goodman, Y. Roots of literacy. In M. Douglass (Ed.), *Claremont Reading Conference Forty-fourth Yearbook.* Claremont, Calif., 1980.

Goodman, Y., & Burke, C. *Reading strategies: Focus on comprehension.* New York: Holt, Rinehart, and Winston, 1980.

Piaget, J. *Psychology and epistemology* (A. Rosin, trans.) New York: Grossman, 1971.

Publications by Kenneth S. Goodman

Articles

1963

1. "A Communicative Theory of the Reading Curriculum." *Elementary English* (40)3 (March 1963): 290–298.

2. With Yetta M. Goodman. "Spelling Ability of a Self-Taught Reader." *The Elementary School Journal* (64)3 (December 1963): 149–154.

1964

3. "The Linguistics of Reading." *The Elementary School Journal* (64)8 (April 1964): 355–361.
   Also in Durr (ed.), *Readings on Reading.* Boston: Houghton Mifflin, 1968.
   Also in Frost (ed.), *Issues and Innovations in the Teaching of Reading.* Chicago: Scott, Foresman, 1967.

1965

4. "Cues and Miscues in Reading: A Linguistic Study." *Elementary English* (42)6 (October 1965): 635–642.
   Also in Wilson and Geyer (eds.), *Reading for Diagnostic and Remedial Reading,* pp. 103–110. Columbus, OH: Merrill, 1972.
   Also in Gentile, Kamil, and Blanchard (eds.), *Reading Research Revisited,* pp. 129–134. Columbus, OH: Merrill, 1983.
   Also in Singer and Ruddell (eds.), *Theoretical Models and Processes of Reading,* 3rd ed. Newark, DE: International Reading Association, 1985.

5. "Dialect Barriers to Reading Comprehension." *Elementary English* (42)8 (December 1965): 852–860.
   Also in Linguistics and Reading. Urbana IL: National Council of Teachers of English, 1966.
   Also in Evertts, E. (ed.), *Dimensions of Dialect.* Urbana, IL: National Council of Teachers of English, 1967.
   Also in Kosinski, L. (ed.), *Readings on Creativity and Imagination in Literature and Language.* Urbana, IL: National Council of Teachers of English, 1969.
   Also in Baratz-Snowden, J., & Shuy, R. (eds.), *Teaching Black Children to Read.* Washington, DC: Center for Applied Linguistics, 1969.

Also in Binter, A., Dlabal, J. & Kise, L. (eds.), *Readings on Reading*, 241–251. Scranton, PA: International Textbook Co., 1969.
Also in Cayer, R., Green, J. & Baker, E. (eds.), *Listening and Speaking in the English Classroom: A Collection of Readings.* New York: Macmillan, 1971.
Also in Shores, D., (ed.), *Contemporary English; change and variation.* Philadelphia: Lippincott, 1972.
Also in Ruddell, R. (ed.), *Resources in Reading-Language Instruction.* Englewood Cliffs, N.J.: Prentice-Hall, 1974.
Also in DeStefano, J., (ed.), *Language, Society, and Education: A Profile of Black English.* Worthington, Ohio: C. A. Jones Pub. Co., 1973.

1967

6. With Yetta M. Goodman, "References on Linguistics and the Teaching of Reading." *Reading Teacher* (21)1 (October, 1967): 22–23.

7. "Word Perception: Linguistic Bases." *Education*, Vol. 87 (May 1967): 539–543.

8. "Reading: A Psycholinguistic Guessing Game." *Journal of the Reading Specialist* (6)4 (May 1967): 126–135.
   Also in Ruddell, R., & Singer, H., *Theoretical Models and Processes of Reading*, 259–272. Newark, DE: International Reading Association, 1970.
   Also in Gunderson, L. (ed.), *Language and Reading.* Washington, DC: Center for Applied Linguistics, 1970.
   Also in Harris, A., & Sipay, E. (eds.), *Readings on Reading Instruction.* David McKay, 1972.
   Also in Karlin, R. (ed.), *Perspectives on Elementary Reading; Principles and Strategies of Teaching.* New York: Harcourt Brace Jovanovich, 1973.
   Also in Comprehension and the Use of Context, 30–41. London: Open University Press, 1973.
   Also in Johnson, N. (ed.), *Current Topics in Language: Introductory Readings.* Cambridge, Mass.: Winthrop Publishers, 1976.
   Also in Reading Development. London: Open University Press, 1977.
   Also in The English Curriculum: Reading I, 21–24. London: The English and Media Centre, 1990.

1968

9. "Linguistic Insights Teachers May Apply." *Education* (88)4 (April–May 1968): 313–316.
   Also in What About Linguistics and the Teaching of Reading. Scott, Foresman, 1968.

10. "Reading Disability: A Challenge." *The Michigan English Teacher* (October–November, 1968).

1969

11. "Linguistics in a Relevant Curriculum." *Education* (April–May 1969): 303–307.
    Also in Savage J. (ed.), *Linguistics for Teachers*, 92–97. Chicago: Science Research Associates, 1973.

12. "Building on Children's Language." *The Grade Teacher* (March 1969): 35–42.

13. "Let's Dump the Up-Tight Model in English." *Elementary School Journal* (October 1969): 1–13.
    Also in Education Digest (December 1969): 45–48.
    Also in Savage, J. (ed.), *Linguistics for Teachers: Selected Readings.* Chicago: Science Research Associates, 1973.
    Also in Burns, P. & Schell, L. (eds.), *Elementary School Language Arts; Selected Readings.* Chicago: Rand McNally, 1969.
    Also in Harris, *Handbook of Standard and Non-Standard Communication.* Alabama Assistance Center, University of Alabama, 1976.

14. "Language and the Ethnocentric Researcher." *SRIS Quarterly* (Summer, 1969).
    Also in The Reading Specialist (Spring, 1970).

15. "What's New in Curriculum: Reading." *Nations Schools,* 1969.

16. "Analysis of Oral Reading Miscues: Applied Psycholinguistics." *Reading Research Quarterly* (5)1 (Fall, 1969): 9–30.
    Also in Smith, F. (ed.), *Psycholinguistics and Reading.* New York: Holt, Rinehart and Winston, 1973.
    Also in Emans and Fishbein, *Competence in Reading.* Chicago: Science Research Associates, 1972.
    German translation in Hofer, *Lesenlernen: Theorie and Unterricht,* 298–320. Schwann: Dusseldorf, 1976.
    Also in Current Comments (21)6 (February 6, 1989): 20. (Cited as "Classic Citation" in *Social Science Abstracts.*)

17. "A Psycholinguistic Approach to Reading. Implications for the Mentally Retarded." *The Slow Learning Child* (Australia)(Summer 1969).
    Also in Selected Academic Readings. Simon and Schuster.

18. "On Valuing Diversity in Language: Overview." *Childhood Education* (1969): 123–126.
    Also in Strickland, R. (ed.), *The Language Arts in the Elementary School.* 3d ed. Lexington, MA: Heath, 1969.
    Dutch translation in "Het Belag Van De Verscheidenbled in de Tall." *Kleuterwereld* (April 1973): 170–171.
    Also in Harris, A., (ed.), *A Handbook of Standard and Non-Standard Communication.* Alabama Assistance Center, University of Alabama, Tuscaloosa, AL 1976.

1970

19. With Carolyn L. Burke, "When a Child Reads: A Psycholinguistic Analysis." *Elementary English,* Vol. 47 (January 1970): 121–129.
    Also in Harris, L., & Smith, C. (eds.), *Individualizing reading instruction; A reader,* 231–243. New York: Holt, Rinehart and Winston, 1972.
    Also in Ruddell et al., *Resources in Reading-Language Instruction.* Englewood Cliffs, NJ: Prentice-Hall, 1974.

20. "Psycholinguistic Universals in the Reading Process." *Journal of Typographic Research* (4)2 (Spring 1970): 103–110.

Also in Pimslear and Quinn (eds.), *Papers on the Psychology of Second Language Learning,* 135–142. NY: Cambridge University Press, 1971.
Also in Smith, F., (ed.), *Psycholinguistics and Reading,* 21–27. New York: Holt, Rinehart and Winston, 1972.

21. "Dialect Rejection and Reading: A Response." *Reading Research Quarterly* (5)4 (Summer 1970): 600–603.
    Also in Selected Academic Readings, Simon and Schuster.

22. With Frank Smith, "On the Psycholinguistic Method of Teaching Reading." *Elementary School Journal* (70)4 (January 1971): 177–181.
    Also in Ekwall, E., (ed.), *Psychological factors in the teaching of reading.* Columbus, OH: Merrill, 1973.
    Also in DeStefano, J., & Fox, S., (eds.), *Language and the language arts.* Boston: Little, Brown, 1973, 239–243.
    Also in Smith, F., (ed.), *Psycholinguistics and Reading,* 177–182. New York: Holt, Rinehart and Winston, 1973.
    German translation in Hofer, *Lesenlernen: Theories und Unterricht,* 232–237. Schwann: Dusseldorf, 1976.

1971

23. "Promises, Promises." *The Reading Teacher* (24)4 (January 1971): 356–367.
    Also in DeStefano, J., & Fox, S., (eds.), *Language and the Language Arts.* Boston: Little Brown, 1973.
    Also in Malberger et al., *Learning.* Shoestring Press, 1972.

24. "Who Gave Us the Right?" *The English Record* (21)4 (April 1971): 44–45.

25. With D. Menosky, "Reading Instruction: Let's Get It All Together." *Instructor* (79)2 (March 1971): 44–45.

26. "Decoding–From Code to What?" *Journal of Reading* (14)7 (April 1971): 455–462.
    Also in DeStefano, J., & Fox, S., (eds.), *Language and the Language Arts,* 230–236. Boston: Little Brown, 1973.
    Also in Beery, A., Barrett, T., & Powell, W. (eds.), *Elementary reading instruction; selected materials II.* [2d ed.] Boston: Allyn and Bacon, 1974.

1972

27. "Oral Language Miscues." *Viewpoints* (48)1 (January 1972): 13–28.

28. "Reading: The Key Is in Children's Language." *The Reading Teacher* (25)1 (March 1972): 505–508.
    Also in Reid, Jesse, and Donaldson (eds.), *Reading: Problems and Practices,* 2nd ed., 358–362. London: Ward Lock Educational Limited, 1977.

29. "Orthography in a Theory of Reading Instruction." *Elementary English* (49)8 (December 1972): 1254–1261.

30. "Up-Tight Ain't Right." *School Library Journal* (19)2 (October 1972): 82–84.
    Also in Trends and Issues in Children's Literature. New York: Xerox, 1973.

1973

31. "The 13th Easy Way to Make Learning to Read Difficult." A reaction to Gleitman and Rozin, *Reading Research Quarterly* (8)4 (Summer 1973).

32. With Catherine Buck, "Dialect Barriers to Reading Comprehension Revisited." *Reading Teacher* (27)1 (October 1973): 6–12.
    Also in Mental Health Digest (5)12 (December 1973): 20–23.
    Also in Johnson, N., (ed.), *Current Topics in Language,* 409–417. Cambridge, MA: Winthrop, 1976.
    Reprinted as classic article in The Reading Teacher (50)6 (March 1997): 454–459.

33. With Yetta M. Goodman and Carolyn L. Burke, "Language in Teacher Education." *Journal of Research and Development in Education* (7)1 (Fall 1973): 66–71.

1974

34. "Military-Industrial Thinking Finally Captures the Schools." *Educational Leadership* (February 1974): 407–411.

35. "Effective Teachers of Reading Know Language and Children." *Elementary English* (51)6 (September 1974): 823–828.
    Also in Education Digest (December 1974).
    Also in NJEA Review.

36. "Reading: You Can Get Back to Kansas Anytime You're Ready, Dorothy." *English Journal* (63)8 (November 1974): 62–64.
    Also in Reading in Focus, National Council of Teachers of English Newsletter, Australia, October 1976.

1975

37. "Do You Have to Be Smart to Read? Do You Have to Read to Be Smart?" *Reading Teacher* (28)2 (April 1975): 625–632.
    Also in Education Digest (41) (September 1975): 41–44.
    Also in ABH Reading Pacesetter, Manila, Philippines, 1975.
    Also Spanish translation in Enfoques Educacionales, 40–47. Chile, no. 5, 1979.

38. "Influence of the Visual Peripheral Field in Reading." *Research in Teaching of English* (9)2 (Fall 1975): 210–222.

1976

39. "A Bicentennial Revolution in Reading." *Georgia Journal of Reading* (2)1 (Fall 1976): 13–19.

40. "From the Strawman to the Tin Woodman, a Response to Mosenthal." *Reading Research Quarterly* (12)4: 575–585.

41. "And a Principled View from the Bridge." *Reading Research Quarterly* (12)4: 604.

42. With Yetta M. Goodman, "Lesenlernen—Ein funktionaler Ansatz." *Die Grundschule* (9)6 (June 1977): 263–267.

43. With Yetta M. Goodman, W. McGinnitie, Michio Namekawa, Eikkchi Kurasawa, Takashiko Sakamoto, "Tokubetsu Zadankai: Eizo Jidai ni okero Dokusho Shido" (Reading Instruction in the Era of Visual Imagery). *Sogo Kyuiku Gijutso* (Unified Educational Theory) (31)11 (December 1976): 116–125.

1977

44. With Yetta M. Goodman, "Learning about Psycholinguistic Processes by Analyzing Oral Reading." *Harvard Educational Review* (40)3 (1977): 317–333.
Also in McCullough, (ed.), *Inchworm, Inchworm: Persistent Problems in Reading Education*, 179–201. Newark, DE: International Reading Association, 1980.
Also in Thought and Language/Language and Reading (eds.), Cambridge, MA: Harvard University Press, 1980.

45. "Acquiring Literacy Is Natural: Who Skilled Cock Robin?" *Theory Into Practice* (16)5 (December 1977): 309–314.
Also in 25th Anniversary Issue, Theory Into Practice (26)5 (December 1987): 368–373.

46. "And Good Luck to Your Boy." *Arizona English Bulletin* (20) (October 1977): 6–10.

1978

47. "Open Letter to President Carter." *SLATE* (3)2 (March 1978).
Condensed in Ohio Reading Teacher (January 1979).
Also in Michigan English Teacher (May 1978).
Also in Wisconsin Reading Teacher (May 1979).
Also in Wisconsin Administration Bulletin (May 1979).

48. "Minimum Competencies: A Moral View." *Minimum Competency Standards, Three Points of View.* Newark, DE: International Reading Association, 1978.

49. "What Is Basic About Reading." In *Reading, the Arts and the Creation of Meaning,* edited by E. W. Eisner, 55–70. National Art Education Association, Reston, VA, 1978.

50. "Commentary: Breakthroughs and Lock-outs." *Language Arts* (55)8 (November–December 1978): 911–920.
Also in Connecticut Council of Teachers of English Newsletter (12)2 (December 1978).

1979

51. "The Know-More and Know-Nothing Movements in Reading: A Personal Response." *Language Arts* (56)8 (September 1979): 657–663.
Also in Georgia Journal of Reading (5)2 (Spring 1980): 5–12.

Translation in Danish in Laesepaedogogen 1981 and as *Laese Rapport 4* under the title, "Laesning Efter Mening-Eller Laesning Som Teknik." Undated.

52. With Yetta M. Goodman, "Learning to Read Is Natural." In *Theory and Practice of Early Reading,* edited by L. B. Resnick and P. A. Weaver, pp. 137–155. Hillsdale, NJ: Erlbaum, 1979.
    Translation in French in Apprentissage et Socialisation (3)2 (1980): 107–123.
    Translation in Spanish in Enfoques Educasionales. Chile, 1980.

1980

53. "Revisiting Research Revisited." *Reading Psychology* (Summer 1980): 195–197.
    Also in Gentile, Kamil, and Blanchard (eds.), *Reading Research Revisited.* Columbus, OH: Merrill, 1983.

54. "On the Ann Arbor Black English Case." *English Journal* (69)6 (September 1980): 72.

55. With Frederick V. Gollasch, Word-Level Omissions in Reading: Deliberate and Non-Deliberate. Tucson, AZ, University of Arizona Occasional Paper #2, 1981. *Reading Research Quarterly* (16)1 (1980): 6–31.

1981

56. With Yetta M. Goodman, "Twenty Questions About Teaching Language." *Educational Leadership* (38)6 (March 1981): 437–442.

57. "A Declaration of Professional Conscience for Teachers." *Childhood Education* (March–April 1981): 253–255.
    Also in Labinowicz, E., (ed.), *Learning from children: new beginnings for teaching numerical thinking: a Piagetian approach.* Menlo Park, CA: Addison-Wesley, 1985.
    Also in Goodman, Bird, and Goodman (eds.), *The Whole Language Catalog,* inside front cover. Santa Rosa, CA: American School Publishers, 1991.
    Also in Kaufmann (ed.), *Council-Grams* (54)4 (1991): 8.
    Also in Society for Developmental Education News (2)2 (Fall 1992): 6.
    Also in Sumner (ed.), *Into Teachers' Hands,* inside front cover. Peterborough, NH: Society for Developmental Education, 1992.
    Also in Whole Teaching, Society for Developmental Education Sourcebook, 6th ed., inside front cover. Peterborough, NH: Society for Developmental Education, 1993.

58. With Yetta M. Goodman, "To Err Is Human." *NYU Education Quarterly* (12)4 (Summer 1981): 14–19.

59. "Response to Stott." *Reading-Canada-Lecture* (1)2 (April 1981): 18–20.

60. "Lukemisprosessi: Monikielinen, Kehityksellinen Nakokulma." *Jasenlehti,* no. 3 8–9. (Finland), 1981.

1982

61. "Revaluing Readers and Reading." *Topics in Learning and Learning Disabilities* (1)4 (January 1982): 87–93.

1983

62. With Yetta M. Goodman, "Reading and Writing Relationships: Pragmatic Functions." *Language Arts* (60)5 (May 1983): 590–599.
    Also in Jensen, J. (ed.), *Composing and Comprehending*, 155–164. Urbana, IL: National Council for Research in English/Educational Resource Information Centre, 1984.

63. "The Solution Is the Risk: A Reply to the Report of the National Commission on Excellence in Education." *SLATE* (9)1 (September 1983).

1984

64. With L. Bird, "On the Wording of Texts: A Study of Intra-Text Word Frequency." *Research in Teaching English* (18)2 (May 1984): 119–145.

65. "Growing into Literacy." *Prospects, Education Quarterly of UNESCO* (16)1 (1985).
    Also in French, Spanish, Arabic, and Russian translations.

66. "On Being Literate in an Age of Information." *Journal of Reading* (28)5 (February 1985): 388–392.
    Also in Mayor, B. & Pugh, A.K., (eds.), *Language, communication, & education.* London: Open University, and Croom Helm: Wolfeboro, NH, 1987.

67. Introduction to "A Glimpse at Reading Instruction in China" by Shanye Jiang, Bo Li. *The Reading Teacher* (38)8 (April 1985): 762–766.

68. "Chicago Mastery Learning Reading: A Program with 3 Left Feet," *Education Week* (October 9, 1985): 20.

69. "Un Programma Olistico Per L'apprendimento e lo Sviluppo Della Lettura." *Educazione e Scuola* (Italy) (4)15 (September 1985): 11–24.
    Also see Occasional Paper No. 1.

70. "Response to Becoming a Nation of Readers." *Reading Today* (63)1 (October 1985).

1986

71. "Basal Readers: A Call for Action." *Language Arts* (63)1 (April 1986).

72. With Mira Beer-Toker, "Questions About Children's Language and Literacy: An Interview with Kenneth S. Goodman." *Mother Tongue Education Bulletin* (Quebec, Canada) (1)2 (Spring and Fall 1986): 19–22.

1987

73. "You and the Basals: Taking Charge of Your Classroom." *Learning 87* (16)2 (September 1987): 62–65.

Also in Manning and Manning (eds.),*Whole Language: Beliefs and Practices, K-8,* 217–219. Washington, DC: National Education Association, 1989.

74. "Determiners in Reading: Miscues on a Few Little Words." *Language and Education* (1)1 (1987): 33–58.

75. "Who Can Be a Whole Language Teacher?" *Teachers Networking* (1)1 (April 1987): 1.

76. "To My Professional Friends in New Zealand." *Reading Forum NZ* (June 1987).

77. "The Reading Process: Ken Goodman's Comments." *ARA Today* (August 1987).

1988

78. "Look What They've Done to Judy Blume!: The 'Basalization' of Children's Literature." *The New Advocate* (1)1 (1988): 29–41.

79. "Reflections: An Interview with Ken and Yetta Goodman." *Reading-Canada-Lecture* (6)1 (Spring 1988): 46–53.

1989

80. "On Writing 'Reading Miscues—Windows on the Psycholinguistic Guessing Game.'" *Current Comments* (21)6 (February 6, 1989): 20.

81. "Whole Language Is Whole: A Response to Heymsfeld." *Educational Leadership* (46)6 (March 1989): 69–71.

82. "The Whole Language Approach: A Conversation with Kenneth Goodman." *Writing Teacher* (3)1 (August–September 1989): 5–8.

83. "Access to Literacy: Basals and Other Barriers." In *Theory Into Practice,* P. Shannon and K.S. Goodman (eds.) (39)4 (Autumn 1989): 300–306.

84. "Latin American Conference Is Successful." *Reading Today* (7)3 (December 1989).

1990

85. With Ira E. Aaron, Jeanne S. Chall, Dolores Durkin, and Dorothy S. Strickland, "The Past, Present, and Future of Literacy Education: Comments from a Panel of Distiguished Educators, Part I." *The Reading Teacher* (43)4 (January 1990): 302–315.

86. "Whole Language Research: Foundations and Development." *Elementary School Journal* (90)2 (November 1989): 207–221.
Japanese translation by Takashi Kuwabara. *Journal of Language Teaching* (17) (1990): 99–116.

87. "Managing the Whole Language Classroom." *Instructor* (99)6 (February 1990): 26–29.

88. "A Rebuttal to Priscilla Vail." *Whole Language Special Interest Group Newsletter* (Spring 1990): 4.

89. "El Linguaje Integral: Un Camino Facil para el Desarrollo del Lenguaje." *Lectura Y Vida* (9)2 (June 1990): 5–13.

90. With Dorothy F. King, "Whole Language: Cherishing Learners and Their Language," *LSHSS* (21)4 (October 1990).

1991

91. "An Open Letter to President Bush." *Whole Language Umbrella Newsletter* (Summer 1991): 1–4.

92. With Yetta M. Goodman, "About Whole Language." *Japanese (First Language) Education Research Monthly* (233) (October 1991): 64–71.

93. With Diane de Ford, Irene Fountas, Yetta M. Goodman, Vera Milz, and Sharon Murphy, "Dialogue on Issues in Whole Language." *Orbit* (Canada) (22)4 (December 1991): 1–3.

94. With Richard J. Meyer, "Whole Language: Principles for Principals." *SAANYS Journal,* (22)3 (Winter 1991–1992): 7–10.

1992

95. "Why Whole Language Is Today's Agenda in Education." *Language Arts* (69)5 (September 1992): 354–363.

96. "I Didn't Found Whole Language." *The Reading Teacher* (46)3 (November 1992): 188–199.
    Also in The Education Digest (59)2 (October 1993): 64–67.

97. "Gurus, Professors, and the Politics of Phonics." *Reading Today* (December 1992/January 1993): 8–10.

1993

98. "Phonics Phacts." *Nebraska Language Arts Bulletin* (5)2 (January 1993): 1–5.

1994

99. With Lisa Maras and Debbie Birdseye, "Look! Look! Who Stole the Pictures from the Picture Book?" *The New Advocate* (7)1 (Winter 1994): 1–24.

100. "Standards, Not!" *Education Week* (September 7, 1994): 39, 41.
    Also in The Council Chronicle (4)2 (November 1994): 17 and back page.

101. "Deconstructing the Rhetoric of Moorman, Blanton, and McLaughlin: A Response." *Reading Research Quarterly* (29)4 (October/November/December 1994): 340–346.

1995

102. "Is Whole-Language Instruction the Best Way to Teach Reading?" *CQ Researcher* (5)19 (May 19, 1995): 457–461.

103. "Forced Choices in a Non-Crisis, A Critique of the Report of the California Reading Task Force." *Education Week* (15)11 (November 1995): 39, 42.

104. With Elizabeth Noll, "Using a Howitzer to Kill a Butterfly: Teaching Literature with Basals." *The New Advocate* (8)4 (Fall 1995): 243–254.

1996

105. With Yetta M. Goodman, "Possible Lives: The Promise of Public Education in America." Reviewed by Mike Rose, *Rhetoric Review* (14)2 (Spring 1996): 420–424.

106. "An Open Letter to Richard Riley and Bill Clinton." *Reading Today* (13)6 (June/July 1996): 39.

107. "The Reading Derby: An Open Letter to Wisconsin Teachers." *WSRA Journal* (40)3 (Summer/Fall 1996): 1–5.

108. "Educar, Como se Enseña a Vivir" (Interview with Ken and Yetta Goodman). *Para Ti* 3844 (March 11, 1996): 92–93.

109. "Ken and Yetta Goodman: Exploring the Roots of Whole Language." Interview with Ken and Yetta Goodman by Jerome Harste and K. Short. *Language Arts* (73)7 (November 1996): 508–519.

1997

110. "The Reading Process: Insights from Miscue Analysis." A summary adapted from *The 1996–97 Dean's Forum, the Advancement of Knowledge and Practice in Education Proceedings.* Tucson, University of Arizona, January, 1997.

111. "California, Whole Language, and the NAEP." *CLIPS* (3)1 (Spring 1997): 53–56.

112. "Capturing 'America Reads' for a Larger Agenda?" *Education Week* (17)4 (September 1997): 34–35.

113. "Putting Theory and Research in the Context of History." *Language Arts* (74)8 (December 1997): 595–599.

1998

114. "Parental Choice Bill Requires a State-Mandated Curriculum." *Arizona Daily Star,* section A (February 20, 1998): 11.

115. "Good News from a Bad Test: Arizona, California and the National Assessment." *Arizona Reading Journal* (25)1 (Spring/Summer 1998): 13–23.

116. "The Phonics Scam: The Pedagogy of the Absurd." *Talking Points* (10)1 (October/November 1998): 8–10.

117. "Ten Reasons for Hope for Success In Educating All Learners." *Talking Points* (10)1 (October/November 1998): 18.

118. "Comments on the Reading Excellence Act (U.S.) 1998." *Reading Online,* Available from World Wide Web: <http://www.readingonline.org/critical/ACT.html>.

119. "On Reading." In *The Science of Reading,* translated by R. Yokota (42)1 (April 1998): 27–42.

1999

120. "Teaching Mid the Rockets Red Glare." *Tucson Teachers Applying Whole Language News* (November 1999): 5–6.

121. "Mean Times for Teachers and Learners in California." *Talking Points* (11)1 (October/November 1999): 18–19.

122. "On Reading." In *The Science of Reading,* translated by R. Yokota (43)4 (December 1999): 152–158.

2000

123. "Ken Goodman on His Life in Reading." *History of Reading News* (23)2 (Spring 2000): 1, 2, 7.

124. "Ken's Kolumn." *Talking Points* (11)2 (April/May 2000): 18–19.

125. "Teaching Amid the Rocket's Red Glare." *Minnesota English Journal* (Fall, 2000): 107–110.

126. "Defending Teachers and Learners from Mandates." *Minnesota English Journal* (Fall, 2000): 111–114.

127. With Eric J. Paulson, "Influential Studies in Eye-Movement Research." *Reading Online.* December, 1998. Available on the World Wide Web: <http://www.readingonline.org/research/eyemove.html>.

128. "On Reading." In *The Science of Reading,* translated by R. Yokota (July 2000): 73–82.

129. "On Reading." In *The Science of Reading,* translated by R. Yokota (44)3 (October 2000): 83–104.

2001

130. "Aims." *Arizona Daily Star* (October 28, 2001): B-11.

131. "On Reading." In *The Science of Reading,* translated by R. Yokota (45)3 (October 2001): 103–125.

Books and Monographs

1. With Hans Olsen, Cynthia Colvin, and Louis Vanderlinde, *Choosing Materials to Teach Reading*, 2nd ed. Detroit: Wayne State University Press, 1973.

2. As editor of *The Psycholinguistic Nature of the Reading Process*. Detroit: Wayne State University Press, 1968.
   Lead article translation in German, Hofer, *Lesenlernen: Theorie und Unterricht*, 139–151. Schwann: Dusseldorf, 1976.

3. With J. Fleming (eds.), *Psycholinguistics and the Teaching of Reading*. Newark, DE: International Reading Association, 1969.

4. With Olive Niles, *Reading: Process and Program*. Champaign, IL: National Council of Teachers of English, 1969.
   Excerpt in Reading: Today and Tomorrow. London: Open University, 1972.
   Also in Singer and Ruddell, *Theoretical Models and Processes in Reading*, 2nd ed., Newark, DE: International Reading Association, 1976.
   Also in German edition of M. Angermair, *Theoretical Models*.

5. With E. Brooks Smith and Robert Meredith, *Language and Thinking in the Elementary School*. New York: Holt, Rinehart and Winston, 1970.
   Chapter reprinted in Ruddell, R. (ed.), *Resources in Reading-Language Instruction*. Englewood Cliffs, NJ: Prentice Hall, 1973.
   Also in Language and Thinking in School, 2nd ed., New York: Holt, Rinehart and Winston, 1976.
   Also in Smith, Meredith, and Goodman, *Language and Thinking in School, A Whole-Language Curriculum*, 3rd ed. New York: Richard C. Owen, 1987.

6. With Yetta M. Goodman, *Annotated Bibliography on Linguistics, Psycholinguistics and the Teaching of Reading*, 3rd ed. Newark, DE: International Reading Association, 1980.

7. As editor of *Miscue Analysis: Applications to Reading Instruction*. National Council of Teachers of English-ERIC, 1973.
   Excerpt in Plackett (ed.), *The English Curriculum: Reading 2, Slow Readers*, 79–83. London: The English Centre, 1990.

8. *Reading: A Conversation with Kenneth Goodman*. Chicago: Scott, Foresman, 1976.
   Digest in TSI Repeater-Cable, Telesensory Systems. Palo Alto, September, 1977.

9. With Yetta M. Goodman and Barbara Flores, *Reading in the Bilingual Classroom: Literacy and Biliteracy*. Rosslyn, VA: National Clearinghouse for Bilingual Education, 1979.

10. *Reading and Readers* (The 1981 Catherine Molony Memorial Lecture). New York, City College School of Education, Workshop Center for Open Education, 1981.

11. *Language and Literacy, the Selected Writings of Kenneth S. Goodman, Volume 1: Process, Theory, Research*, F. V. Gollasch (ed.). Boston and London: Routledge and Kegan Paul, 1982.

12. *Language and Literacy, the Selected Writings of Kenneth S. Goodman, Volume II: Reading, Language and the Classroom Teacher,* F. V. Gollasch (ed.). Boston and London: Routledge and Kegan Paul, 1982.

13. *What's Whole in Whole Language.* Richmond Hill, Toronto: Scholastic, 1986, and Portsmouth, NH: Heinemann Educational.
    Spanish edition in Lenguaje Integral. Editorial Venezolana C.A., Toronto, 1989.
    French edition in Le Comment et Pourqois de la Langage Integre. Scholastic, Toronto, 1989.
    Japanese edition in Kyoku e no atarashi chosen: Eigo ken ni okeri zentai gengo kyoiku. Tokyo: Ozora Sha, 1990.
    Spanish edition in El lenguaje Integral, Grupo (ed.). S.A.: Libro De Edición Argentina, 1995.
    Portuguese edition in Linguagem Integral. Traducao: Marcos A.G. Domingues, Porto Alegre: Artes Medicas, 1997.

14. With Patrick Shannon, Yvonne Freeman, and Sharon Murphy, *Report Card on Basal Readers.* Katonah, NY: Richard C. Owen, 1988.

15. With Yetta M. Goodman and Wendy Hood, *The Whole Language Evaluation Book.* Portsmouth, NH: Heinemann, 1989.

16. With Yetta M. Goodman and Wendy Hood, *Organizing for Whole Language.* Portsmouth, NH: Heinemann, 1991.

17. With Lois Bird and Yetta M. Goodman, *The Whole Language Catalog.* Santa Rosa, CA: American School Publishers, January, 1991.

18. *Eminent Scholar Conversation #15* by Rudine Sims Bishop, pp. 1–35. Ohio State University, Columbus, OH: Martha L. King Language and Literacy Center, 1991.

19. With Lois B. Bird and Yetta M. Goodman, *The Whole Language Catalog: Authentic Assessment Supplement.* Santa Rosa, CA: American School Publishers, May 1992.

20. *Ken Goodman Phonics Phacts.* Richmond Hill, Ontario: Scholastic Canada and Portsmouth, NH: Heinemann, 1994.

21. With Lois Bird and Yetta M. Goodman, *The Whole Language Catalog: Forms for Authentic Assessment.* New York: SRA Division Macmillan/McGraw-Hill School Publishing, 1994.

22. With Patrick Shannon, *Basal Readers, a Second Look.* Katonah, NY: Richard C. Owen, 1994.

23. *Ken Goodman on Reading.* Richmond Hill, Ontario: Scholastic Canada and Portsmouth, NH: Heinemann, 1996.

24. With Joel Brown and Ann M. Marek, *Studies in Miscue Analysis: An Annotated Bibliography.* Newark, DE: International Reading Association, 1996.

25. *In Defense of Good Teaching,* K. S. Goodman (ed.). York, ME: Stenhouse, 1998.

26. *Reflections and Connections Essays in Honor of Kenneth S. Goodman's Influence on Language Education,* A. M. Marek and C. Edelsky (eds.). Cresskill, NJ: Hampton Press, 1998.

Book Chapters

1. "A Psycholinguistic View of Reading Comprehension." In *New Frontiers in College-Adult Reading.* 15th Yearbook of the National Reading Conference, Milwaukee, 1966.

2. "Elementary Education." In *Foundations of Education,* rev. ed., edited by G. Kneller, 493–521. New York: John Wiley and Sons, 1967.

3. "Is the Linguistic Approach an Improvement in Reading Instruction: Pro." In *Current Issues in Reading,* edited by N. Banton Smith, 268–276. Newark, DE: International Reading Association, 1969.

4. "Words and Morphemes in Reading." In *Psycholinguistics and the Teaching of Reading,* edited by Goodman and J. Fleming, 25–33. Newark, DE: International Reading Association, 1969.

5. "The Interrelationships Between Language Development and Learning to Read." In *The Impact of Society on Learning to Read,* edited by M. Schleich. Hofstra University, 1970.

6. "Comprehension-Centered Reading Instruction." In *Proceedings of the 1970 Claremont Reading Conference,* 125–135.
   Also in Ekwell, E. (ed.) *Psychological Factors in the Teaching of Reading,* 292–302. Columbus, OH: Merrill, 1972.

7. "Psycholinguistics in Reading." In *Innovations in the Elementary School: An IDEA.* Occasional Paper. Melbourne, FL, 1970.

8. "Urban Dialects and Reading Instruction." In *Teaching Reading–Not by Decoding Alone,* edited by J. P. Kender, 61–75. Interstate: Danville, 1971.

9. "The Search Called Reading." In *Coordinating Reading Instruction,* edited by H. Robinson, 8–14. Glenview, IL: Scott, Foresman, 1971.

10. "Children's Language and Experience: A Place to Begin." In *Coordinating Reading Instruction,* edited by H. Robinson, 46–52. Glenview, IL: Scott, Foresman, 1971.

11. "Linguistics and Reading." In *Encyclopedia of Education,* edited by L. C. Deighton. New York: Macmillan, 1971.

12. "Psycholinguistics and Reading." In *Proceedings of the Maryland Reading Institute,* 1971.

13. "The Reading Process: Theory and Practice." In *Language and Learning to Read: What Teachers Should Know About Language,* edited by Hodges and Rudorf, 143–159. Boston: Houghton-Mifflin, 1972.

14. "Testing in Reading: A General Critique." In *Accountability and Reading Instruction,* edited by R. Ruddell. Urbana, IL: National Council of Teachers of English, 1973.

15. "Strategies for Increasing Comprehension in Reading." In *Improving Reading in the Intermediate Years,* edited by H. Robinson, 59–71. Glenview, IL: Scott, Foresman, 1973.
   Also available as a separate monograph, Glenview, IL: Scott, Foresman, 1974.

16. "The Reading Process," In *Proceedings of the Sixth Western Symposium on Learning: Language and Reading*. Bellingham, WA, 1975.

17. "Miscue Analysis: Theory and Reality in Reading." In *New Horizons in Reading, Proceedings of Fifth IRA World Congress on Reading*, edited by J. E. Merritt, 15–26. Newark, DE: International Reading Association, 1976.

18. "Linguistically Sound Research in Reading." In *Improving Reading Research*, edited by Farr, R., Weintraub, S., and Tone, B., 89–100. Newark, DE: International Reading Association, 1976.

19. "What's Universal About the Reading Process." In *Proceedings of 20th Annual Convention of the Japan Reading Association*, Tokyo, 1976.

20. "Manifesto for a Reading Revolution." In *40th Yearbook Claremont Reading Conference*, edited by M. Douglas, 16–28. Claremont, CA, 1976.

21. "What We Know About Reading." In *Findings of Research in Miscue Analysis: Classroom Implications*, edited by P. D. Allen and D. Watson, 57–69. Educational Resources Information Centre-National Council of Teachers of English, 1976.

22. "The Goodman Taxonomy of Reading Miscues." In *Findings of Research in Miscue Analysis: Classroom Implications*, edited by P. D. Allen and D. Watson, 157–244. Educational Resources Information Centre-National Council of Teachers of English, 1976.

23. With Yetta M. Goodman, "Reading and Reading Instruction: Insights from Miscue Analysis." In *English in Secondary Schools: Today & Tomorrow*, edited by K. D. Watson and R. D. Eagleson, 254–259. Sydney: English Teachers Association of New South Wales, 1977.

24. With Carolyn Burke, "Reading for Life: The Psycholinguistic Base." *Conference Proceedings Reading*.

25. "Bridging the Gaps in Reading: Respect and Communication." In *New Perspectives on Comprehension*, edited by J. Harste and R. Carey. Bloomington: Indiana University, 1979.

26. With Yetta M. Goodman and Barbara Flores, "Reading in the Bilingual Classroom: Literacy and Biliteracy." Rosslyn, VA: National Clearinghouse for Bilingual Education, 1979.

27. "Needed for the '80's: Schools That Start Where Learners Are." *Needs of Elementary and Secondary Education in the 1980's; Sub-committee on Elementary Secondary and Vocational Education, House of Representatives, 96th Congress*. Washington, DC: Government Printing Office, January 1980.

28. "El Proceso Lector en Ninos Normales." In *El Nino con Dificultades para Aprender*, edited by L. Bravo Valdiviesco. Santiago de Chile: Unicef/Pontificia Universidad Catolica, 1980.

29. "Linguistic Diversity, Teacher Preparation and Professional Development." In *Black English and the Education of Black Children Youth*, edited by G. Smitherman, 171–189. Detroit, MI: Center for Black Studies, Wayne State University, 1981.

30. "Miscue Analysis and Future Research Directions." In *Learning to Read in Different Languages, Linguistics and Literacy,* series 1, edited by S. Huddleson. Washington, DC: Center for Applied Linguistics, 1981.

31. "Language Development: Issues, Insights, and Implementation." In *Oral and Written Language Development Research: Impact on the Schools,* edited by Goodman, Y., Haussler, M., and Strickland, D. National Council of Teachers of English and International Reading Association, 1982.

32. "El Proceso de Lectura: Consideraciones a Traves de las Lenguas y del Desarrollo." In *Nuevas Perspectivas Sobre Los Procesos de Lectura y Escritura,* edited by E. Ferreiro and M. Gomez, 13–28. Mexico Editorial Siglo XXI, Mexico City, 1982.

33. "The Reading Process, a Multi-Lingual Developmental Perspective." In *Full Participation, Proceedings of the Second European Conference on Reading,* edited by K. Tuunainen and A. Chiaroni. Joensuu Finland, 1982.

34. With Yetta M. Goodman, "A Whole-Language Comprehension-Centered View of Reading Development." In *Basic Skills: Issues and Choices,* vol. 2, edited by L. Reed and S. Ward, 125–134. St. Louis: Cemrel, 1982.

35. "On Research and the Improvement of Reading." In *Forty-Seventh Yearbook of the Claremont Reading Conference,* edited by M. Douglas, 28–36. Claremont Graduate School, Claremont, CA, 1983.

36. "A Conversation with Kenneth Goodman." In a guide accompanying three program video series of *Out of the Shadows,* edited and produced by L. Rainsberry, 17–20. Toronto: TV Ontario, 1983.

37. With Yetta M. Goodman, "Everything You Wanted to Know But Didn't Have the Opportunity to Ask." In a guide accompanying three program video series of *Out of the Shadows,* edited and produced by L. Rainsberry, 28–44. Toronto: TV Ontario, 1983.

38. "Unity in Reading." In *Becoming Readers in a Complex Society, 83rd Yearbook of the National Society for the Study of Education,* edited by O. Niles and A. Purves. Chicago, IL, 1984.
Also in Singer, H., and Ruddell, R. (eds.). *Theoretical Models & Processes of Reading,* 3rd ed. Newark, DE: International Reading Association, 1985.
Also in Portuguese as "Unidad na Leitura."*Letras de Hoje* 86 (December 1991): 9–44.

39. "Literacy: For Whom and for What." In *Language in Learning,* edited by M.L. Tickoo. Singapore: SEAMEO Regional Language Centre, 1986.

40. "A Holistic Model of Reading." In *Aspects in Reading Processes,* edited by Trondhjem. 12th Danavox Symposium, Klarskovgard, Denmark, 1986.

41. "Foreword." In *Making Connections with Writing,* edited by M. and C. Kitagawa. Portsmouth, NH: Heinemann, 1987.

42. "Teachers Detechnologizing Reading." In *Ideas and Insights,* edited by D.J. Watson, x–xi. Urbana, IL: National Council of Teachers of English, 1987.

43. "Reading for Life: The Psycholinguistic Base." In *Reading Concerns: Selected Papers from UKRA Conferences 1972–1980*. London: United Kingdom Reading Association, 1988.

44. "Language and Learning: Toward a Social-Personal View." In *Proceedings of the Brisbane Conference on Language and Learning*, July, 1988.

45. "Afterword." In *Counterpoint and Beyond*, edited by J. L. Davidson, 105–108. Urbana, IL: National Council of Teachers of English, 1988.

46. "Language Development: Issues, Insights and Implementation." In *Teachers and Research: Language Learning in the Classroom*, edited by G. Pinnell and M. Matlin, 130–141. Newark, DE: International Reading Association, 1989.

47. With Yetta M. Goodman, "Vygotsky in a Whole Language Perspective." In *Vygotsky and Education*, edited by L. Moll, 223–250. New York: Cambridge University Press, 1990.

48. "The Whole Language Curriculum." In *Whole Language: Empowerment at the Chalk Face*, edited by J. Hydrick and N. Wildermuth, 191–211. New York: Scholastic, 1990.

49. With Yetta M. Goodman, "Our Ten Best Ideas for Reading Teachers." In *10 Best Ideas for Reading Teachers*, edited by E. Fry, 60–64. Menlo Park, CA: Addison Wesley, 1991.

50. "Whole Language: What Makes It Whole." In *Literacy in Process*, edited by B. Power and R. Hubbard. Portsmouth, NH: Heinemann, 1991.

51. "The Teacher Interview" Toby Kahn Curry and Debra Goodman. An interview by Yetta M. Goodman, commentary by Ken Goodman. In *Workshop 3: The Politics of Process*, edited by N. Atwell, 81–93. Portsmouth, NH: Heinemann, 1991.

52. With Yetta M. Goodman, "Whole Language: A Whole Educational Reform." *Schools of Thought, Pathways to Educational Reform* (16)2 (Spring 1991): 59–70.

53. "Whole Language Research: Foundations and Development." In *What Research Has to Say About Reading Instruction*, 2nd ed., edited by S. J. Samuels and A. Farstrup. Newark, DE: International Reading Association, 1992.
Also in Japanese *Horu Rangegi*, edited and translated by T. Kuwabara, 112–157. Tokyo: Kokudo sha, 1992.

54. "A Question About the Future." In *Questions & Answers About Whole Language*, edited by O. Cochrine, 137–140. Katonah, NY: Richard C. Owen, 1992.

55. "Foreword." In *Read Any Good Math Lately?*, edited by D. J. Whitin and S. Wilde, xi–xii. Portsmouth, NH: Heinemann, 1992.

56. With D. Freeman, "What's Simple in Simplified Language?" In *Simplification: Theory and Application*, edited by M. L. Tickoo, 69–81. Singapore: SEAMEO Regional Language Centre, 1993.

57. "Ponencias Primero Conferencia." In *Memorias Del Primer Congreso de las*

Americas sobre Lectoescritura, 4–15. Maracaibo, Venezuela: Universidad de Los Andes, 1993.

58. "El Lenguaje Integral Como Filosofia Educativa." In *Memorias Del Primer Congreso de las Americas sobre Lectoescritura,* 16–29. Maracaibo, Venezuela: Universidad de Los Andes, 1993.

59. With Yetta M. Goodman, "Vygotsky Desde la Perspective del Lenguaje Total (Whole-Language)." In *Vygotsky Y La Educación,* edited by L. Moll, 263–292. Méndez de Andés: Aique Grupo Editor S.A., 1993. (*Spanish translation of* "Vygotsky in a Whole Language Perspective" in *Vygotsky and Education.*)

60. With Yetta M. Goodman, "To Err Is Human: Learning About Language Processes by Analyzing Miscues." In *Theoretical Models and Processes of Reading,* 4th ed., edited by R. B. Ruddell, M. R. Ruddell, and H. Singer. Newark, DE: International Reading Association, 1994, pp. 104–123.

61. "Reading, Writing and Written Texts: A Transactional Sociopsycholinguistic View." In *Theoretical Models and Processes of Reading,* 4th ed., edited by R. B. Ruddell, M. R. Ruddell, and H. Singer. Newark, DE: International Reading Association, 1994, pp. 1093–1130.

62. "Universals in Reading: A Transactional Socio-Psycholinguistic Model of Reading, Writing and Texts." A summary by Patrick Gallo, in *Report of the Regional Seminar on Reading and Writing Research: Implications for Language Education,* 6. Singapore, 1994.

63. "Lots of Changes, But Little Gained." In *Basal Readers: A Second Look,* edited by P. Shannon and K. S. Goodman. Katonah, NY: Richard C. Owen, 1994.

64. With Lisa Maras and Debbie Birdseye, "Look! Look! Who Stole the Pictures from the Picture Book?" In *Basal Readers: A Second Look,* edited by K. S. Goodman and P. Shannon. Katonah, NY: Richard C. Owen, 1994.

65. With Yetta M. Goodman, "Preface." In *Leadership in Whole Language, the Principal's Role,* ix–xi. York, ME: Stenhouse, 1995.

66. With Kathryn F. Whitmore, "Practicing What We Teach: The Principles That Guide Us." In *Whole Language Voices in Teacher Education,* edited by K. F. Whitmore and Y. M. Goodman, 1–16. York, ME: Stenhouse, 1996.

67. With Richard Meyer and Yetta M. Goodman, "Continuous Evaluation in a Whole Language Preservice Program." In *Whole Language Voices in Teacher Education,* 256–267. York, ME: Stenhouse, 1996.

68. "Lines of Print." In *Whole Language Voices in Teacher Education,* 134–135. York, ME: Stenhouse, 1996.

69. "The Boat in the Basement." In *Whole Language Voices in Teacher Education,* 136–137. York, ME: Stenhouse, 1996.

70. "Nonsense Texts to Illustrate the Three Cue Systems: 'A Mardsan Giberter for Farfie,' 'Gloopy and Blit,' and 'The Marlup.'" In *Whole Language Voices in Teacher Education,* 138–140. York, ME: Stenhouse, 1996.

71. "Real Texts to Illustrate the Three Cue Systems: Downhole Heave Compensator." In *Whole Language Voices in Teacher Education,* 141–143. York, ME: Stenhouse, 1996.

72. "Real Texts to Illustrate the Three Cue Systems: Poison." In *Whole Language Voices in Teacher Education*, 144–145. York, ME: Stenhouse, 1996.

73. "Principles of Revaluing." In *Retrospective Miscue Analysis*, edited by Goodman, Y., & Marek, A., 13–20. Katonah, NY: Richard C. Owen, 1996.

74. With Yetta M. Goodman, "Vygotsky Em Uma Perspectiva da Linguagem Integral." In *Vygotsky e a educação*, edited by L. Moll, 219–224. Porto Alegre RS, Brazil: Artes Médicas, 1996. (*Portuguese translation of* "Vygotsky in a Whole Language Perspective" in *Vygotsky and Education.*)

75. "Preface." *Studies in Miscue Analysis: An Annotated Bibliography,* Brown, J., Goodman, K., & Marek, A., (eds.). iv–x. Newark, DE: International Reading Association, 1996.

76. "Oral and Written Language: Functions and Purposes." In *Many Families, Many Literacies: An International Declaration of Principles,* edited by D. Taylor, 43–46. Portsmouth, NH: Heinemann, 1997.

77. With Yetta M. Goodman, "Foreword." In *Multiple Voices, Multiple Texts,* edited by R. Dornan, L. Rosen, and M. Wilson, pp. ix-xi. Portsmouth, NH: Boynton/Cook, Heinemann, 1997.

78. "¿Por Qué es Importante el Lenguaje?" In *Una Historia Sin Fin. Crear Y Recrear Texto,* edited by G. Ynclán, 15–17. México, D.F., 1997.

79. With Yetta M. Goodman, "To Err Is Human: Learning About Language Processes by Analyzing Miscues." In *Reconsidering a Balanced Approach to Reading,* edited by C. Weaver, 101–123. Urbana, IL: National Council of Teachers of English, 1998.

80. "California, Whole Language, and National Assessment of Educational Progress (NAEP)." In *Reconsidering a Balanced Approach to Reading,* edited by C. Weaver, 467–491. Urbana, IL: National Council of Teachers of English, 1998.

81. "The Phonics Scam: The Pedagogy of the Absurd." In *Perspectives on Reading Instruction,* 27–31. Alexandria, VA: Association for Supervision and Curriculum Development, 1998.

82. "The Reading Process." In *Encyclopedia of Language and Education,* vol. 2, edited by V. Edwards and D. Corson, 1–7. Dordrecht, The Netherlands: Kluwer Academic Publishers, 1997.

83. With Catherine Buck, "Dialect Barriers to Reading Comprehension Revisited." In *Literacy Instruction for Culturally and Linguistically Diverse Student,* 139–145. Newark, DE: International Reading Association, 1998.

84. "Teachers Supporting Learners: A Transactional View," *Australian Journal of Remedial Education,* Vol. 21:2, 1989, pp. 14–19.

85. "I Didn't Found Whole Language." In *Distinguished Educators on Reading,* edited by N. Padak, 2–19. Newark, DE: International Reading Association, 2000.

86. "Update: Forward 8 Years and Back a Century." In *Distinguished Educators on Reading,* edited by N. Padak, 20–27. Newark, DE: International Reading Association, 2000.

Reviews

1. "The Psychology of Language Thought and Instruction." Readings by DeCecco in *Journal of Reading.*

2. "Research Critique: Oral Language of Kindergarten Children." *Elementary English*(43)8 (December 1966): 897–900.

3. Buros, "Reading Tests and Reviews." *American Educational Research Journal,* (January 1971): 169–171.

4. "Linguistics in Language Arts and Reading." *Journal of Reading* (November 1972).

5. Williams, F., Hopper, R., and Natalicio, W. "The Sounds of Children." *Reading Teacher* (31)5 (February 1978): 578–580.

School Materials

Co-author, *Scott, Foresman Reading Systems: Scott Foresman, Levels 1–21 (Grades K-6), 1971–73. Levels 22–27, 1974.* Chicago: *Reading Unlimited,* rev. ed. Levels 1–27, 1976.

Research Reports

1. *A Study of Children's Behavior While Reading Orally,* Final Report, Project No. S-425, Contract No. OE-6-10-136. Washington, DC: U.S. Department of Health, Education and Welfare, Office of Education, Bureau of Research.

2. *A Study of Oral Reading Miscues that Result in Grammatical Re-Transformations,* Final Report, Project No. 7-E-219, Contract No. OEG-O-8-070219-2806 (010). Washington, DC: U.S. Department of Health, Education and Welfare, Office of Education, Bureau of Research.

3. *Theoretically Based Studies of Patterns of Miscues in Oral Reading Performance,* Final Report, Project No. 9-0375, Grant No. OEG-0-9-320375-4269, May 1973. Washington, DC: U.S. Department of Health, Education and Welfare, Office of Education, Bureau of Research. Abstracted in ERIC.

4. With William Page, *Reading Comprehension Programs: Theoretical Bases of Reading Comprehension Instruction in the Middle Grades,* Contract No. NIE C-74-0140, August 1976. Washington, DC: U.S. Department of Health, Education and Welfare, National Institute of Education.

5. *Reading of American Children Whose Reading is a StableRural Dialect of English or a Language Other Than English,* Grant No. NIE-C-00-3-0087, August 1978. Washington, DC: U.S. Department of Health, Education and Welfare, National Institute of Education.

6. With Suzanne Gespass, *Analysis of Text Structures as They Relate to Patterns of Oral Reading Miscues,* Project NIE-G-80-0057, February 1982. Washington, DC: Department of Health, Education and Welfare, National Institute of Education.

Audio/Visual Tapes

With Janet Emig and Yetta M. Goodman, *Interrelationships of Reading and Writing.* Urbana, IL: National Council of Teachers of English, No. 7250R, 1975.

With Barbara Bonder and Jean Malmstram, *Psycholinguistics and Reading.* Urbana, IL: National Council of Teachers of English, No. 73276R, 1976.

With Yetta M. Goodman, *Reading for Meaning: The Goodman Model.* Sydney: Film Australia, 1977 (16mm film).

With DeWayne Triplett and Frank Greene, *The Right Not To Read.* Urbana, IL: National Council of Teachers of English, No. 71311R, 1979.

With Yetta M. Goodman, *Watching Children Reading.* British Broadcasting Company, London, 1986.

What's Whole in Whole Language? Association for Supervision and Curriculum Development, Alexandria, Virginia, 1992.

With Constance Kamii, *Constructivism & Whole Language.* Association for Supervision and Curriculum Development, Alexandria, Virginia, 1993.

Occasional Papers

Program in Language and Literacy
College of Education
University of Arizona, Tucson

No. 1   With Yetta M. Goodman, *A Whole-Language Comprehension Centered View of Reading Development.* February, 1981.

No. 2   With F.V. Gollasch, *Word Omissions: Deliberate and Non-Deliberate.* March, 1980.

No. 3   With Bess Altwerger, *Studying Text Difficulty Through Miscue Analysis.* June, 1981.

No. 6   With Lois Bridges Bird, *On the Wording of Texts: A Study of Intra-Text Word Frequency.* March, 1982.

No. 7   With Suzanne Gespass, *Text Features as They Relate to Miscues: Pronouns.* March, 1983.

No. 8   *Text Features as They Relate to Miscues: Determiners.* July, 1983.

No. 15 With G. Williams and J. David, *Revaluing Troubled Readers.* February, 1986.

No. 16 With J. Brown and A. Marek, *Annotated Chronological Bibliography of Miscue Analysis.* August, 1994.

Index